Healthcare Crime

Investigating Abuse, Fraud, and Homicide by Caregivers

Healthcare Crime

Investigating Abuse, Fraud, and Homicide by Caregivers

Kelly M. Pyrek

CRC Press
Taylor & Francis Group
Boca Raton   London   New York

CRC Press is an imprint of the
Taylor & Francis Group, an **informa** business

CRC Press
Taylor & Francis Group
6000 Broken Sound Parkway NW, Suite 300
Boca Raton, FL 33487-2742

Printed in the United States of America on acid-free paper
10 9 8 7 6 5 4 3 2 1

International Standard Book Number: 978-1-4398-2033-9 (Hardback)

Library of Congress Cataloging-in-Publication Data

Pyrek, Kelly.
   Healthcare crime : investigating abuse, fraud, and homicide by caregivers / Kelly M. Pyrek.
      p. cm.
   Includes bibliographical references and index.
   ISBN 978-1-4398-2033-9 (hardcover : alk. paper)
   1. Medical ethics. 2. Medical personnel--Malpractice. 3. Caregivers. I. Title.

R724.P97 2011
174.2--dc22   2010045941

Visit the Taylor & Francis Web site at
http://www.taylorandfrancis.com

and the CRC Press Web site at
http://www.crcpress.com

To Judi Pyrek and Tony Hettinger,
with love and appreciation.

Table of Contents

Acknowledgments

Successful journalism requires an interviewer who knows how to get to the heart of an issue and an interviewee who is not afraid of the hard questions. I am fortunate to have had the opportunity to interview experts in the fields of forensic science investigation, forensic nursing, and forensic psychology, as well as healthcare administration and public policy, healthcare human relations, and healthcare law. The following individuals have graciously given of their time to share their expertise with me to augment that research and perspective that I bring to this book:

- Janet Barber, RN, MS, FAAFS
- Norman Bates, JD
- Joseph Bellino
- Marshall Kapp, JD
- Kenneth W. Kizer, MD
- Jeffery Payne
- Katherine Ramsland, PhD
- Louis Saccacio
- Bruce Sackman
- Beatrice Crofts Yorker, JD, MS, RN

Introduction

Justice will not come ... until those who are not injured are as indignant as those who are.

Thucydides

At the time of writing, the U.S. Congress had just passed sweeping reform for the nation's healthcare system, but the proposed legislation does little to ameliorate or even address an aspect of healthcare that is increasingly pervasive—crime perpetrated by healthcare professionals. For the purposes of this book, these crimes will be divided into four broad categories—(1) exploitation, (2) fraud, (3) abuse, and (4) murder—each of which encompass a wide range of criminal behaviors against patients, coworkers, and employers.

Can an entire book be dedicated to the concept of crime committed by healthcare practitioners? I was initially skeptical until I started digging deeper into the medical and legal literature, perusing reports in the mainstream media and talking to experts in the fields of healthcare, medicine, law, economics, social sciences, and human resources. Although not entirely pervasive, there is sufficient evidence that crime may be on the upswing in U.S. healthcare institutions. It may not be as high profile as medical errors and adverse events, but it is occurring, and it is certainly not on every facility's radar—as the cases of healthcare serial killers Michael Swango, Kristen Gilbert, and Charles Cullen clearly demonstrate.

Healthcare institutions are intended to be places of healing, not houses of horror. So, why are so many individuals being harmed by or dying at the hands of healthcare professionals? That is the journey of discovery in this book that I hope you will take with me. There are five thoughts about crime perpetrated by healthcare professionals that I endeavor to express in this book:

It is perturbing.
1. The breach of trust that occurs every time that a patient is exploited, defrauded, abused, or murdered is horrifying to contemplate. Healthcare practitioners take oaths to heal, not harm, yet some of the most prolific serial killers have been healthcare professionals. Their motives vary, but their malfeasance results in morbidity and mortality that creates fear among healthcare consumers, erodes confidence in the healthcare system, and adds

to an already overburdened U.S. investigatory and prosecutorial system.

It is precedented.

2. Abuse by individuals in the helping and healing professions is not a new phenomenon. Sexual abuse of minors by members of the clergy as well as teachers, coaches, and daycare workers has been well-documented in the media and vetted by the courts.

It is precluded.

3. Skepticism about whether these crimes are actually committed makes it impossible for this subject matter to be discussed candidly by healthcare providers, healthcare institution leaders, members of law enforcement, and prosecutors. Whistle-blowers are squelched or punished, hospital chief executive officers (CEOs) cover it up, authorities are hampered by obstacles to investigation, and prosecutors have trouble making charges stick. This is, of course, assuming that the perpetrator is even caught; in so many instances, healthcare colleagues are not willing to act upon their suspicions or observations for fear of recrimination, termination, or legal action. Not only is crime committed by healthcare professionals being covered up, when it is brought to light, many people have a difficult time accepting it as fact, let alone doing anything about it because it seems so preposterous. Until, that is, in the early 2000s, when there were a number of cases in which nurses and doctors were convicted of killing their patients. In 2006, one of the most authoritative examinations of the topic of healthcare serial killers was published by health-care experts Beatrice Yorker and Kenneth Kizer in the *Journal of Forensic Science.*

When I interviewed Yorker for this book, she said that she was disappointed that the topic was not taken seriously by the medical community or the general public. As Yorker told me,

> We stand behind our conclusions, and it is a shame that since the article was published, there has not been enough public outcry over healthcare serial killers. We believe we would have gotten a lot more mileage on the topic if the article had been published in the *Journal of the American Medical Association* or in the *New England Journal of Medicine.* Both journals declined to publish the article. The reviewers indicated the problem was too isolated, yet our whole point was that it is *not* isolated. With a body count over 2000, just of convicted healthcare killers, that is as high as non-healthcare

serial murderers, it's a significant issue and it warrants significant resources to address and resolve. (Interview with author.)

It is preventable.

4. As you will see in Chapter 7, there are many common-sense strategies that can help curtail malfeasance by healthcare professionals, including better equipping and educating these workers to do their jobs; training healthcare institutions and law enforcement about the warning signs; and ensuring that the appropriate level of legislation is in place to "add teeth" to the regulation and oversight of the healthcare industry with regard to ensuring that repeat offenders do not find their way back into the system to continue their nefarious acts. It is not readily evident who the perpetrators are; in many cases, they appear to be as competent and compassionate as possible; healthcare institutions must be vigilant about removing problematic individuals, and the legal system must have the mechanisms in place to ensure swift due process. In addition, the licensing and regulatory boards for the healthcare profession must ensure that they can shut down those whose sole purpose in the world is to harm healthcare's most vulnerable populations.

It is personal.

5. Yorker also believes that the kind of crime perpetrated by healthcare professionals—assault, abuse, neglect, exploitation, and fraud—is where crime in general is headed. "It's an interpersonal crime and it's definitely happening in the healthcare workplace." For as much as the U.S. healthcare system has tried to become more transparent, there are more places to hide than ever before, and the very nature of the crime makes it far more personal for the crime victim. No patient enters the hospital thinking he or she will have his or her identity stolen, or will be abused or defrauded, or even murdered.

This book is personal for another reason. More than 25 years ago, I worked as a certified nursing assistant in long-term care and home healthcare while I was a student in high school and college. My mother is a career nurse, and so I grew up knowing and respecting the people who work in medicine and healthcare. As such, I have witnessed and experienced firsthand many of the stressors mentioned in this book, and I know the dedication it takes to endure—because it is your job, and because it is the right thing to do. Among healthcare providers, I have seen the corners cut, the thinly veiled disgust, and the exasperation with a needy patient. There are days and nights when healthcare professionals believe they can no longer function in this high-stress environment, with low pay and little autonomy with which to change their circumstances. I also know what it feels to be my patients' advocate, even if it is only for an 8-hour shift. And I know that the healthcare community is a very special place—I worked in it, and as a career journalist, I write about it, so it is very much my home. And I become righteously indignant when I catalog the horrific abuses that persist in the system.

This book is not an indictment of the healthcare profession, but it is an objective look at an industry that seems to attract its share of miscreants. It was written out of respect and concern for practitioners, patients, and the public. And it was written from a desire to help draw attention to the issue of malfeasance by healthcare professionals as much as it was to explain the stressors and extenuating circumstances under which so many practitioners operate today. As with any profession, there are individuals who give their industry a bad name, and there are thousands and thousands of professionals who endeavor to earn our trust. As Runciman et al. (2007) observed:

The vast majority of humans have a spontaneous urge to help their fellow beings when they are in trouble. Attempts to alleviate pain, sickness and suffering are evident from the beginning of recorded history. A considerable number of people systematically set out to help their fellow humans by training for roles in healthcare. Our overwhelming experience has been that almost all of these people, all over the world, are highly motivated to help those afflicted by disease and injury....All involved in healthcare want to be able to do the right thing at the right time, in the right way, for the right people. (p. xvii)

However, as Runciman et al. (2007) rightly pointed out, "How can one be sure that one is doing the right thing when faced with having to practice an uncertain science on vulnerable patients in a complex system under ever-changing conditions?" and noted further, "There is a minefield of often conflicting considerations that has to be navigated in the everyday work of a healthcare professional. Politicians put pressure on administrators, administrators put pressure on managers, and managers and patients (and their families) make demands of frontline clinicians. These pressures and demands are sometimes difficult to reconcile" (p. 3).

Patients are victims of exploitation, abuse, neglect, injury, and homicide. There is a plethora of information about medical errors but a paucity of information about patients who are harmed intentionally. It is my hope to add to what is already known about healthcare crime and to advance the dialog necessary to address medical malfeasance.

Reference

Runciman B, Merry A, and Walton M. *Safety and Ethics in Healthcare: A Guide to Getting It Right.* Guildford, UK: Ashgate. 2007, pp. xvii, 3.

Healthcare Trends, Stressors, and Workplace Violence

1

This book addresses *medical malfeasance*, defined generally as the performance by an individual working in the healthcare profession of an act that is legally unjustified, harmful, or contrary to law; at its core is wrongdoing conducted especially in violation of a public trust. That breach of trust is what makes crime committed by healthcare professionals so abhorrent.

In polls, healthcare professionals are frequently cited as some of the most trusted individuals. For example, a Harris Interactive poll in 2006 revealed that physicians were at the top of its most trustworthy occupations list; physicians scored 85 percent, beating out teachers, scientists, and police officers (Harris, August 2006). In 2008, for the seventh consecutive year, nurses received top accolades in Gallup's annual *Honesty and Ethics of Professions* survey. Eighty-four percent of Americans characterize nurses' honesty and ethical standards as either "high" or "very high." Physicians are ranked fourth, with close to two-thirds of Americans rating them highly (Gallup, 2008).

This trust is betrayed when healthcare professionals engage in activities that run counter to their oaths to heal, not harm. The question seems to be, whatever happened to ethics in healthcare? Practitioners are expected to adhere to stringent codes of ethics and conduct because it is the right thing to do, not simply because it is a condition for licensure or employment.

More than 2,000 years ago, Hippocrates realized that a patient's willingness to trust his or her physician was absolutely essential to the practice of medicine. Physicians are bound by the tenets of the Hippocratic Oath to respect the patient and one's profession enough to endeavor to the highest levels of skill, competency, and dedication. The most famous code of all, of course, is *primum non nocere*, or "above all, do no harm." The American Medical Association (AMA)'s Principles of Medical Ethics directs physicians to be "dedicated to providing competent medical care, with compassion and respect for human dignity and rights" and to "uphold the standards of professionalism, be honest in all professional interactions, and strive to report physicians deficient in character or competence, or engaging in fraud or deception, to appropriate entities." The principles also state that a physician "shall respect the rights of patients, colleagues and other health professionals, and shall safeguard patient confidences and privacy within the constraints of the law" and that while caring for a patient, "regard responsibility to the patient as paramount."

Every state has a Nurse Practice Act (NPA), which is a set of laws designed to protect the general public from harm, define the formal education needed for a particular level of nursing, and establish licensure regulations. Further, the NPA defines the nurse's scope of practice based on the content of the formal education and level of nursing required. The Code of Ethics for Nurses, from the American Nurses Association (ANA), states, "The nurse, in all professional relationships, practices with compassion and respect for the inherent dignity, worth and uniqueness of every individual, unrestricted by considerations of social or economic status, personal attributes or the nature of health problems." It indicates that the nurse's primary commitment is to the patient, and that the nurse "promotes, advocates for and strives to protect the health, safety and rights of the patient." The code also indicates that, "The nurse participates in establishing, maintaining and improving healthcare environments and conditions of employment conducive to the provision of quality healthcare and consistent with the values of the profession through individual and collective action." The code also addresses questionable practice by stating, "As an advocate for the patient, the nurse must be alert to and take appropriate action regarding any instances of incompetent, unethical, illegal or impaired practice by any member of the healthcare team or the healthcare system or any action of others that places the rights or best interests of the patient in jeopardy."

The Hippocratic tradition has taken its hits over the centuries, with serious breaches in truthfulness, privacy, justice, and responsibility. Beauchamp (2007) asserted there are four principles in healthcare ethics that must be followed: respect for the decision-making capabilities of autonomous individuals; nonmaleficence (a principle of not causing harm to others); beneficence (a set of principles requiring the prevention of harm, balancing benefits against risks and costs); and justice (appropriate distribution of benefits, risks, and costs). Essentially, these principles dictate that healthcare professionals must respect the rights of individuals "to hold certain views, to make certain choices, and to take certain actions based on personal values and beliefs" (Beauchamp, 2007). They must also uphold the intention to do no harm, which, as Beauchamp (2007) points out, involves the rules of "do not kill, do not cause pain, do not disable, do not deprive of pleasure, do not cheat and do not break promises." In showing beneficence, or compassion, one would argue that not only is it incumbent upon the healthcare provider to do so, but that it is perhaps a moral imperative of the highest order.

Beauchamp (2007) observes that "health professionals' obligations and virtues have for centuries been framed by professional commitments to provide medical care and to protect patients from disease, injury and system failure. Our principles build on this tradition." He describes these principles as the building blocks of what he calls the "common morality," or a set of norms and mores that society deems as appropriate for right living and rewards as virtuous acts, such as preventing harm from occurring or tell-ing the truth. Beauchamp states that society has adopted this code of morals because it strives to perpetuate the human race and counteract conditions that cause the quality of people's lives to deteriorate. "The goal is to prevent or limit problems of indifference, conflict, suffering, hostility, scarce resources, limited information and the like. Centuries of experience have demonstrated that the human condition tends to deteriorate into misery, confusion, vio-lence and distrust unless…the norms of the common morality are observed" (Beauchamp, 2007).

So, how and why do some healthcare professionals misplace their moral compass? Absent the individuals who are truly malevolent and utterly lacking in conscience, this slip in moral fortitude could be explained by a number of factors impacting the healthcare system pres-ently, including increased healthcare utilization at a time of chronic healthcare practitioner shortages. To understand the issue of crime per-petrated by healthcare professionals requires an understanding of the convergence of factors exacerbating the stress that they already feel, as we shall see. It may be helpful to examine the current trends in healthcare to better understand the issues and factors relating to healthcare profes-sionals' stressful world.

The U.S. healthcare industry is an entity of monstrous proportions and complexity.

According to the Bureau of Labor Statistics (BLS), in 2008 (the year for which the latest figures are available), healthcare pro-vided approximately 14.3 million jobs in about 595,000 health-care institutions. As we will see, this contributes to providing adequate places to hide for individuals who are intent on defraud-ing the system or harming patients.

Healthcare utilization is on the rise, which contributes to the chaos and creates opportunities for medical mischief. In 2006, U.S. hospitals discharged nearly 35 million people after an aver-age stay of almost 5 days during which 46 million procedures were performed, according to the National Center for Health Statistics of the Centers for Disease Control and Prevention (CDC) (Merrill and Elixhauser, 2006). This does not take into account the 102 million visits to hospital outpatient depart-ments, which is nearly 35 visits for every 100 persons, according to the National Hospital Ambulatory Medical Care Survey for 2006. Visits to hospital emergency departments (EDs) in 2006 were 119.2 million, or 40.5 ED visits per 100 persons. These visits translated into 15.3 million hospital admissions and 2.3 million admissions to a critical care unit. And according to the Agency for Healthcare Research and Quality (AHRQ), in 2007, the number of hospital discharges rose to 39.5 million with an average length of stay of 4.6 days. Essentially, more patients moving through the system means more possibilities to conduct medical malfeasance.

Apparently, risk adjusters already expect things to go wrong in hospitals. According to Runciman et al. (2007), 10 percent of admissions to acute-care hospitals are associated with an adverse event. If you consider death rates by exposure to various activities, being a patient in an acute-care hospital can be dangerous; there are 33,000 healthcare-associated deaths per 100 million people per year. As Runciman et al. (2007) noted, safety has been defined as liberty from hazard where hazard is "a circumstance or agent that can lead to harm damage or loss" (p. 20). Runciman et al. (2007) explained further that there must be a balance between the potential for harm, the likelihood that a healthcare worker will do what is right, and the choices that are present at the time of ethical decision making: "What is within the power of individual healthcare professionals is to ensure that they consistently behave, in their everyday activities, in a manner that is safe, and understood by and acceptable to their patients. This individual behavior will translate, collectively, into a culture change, and unsafe practices will become unacceptable" (p. 20).

A chronic shortage of healthcare professionals persists, which exacerbates the stressors that healthcare professionals are already experiencing as new healthcare jobs cannot be filled. According to the BLS, healthcare will generate 3.2 million new wage and salary jobs between 2008 and 2018, more than any other industry, yet there are fewer qualified healthcare providers than ever before; industry associations predict up to a 20 percent shortage of qualified individuals. Driving this job growth is the growing patient population; the number of people with much greater than average healthcare needs will grow faster than the total population between 2006 and 2016; as a result, the demand for healthcare will increase. In addition, advances in medical technology will continue to improve the survival rate of severely ill and injured patients, who will then need extensive therapy and care, and new technologies will make it possible to identify and treat conditions that were previously not treatable.

Probably one of the most critical reasons that healthcare professionals succumb to the temptations of medical misbehavior is the stressors of the occupation brought upon by these chronic personnel shortages. The American Hospital Association (AHA) reports that 89 percent of hospitals have openings for registered nurses (RNs) that are unfilled, and 75 percent of hospitals today are finding it more difficult to recruit nurses than in the past. The national vacancy rate for RNs is 11 percent, according to the AHA, and this shortage contributes to delays in care and makes it more difficult for patients to receive the care they need (AFT Healthcare, undated 1). And the American Academy of Family Physicians is predicting a shortage of 40,000 primary-care doctors by 2020, with medical schools graduating only half the number needed to meet demand (AFT Healthcare, undated 2). The statistical figure on the number of required healthcare workers estimated by the BLS is estimated to be around 2.2 million as replacements and 3.1 million for new positions by the end of 2010. The Department of Health and Human Services estimates that the nursing shortage would reach 1 million by the end of 2020 (S&P, 2004).

Shortages are exacerbated by a shrinking experienced workforce, as an increasing number of nurses retire and a significantly reduced number of new nurses enter the field. The American Association of Colleges of Nursing reports that students entering baccalaureate nursing programs fell almost 21 percent between 1995 and 2000 (AFT Healthcare, undated 2). Recruitment and retention of qualified individuals are problematic for many healthcare institutions due to the aforementioned factors as well as the challenging nature of the work. A national survey of nurses in 2000 showed that the majority of nurses who left their jobs did so in order to take less stressful and less physically demanding positions that also offered more regular hours. Many of these nurses cited stressful, intolerable conditions in the workplace as the impetus for their departures (AFT Healthcare, undated 2).

Cost containment and reform are continuing to shape the healthcare industry.

The way healthcare is delivered is being impacted by the need to cut costs and boost healthcare institutions' profit margins. The cost of care is rising, and healthcare facilities are attempting to do more with less. The ramifications of fiscal belt-tightening and organizational culture change can manifest themselves in the clinical arena as additional stressors for healthcare providers. Hockley (2005a) said that an organizational culture that does not support staff members who are experiencing stressors in their personal or professional lives may lead to them being violent. Conlin-Shaw (1998) assigned much of the blame for abuse and neglect by staff on the financially driven medical model with productivity and efficiency as its primary goals rather than caring and human relationships. Hockley (2005a) said that individuals who enter healthcare facilities have the right to expect a safe environment that is free from violence and abuse by healthcare professionals. Most patients would never conceive that they may be placed in harm's way intentionally, and staff violence is a professional issue that is "under-recognized and poorly reported," according to Hockley, who observed that "it is accepted that most health professionals are non-violent and caring. Unfortunately, there is a small element within healthcare that exhibits violent acts toward those they care for. Furthermore, many of these acts are so horrendous…because they target some of the most vulnerable people in our society and because the perpetrator is often a repeat offender." Hockley (2005a) said that medical malfeasance by healthcare professionals is exacerbated by institutional factors such as the workplace's organizational culture that may discourage the reporting of unprofessional conduct. "Until these factors are addressed, including revamping healthcare institutions' culture, this kind of violence will continue."

And finally, the healthcare work environment is becoming more hazardous. In 2006, the incidence of occupational injury and illness in hospitals was 8.1 cases per 100 full-time workers, compared with an average of 4.4 for private industry overall. As we will see, burnout and workplace violence pose significant threats to healthcare professionals.

Stressors of Healthcare and Workplace Violence

The medical literature contains a significant number of studies documenting occupational stress among healthcare professionals. Many studies indicate that job dissatisfaction and burnout are significantly higher in occupations with high workload demands and complex organizational cultures such as healthcare. Occupational stress has been a long-standing concern of the healthcare industry. Studies indicate that healthcare workers have higher rates of substance abuse and suicide than other professions and elevated rates of depression and anxiety linked to job stress. In addition to psychological distress, other outcomes of job stress include burnout, absenteeism, employee intent to leave, reduced patient satisfaction, and diagnosis and treatment errors. The National Institute for Occupational Safety and Health (NIOSH) defines *occupational stress* as "the harmful physical and emotional responses that occur when the requirements of the job do not match the capabilities, resources, or needs of the worker" (NIOSH, 2008).

Contributing to stress are workplace factors such as oppressive job demands and workload or poor organizational climate. Stressors common in healthcare settings include inadequate staffing levels, long work hours or shift work, role ambiguity, and exposure to occupational hazards. Stressors vary among healthcare occupations and even within occupations, depending on the task being performed. In general, studies of nurses have found the following factors to be linked with stress: work overload; time pressure; lack of social support at work (especially from supervisors, head nurses, and higher management); exposure to work-related violence or threats; sleep deprivation, role ambiguity, and conflict; understaffing; career development issues; and dealing with difficult or seriously ill patients. Among physicians, stressors include long hours, excessive workload, dealing with death and dying, interpersonal conflicts with other staff, patient expectations, and threat of malpractice litigation (NIOSH, 2008).

According to the 2009 CareerCast "Jobs Rated" survey, a registered nurse's stress score is 62 on a scale of 1 to 100. According to the Department of Health and Human Services, medicine is Number 2 on the 10 most stressful jobs list, coming after teaching at Number 1 and fire/police services at Number 3. The University of Manchester Institute of Science and Technology established a list of occupations that equal or exceed the rate of 6 on a stress-rating scale of 0 to 10: doctors came in at 6.8 and nurses at 6.5, behind miners at 8.3, police officers at 7.7, and airline pilots at 7.5. Chronic stress can take its toll, as Ulrich et al. (2007) summarize: "As healthcare becomes increasingly complex, these providers encounter difficult ethical issues in patient care.... The severity of patient problems, paperwork, caseload size, undervalue of work and decreases in job security, staffing levels, wages, skill mix, resources, and other factors continue to affect the satisfaction and retention of healthcare providers."

Respect is the glue that keeps professional relationships together, but a recent study revealed that doctors and nurses are still feuding, which adds to an already volatile environment. Johnson (2009) reported on a survey conducted by the American College of Physician Executives (ACPE) illustrating how pervasive the problem of bad behavior from doctors and nurses has become. More than 2,100 physicians (33 percent) and nurses (67 percent) who participated in the survey told tales of doctors groping nurses and technicians as they tried to perform their jobs, surgical instruments being hurled by surgeons at nurses in the operating room, personal grudges interfering with patient care, and rampant accusations of incompetence or negligence in front of patients and their families. Johnson (2009) noted, "According to the respondents, the fundamental lack of respect between doctors and nurses is a huge problem that affects every aspect of their jobs. Staff morale, patient safety and public perception of the industry all suffer as a result."

According to the survey, nearly 98 percent of respondents reported witnessing behavior problems between doctors and nurses in the past year. About 30 percent of participants said bad behavior occurred several times a year, another 30 percent said it occurred weekly, about 25 percent said monthly, and 10 percent said they witnessed problems between doctors and nurses daily. The survey found that the most common complaint was about degrading comments and insults that nearly 85 percent of participants reported experiencing at their organizations; yelling was reported by 73 percent; and other problems included cursing, inappropriate jokes, and refusing to work with one another. The survey revealed doctors to be at the heart of the unrest, with both doctors and nurses saying physicians were to blame for a significant amount of the disruptive behaviors, including patronizing and belittling nurses. Thirteen percent of respondents reported witnessing acts of sexual harassment in the past year.

One of the most significant stressors for healthcare providers is experiencing workplace violence.

When Healthcare Professionals Are the Abused

Workplace violence is a significant stressor for healthcare professionals. News headlines convey incidents ranging from aggression, to assault and rape, to murder. Healthcare professionals have the highest rate of nonfatal assault injuries, and nurses are three times more likely to experience workplace violence than any other professional group, according to the BLS (American Association of Critical Care Nurses [AACN], 2004). Within the medical profession, nurses are more likely to be victims of workplace violence than any other staff worker (Warchol, 1998). A study of ED nurses revealed that 50 percent reported having been assaulted during their careers (UPI, 2009). Data from the BLS confirm that the healthcare sector continues to lead all other industry sectors in incidence of nonfatal workplace assaults. In 2000, 48 percent of all nonfatal injuries from violent acts against workers occurred in the healthcare sector, with nurses, aides, and orderlies taking the brunt of the abuse (BLS, 2001).

It is vital to note that healthcare providers are primarily experiencing this violence at the hands of their patients. A report from NIOSH indicated that healthcare providers face a number of risk factors contributing to occupational violence, including working directly with volatile people, being understaffed during busier times such as visiting hours, and being in places, such as EDs, where patients are more agitated from their injuries and from waiting to be seen by healthcare providers (NIOSH, 2002).

As McPhaul and Lipscomb (2004) noted, "Transporting patients, long waits for service, inadequate security, poor environmental design and unrestricted movement of the public are associated with increased risk of assault in hospitals and may be significant factors in social services workplaces as well." They added, "The presence of agitated, demented individuals or individuals with a history of violent behavior, the absence of violence prevention programs and training, and staffing shortages magnified by increased patient acuity are factors that contribute to workplace violence."

Workplace violence ranges from offensive or threatening language to homicide. NIOSH (2002) defined *workplace violence* as violent acts (including physical assaults and threats of assaults) directed toward persons on duty. According to NIOSH, examples of violence include threats (expressions of intent to cause harm, including verbal threats, threatening body language, and written threats); physical assaults (attacks ranging from slapping and beating to rape, homicide, and the use of weapons such as firearms, bombs, or knives); and aggravated assaults (usually conducted by surprise and with intent to rob or harm).

Although anyone working in a hospital may become a victim of violence, nurses and aides who have the most direct contact with patients are at higher risk. Violence may occur anywhere in the healthcare institution, but it is most frequent in psychiatric wards, emergency rooms, waiting rooms, and geriatric units (NIOSH, 2002). The effects of violence can range in intensity and include both minor and major physical injuries, temporary and permanent physical disability, psychological trauma, and even death. Violence may also have negative organizational outcomes such as low worker morale, increased job stress, increased worker turnover, reduced trust of management and coworkers, and a hostile working environment (NIOSH, 2002).

The problem of workplace violence against healthcare professionals is significant, as it creates injury and disability among its victims while also triggering treatment and legal costs for the hospital, as well as reduced productivity and high staff turnover. McPhaul and Lipscomb (2004) said that workplace arises, in part, from a healthcare culture that resists the idea that violence is a reality, combined with the notion that violence is merely part of the healthcare professional's job. As McPhaul and Lipscomb (2004) explained, "The dangers arise from the exposure to violent individuals combined with the absence of strong violence prevention programs and protective regulations. These factors together with organizational realities such as staff shortages and increased patient acuity create substantial barriers to eliminating violence in today's healthcare workplace."

Even though workplace violence has been identified as an "emerging hazard" (Lipscomb and Love, 1992), very little action has been taken, according to McPhaul and Lipscomb (2004), who assert that even though the government has voluntary guidelines for healthcare employers which describe a comprehensive approach to violence prevention based on proven principles of occupational safety and health, "there are very few violence prevention intervention studies on how to prevent violence toward healthcare workers."

Long-standing codes of ethics for nurses established by organizations such as the ANA, the American Academy of Nursing (AAN), and the International Council of Nurses (ICN) indicate that nurses should look out for the safety and welfare of their patients; the ICN (2000) says that nurses must take "appropriate action to safeguard individuals when their care is endangered by a co-worker or any other person." However, these codes cannot prevent medical malfeasance on their own. In its policy on violence against nurses, the ICN (2000) acknowledges that "regrettably, a small number of nurses have also been known to be perpetrators of violence, patient or colleague abuse in violation of nursing's code of conduct."

Although organizations have called for increased intervention-effectiveness research and more widespread protective regulations, putting these interventions into practice has been challenging for healthcare institutions. Hockley (2005a) suggests that the law is most likely a more suitable arbitrator of professional conduct relating to negligence, discrimination, assault, and homicide. The first step is actually identifying workplace violence, as it encompasses the more subtle forms of bullying, escalating into more blatant exhibitions of physical and psychological violence, abuse, and harassment. Violence can occur during interactions between coworkers, supervisors, patients, families, visitors, and others (McPhaul and Lipscomb, 2004).

A significant challenge to the ability to resolve workplace violence is the vast amount of underreporting of violence. Chapman et al. (2010) reported that three-quarters of nurses experienced workplace violence, but only one in six incidents were formally reported. The majority (92 percent) said they had been verbally abused; 69 percent had been physically threatened; and 52 percent had been physically assaulted. Nurses reported 2,354 incidents to the research team, with nurses facing an average of 2 to 46 incidents a year. "Many of the nurses who took part in the research said that they did not report incidents because they felt that workplace violence was just part of the job," said lead author Rose Chapman, MD, from Curtin University of Technology in Perth, Western Australia.

The 113 nurses who took part in the study were mainly female, in their early 40s, and had been in the profession for between 6 months and 40 years, with an average service of just under 18 years. Nearly two-thirds worked part-time. The number and nature of incidents varied depending on which department the nurses worked in: 25 percent of the nurses experienced weekly events, 27 percent experienced monthly events, and 25 percent experienced one event every 6 months. The remainder had not experienced any violence. Incidents were highest in the emergency department, where staff reported an average of 46 incidents over the previous year, and in mental health, where the average was 40 incidents. The lowest incidents were reported by midwives (an average of two incidents each) and surgical staff and pediatric staff (an average of four incidents each). Forty percent of staff had been involved in an incident with a weapon, and 3 percent said it was a weekly occurrence. Weapons included guns (6 percent); knives (3 percent); and hospital equipment (32 percent). Weapon-related incidents were more common in the ED (weekly) and mental health (monthly). Reporting practices also varied; despite experiencing more problems, nurses working in the ED were much less likely to report any incidents (42 percent) than staff in other areas (76 percent). Half of all the nurses (50 percent) said they had reported an incident verbally—to their immediate manager (29 percent), other senior nursing staff (14.5 percent), or to their friends or colleagues (6 percent). But only 16 percent of incidents were officially reported. Thirty percent did not report incidents because they felt workplace violence was part of the job, and 50 percent said that when they reported an event, senior managers failed to take action. However, 70 percent said they would report an incident if they or a colleague were injured or there was a chance they would be laying charges or making a claim for compensation.

"The nurses in our study were reluctant to report episodes of workplace violence unless they considered the event to be serious," said Chapman. "This finding was supported by a retrospective audit of the hospital's formal incident reports, which showed that 96 percent of the reporting nurses had received one or more injuries as the result of a violent incident in the workplace. Understanding why nurses do or do not report incidents is very important as it can help educators and administrators to develop programs that help to reduce workplace violence. Further research on how individuals adapt to violence in the workplace is also warranted."

When healthcare organizations do not establish effective measures to prevent violence and protect nurses, the result is compromised quality of care for patients. Establishing a zero tolerance policy for violence is the first step, according to Jean Henry, assistant professor of health science in the College of Education and Health Professions at the University of Arkansas, Fayetteville. "There must be an organizational culture established that has a zero tolerance policy for violence," Henry said. "When it comes to protecting healthcare workers, administrators must make it clear that they won't tolerate any violence—verbal or physical—against workers."

Such a commitment sets the tone for developing policies and procedures to ensure a safe workplace. Henry and Ginn (2006) emphasize the importance of implementing a risk-management system throughout healthcare facilities to protect people and property from violence and prevent problems. "A lot of what you see now in patient violence comes from frustration with the healthcare system in general. The system is not doing a good job in providing adequate care," Henry adds. "Nurses are on the front line, so patients vent at the nurse."

General frustration with the system is compounded by problems with maintaining sufficient staffing levels. Henry uses an example of an inexperienced emergency room nurse who misreads a situation with an angry individual in the waiting room. "Even with maturity and experience, emergency room nurses are often swamped and stressed and can miss what is going on in the waiting room," Henry said. She suggests ways to handle emergency rooms to lessen the potential for patient violence. Staffing an emergency room with a patient advocate, who may be a trained volunteer, can help ensure that patients do not feel "invisible and forgotten." Procedures requiring that regular and frequent contact with patients be noted on a chart can facilitate follow-up and reduce patient frustration.

Henry notes that nurses are the most common perpetrators of some forms of violence, for example, "horizontal violence" directed against other nurses, which usually takes the form of psychological harassment. As Henry and Ginn (2006) explain, "The literature reveals that nurses are the most common perpetrators of some forms of violence, such as bullying. Some researchers suggest that the workplace environment and nursing culture allow this horizontal violence to occur unimpeded and actually accept it as a normal part of workplace culture. This seems to be particularly evident in regard to nursing experience; bullying is most often reported to be directed toward new nurses by more seasoned nurses." Such actions often seem to be precipitated by staffing shortages and increasing workloads.

Once again, institutions must establish a culture that does not tolerate violence, including bullying and harassment, which in some workplaces "may be so endemic that it is taken for granted and dismissed as inconsequential" (Henry and Ginn, 2006). Permitting bullying and harassment to go on has significant negative consequences, including demoralization and loss of confidence as well as negative attitudes and impaired work performance. The goal, Henry said, is an organizational culture that can be characterized as "caring, trusting and collaborative." In addition to assessing the risks and making changes in policies, procedures, and physical environment to protect against violence, healthcare administrators need to develop procedures for responding to incidents of violence that both support the victim and lead to improvements in the workplace. "Nurses have to know that the organization will protect them and that if something happens, they will not be treated as though they did something wrong," Henry said. "When people are victims of violence, we don't want to further victimize them during the investigation."

Henry notes that workplace violence has a broader impact than what was done to any one victim. Henry and Ginn (2006) note, "It damages trust, community and the sense of security that every employee has a right to feel while at work." Healthcare administrators and the educational institutions that prepare nurses both have a responsibility in the face of increasing violence, Henry and Ginn (2006) add. Employers need to show a commitment to providing a safe workplace in all clinical areas and other high-risk settings. Educators and employers both need to prepare nurses to deal with potentially violent situations.

Workplace violence can be classified into one of four categories, according to the University of Iowa Injury Prevention Research Center:

- *Type I (criminal intent)*: This type results while a criminal activity is being committed, and the perpetrator has no legitimate relationship to the workplace.
- *Type II (customer/client)*: The perpetrator is a customer or client at the workplace (e.g., healthcare patient) and becomes violent while being served by the worker.
- *Type III (worker-on-worker)*: Employees or past employees of the workplace are the perpetrators.
- *Type IV (personal relationship)*: The perpetrator usually has a personal relationship with an employee.

McPhaul and Lipscomb (2004) state that although healthcare providers may be exposed to all four types in the course of their work, a significant majority of threats and assaults against caregivers come from patients or their families and visitors. But as we shall see, that may be changing, as healthcare providers become the aggressors. Some criminal justice experts believe that ignoring or tolerating low-level crime creates an environment conducive to more serious crime. To this end, Hesketh et al. (2003) says that when verbal abuse, threats of assault, and low-level daily violence are tolerated in healthcare institutions, more serious forms of violence will follow.

It is impossible to say with certainty that stressed healthcare professionals engage in retribution against patients. There is little to nothing in the medical literature that suggests this connection, yet some experts believe it is a concept worth exploring to try to explain the occurrences of abuses of patients and other healthcare practitioners at the hands of healthcare providers.

When Healthcare Professionals Are the Abusers

Even as healthcare workers experience violence from patients, they are at risk for being victims of aggression from their coworkers. Hockley (2003) states that antisocial workplace practices such as abuse, bullying, and harassment among nurses in healthcare institutions are the "dark side of the caring profession." She adds that not only are nurses capable of being violent toward each other, but they use a variety of violent strategies to reach personal goals in the workplace, and they learn how to be violent to each other as a part of their socialization when they enter nursing. Najjar et al. (2009) documented the phenomenon known as *compassion fatigue*, wherein healthcare providers experience burnout related to their capacity for showing empathy to their patients and to others. Gardner (2009) explained that this term emerged in the 1990s to describe the mental distancing some healthcare professionals develop as a way to protect themselves, and that as healthcare becomes busier and more complex and as patient volumes rise, many healthcare providers can shut down and pull back from the emotional impact of seeing people suffering.

Whatever the triggers, healthcare providers seem to be capable of violence toward their charges—to the horror of other practitioners and society. Hockley (2005a) observed, "It is paradoxical that those whose overriding responsibility is to provide care and promote an environment in which the human rights, values, customs and spiritual beliefs of those in their care should be respected, should at the same time be also potentially capable of violent actions against those they are committed to care for." Hockley (2003) noted, "Acts of violence pervade human society but there is an expectation that when individuals enter a health setting they are going to be cared for in a professional and safe manner. It is ignoring these two principles that make unprofessional conduct toward patients so disturbing and dangerous."

Hockley (2005a) states that violence is no respecter of location, age, and so forth: "When a person requires healthcare they can become a target at any time. The targeted person could be mentally ill, a resident in an aged-care facility...Staff violence in the healthcare system can occur across the age spectrum as well as in different settings and locations wherever health professionals work."

As we will see in Chapter 3, much of the violence perpetrated by healthcare professionals is against vulnerable populations such as the very young, the very old, the mentally ill, or the medically incapacitated. Hockley (2005a) indicates that the literature shows that most of the research on staff-initiated violence is toward the elderly and therefore has different characteristics compared to other forms of workplace violence. For example, unlike other studies into workplace violence, the victims in this context are generally elderly women, in ill health, residing in a care facility. Conlin-Shaw (1998) confirmed that those at high risk are women, are generally mentally impaired by a disease such as dementia, have suffered a stroke, or have been diagnosed with Parkinson's disease; they are aged 75 years or older and are highly dependent on others. Hockley (2003) said that although there is the potential for patients of any age and health status to be victims of this form of violence, the elderly and the mentally ill are particularly at risk. Their inability to report this behavior may be one of the reasons why these groups of people are targeted, or it may be because of their mental state, or that they are vulnerable, or because they do not have people to advocate on their behalf.

Experts believe that any healthcare professional could become an abuser, from an untrained aide to a highly skilled and educated practitioner (Speaks, 1996; Hockley, 2003) Conlin-Shaw (1998) categorized healthcare abusers into three types: sadistic, reactive, and negligent, and indicated that sadistic and reactive abusers could be identified by their ability to develop psychological immunity, a self-protecting mindset that permits them to continue to work and actually feel good about the outcomes of their work. Citing Conlin-Shaw's work, Hockley (2005a) explained that sadistic abusers methodically and repeatedly abuse residents, are not remorseful, and are incapable of developing this immunity and often deny or blame others for their abusive behaviors. In comparison, Conlin-Shaw (1998) said that reactive abusers are "unable to control their impulses, lose their immunity suddenly and without thinking. They react negatively toward the resident with impulsive, almost instinctive reactions, often related to invasion of their personal body space."

Some healthcare workers, when faced with mounting workloads and difficult patients, react by taking out their frustrations on their charges. Hockley (2005a) said that patients can be victimized because they have complicated and sometimes off-putting medical needs, such as patients who smell because of their fungating wounds: "On one level, nurses may pity them and on another, they avoid them. I think victimization in terms of nurses to patient, is usually avoidance."

Hockley (2005a) urges healthcare institutions to watch for "invisible" violence toward patients which may be much more difficult to prove that it occurred. Hockley (2005a) explained, "Many of the non-physical types of violence…are similar to acts of neglect, abuse of power, humiliation and intimidation. For example, there have been documented cases of patients in mental institutions that have been made to perform for the amusement of staff members."

Speaks (1996) documented examples of neglect in a nursing home, such as not fixing patient call bells, allowing patients to become dehydrated, allowing decubitus ulcers to fester, or not changing wound dressings. Hockley (2005a) pointed to healthcare professionals withholding medications, allowing patients' meals to go cold, or leaving incontinent patients wet or soiled for long periods of time. Speaks (1996) emphasized that undetected neglect and abuse, over time, can escalate and lead to greater injury or even death. As we will see, medical malfeasance encompasses everything from exploitation to abuse to homicide, and it is this extreme that we will explore further in Chapter 5.

Healthcare professionals can become abusers when trying to cope with unsatisfactory circumstances in their lives, such as disappointing experiences, a lack of satisfaction at home or at work, financial stress, physical and emotional fatigue, domestic problems, and substance use and abuse. Hockley (2005a) explains that abusive caregivers often have experienced abuse in their personal lives; are not fully integrated from a social standpoint; have some history of arrests, hospitalizations for mental illness, violent behavior, or alcoholism or drug abuse; have poor coping skills and fragile emotional states; and have personality traits that are unrealistic, hypercritical, demanding, and rigid.

These troubles are compounded by organizational factors previously alluded to in this chapter, such as staffing shortages or a substandard work environment (Speaks 1996; Conlin-Shaw 1998). Engel (2004) and Hockley (2005a) proposes that healthcare professionals become abusers because they are victims themselves and then in turn become perpetrators when there is a buildup of anger, tension, or emotion that is released, and their patient is abused. Engel (2004) also proposes that numerous demands placed on healthcare providers can make them crack. Hockley (2005a) notes, "Another factor that allows healthcare workers to behave in this manner is because of their position of power, by taking an advantage of the situation and by breaking the trusting relationship."

There is no absolute documentation of the number of patients harmed at the hands of healthcare professionals. Pavlik et al. (2001) have reported that mistreatment of adults, including abuse, neglect, and exploitation, affects more than 1.8 million Americans. The potential for this kind of violation of patients' rights was recognized in 1973, when the AHA first crafted the Patient's Bill of Rights, with revisions in 1992. The AHA says hospitals must maintain and protect an institutional ethic that respects patients in all aspects of their care, and that this bill of rights will "contribute to more effective patient care and be supported by the hospital on behalf of the institution, its medical staff, employees, and patients."

First and foremost, and for our purposes in this book, the Patient's Bill of Rights asserts that "the patient has the right to considerate and respectful care." A second important tenet is the patient's "right to every consideration of privacy. Case discussion, consultation, examination, and treatment should be conducted so as to protect each patient's privacy." But equally important is the mandate that "the patient has the right to expect that all communications and records pertaining to his/her care will be treated as confidential by the hospital, except in cases such as suspected abuse and public health hazards when reporting is permitted or required by law. The patient has the right to expect that the hospital will emphasize the confidentiality of this information when it releases it to any other parties entitled to review information in these records." As we will see in Chapter 2, this right is being violated in many disturbing ways.

The Patient's Bill of Rights notes, "Hospitals have many functions to perform, including the enhancement of health status, health promotion and the prevention and treatment of injury and disease; the immediate and ongoing care and rehabilitation of patients; the education of health professionals, patients, and the community; and research. All these activities must be conducted with an overriding concern for the values and dignity of patients."

The violation of patient rights has not been lost on Congress, but some may say that enough action has not yet been taken to resolve the issue. A Senate bill known as the 2007–2008 Patient Safety and Abuse Prevention Act was introduced in the 110th Congress, and it sought to require screening, including national criminal history background checks, of care providers in skilled nursing facilities and other long-term care facilities and providers, and to provide for nationwide expansion of the pilot program for national and state background checks on direct patient-access employees of long-term care facilities or providers. Sponsored by Senator Herbert Kohl and a number of bipartisan cosponsors, the bill never became law. However, in the 111th Congress, a bill known as the 2009–2010 Patient Safety and Abuse Prevention Act is being considered by lawmakers at the time of writing. This newer bill also seeks to provide for nationwide expansion of the pilot program for national and state background checks on direct patient-access employees of long-term care facilities or providers. The measure would add a federal component to the background check process by screening applicants against the Federal Bureau of Investigation's (FBI) national database of criminal history records.

The bill has been riding on a wave of renewed interest on the part of legislators thanks to an endless stream of stories in the media about health-care providers who commit criminal misconduct on the job, and it was later discovered that these individuals have a history of convictions which a background check would have flagged. In 2002, a Government Accountability Office (GAO) report, which was requested by members of the Senate Aging Committee, recommended that individuals "applying to work in long-term care settings also undergo background checks because the elderly, like children, are a highly vulnerable population." More than 9,500 applicants with a history of substantiated abuse or a violent criminal record were prevented from working with elders and individuals with disabilities during a 3-year, seven-state demonstration project.

A 2006 study conducted by the Department of Health and Human Services determined that criminal background checks are a valuable tool for employers during the hiring process, that the use of criminal background checks during the hiring process does not limit the pool of potential job applicants, that a correlation exists between criminal history and incidences of abuse, and that the long-term care industry supports the practice of conducting background checks on potential employees in order to reduce the likelihood of hiring someone who has the potential to harm residents of long-term care facilities.

Furthermore, a national survey of State Adult Protective Services agencies identified more than 500,000 reports of elder and vulnerable adult abuse in 2004, and a national report concluded that more than 15,000 nursing home complaints involved abuse, including nearly 4,000 complaints of physical abuse, more than 800 complaints of sexual abuse, and nearly 1,000 complaints of financial exploitation. The Department of Health and Human Services has determined that even though 41 states now require criminal background checks on certified nurse aides prior to employment, only half of those require criminal background checks at the federal level. The subject of healthcare employee screening, background checks, and negligent hiring will be explored further in Chapter 6.

Breaking Professional Boundaries

Perhaps criminal activity begins the moment a healthcare professional crosses the boundary that exists between right and wrong, even with the smallest infraction that opens the door to escalating negligent behavior. Hundreds of case histories show that sex offenders often "operate" in places where they can take advantage of vulnerable targets. Examples of these offenders have included teachers and other school employees, as well as the clergy, and so it is no surprise that healthcare professionals are counted among the individuals who violate professional boundaries they are sworn to uphold.

The concept of establishing and maintaining sacrosanct boundaries is the hallmark of all relationships between care and counseling professionals such as healthcare providers or the clergy. Norris et al. (2003) defined a *boundary* as "the edge of appropriate professional behavior, a structure influenced by therapeutic ideology, contract, consent, and, most of all, context." They added further that "Boundary violations are typically harmful and are usually exploitive of patients' needs. Examples include having sex with patients, exploiting patients to perform menial services for the treater, exploiting patients for money…and generally using patients to feed the treater's narcissistic, dependent, pathologic or sexual needs."

It may be helpful to take a quick look at sexual abuse cases relating to the other helping professions, to place medical malfeasance in context. In the mid-2000s, the United States was rocked by a series of news reports of members of the Catholic clergy sexually abusing minors. The U.S. Conference of Catholic Bishops (USCCB) commissioned researchers at the John Jay College of Criminal Justice to conduct a study to examine the nature and scope of the problem of child sexual abuse in the Catholic Church. The data—based upon surveys provided by 195 dioceses, representing 98 percent all diocesan priests in the United States—attempted to pinpoint the number and nature of allegations of sexual abuse of minors under the age of 18 by Catholic priests between 1950 and 2002. The analysis by Lynch et al. (2004) revealed a range of 3 percent to 6 percent in the rates of alleged abuse across regions of the Catholic Church in the United States, and that a total of 10,667 individuals made allegations of child sexual abuse by priests. Less than 13 percent of allegations were made in the year in which the abuse allegedly began, and more than 25 percent of the allegations were made more than 30 years after the alleged abuse began. The largest group of alleged victims (50.9 percent) were between the ages of 11 and 14; 27.3 percent were 15 to 17; 16 percent were 8 to 10; and nearly 6 percent were under the age of 7. Overall, 81 percent of the victims were male and 19 percent were female. The majority of priests (56 percent) were alleged to have abused 1 victim; nearly 27 percent were alleged to have abused 2 or 3 victims; nearly 14 percent were alleged to have abused 4 to 9 victims; and 3.4 percent were alleged to have abused more than 10 victims. The 149 priests (3.5 percent) who had more than 10 allegations of abuse were allegedly responsible for abusing 2,960 victims, thus accounting for 26 percent of the allegations. Therefore, a very small percentage of accused priests are responsible for a substantial percentage of the allegations. The most frequent acts allegedly committed were touching over the victim's clothing (52.6 percent); touching under the victim's clothes (44.9 percent); cleric performing oral sex (26 percent); victim disrobed (25.7 percent); and penile penetration or attempted penile penetration (22.4 percent). Abuse is not limited to the Catholic Church; in 1984, a Fuller Seminary survey of 1,200 ministers found that 20 percent of theologically "conservative" pastors admitted to some sexual contact outside of marriage with a church member; the figure jumped to more than 40 percent for "moderates" and 50 percent for "liberal" pastors confessing to similar behavior (Catholic League, 2004).

Teachers and other school employees have been significant perpetrators of sexual abuse of children. Shakeshaft (2004) examined the existing research on educator sexual misconduct in U.S. schools and reported a preponderance of studies addressing the incidence and the prevalence of child sexual abuse, as well as that these studies presented a wide range of estimates of the percentage of U.S. students subject to sexual misconduct by school staff and varying from 3.7 percent to 50.3 percent. Studies often revealed that teachers who sexually abuse believe the stereotype of an abuser as an easily identifiable danger to children, that many are those most celebrated in their profession, and that they are chronic predators. Teachers are reported most often, followed by coaches, in the studies. And as with members of the clergy, there is a power struggle at play here, too. As Shakeshaft (2004) explains, "Sexual abuse of students occurs within the context of schools, where students are taught to trust teachers. Schools are also a place where teachers are more often believed than are students and in which there is a power and status differential that privileges teachers and other educators." Shakeshaft said that sexual predators, no matter where they are or who they target, engage in strategies that trap their victims by lying to them, isolating them, and manipulating them. What's more, the abuse continues, because frequently, when children report abuse, they are not believed. "Because of the power differential, the reputation difference between the educator and the child, or the mindset that children are untruthful, many reports by children are ignored or given minimal attention," explains Shakeshaft (2004).

Addressing sexual abuse by educators has also traveled a similar trajectory, as has the punitive aspects of members of the clergy who are child abusers—sometimes the perpetrators are stopped and punished, while others are allowed to work and continue their criminal behavior. Shakeshaft and Cohan's (1994) study of 225 cases of educator sexual abuse in New York revealed that all of the accused had admitted to sexual abuse of a student, but none of the abusers was reported to authorities, and only 1 percent lost their license to teach. All of the accused had admitted to physical sexual abuse of a student, but only 35 percent received a negative consequence for their actions: 15 percent were terminated or, if not tenured, they were not rehired; and 20 percent received a formal reprimand or suspension. Another 25 percent received no consequences or were reprimanded informally and off-the-record. Nearly 39 percent chose to leave the district, most with positive recommendations or even retirement packages intact.

Experts say that there are two types of predators—the fixated predator and the situational predator. The fixated predator has essentially gravitated toward and become a part of the environment that houses his or her favorite kind of victim. If it is children, the fixated predator most commonly makes a conscious decision to become a teacher, pastor, or daycare educator to have easy access. The situational predator will take advantage of an opportunity that presents itself if the victim is available and the conditions are right. Whether fixated or situational, many healthcare professionals who intentionally harm their patients cross their professional boundaries with ease and with skill, using their status, power, and access to vulnerable populations as a springboard for their malfeasance.

It is difficult to imagine healthcare professionals as predators, but they do exist. Bloom et al. (1999) pointed to a statement from the Medical Council of New Zealand (MCNZ, 1992) that summarizes a credo to which all healthcare professionals should subscribe:

> The ethical doctor–patient relationship depends on the doctor creating an environment where mutual respect and trust can exist and where the patient can have confidence and safety. The onus is always on the doctor to behave in a professional manner. The community must be confident that personal boundaries will be maintained and that as patients they will never be at risk. It is never acceptable to blame the patient for sexual misconduct. The doctor is in a uniquely privileged position regarding physical and emotional proximity. Boundaries can easily be broken in this environment.

Breaches of the doctor–patient relationship risk causing psychological damage to the patient. Sexual misconduct by a doctor inevitably harms the patient. The doctor–patient relationship is not one of equality. In seeking assistance, guidance and treatment, the patient is vulnerable. Exploitation of the patient is an abuse of power. Because of the power imbalance patient consent can never be a defense.

Although it is often said that life imitates art, is there a connection between Hollywood's version of medicine and the breach of boundaries by healthcare professionals in real life? A medical student and faculty directors from the Johns Hopkins Berman Institute of Bioethics analyzed depictions of bioethical issues and professionalism over a full season of two popular medical dramas, *Grey's Anatomy* and *House, M.D.*, and found that the shows were rife with ethical dilemmas and actions that often ran afoul of professional codes of conduct. The authors of the review say they were well aware that their findings would end up stating the obvious, but they nonetheless wanted to provide data that would shed light on the relationship of these depictions on the perceptions of viewers, both healthcare professionals and members of the public. "I think the utility in our study is that it provides a starting point for a discussion," says fourth-year medical student Matthew Czarny, a researcher at the Berman Institute. "In no way are we saying that these shows are educational in and of themselves."

An earlier analysis by the coauthors, along with fellow Berman Institute faculty member Marie Nolan, PhD, found that more than 80 percent of medical and nursing students watch television medical dramas. That study also concluded that the programs might prompt students to think and talk about bioethical issues. In analyzing the second seasons of *Grey's Anatomy* and *House*, Czarny counted 179 depictions of bioethical issues, fewer than 11 different topics, ranging from informed consent to organ-transplant eligibility to human experimentation. Berman Institute director Ruth Faden, PhD, and the institute's deputy director for medicine, Jeremy Sugarman, MD, designed the study, helped develop the coding, and ensured the quality of the findings.

Given the vivid portrayals of clinical practice and bioethical issues in medical dramas, albeit through storylines that sometimes stray into the realm of outlandish, Czarny et al. (2010) began systematically eyeing the programs in the genre several years ago to assess the nature and extent of the depictions. *Grey's Anatomy*, now in its sixth season on the ABC Network, is one of the most watched prime-time television series in the country and chronicles the lives of five surgical interns and their attending and resident physicians. *House*, which airs on the Fox Network and is also in its sixth season, follows the medical maverick Dr. Gregory House and his trainees, as they diagnose and treat the most complex and perplexing cases.

Informed consent was the most frequently observed bioethical issue. Of 49 total incidents, 43 percent involved "exemplary" consent discussions, while the remaining instances were "inadequate." In general, exemplary depictions portrayed "compassionate, knowledgeable physicians participating in a balanced discussion with a patient about possible treatment options." Conversely, inadequate depictions were "marked by hurried and one-sided discussions, refusal by physicians to answer questions" and "even an entire lack of informed consent for risky procedures," the authors stated (Czarny et al., 2010).

They also tallied 22 incidents of "ethically questionable departures from standard practice," most of them depicting doctors endangering patients unnecessarily in their pursuit of a favorable outcome. "In almost all of these incidents (18 out of 22), the implicated physician is not penalized," the authors noted. Czarny recalled an episode of *Grey's Anatomy* in which an intern forged an attending physician's signature. "When this is discovered, the attending seems somewhat grateful that that was pursued," Czarny said. He cited another egregious example from the show, in which an intern administers medical care while intoxicated. The study also examined 400 incidents of professionalism, which included interactions among professional colleagues, as well as those with patients. The authors limited their count to incidents they defined as either "exemplary" or "egregious."

"Incidents related to respect were the most frequently observed across both series, and depictions were largely negative," Czarny et al. (2010) concluded. The next most commonly observed departure from professionalism was sexual misconduct, with 58 incidents notched by the second season of *Grey's Anatomy* and 11 in *House*. Out of 178 interactions between professionals, across all issues, the authors deemed just 9 exemplary in nature.

Acknowledging that both series are intended for entertainment purposes, the Berman Institute group said none of the findings was unexpected. In addition, because the study was a content analysis, the authors did not set out to determine the value of these medical dramas as educational tools. Rather, their goal was to inform discussions about whether medical dramas should be shown in a classroom to spur conversations about ethics and professionalism among medical and nursing students.

References

AFT Healthcare. "Empty hallways: The hidden shortage of healthcare workers." Undated 1.

AFT Healthcare. "The vanishing nurse ... and other disappearing healthcare workers." Undated 2.

American Association of Critical Care Nurses (AACN). "Workplace violence prevention." 2004.

American Medical Association (AMA). "Principles of medical ethics." 2001.

American Nurses Association (ANA). "Code of ethics for nurses." 2001.

Beauchamp TL. The four principles approach to healthcare ethics. In: *Principles of Health Care Ethics*, second edition. Ashcroft RE et al., eds. New York: John Wiley & Sons. 2007, p. 7.

Bloom JD, Nadelson CC, and Notman MT, eds. *Physician Sexual Misconduct*. Washington, DC: American Psychiatric Association. May 1999.

Bureau of Labor Statistics (BLS). "U.S. Department of Labor Career Guide to Industries," 2010–2011 Edition.

Catholic League for Religious and Civil Rights. "Sexual abuse in social context: Catholic clergy and other professionals." February 2004.

Chapman R, Styles I, Perry L, and Combs S. Examining the characteristics of workplace violence in one non-tertiary hospital. *J Clin Nurs*. 19(3–4):479–488. 2010.

Conlin-Shaw MM. Nursing home resident abuse by staff. *J Elder Abuse Neglect*. 9(4):1–21. 1998.

Czarny MJ, Faden RR, and Sugarman J. Bioethics and professionalism in popular television medical dramas. *J Med Ethics*. 36(4):203–206. 2010.

Emergency Nurses Association (ENA). "Prevalence of violence in emergency departments." 1994.

Engel F. *Taming the Beast: Getting Violence Out of the Workplace*, second edition. Montreal, Canada: Ashwell. 2004.

Gallup Poll. "Nurses shine, bankers slump in ethics ratings: Annual honesty and ethics poll rates nurses best of 21 professions." November 24, 2008.

Gardner A. Stressed healthcare workers battle compassion fatigue. *U.S. News & World Report*. April 10, 2009.

Hampson R. "Angels of mercy: The dark side." *USA Today*. December 16, 2003.

Harris Poll No. 58. July 26, 2006.

Harris Poll No. 61. August 8, 2006.

Healthgrades. "Sixth annual patient safety in American hospitals study." April 7, 2009.

Henry J, and Ginn GO. Prevention of workplace violence for nurses. In: *Leadership and Nursing Care Management*. Huber D, ed. Philadelphia: Saunders. 2006. (Accessed October 23, 2010, at: http://books.google.com/books?id=MgSgz-q mlQEC&printsec=frontcover&dq=%22Leadership+and+Nursing+Care+Managem ent%22&hl=en&src=bmrr&ei=36AGTbKrNo3AsAP9gu2BBw&sa=X&oi=book_res-ult&ct=result&resnum=1&ved=0CDMQ6AEwAA#v=onepage&q=%22prevention%20 of%20workplace%20violence%20for%20nurses%22&f=false.)

Hesketh K et al. Workplace violence in Alberta and British Colombia Hospitals. *Health Policy*. (63):311–321. 2003.

Hockley C. *Silent Hell: Workplace Violence and Bullying*. Itasca, IL: Peacock. 2003.

Hockley C. Staff violence against those in their care. In: *Workplace Violence: Issues, Trends, Strategies*. Bowie V, and Fisher BS, eds. Cullompton, England: Willan. Pp. 77–96. 2005a.

Hockley C. Violence in nursing: The expectations and the reality. In: *Professional Issues in Nursing: Challenges and Opportunities*. Philadelphia: Lippincott Williams & Wilkins. Huston C, ed. 2005b.

International Council of Nurses (ICN). "Code of ethics for nurses." 2000.

Johnson C. Bad blood: Doctor–nurse behavior problems impact patient care. Special report: 2009 Doctor–nurse behavior survey. *Phys Exec J.* November/December. 2009.

Lipscomb J, and Love C. Violence toward healthcare workers: An emerging occupational hazard. *AAOHN J.* 40(5):219–228. 1992.

Lynch GW, Levine J, and Terry K. "John Jay College of Criminal Justice research report: The nature and scope of the problem of sexual abuse of minors by Catholic priests and deacons in the United States." 2004. (Accessed October 23, 2010, at: http://usccb/org/nrb/johnjaystudy.)

McPhaul K, and Lipscomb J. Workplace violence in healthcare: Recognized but not regulated. *J Issues Nurs.* 9(3). 2004.

Medical Council of New Zealand (MCNZ). *Bulletin of the Medical College of New Zealand.* 6:4–5.1992.

Merrill CT, and Elixhauser A. Procedures in U.S. hospitals, 2003: HCUP Fact Book no. 7. Agency for Healthcare Research and Quality (AHRQ) Publication 06-0039. May 2006.

Najjar N, Davis LW, Beck-Coon K, and Doebbeling CC. Compassion fatigue. *J Health Psych.* 14(2):267–277. 2009.

NIOSH Publication 2002-101: "Violence occupational hazards in hospitals." April 2002.

NIOSH. Publication 2008-136. "Exposure to stress: Occupational hazards in hospitals." July 2008.

Norris DM, Gutheil TG, and Strasburger LH. This couldn't happen to me: Boundary problems and sexual misconduct in the psychotherapy relationship. *Psychiatr Serv.* 54:517–522. April 2003.

Pavlik VN, Hyman DJ, Festa NA, and Dyer CB. Quantifying the problem of abuse and neglect in adults—Analysis of a statewide database. *J Am Geri Soc.* 49:45–48. 2001.

Runciman B, Merry A, and Walton M. *Safety and Ethics in Healthcare: A Guide to Getting It Right.* Guildford, UK: Ashgate. 2007, p. 2007.

Shakeshaft C. "Educator sexual misconduct: A synthesis of existing literature." Prepared for the U.S. Department of Education's Office of the Under Secretary Policy and Program Studies Service by Hofstra University and Interactive, Inc. June 2004.

Shakeshaft C, and Cohan A. "*In loco parentis*: Sexual abuse of students in schools; what administrators should know." Report to the U.S. Department of Education. 1994.

Speaks GE. Documenting inadequate care in the nursing home: The story of an undercover agent. *J Elder Abuse Neg.* 8(3):37–45. 1996.

Standard & Poor's Industry Surveys: Health Care. 2004.

Stultz MS. Crime in hospitals 1986–1996: The latest IAHSS surveys. *J Health Pro Man.* (2):1–25. 1993.

United Press International. Half of ER nurses assaulted on the job. July 29, 2009.

U.S. Department of Labor. 1996.

U.S. Department of Labor. 2004.

Wallace M. *Healthcare and the Law*, third edition. North Ryde, NSW: Law Book. Pg. 185. 2001.

Patient Privacy and Exploitation

2

As discussed in Chapter 1, healthcare has some of the most trusted practitioners of any industry. Perhaps that is why it is so disheartening to hear about breaches of that trust in ways that make a mockery of healthcare practitioners' codes of ethics. In an age of technological advances, the Internet, cell phones, and other portable electronic devices, there are numerous new ways to invade patients' privacy, endanger their personal health information, and exploit them when they are most vulnerable.

In a Harris Poll of 2,392 Americans conducted in September 2007, 83 percent of respondents agreed with the statement, "I generally trust my healthcare providers—doctors and hospitals—to protect the privacy and confidentiality of my personal medical records and health information" (Westin, 2007). However, 12 percent believe that a healthcare provider had disclosed their personally identified medical information in a way they felt was improper. When it came to the statement, "The privacy of personal medical records and health information is not protected well enough today by federal and state laws and organizational practices," 58 percent agreed, while 42 percent disagreed (Westin, 2007).

What Americans do not seem to trust is the U.S. government's control over their electronic health records—an intriguing trend as the country's healthcare institutions plod slowly toward a paperless medical record. In a recent national survey of 883 adult-aged Americans, the Ponemon Institute (2010) found that 84 percent of respondents are not aware that the U.S. government is considering the implementation of national databases for managing their personal health records. Respondents were unsure about who should be responsible for managing this national database; 45 percent would not pick any of the options offered in the study to manage the government database. Just 6 percent say it should be an existing federal department or agency, while 8 percent say it should be a new government department or agency especially charged with managing the national database; 10 percent would like to see one private company with government contracts; and 31 percent prefer many private companies with government contracts. And, 75 percent of respondents think the national database is not a good idea. However, if such a database were to be created, almost all respondents (98 percent) believe the individual's primary-care physician and 90 percent of respondents believe all medical personnel treating them should have access to their health records.

Interestingly, according to the Ponemon Institute study, more than 73 percent of respondents do not trust the federal government to protect the privacy of their health records, while 71 percent of respondents do trust healthcare providers to do so. The Ponemon Institute study also found that respondents considered two measures the most important for protecting the privacy of their health records: ensuring that only professionally trained medical practitioners have access to their health records (74 percent) and allowing their direct control of individual health records (71 percent).

At the core of the country's privacy and security of medical information is federal legislation known as the Health Insurance Portability and Accountability Act (HIPAA). Rolled out in several phases beginning in 2003, HIPAA established new requirements for the handling, processing, and storage of patient health information, and it was intended to strengthen existing commitments to keep patient information secure and private. It requires that all healthcare professionals be trained on the legislation's three regulations encompassing privacy rules, standard transactions, and security rules.

HIPAA's privacy rule identifies certain patient information as protected health information (PHI), designated as any information, whether oral or recorded in any form, that is created or received by a healthcare provider and relates to a past, present, or future medical condition or payment for services of an individual. Examples of PHI include Social Security numbers, birth dates, and driver's license numbers. The HIPAA privacy rule gives healthcare providers guidance on how, when, and with whom PHI can be shared. The privacy rules ensure that patients have the right to see their own medical records and to request changes to the records, as well as levy penalties for violation of these rules. In addition, HIPAA provides that national health priorities such as public health, medical research, fraud and abuse investigations, clinical quality assessments, and improvements may require the sharing of PHI without patient authorization; all other sharing of PHI must be authorized by the patient. HIPAA requires that a signed authorization form must be submitted before any information is disclosed to another person or company. HIPAA also establishes rules and standards for keeping patient information, whether written or electronic, confidential and protected from all unnecessary disclosure. A critical note to make is that privacy rules cover more than just written information; the rules can be extended to electronic and computer information, paper records, film (such as X-rays), and verbal information.

HIPAA is updated by the Health Information Technology for Economic and Clinical Health (HITECH) Act, effective February 2010, which extends HIPAA's rules for security and privacy safeguards, including increased enforcement, penalties, and audits; this new act was approved under the American Recovery and Reinvestment Act (ARRA) of 2009. Essentially, the HITECH Act introduces the first federally mandated data-breach notification requirement, as well as extends the reach of HIPAA's privacy and security rules to cover the "business associates" of HIPAA-accountable entities, such as healthcare providers, pharmacies, and billing agencies. These business associates will now face governmental penalties if they fail to meet HIPAA provisions as of February 2011.

In summary, the HITECH Act establishes a federal breach notification requirement for health information that is not encrypted or otherwise made indecipherable, and it requires that an individual be notified if there is an unauthorized disclosure or use of their health information. It ensures that new entities that were not contemplated when the federal privacy rules were first written, as well as those entities that work on behalf of providers and insurers, are subject to the same privacy and security rules as providers and health insurers. The act requires that providers attain authorization from a patient in order to use their health information for marketing and fund-raising activities. It also provides transparency to patients by allowing them to request an audit trail showing all disclosures of their health information made through an electronic record, and it is designed to shut down the secondary market that has emerged around the sale and mining of patient health information by prohibiting the sale of an individual's health information without his or her authorization. Day and Kizer (2009) note that the HITECH Act adds teeth to HIPAA: "Previously, HIPAA's enforcement approach resulted in few investigations, and the imposition of penalties was exceptionally rare. Now, the sanctions for noncompliance will raise the risk and business impact for both covered entities as well as newly affected business associates."

A study of 260 healthcare organizations conducted by the Ponemon Institute (2009) revealed that 94 percent are not in substantial compliance with HITECH, but existing covered entities under HIPAA are far more prepared than the business associates that the HITECH Act targets. According to the Poneman Institute study conducted in the fall of 2009, 27 percent had not started working toward compliance with the HITECH Act and are barely aware of what they need to do; 32 percent had been waiting for more detail; 14 percent had a plan but were waiting for more detail; and 21 percent were just starting to act. Only 1 percent of organizations reported being ready, and 4 percent were almost ready to meet the 2010 effective date. The Poneman Institute (2009) reported that of those healthcare organizations that have a privacy and security compliance program in place, 20 and 21 percent, respectively, have an independent party test the program for adequacy annually or at least every 2 years. Forty-two percent of participating organizations had updated their privacy programs at least once since inception, and 38 percent had similarly updated their security compliance program. In terms of owning up to potential deficiencies, the study found that smaller healthcare organizations were more likely to report deficiencies in their HIPAA privacy rule or security rule compliance programs.

A significant barrier to compliance with HIPAA and to HITECH, according to the Poneman Institute (2009), is a lack of buy-in by the healthcare organization's management or by leaders in the "business associate" organizations, as well as insufficient budgets and resources to ensure compliance. This is distressing in light of the Poneman Institute's findings that most healthcare organizations reported that they had experienced one or more data-breach incidents involving the loss or theft of patient information during the past 2 years. In fact, 90 percent of respondents admit their organizations experienced one or more data breaches over the past 2 years involving the loss or theft of patient information, and all covered entities in the Ponemon study say their organizations had at least one breach involving one or more compromised records. Similarly, 80 percent of business associates admit to experiencing a data breach involving at least one or more compromised records. The estimated cost of data breach varied by organizational size; according to the Ponemon study, healthcare organizations with less than 100 employees experienced an average cost of $130,000, while organizations with more than 25,000 employees experienced an average cost of $4.1 million.

There is certainly good reason to strive toward HITECH Act compliance; according to Day and Kizer (2009), the act establishes new tiered penalties with a new potential maximum of up to $1.5 million; state attorneys general can now bring civil actions to enforce HIPAA; and a provision is pending to permit affected individuals to share in civil monetary penalties imposed under HIPAA. Day and Kizer (2009) emphasized that despite the safeguards designed to protect the privacy and security of PHI, healthcare organizations must reexamine the protections they have in place as well as know where sensitive patient data are being stored and who has access to the data. They note, "To achieve the goals of the new legal requirements, healthcare-related organizations will need to execute a strategic data classification program and utilize a more holistic approach to information security management to better safeguard protected health information."

Some assert that HIPAA—designed to engender confidence in national health privacy protection—falls short of the intended goal and that widely reported medical data breaches may be a factor in the public's mistrust, with or without the new HITECH Act provisions, protections, and penalties. Others point to the lack of systematic data to determine the frequency, scope, and severity of the security and privacy incidents involving PHI. One healthcare professional, who remains anonymous, started the Web site PogoWasRight.org in 2006, to increase awareness of privacy issues. (The name is derived from the Pogo cartoon character who remarked, "We have met the enemy and he is us," because the creator felt it applied equally well to privacy concerns.) In July 2007, PogoWasRight.org released results from a review of media reports that attempted to enumerate incidents that occurred after the HIPAA privacy rule was implemented in April 2003. PogoWasRight.

org report that out of 291 incidents meeting inclusion criteria in the study, 249 incidents for which sufficient data were available for analysis accounted for the potential or actual exposure, loss, or compromise of health information of more than 16 million people in the approximately 4-year study period. For the entire sample, 36 of the reported incidents (12 percent) resulted in fraud or identity theft, including medical identity theft. Dishonest healthcare employees who acquired and then used or sold the individual's data to others accounted for 75 percent of all incidents that were reported to have resulted in misuse of information.

PogoWasRight.org (2007) says that hospital databases are particularly vulnerable to breaches: "A number of hospitals have reported hacks of their patient database servers. To date, however, none of the publicized incidents reported in the media have been definitively linked to any financial fraud or identity theft." However, PogoWasRight.org (2007) cautions that because perpetrators may not use the stolen patient information immediately, fraud may not be detected until months or even years later, and that assurances about a lack of evidence of misuse of information are "false reassurance to those whose information was exposed or compromised."

The Government Accountability Office (GAO, 2007) report analyzed breach reports or incidents where the nature of the data might lend itself to identity theft, in order to determine the extent to which incidents resulted in identity theft and whether it would be appropriate for Congress to incorporate some risk-based criteria in any mandatory disclosure and notification law. As part of its analysis, the GAO asked the American Hospital Association (AHA) to ask a nonrepresentative sample of 78 large hospitals whether they had experienced any breaches of sensitive personal information (excluding medical records) since January 2003. Of the 46 hospitals responding to the query, 13 reported a total of 17 data breach incidents. No additional information about the incidents was provided in the GAO report, and the agency did not make recommendations.

According to PogoWasRight.org, the U.S. Healthcare Industry Quarterly HIPAA Survey Results is one source of data-breach information. In 2003, 77 percent of respondent providers reported being (mostly) in compliance; in 2004, the self-reported compliance rate was 78 percent; and in 2005 and 2006, the compliance rate remained at 78 percent. In contrast to these findings of a plateau in provider compliance, a January 2006 survey conducted by the American Health Information Management Association (AHIMA) reported that provider compliance actually decreased in 2006 compared to 2005. AHIMA reported that the percentage of healthcare privacy officers and others whose jobs relate to HIPAA privacy who believe their institution is more than 85 percent compliant dropped to 85 percent in 2006, down from 91 percent in 2005. As a result, the percent who believe they are less than 85 percent compliant increased from 9 percent in 2005 to 15 percent in 2006.

Respondents to AHIMA's survey listed a lack of resources and lack of administrative support as their main challenges to greater compliance.

HIPAA's second rule, which addresses security, went into effect in April 2005. The U.S. Healthcare Industry Quarterly HIPAA Survey indicates less provider compliance with the HIPAA security rule than with the privacy rule: in 2005, 43 percent of providers and 74 percent of payers reported compliance with the security rule; in 2006, 56 percent of providers and 80 percent of payers reported compliance. AHIMA data show different compliance rates: in 2006, 25 percent of survey respondents reported full compliance with the security rule, while an additional 50 percent indicated that they were between 85 percent and 95 percent compliant.

Regarding breaches of the HIPAA security rule, the U.S. Healthcare Industry Quarterly HIPAA Survey respondents reported that in 2004 (before compliance was required), 28 percent of providers and 17 percent of payers reported that they had experienced one to five data security breaches in the first 6 months of the year. In 2005, 57 percent of providers and 68 percent of payers reported no incidents, but 32 percent of providers and 27 percent of payers experienced at least one security breach, including an average of 4 percent of both providers and payers that experienced between 6 and 10 security breaches in the first 6 months of the year. In 2006, 32 percent of providers experienced between one and five incidents, and another 7 percent reported 6 to 11 incidents. Additionally, 29 percent of payers experienced between one and five security incidents, and another 4 percent experienced between 6 and 11 breaches.

PogoWasRight.org (2007) have observed that compliance with the HIPAA privacy rule has plateaued or even declined, and that the data indicate numerous breaches occurring daily across the United States, "each of which has the potential to harm an individual or many individuals and each of which may be lessening the public's trust in the healthcare system to protect privacy, confidentiality, and security of health information."

A November 2006 survey conducted by Lake Research Partners and American Viewpoint for the Markle Foundation on attitudes toward electronic health records found that 80 percent of the Americans sampled said they are very concerned about identity theft or fraud. As we have seen, for all of its protections, HIPAA could be providing patients with a false sense of security about how well their PHI is safeguarded by their healthcare providers. An industry white paper, "Privacy Surveillance in Healthcare," (FairWarning, undated) observes that the healthcare system is experiencing an "epidemic of high-profile privacy incidents involving employees and affiliates using electronic health records (EHRs) to conduct unlawful activities." These offenses include snooping in medical records and identity theft, with serious consequences for patients and healthcare institutions alike. The white paper authors observed, "Compounding the situation is increasingly aggressive enforcement of privacy and security legislation which carries punitive damages for healthcare institutions and in the case of some states, fines for individual employees involved."

Some experts suggest that perhaps the increase in reported privacy breaches is merely a result of improved reporting in recent years, as individuals are better able to identify and act on privacy breaches as a result of the passage of state data-breach notification laws. Day and Kizer (2009) have said that although these assertions are viable, "the growing number of reported privacy breaches also reflects an actual rise in breach incidents. Despite the significant efforts made to comply with HIPAA, the implementation and management of privacy and information security programs remain problematic." Based on the number of reported data breaches and affected individuals, the healthcare industry has only a slightly better record than other industries, representing just 11 percent of all reported data breaches in the United States from 2000 to 2007. However, Day and Kizer (2009) caution that the number of reported healthcare privacy breaches is expected to increase due to pending HIPAA modifications. They noted, "As difficult as it has been to get compliance in the past, the new ARRA provisions related to HIPAA will make future compliance even more challenging."

Patients' PHI is increasingly vulnerable because it is generally accessible to all personnel who may need access, including administrative and accounting staff, as well as clinicians and technicians. This access has led to a number of high-profile privacy-related incidents at healthcare institutions, perpetrated by insiders at prestigious health systems—demonstrating that privacy breaches can happen anywhere, regardless of the sophistication of healthcare information technology systems. Consider these incidents:

- At New York–Presbyterian Medical Center in New York City, patients' names, phone numbers, and Social Security numbers were stolen by an admissions department employee and sold to organized crime groups specializing in identity theft.
- At the University of California–Los Angeles (UCLA) Medical Center, an employee accessed actress Farrah Fawcett's cancer treatment records and sold information to several tabloid publications. It was later discovered that this employee had accessed the records of more than 30 other celebrity patients.
- At Baptist Health Medical Center in Little Rock, Arkansas, an admissions clerk stole patient information and used it to secure temporary account authorization numbers that were then used to purchase Wal-Mart gift cards.

Other types of incidents include the following:

- Credit card information was stolen and used to make unauthorized purchases.
- Patient information was used to create fake identifications.
- Faxes from medical centers and physician offices were mistakenly sent in error to unintended recipients.
- Boxes of unshredded patient medical records were found in dumpsters.
- Patient medical forms were found in the backyards of people's homes, evidently carried by the wind and coming from a local nursing home.
- Unencrypted laptops, desktop computers, and personal digital assistants (PDAs) holding patient information were stolen or lost.
- Hackers breached health institutions' computer systems.
- PHI was exposed and cached on Google.
- Before-and-after photos were posted to Web sites without patient consent.

These aforementioned breaches are appalling, and they are compelling patients to wonder what healthcare institutions are doing to better protect sensitive health information. Although security measures are put into place, they are still prone to breaches by insiders, who are becoming the most significant source of risk. As Day and Kizer (2009) have explained, healthcare privacy breaches most frequently are triggered by hackers, employees with malicious intent, or by the theft of laptop computers or USB drives: "Hackers typically exploit vulnerabilities in IT systems or embed malicious code in Web sites or files, such as free MP3s, videos, or games. They target relatively poorly protected systems rather than attempting to penetrate highly secured systems. Their motive is usually to commit fraud by stealing a patient's PHI." Day and Kizer (2009) have also stated that employees with illicit intent account for just 10 percent of breaches but are responsible for nearly 25 percent of all compromised health records, and they added, "These persons typically are healthcare administrators or IT staff who have become disgruntled, have criminal intentions or simply cannot control their curiosity. They have access to sensitive patient information because of their jobs, but they abuse the trust and access, sometimes causing serious damage."

There are limitations to hospitals' existing security measures. For example, encryption on computers can be bypassed by insiders with authorized access to EHRs and their applications. Even though single sign-on (SSO) technology can enforce passwords, again, it does not prevent authorized users with malicious intention from accessing data. Identity management and provisioning technology can help deny access to former employees, but it does not stop authorized users from abusing their access privileges. Finally, security information management (SIM) technology can collect information about security-related events from infrastructure systems such as firewalls, routers, servers, and virtual private networks, but it was not designed to support EHRs. The Enterprise Strategy Group (2006) estimates that as much as 85 percent of all business data is unstructured, such as the information contained in e-mails, text documents, spreadsheets, and presentations, and therefore is more susceptible to unauthorized access.

Day and Kizer (2009) have reported that some of the most frequent causes of a data breach include the introduction of malicious code into an information system; internal staff actions such as intentional and accidental inappropriate disclosures; data exposure caused by deficient system design; and theft or loss of laptops or portable storage devices. As Day and Kizer (2009) explain, "Individual carelessness and non-adherence to established security procedures have been the reasons behind a number of incidents. In other cases, the root causes have been procedural irregularities involving nonstandard or poorly documented confidential data storage, unauthorized or unknown network connections, and unknown accounts or data access privileges."

So, what if PHI suddenly develops "legs," so to speak? Portable electronic devices are being implicated in a number of patient privacy breaches. A recent survey of 1,000 healthcare professionals in the United States and in the United Kingdom revealed that more than one-third keep confidential information on laptops, smartphones, and portable drives without adequately securing the data. The Mobile Device Usage in the Healthcare Sector survey, conducted by mobile security firm Credent Technologies, found that one-fifth of respondents admitted to using their own devices to transport patient information (including patient demographics, medical research data, diary and patient records, and laboratory and operation procedures). A little more than one-third of those surveyed rely solely on passwords to secure their work laptops and other mobile devices. Eighteen percent of U.S. respondents and 6 percent of UK respondents admitted to storing sensitive patient details with no security measures taken. About 56 percent of healthcare professionals in the United Kingdom use strong security to protect their devices, with 35 percent using encryption, 17 percent using two-factor authentication, 3 percent using biometrics, and 1 percent using smart cards. Only 23 percent of U.S. respondents report using strong security measures to protect their mobile devices. When asked why they were using these devices, the majority cited convenience, capacity, and speed of removal as the primary reasons.

To combat privacy breaches, healthcare organizations have been placing restrictions on the use of mobile devices in the workplace, such as placing blocks on USB connections, disabling cameras on phones, or preventing people from downloading information from a hospital's network onto a mobile device. However, the privacy breaches seem to continue nonetheless.

Exploitation via Photography

Photography in the healthcare setting has its place, of course. As Hjort et al. (2001) have observed, "The use of patient photography, videotaping, digital imaging and other visual recordings during patient care is commonplace.... Although patient photography may be fairly common, liability issues need to be considered and federal regulations observed. Without proper precautions during a healthcare encounter, patient photography may make a healthcare provider liable for invasion of privacy." The legal system has punished providers who exploit patients for financial gain, as well as when a patient's name or picture was used for noncommercial purposes, maintaining that even taking a photograph without the patient's consent was an invasion of privacy.

Hjort et al. (2001) add that photography is addressed by the HIPAA privacy rule in that it defines *health information* in a manner that implies inclusion of patient photography: "Health information means any information... that is created or received by a healthcare provider...and relates to the past, present or future physical or mental health of an individual; the provision of healthcare to an individual; or the past, present or future payment for the provision of healthcare to an individual." In addition, Hjort et al. (2001) note that "Still photographs and scanned printouts taken for medical reasons may be filed with the patient's record for safekeeping. The issue of patient privacy and confidentiality needs to be addressed when maintaining patient images. Sensitive images...need to be available for patient care, but also need to be maintained in a manner that protects the patient from unauthorized viewing."

Exploitation via Cell Phone Photos

The presence of cell phones in healthcare facilities poses the liability of invasion of patient privacy. As Barber (2010) notes, healthcare professionals should be aware of any digital media devices in patients' possession that could be used to download information from the hospital's computer network: "Many individuals have cell phones with cameras and other mobile storage devices, and when these are brought into the hospital environment, they pose a real threat to patient privacy and overall hospital security" (pp. 97–104).

A survey conducted by the College of Healthcare Information Management Executives (CHIME, 2007) revealed that an increasing number of hospitals are loosening restrictions on cell phone usage, even allowing cell phones in the emergency department (ED) and the intensive care unit (ICU). According to the survey, 23 percent of the 185 CHIME members responding to the survey reported that their hospital lifted all restrictions on cell phone use, up 5.5 percent from a similar survey conducted in 2004. Respondents commented that restrictions were being lifted after numerous studies indicated that cell phone interference with medical equipment is negligible; lifting restrictions is also seen as a way to improve patient care and patient satisfaction. Sixty-nine percent reported that cell phone use is restricted only in certain areas, such as the ED and ICU, while only 11 (0.06 percent) of the respondents indicated that cell phone use is strictly prohibited in their hospital.

Incidents of high-profile cell phone invasions of privacy are numerous:

- In September 2009, the Tennessee Bureau of Investigation (TBI) arrested two former employees of a Tennessee rehabilitation center for taking with their cell phones degrading photos of elderly patients in their care. They were each indicted by the county grand jury on four counts of healthcare abuse (TBI, 2009).
- In 2009, a photo of a partially nude patient at a North Carolina mental hospital was found on a hospital-provided cell phone. Two state employees were placed on leave while allegations were investigated (Associated Press, 2009).
- In 2008, two University of New Mexico Hospital employees were fired and others were disciplined for using their cell phone cameras to take photos of patients receiving treatment for injuries and then posting the images to a social networking Web site (Clark/AP, 2008).
- In 2007, a chief resident of general surgery at Mayo Clinic's Phoenix Hospital used his cell phone to take an inappropriate photograph of a patient under anesthesia and then showed the picture to his colleagues (Markus and Zuiker, 2009).
- In 2007, Tri-City Medical Center in Oceanside, California, fired nine employees, including emergency-medical technicians, nurses, and secretaries, who took or looked at camera-phone photos of a patient's X-ray (Dotinga, 2007).
- In 2006, a hospital-based respiratory therapist in San Diego was accused of molesting brain-damaged, comatose children, taking cell phone photos of himself in the act, and posting them on the Internet (Hughes, 2006).
- In 2007, in Kentucky, a county ambulance employee took pictures at accident scenes with his cell phone and then uploaded pictures of some of the victims and accidents to MySpace, where he blogged about his work as a paramedic. One of the pictures was of a fatal accident involving a teenager. The paramedic was assaulted by the teen's grieving family, he was fired from his job for the privacy breach and unethical conduct, and the family members were charged with felony assault (Sanders, 2007).

Markus and Zuiker (2009) have noted that healthcare facilities have understood that photographs constitute personal health information and have therefore prohibited their employees from photographing a patient without his or her consent: "With the ever-increasing popularity of cell phone cameras and online social networking Web sites, the potential for inappropriate use of such cameras in healthcare settings is tremendous." Dotinga (2007) has stated that most hospitals have regulations that ban photography without permission, forbid employees from using cell phones on the job, and remind visitors not to use cameras. Dotinga (2007) reports that "It's unclear how many hospitals have policies regulating camera phones, but their numbers seem to be growing. Last year, the Southern California hospital chain Scripps Health added camera phones and PDAs to its policies restricting photography, although they are not officially banned. Scripps Health, which runs five hospitals and 13 outpatient clinics, told Wired News it has fired employees in the last month for violating photography rules, although fewer than a dozen of its 11,000 employees have been sacked for privacy violations over the past year." Ornstein (2008) has reported that UCLA's neuropsychiatric hospital banned all cell phones and laptop computers after a patient posted group photos of other patients on a social networking Web site. Other hospitals have banned cell phone cameras as well. Rady Children's Hospital in San Diego prohibited employees from carrying cell phones in patient-care areas after investigators found images of children, taken at the hospital, on a respiratory therapist's computer and cell phone. The therapist later pleaded guilty to child molestation and exhibiting a minor in pornography.

Cell phone camera voyeurism became a federal offense when former President George W. Bush signed into law the Video Voyeurism Prevention Act of 2004. The legislation amended the federal criminal code to prohibit knowingly videotaping, photographing, filming, recording by any means, or broadcasting an image of a private area of an individual, without that individual's consent, under circumstances in which that individual has a reasonable expectation of privacy. Punishment for violation includes fines of up to $100,000 or up to a year in prison, or both. The Senate version of the bill was introduced in 2000, several years before the first generation of cell phones equipped with a camera function debuted, so the legislation primarily focused on the use of hidden video cameras. New language was added to the bill in Congressional sessions in 2002 and 2003 to address potential privacy violations posed by cell phone cameras.

The challenge is that most phones now have features capable of sending and receiving files, photographs, and videos, making the distribution of illicit images easy for owners of cellular phones. The cell phone industry estimates that as of 2008, the number of cell phones in use surpassed 100 million, and there are millions more video cameras, so it is an impossible feat to apprehend voyeurs. Healthcare facilities must safeguard their patients from this threat. But what if the perpetrator is one of healthcare's own? In one case, a board-certified emergency medicine physician in Utah was arrested after he was allegedly caught videotaping and taking photographs of females who were undressing in an exam room in an urgent care clinic. The women saw the camera, called police, and law enforcement officers found the camera and video equipment containing images of the women, as well as additional images saved on the physician's computer. The physician was arrested for investigation of two counts of voyeurism and one count of evidence tampering because the physician allegedly attempted to delete and destroy evidence during the investigation (Morgan, 2009).

In January 2009, the United Kingdom's Department of Health published guidelines to help hospitals deal with the issue. Essentially, the document said that while phones should be allowed, hospitals must familiarize themselves with the risks and issues when preparing their cell phone usage policy, and that patient privacy and dignity must be upheld at all times. The guidelines also suggested that hospitals have a written policy regarding the use of cell phones, cameras, and video recording devices which is easily accessible to staff, patients, and visitors, and that all areas of the hospital that are off-limits to recording devices be clearly marked with appropriate signage (DH, 2009). In the United States, hospitals and healthcare systems are left to devise their own policies and procedures, with most institutions including the aforementioned commonsense practices in their policies.

Markus and Zuiker (2009) have observed that healthcare facilities are not the only institutions "navigating the privacy issues arising from ongoing technological advancements. However, given the strict regulatory environment in which they operate and the increasing industry concern for patient privacy, healthcare facilities must be proactive in addressing cell phone camera use" (pp. 12–14). Markus and Zuiker (2009) suggest that healthcare institutions address these concerns and avoid potential liability by adopting written policies that:

- Outline in detail to patients, staff, and visitors the facility's limitations on cell phone camera use and the consequences for failure to abide by the policy.
- Emphasize that cell phone cameras are never to be used to record images of patients (and that such images, if needed for purposes of care or training, should be obtained only by authorized practitioners using specified equipment and pursuant to a specific facility policy).
- Prohibit the distribution of photographs or other images to any person outside the facility, absent written authorization for a permissible use.

Markus and Zuiker (2009) also suggest that facility staff, including volunteers and members of the medical staff, should be trained annually on the policy in conjunction with other compliance training sessions, and attendance should be made a condition of employment. In addition, whatever policy a health-care institution adopts, it should conspicuously post signs that clearly state the nature and extent of the ban on cell phone or cell phone camera usage within the facility. If the policy is violated, Markus and Zuiker (2009) have stated that facilities train staff to require any patient, visitor, employee, or any other individual who is observed taking photographs with a cell phone to immediately erase the photographs from the phone. "As technology advances and wireless handheld devices, phones, cameras, and computers become ever smaller and add new features, healthcare facilities need to proactively respond to the potential privacy violations that the use of such devices presents," Markus and Zuiker (2009) noted. "Cameras on cell phones, PDAs, and laptops are particularly troublesome because they can be used without anyone knowing that a photograph is being taken. Further, the user can instantaneously transmit the photograph to the Internet, at which point the subject's PHI is no longer protected or private. Although the inconveniences are real, and patient and practitioner push-back is likely, a complete ban on the use of cell phones may be the safest policy to ensure that patient privacy is protected. Healthcare facilities should be known for the patient care they provide, not the unauthorized or inappropriate photographs of their patients that surface on Facebook."

Exploitation via Internet Improprieties

A proclivity toward breaches of privacy apparently begins in medical school for some would-be physicians. One study found that a majority of medical schools report they have experienced incidents of students posting unprofessional content online, including incidents involving violation of patient confidentiality, with few schools having policies to address these types of postings (Chretien et al., 2009). An anonymous survey was sent to deans of student affairs at each institution in the Association of American Medical Colleges; data were collected in March and April 2009, with 60 percent of U.S. medical schools responding (78 out of 130). Chretien et al. (2009) wrote: "Medical schools are tasked with establishing the foundation of professional behavior in a generation of students who use Web 2.0 and expect digital connectedness. There are few data to document unprofessional behavior in medical student–posted online content. Also, the adequacy of current institutional professionalism policies, given these new challenges, is unknown."

Internet applications built around user-generated content, including social networking sites such as Facebook and Twitter, media-sharing sites such as Flickr and YouTube, blogs, wikis, and podcasts, are proliferating and providing vehicles for the posting of inappropriate material. The researchers found that of the schools that responded to the survey, 60 percent (47/78) reported ever having incidents involving students posting unprofessional content to social networking sites. Chretien et al. (2009) wrote: "In the past year, 13 percent (6/47) of these had no incidents, 78 percent (36/47) had fewer than five incidents, 7 percent (3/47) had 5 to 15 incidents, and 2 percent (1/47) had some incidents but did not know how many. Incidents involving violation of patient confidentiality in the past year were reported by 13 percent (6/46). Student use of profanity, frankly discriminatory language, depiction of intoxication, and sexually suggestive material were more commonly reported. Issues of conflict of interest were rare." Chretien et al. (2009) add, "Of 45 schools that reported an incident and responded to the question about disciplinary actions, 30 gave informal warning (67 percent) and 3 reported student dismissal (7 percent). Policies that cover student-posted online content were reported by 38 percent (28/73) of deans. Of schools without such policies, 11 percent (5/46) were actively developing new policies to cover online content. Deans reporting incidents were significantly more likely to report having such a policy (51 percent versus 18 percent), believing these issues could be effectively addressed (91 percent versus 63 percent), and having higher levels of concern." According to the researchers, there are a number of actions that medical schools could take that might address some of the concerns raised by these findings. "The formal professionalism curriculum should include a digital media component, which could include instruction on managing the 'digital footprint,' such as electing privacy settings on social networking sites and performing periodic Web searches of oneself. This is important given that residency program directors, future employers, and patients may access this information. Discussions among students, residents, and faculty should occur to help define *medical professionalism* in the era of Web 2.0."

Exploitation via Medical Records Snooping

It could be argued that a reckless disregard for personal privacy in general could foster the temptation to be reckless with others' privacy, namely, their patients. It certainly did not stop the healthcare providers who decided that snooping in private medical records was acceptable. Ornstein (2009) has described the saga of Kaiser Permanente's Bellflower Medical Center, California, that was fined $250,000 by California health regulators in May 2009 for failure to prevent employees from accessing the medical records of media curiosity Nadya Suleman, the woman who gave birth to octuplets in January 2009, and noted, "The fine is the first monetary penalty imposed and largest allowed under a new state law enacted last year after widely publicized violations of privacy at UCLA Medical Center involving Farrah Fawcett, Britney Spears, California First Lady Maria Shriver and other celebrities." The law allows the Department of Public Health to impose fines against health-care facilities of up to $25,000 per patient for the first violation and $17,500 for each additional violation, up to $250,000. A separate law allows fines to be imposed against individual healthcare workers. In a written statement, California Governor Arnold Schwarzenegger stated, "The fine issued today should be a reminder that there are consequences for violations of medical privacy" (Ornstein, 2008).

On September 30, 2008, Governor Schwarzenegger signed two bills, AB 211 and SB 541, to address healthcare-related security breaches and add teeth to the federal Health Insurance Portability and Accountability Act (HIPAA) (and its Security Rule regulations), and the California Confidentiality of Medical Information Act. AB 211 requires that healthcare providers implement appropriate administrative, technical, and physical safeguards to protect the privacy of patients' medical information and to reasonably safeguard confidential medical information from any unauthorized access or unlawful access, use, or disclosure. Similar to AB 211, SB 541 requires healthcare facilities to prevent unlawful or unauthorized access to, and use or disclosure of, patients' medical information. It also imposes new breach-notification requirements on covered entities.

Around the time that this legislation was circulating in the state capitol, the California Department of Public Health identified 349 confidentiality violations in acute-care hospitals involving 5,235 patients in a 2-year period. Ornstein (2009) reported, "Since the law took effect Jan. 1, hospitals have reported about 300 incidents in which patient records were inappropriately accessed or disclosed. Most of those were inadvertent, such as giving discharge instructions or medication orders to the wrong patients, but some involved prying into patients' records without permission."

The California Department of Public Health declared that the breaches of Suleman's records extended beyond the Bellflower Hospital and continued even after Kaiser first informed regulators it had a breach. In early February, two employees breached Suleman's records; by the end of the month, six employees had been identified as having accessed records without authorization. By late March, 17 additional employees—including two doctors—were added to the list, for a total of 23. Of those, 15 were either terminated or resigned under pressure and eight faced other disciplinary actions, the state said in a report. The doctors were among those disciplined, not fired (Ornstein, 2009). While the department of health asserted that efforts to protect Suleman's privacy were not aggressive enough, Ornstein (2009) reported that Kaiser insisted that it had taken a number of measures to protect Suleman's privacy, including reminding staff members about privacy laws, and added a prompt to her computerized records warning employees of the consequences for accessing her records without permission.

Fawcett's case, in which a low-level UCLA employee "accessed her records more often than her own doctors," Ornstein (2009) said, prompted the new legislation. The employee pleaded guilty to federal felony charges of selling information to a tabloid publication, but she died of cancer before she could be sentenced. Because the privacy breaches at UCLA occurred before the law took effect, the medical center cannot be cited and fined. UCLA Medical Center was the site of another high-profile breach when it was discovered that employees had snooped in the medical records of singer Britney Spears during her hospitalization in its psychiatric unit. Six employees were suspended, at least 13 others were fired, and six physicians were disciplined for their actions. UCLA had hoped to head off such an incident when it sent a memo to employees the morning Spears was hospitalized to remind them that they could not access patient information unless directly caring for a patient; Spears' name had not been included in this memo. This incident was preceded in 2005 by a snooping incident perpetrated by employees when Spears gave birth at Santa Monica–UCLA Medical Center and Orthopedic Hospital. In addition to snooping, there are other examples of healthcare professionals' carelessness with patient information. For example, four HIV-positive patients whose records were left behind on a train by a Massachusetts General Hospital employee are suing the hospital, contending their privacy was breached (Cooney, 2009).

The Impact of Patient Privacy Breaches

Putting a price tag on patients' privacy is challenging, because the potential costs are so widespread when considering the harm caused to the patient as well as the damage inflicted upon a healthcare organization's image and reputation. Day and Kizer (2009) said that monetary losses resulting from privacy breaches are caused by fines and penalties, legal fees, lost business, and decreased stock valuation, to name a few. According to a recent study conducted by the Ponemon Institute, the average cost per lost healthcare record was projected to be $282 per record in 2008, or nearly $3 million for a breach of 10,000 records. Across all industries, the average per-incident cost of privacy breaches in 2008 was $6.7 million, up from $6.3 million in 2007. As Day and Kizer (2009) pointed out, "More difficult to quantify, but no less real, are consequences from the diminished community and patient trust that frequently result from these incidents. The cost of a tarnished reputation or a damaged brand can be long-lasting."

Day and Kizer (2009) cited an "interplay of cultural, structural and operational security factors" as the culprit for these privacy breaches and assert that in safeguarding PHI, healthcare organizations "face a number of cultural and organizational capacity issues arising from the historical nature of healthcare as a 'cottage industry' in which individual practitioners competed with each other to take care of acute injuries and illnesses. Of note, these same challenges also confound efforts to improve patient safety and healthcare quality. Healthcare's historical culture also includes a tendency to avoid rules and processes that do not add value to patient care, a separation of clinical and administrative activities, and a bias toward caring more about individual patients than organizations or systems." As healthcare evolved, healthcare information technology (HIT) has become the tool uniting a complicated and fragmented system, yet too many organizations have been slow to adopt HIT as well as the systems to protect patients' PHI. Day and Kizer (2009) have explained that the cultural underpinnings of healthcare often confound the implementation of HIPAA and even trigger barriers to patient care: "Therefore, it should not be surprising that many practitioners do not enthusiastically embrace the HIPAA rules and their processes, even when they fully agree with their intent." In addition, they said, many clinicians look askance at what they consider to be mere "paperwork" and prefer that the administrators take care of it. Citing a gap between healthcare institution administrators and clinicians which has grown over time, Day and Kizer (2009) have noted that "Only recently have they started to reintegrate as a result of increasing efforts to link payment to clinical quality. Importantly, as long as information security is portrayed to be an administrative matter instead of a core clinical responsibility, it will be difficult to get clinicians to take ownership of the matter."

Healthcare organizations are busy, chaotic places, which could contribute to the factors that make the environment enticing for perpetrators of privacy breaches. As Day and Kizer (2009) note, "In 25 percent of reported data breaches, the organization did not know how many records were compromised by the breach." Experts acknowledge that healthcare professionals require daily access to patients' private information, and that the majority of them respect patients' privacy. However, "with so many people from so many entities accessing PHI in so many ways, their understanding of both the importance of this protection and how to effectively facilitate it will inevitably vary. Something will undoubtedly fall through the cracks even in the absence of malicious intent," Day and Kizer (2009) explain.

Is Patient Privacy a Fallacy?

The aforementioned incidents of snooping and exploitation demonstrate that even though laws exist to protect against privacy breaches, they cannot stop breaches of privacy and confidentiality. What might come as a surprise to some patients is that the right to privacy, as pointed out by Geiderman and Larkin

(2002), is not specifically articulated in the U.S. Constitution. They explain further, "The origin of the legal term right to privacy is attributed to Warren and Brandeis, who, in 1890, argued that the right to privacy is derived from the fundamental rights of life, liberty and property and concluded that this amounted to 'the right to be let alone.'" In a number of decisions, the U.S. Supreme Court ruled that although the right of privacy was not explicitly identified in the Bill of Rights, the right arose from the tenets found in the First, Third, Fourth, Fifth, Ninth, and Fourteenth Amendments to the Constitution. Geiderman and Larkin (2002) explain that "In other words, a right to privacy exists under the U.S. Constitution because it is implied by so many other amendments. It should be noted, however, that the constitutional right to privacy applies only to the protection of individuals from governmental intrusion." Geiderman and Larkin (2002) said that in order for a claim of intrusion upon a person's seclusion, solitude, or private affairs to succeed, several conditions must be met: the intrusion must be into a private aspect of a person's life; the intrusion must be deliberate; and the intrusion must be extremely objectionable to the average person. They added, "These circumstances may be extant if a patient has not consented in advance to being videotaped in an ambulance, emergency department, hospital room or other healthcare setting."

On its Web site, the organization Coalition for Patient Privacy declares: "Chilling news about health privacy: You have none." The site says that everything from prescriptions for antidepressant medications to sexual impotency, to diagnoses of AIDS or testing for Alzheimer's disease, can become public knowledge because patient consent is no longer required to share personal health information, no matter how embarrassing or intensely personal the contents may be. The coalition faults regulatory changes made to HIPAA as the culprit responsible for destroying patients' rights to control the use and disclosure of their PHI. What makes the situation even worse is that medicine has long been rooted in confidentiality, making breaches even more horrific. The coalition states, "Privacy is the foundation of the entire healthcare system. Without it, we will not trust our doctors enough to tell them about symptoms and illnesses that are painful, frightening, embarrassing, or may cause other people to fear or avoid us. We require absolute privacy to trust our doctors." The coalition emphasizes that had physicians not upheld privacy and confidentiality, "the practice of medicine and our current healthcare system would not even exist," and that "The privacy of medical care is a fundamental human need, guarded zealously by physicians for millennia."

The coalition asserts that privacy breaches will have a chilling effect on Americans' desire to see their healthcare providers: "When the American public realizes that medical privacy no longer exists, they will avoid care, lie, omit sensitive details and seek medical help only as a last resort. The elimination of privacy will destroy the healthcare system."

References

American Health Information Management Association (AHIMA). "The state of HIPAA privacy and security compliance." April 2006.

Associated Press. Nude photo of mental patient found on hospital-issued cell phone. June 23, 2009.

Barber J. Introduction to digital forensics. In: *Forensic Nursing*, second edition. Lynch VA, ed. New York: Mosby. 2010, pp. 97–104.

Chretien KC, Greysen SR, Chretien JP, and Kind T. Online posting of unprofessional content by medical students. *JAMA*. 302(12):1309–1315. 2009.

Clark H. Hospital workers fired for posting patient photos on Web. Associated Press. September 22, 2008.

Coalition for Patient Privacy. "Patient Privacy Rights." Undated. (Accessed July 2009, at: patientprivacyrights.org.)

College of Healthcare Information Management Executives (CHIME) press release: "As hospitals lift cell phone restrictions, new concerns arise." June 25, 2007.

Cooney E. "HIV patients sue after records lost." *Boston Globe*. May 21, 2009.

Day G, and Kizer KW. "Stemming the rising tide of health privacy breaches." A report by Booz Allen Hamilton, Inc. 2009.

Department of Health (United Kingdom). "Using mobile phones in NHS hospitals." January 2009. (Accessed July 2009, at: http://www.dh.gov.uk.)

Dotinga R. "Hospitals nationwide combat employee camera-phone abuse." Wired.com. June 1, 2007.

Enterprise Strategy Group. "Protecting confidential data." Online research report. March 2006.

FairWarning, Inc. "Privacy surveillance in healthcare." (Accessed at: www.FairWarningAudit.com.)

Geiderman JM, and Larkin GL. Commercial filming of patient care activities in hospitals. *JAMA*. 288(3). July 17, 2002.

Government Accountability Office (GAO). "Personal information: Data breaches are frequent, but evidence of resulting identity theft is limited; however, the full extent is unknown." GAO-07-737. June 2007. (Accessed October 23, 2010, at http://library.ahima.org/xpedio/groups/public/documents/ahima/bok2_ 000585.hcsp?dDocName=bok2_000585.)

Hjort B et al. Patient photography, videotaping and other imaging (updated): AHIMA Practice Brief. *J AHIMA*. 72(6). 64M-Q. 2001. (Accessed October 23, 2010, at: http://library.ahima.org/xpedio/groups/public/documents/ahima/bok2_000585.hcsp?dDocName=bok2_000585.)

Hughes J. "Therapist at Children's Hospital accused of child molestation, porn." *San Diego Union-Tribune*. March 10, 2006.

Markus PA, and Zuiker ES. Cell phone camera use in healthcare facilities: Shutter it. *Am Health Law Assoc HIT News*. 12(1):12–14. January 29, 2009.

Morgan E. "Lehi doctor arrested in voyeurism case." *Deseret News*. August 27, 2009.

Ornstein C. "UCLA hospital bans cell phones, laptops." *Los Angeles Times*. March 18, 2008. (Accessed May 15, 2009, at: http://articles.latimes.com/2008/mar/18/local/me-ucla18.)

Ornstein C. "Kaiser Hospital fined $250,000 for privacy breach in octuplet case." ProPublica.com. May 15, 2009. (Accessed October 23, 2010, at: http://jama. ama-asson.org/cgi/content/abstract/302/12/1309.)

PogoWasRight.org. "Medical privacy at risk." July 2007. (Accessed January 2010, at: http://www.pogowasright.org/MedicalPrivacy_2007.pdf.)

Ponemon Institute LLC. "Are you ready for HITECH? A benchmark study of health-care covered entities and business associates." November 10, 2009.

Ponemon Institute LLC. "Americans' opinions about healthcare privacy." February 1, 2010.

Sanders M. "Kentucky paramedic beaten, fired following Internet post." *The Paducah Sun.* May 30, 2007.

Tennessee Bureau of Investigation (TBI) press release. September 23, 2009.

Westin A. "IOM project on health research, privacy, and the HIPAA privacy rule." September 2007.

Abuse and Assault 3

There is increasing awareness among healthcare professionals that routine consultations, examinations, and treatment are ideal opportunities to screen for the signs and symptoms of abuse, particularly in vulnerable populations such as children, women, the disabled, and the elderly. But what if they are the very perpetrators of abuse? Jewkes et al. (1998) have observed that "Although nursing discourse usually emphasizes 'caring,' nursing practice is often quite different and may be more strongly characterized by humiliation of patients and physical abuse." The researchers found that the neglect and abuse perpetrated by healthcare providers was sometimes reactive, and at other times, it was ritualized; regardless, it was a "complex interplay of concerns including organizational issues, professional insecurities, perceived need to assert control over the environment and sanctioning of the use of coercive and punitive measures to do so, and an underpinning ideology of patient inferiority." The researchers also suggest that nurses in particular are "engaged in a continuous struggle to assert their professional and middle class identity and in the process deployed violence against patients as a means of creating social distance and maintaining fantasies of identity and power." Jewkes et al. (1998) have stated that violence has become common due to a lack of personal accountability among healthcare professionals as well as a dearth of action taken against healthcare providers who abuse patients. Jewkes et al. (1998) add, "It also became established as 'normal' in nursing practice because of a lack of powerful competing ideologies of patient care and nursing ethics."

How Patients Are Abused by Healthcare Providers

According to the U.S. Department of Justice, victimization occurs when "a person suffers direct or threatened physical, emotional, and/or financial harm." Victimization can include physical violence, sexual violence, psychological or emotional abuse, and neglect. Victimization can take many forms of violence and abuse. The Centers for Disease Control and Prevention (CDC) defines *physical violence* as "the intentional use of physical force with the potential for causing death, disability, injury or harm." It includes scratching, pushing, shoving, throwing, grabbing, biting, choking, shaking, slapping, punching, burning, use of a weapon, and use of restraints or one's body, size, or strength against another person. *Sexual violence* is defined by the CDC as "the use of physical force to compel a person to engage in a sexual act against his or her will, whether or not the act is completed; an attempted or completed sex act involving a person who is unable to understand the nature or condition of the act, to decline participation, or to communicate unwillingness to engage in the sexual act; and abusive sexual contact." Emotional abuse occurs when a person is "threatened, terrorized, or severely rejected, ignored, or verbally attacked." It includes episodes of yelling, threats, or acts meant to humiliate or hurt feelings, according to the CDC. And finally, the CDC says that neglect can be characterized as a "situation in which the basic needs of a person (such as food, clothing, hygiene, protection, or medical care) are temporarily or permanently not met." It includes preventing a person with disabilities from using a wheelchair, cane, respirator, or other assistive devices as well as failing to address basic needs for food, clothing, shelter, or hygiene.

The bottom line is that patient abuse or neglect is considered to be any action or failure to act which causes unreasonable suffering or harm to the individual. Abuse can encompass physical, verbal, and sexual assault, and it can also include the withholding of necessary food, medication, physical care, and medical attention. Sexual abuse of patients is particularly heinous. Because power can fuel sexual assault and abuse, healthcare providers may have the means and the opportunity to demonstrate their power and dominance over persons of unequal power—their patients—by engaging in sexual victimization. As Burgess and Hartman (1986) state, "Sexual situations in which an adult in an authority position uses sex to take advantage of another person with less power may be termed sexual exploitation. The victim is used primarily for individual gratification, profit or other selfish reasons." There have been innumerable reports of patients who have disclosed sexual misconduct by a healthcare or mental health professional, such as a physician or psychotherapist, and "although there is a professed stringent ethical code among health professionals against sexual encounters with patients, it is acknowledged by health practitioners that these sexual encounters are increasing in number," according to Burgess and Hartman (1986).

The Federation of State Medical Boards (FSMB) of the United States defines *physician sexual misconduct* as behavior that exploits the physician–patient relationship in a sexual way, and this behavior may be verbal or physical, and may include expressions of thoughts and feelings or gestures that are sexual or that reasonably may be construed by a patient as sexual. The FSMB recognizes two primary types of professional sexual misconduct—sexual impropriety and sexual violation—and both are grounds for disciplinary action by a state medical board if it determines that the behavior exploited the physician–patient relationship. According to the FSMB, sexual impropriety may include behavior, gestures, or expressions that are seductive, sexually suggestive, disrespectful of patient privacy, or sexually demeaning to a patient and may include, but are not limited to, the following:

- Neglecting to employ disrobing or draping practices respecting the patient's privacy, or deliberately watching a patient dress or undress.
- Subjecting a patient to an intimate examination in the presence of medical students or other parties without the patient's informed consent or in the event such informed consent has been withdrawn.
- Examining or touching genital mucosal areas without the use of gloves.
- Making inappropriate comments about or to the patient, including, but not limited to, making sexual comments about a patient's body or underclothing, making sexualized or sexually demeaning comments to a patient, criticizing the patient's sexual orientation, or making comments about potential sexual performance during an examination.
- Using the physician–patient relationship to solicit a date or romantic relationship.
- Initiating conversation with the patient regarding the sexual problems, preferences, or fantasies of the physician.
- Performing an intimate examination or consultation without clinical justification and without explaining to the patient the need for such examination or consultation.
- Requesting details of sexual history or sexual likes or dislikes when not clinically indicated for the type of examination or consultation.

Sexual violation may include physical sexual contact between a physician and patient, whether or not initiated by the patient, and engaging in any conduct with a patient that is sexual or may be reasonably interpreted as sexual, including but not limited to sexual intercourse; genital-to-genital contact; oral-to-genital contact; oral-to-anal contact; genital-to-anal contact; kissing; touching breasts, genitals, or any sexualized body part for any purpose other than appropriate examination or treatment, or where the patient has refused or has withdrawn consent; encouraging the patient to masturbate in the presence of the physician or masturbation by the physician while the patient is present; and offering to provide practice-related services, such as drugs, in exchange for sexual favors.

McMurray et al. (1991) state that there appears to be little data indicating the prevalence of sexual misconduct, but that distinctions can be made between the various ways that physicians engage in sexual contact. As McMurray et al. (1991) explain, some physicians fail to manage emotions that arise from the physician–patient relationship, and while some seek rehabilitation for their misconduct, "it is also clear that for some other physicians, sexual misconduct is the conscious use of their professional positions in order to use or exploit their patients' vulnerabilities for their own gratification."

No matter how it is defined, the FSMB emphasizes, "Physician sexual misconduct exploits the physician–patient relationship, is a violation of the public trust, and is often known to cause harm, both mentally and physically, to the patient."

Despite efforts and interventions to address and prevent sexual exploitation by healthcare professionals, the crime continues, leading experts to ask themselves why some practitioners sexually exploit patients. Burgess and Hartman (1986) observed that the cause of sexual exploitation rests heavily within the character of the abusing professional: "In our experience, transgressions are not associated primarily with young, inexperienced health professionals. Instead, older, experienced health practitioners who often have had sexual contact with more than one patient are implicated." Burgess and Hartman (1986) have stated that society responds to the actions of malicious healthcare professionals by suggesting that "the exploitation is transient and reasonably explainable. Rather than addressing the offense, recommendations for dealing with the problem often focus on career change options for the offender. Some health professions, emphasizing compassion, minimize and confuse issues as well as justify acts of exploitation. They blame the victim and accuse colleagues of hysteria and prurient sexual interests." Many experts believe that there is a lack of agreement about how best to identify and sanction abusive professionals.

Who Is Abused: Victimized Patient Populations

Disabled Patients

Numerous studies confirm the likelihood that a disabled person will be abused. Sobsey (1994) estimated that people with disabilities are at least four times more likely to be victimized than people without disabilities. Sorensen (2002) as well as Lumley and Miltenberger (1997) estimated that almost 80 percent of women with developmental disabilities have been sexually assaulted at some point in their lives. Wilson and Brewer (1992) and Baladerian (1991) found the rate for sexual assault was between 2 and 10 times higher for people with disabilities when compared to those without disabilities.

Neufeldt and Mathieson (1995) estimated the prevalence of sexual abuse among people with developmental disabilities to be 70 percent; other studies cite estimates that from 39 percent to 83 percent of girls with developmental disabilities and between 16 percent and 32 percent of boys with developmental disabilities are subjected to sexual assault before the age of 18. The majority of victims were assaulted on more than 10 occasions; only one-fifth of assaults were reported as single offenses (Sobsey and Doe, 1991). Sullivan and Knutson (2000) have shown that the likelihood of maltreatment of disabled children increases nearly fourfold compared to nondisabled children. The researchers found that neglect was 3.8 times as likely, sexual abuse was 3.1 times as likely, physical abuse was 3.8 times as likely, and emotional maltreatment was 3.9 times as likely. Sullivan et al. (1986) have reported a high risk of sexual abuse in children with hearing impairments, with 54 percent of deaf boys and 50 percent of deaf girls sexually assaulted as children. Sobsey and Doe (1991) found that the rate of sexual abuse of hearing-impaired children is doubled for girls and five times higher for boys compared with nondisabled children.

Numerous experts say that healthcare providers represent the majority of abusers of the disabled. Sobsey and Doe (1991) estimate that about 67 percent of perpetrators who abused individuals with severe cognitive disabilities accessed them through their work in disability services. Baladerian (1991) agree that those most likely to sexually abuse the disabled are people known by the victim, such as family members, acquaintances, residential care staff, transportation providers, and personal care attendants, and that as many as 99 percent of abusers are known and trusted by the victim. Baladerian (1992) has emphasized that society has been slow to admit that sexual abuse of people with mental retardation is not only possible, but that it actually occurs. Mullan and Cole (1991) observed that "The most disturbing thing is the increasing evidence of abuse perpetrated by the very people—including healthcare workers—upon whom the person with a disability is posited as dependent." In their search to understand professionals' perceptions of the vulnerability of persons with disability, Mullan and Cole (1991) found that the populations considered "most vulnerable" were persons with long-term cognitive disabilities (that is, combined mental retardation and physical disability, mental illness, and mental retardation). What's more, many caregivers witness abuse. Strand et al. (2003) reported that 35 percent of 122 respondents in their survey admitted they had been implicated in or witnessed a violent incident toward an adult with intellectual disabilities, and 14 percent of the staff members admitted they had been perpetrators. The researchers added that physical violence was most frequently reported in their study, and that most of the aggression occurred in situations when individuals with intellectual disabilities did not cooperate during a caregiving situation.

The ironic paradox of institutionalizing those with disabilities for their "safety" has not been lost on Neufeldt and Mathieson (1995) who noted that "Historically, people at the margins of society in high-income countries, including those with disabilities, have been sent to residential institutions for 'treatment' or 'care.' One rationale for institutionalization is that such settings are safer than community living arrangements. While some may be relatively secure, many place disabled people at high risk for abuse. Indeed, the high probability of physical or sexual assault has been one of the driving forces behind the closing of such institutions." Some experts believe that a revolving door of caregivers can contribute to abuse of patients. Lakin et al. (1982) found that the average annual staff turnover was about one-third in public residential facilities and more than 50 percent in private residential facilities. As Neufeldt and Mathieson (1995) have noted, "Part of the problem is associated with the number of different care-givers who pass through institutions, and who therefore feel little personal accountability to the people with whom they work."

Persons with disabilities are easy targets because they have been forgotten by society in general and frequently left out of protection-planning efforts by agencies. They can have mental and physical impairments that make them vulnerable to abuse, and these same impairments hamper the communication process in a medicolegal proceeding if a case goes to court. Additionally, many care institutions are ill prepared to protect the rights of their disabled charges. Currently, there is little to no incentive—beyond doing the right thing by their patients—for caregivers to report incidents involving individuals with developmental disabilities. Sorensen (2002) explained that many nonabusive staff members do not report incidents of patient abuse for fear of reprisals from supervisors or retribution from their peers. In addition, because care-home administrators may fear negative publicity or loss of licenses for their facilities, they may ignore or minimize allegations of abuse or neglect. Victimization can occur anywhere; however, it usually happens in isolated locations where a person with disabilities has little or no control of the environment and the setting is away from the view of law enforcement. Disabled individuals are abused by a variety of health-care perpetrators in care homes, hospitals, institutions, daycare centers, and even home care. Mansell et al. (1992) found that 26 percent of perpetrators were paid caregivers providing services related to the victim's disability. Sobsey (1994), Furey (1994), and Turk and Brown (1992) found that care homes and residences are the most common setting for abuse. Because many disabled individuals may require assistance with many activities of daily living and hygiene, there are numerous opportunities to sexually abuse the disabled, including during dressing or undressing, baths, changing incontinence underwear, emptying catheters, giving enemas, and toileting. Institutional settings are risk locations for persons with disabilities, because multiple episodes of physical and sexual violence, emotional abuse, or neglect, or violence may be committed against them by staff or other residents and yet go undetected or unreported.

Who commits these acts of victimization? According to the CDC, more men than women, either as intimate partners or as healthcare workers, are reported to commit acts of physical violence, sexual violence, emotional abuse, or neglect against persons with disabilities. Family members have been reported to commit crimes of victimization while caring for a relative with disabilities. Personal home-care attendants or healthcare workers at institutions have been reported to perpetrate emotional abuse and sexual violence against persons with disabilities. In institutional settings, persons with disabilities may commit acts of physical violence or sexual violence against other persons with disabilities. Persons with disabilities are susceptible to victimization due to a number of factors. Societal factors include misperceptions about disability including the assumptions that having a disability protects a person from victimization, or that the risks to a person with disabilities are thought to be less than the risks to a person who has none. Unemployment or underemployment of persons with disabilities restricts their income and limits their choices for caregivers, leading to an increased risk of physical and sexual violence, emotional abuse, or neglect. Community-related factors can include healthcare and law enforcement professionals who are uninformed about victimization of persons with disabilities; thus, they may not have the specialized knowledge or skills to identify and assist these individuals when victimized. Abusers can harm as many as 70 people before being detected, and the levels of underreporting further hamper the arrest and prosecution of offenders. Valenti-Hein and Schwartz (1995) stated that underreporting of sexual abuse of people with disabilities continues to be a major obstacle in preventing this abuse. Sadly, they note that just about 3 percent of sexual abuse cases involving people with developmental disabilities will ever be reported.

Sorensen (2002) said that much of the abuse and neglect inflicted upon people with physical and developmental disabilities can go unreported; Wilson and Brewer (1992) found that almost three-quarters of crimes against people with severe mental retardation go unreported, and Powers, Mooney, and Nunno (1990) found that as much as 85 percent of criminal abuse of residents in institutions never reaches the proper authorities. Studies have also pointed to low rates of prosecution and conviction of crimes against people with disabilities. Sobsey and Varnhagen (1991) found that 65 percent of sexual assault cases reported to police were not prosecuted when the victim had a disability, and Brown and Stein (1997) found that police investigated only 21 percent of sexual assaults on people with intellectual disabilities and only 9 percent were referred by police for prosecution. Reporting can be increased through educating individuals with disabilities and service providers, improving investigation and prosecution, and creating a safe environment that allows victims to disclose, and finally, employment policies must change to increase safety. For example, background checks on new employees should be conducted on a routine basis; those with criminal records should be reported to the police, rather than firing the suspected abuser. Otherwise, the individual will more than likely continue abusing others while working for future employers.

Psychiatric Patients

Movies and media have created indelible images of abuse and neglect occurring in psychiatric institutions. Grubaugh et al. (2007) seem to acknowledge how life and art imitate each other: "There is growing concern over institutional measures of control (e.g., seclusion, restraint) and other potentially harmful or traumatic experiences within psychiatric hospitals." In 1983, the U.S. Justice Department obtained indictments against nine aides at a Pennsylvania state psychiatric care institution on charges of beating and abusing patients; it was believed to be the first federal criminal civil rights prosecutions brought against employees of this kind of institution for patient abuse. The indictments culminated a year-long investigation by the Federal Bureau of Investigation (FBI) and were based in part on the work of an undercover police officer. According to the Justice Department, 90 percent of the patients at the institution had intelligence quotients below 35, 10 percent were over the age of 62 years, 20 percent were blind or visually handicapped, and 20 percent were confined to wheelchairs or had difficulty walking. The aides were accused of beating and assaulting patients (AP, 1983).

Not much seems to have changed in the decades since, and one newspaper proves that sometimes the media is a patient's best advocate. In 2007, *The Atlanta Journal-Constitution* assembled a list of questionable deaths by examining state and federal inspection reports, a database of vital records, autopsies, medical files, court papers, state insurance claims, and other documents. It reported that more than 100 patients from state hospitals had died under suspicious circumstances since 2002 (Judd and Miller, 2007). As a result of this series, a federal investigation was opened; a 65-page report by an assistant Attorney General in 2008 details findings similar to those reported by *The Atlanta Journal-Constitution*.

As Judd and Miller (2007) have reported that "This study revealed a pattern of neglect, abuse and poor medical care in the seven state hospitals, as well as a lack of public accountability for patient deaths. The findings for 2002 through late 2006—from employees beating patients with aluminum pipes to doctors widely prescribing sedatives just to maintain order—evoke images from the mid-20th century at the state hospital in Milledgeville. There, thousands of patients lived and died amid horrific conditions that became synonymous across the nation with mistreatment of people with mental illness." Judd (2009) reported that the deficiencies, such as abuse, neglect, and substandard medical care that contribute to suicide, rape, and murder, continue at state hospitals 2 years since the initial newspaper investigational series, despite a proposal to address these troubled facilities.

In an effort to examine potentially harmful and traumatic psychiatric experiences of patients in psychiatric healthcare settings, Grubaugh et al. (2007) interviewed a number of these individuals and reported that

45.1 percent of patients said they had been to a psychiatric facility to which they would never want to return, and many of these patients had reported adverse events during their care. The researchers noted that 84.5 percent of the patients they interviewed reported that they thought psychiatric facilities have become safer in recent years. The disparity of opinion is puzzling, as news reports of abuse in psychiatric healthcare facilities have not disappeared. As we have seen, much of the alleged and potential abuse in psychiatric healthcare facilities stems from the use of "last-resort" measures such as seclusion, restraint, enforced medications, and handcuffed transport. Other routine procedures, such as confiscation of personal items, being on a locked unit, or being required to take unwanted medication, may, via the associated loss of control, represent a highly distressing or traumatic experience for patients (Grubaugh et al., 2007).

Cusack et al. (2003) found that mental health patients report high rates of lifetime traumatic and potentially harmful experiences occurring within psychiatric settings; witnessing a physical assault (22 percent) and experiencing a physical assault (18 percent) were the most frequent traumatic events reported, while 7 percent of participants reported being sexually assaulted by another patient, and 5 percent witnessed another patient being sexually assaulted. Harmful events reported most frequently included seclusion (58 percent); being around other patients who were very frightening (56 percent); handcuffed transport by police (53 percent); witnessing "take-downs" (being subdued by physical force, 47 percent); and being put in restraints (33 percent). Grubaugh et al. (2007) conducted a study of 142 adult patients from a community mental health center/day-hospital treatment facility and also found high reported rates of potentially harmful or frightening lifetime psychiatric experiences, including handcuffed transport to a psychiatric facility by police (65.2 percent); being placed in seclusion (59.6 percent); being around other patients who were perceived as scary or very violent (55 percent); witnessing a "take-down" (44 percent); being put in restraints (34 percent); receiving a "take-down" (29.1 percent); being forced to take medications against wishes (27 percent); being strip-searched (24.1 percent); having medications used as a threat or punishment (19.9 percent); and staff name-calling (14.3 percent). In addition, high rates of traumatic lifetime psychiatric experiences were reported, including witnessing a physical assault by another patient (39.3 percent); as well as patient-perpetrated physical assault (26.4 percent); staff-perpetrated physical assault (12.9 percent); patient-perpetrated sexual assault (7.8 percent); witnessing a sexual assault by another patient (5.7 percent); and staff-perpetrated sexual assault (2.8 percent).

While not overt abuse, there are many incidents in psychiatric healthcare that could be perceived as bordering on egregious, and Grubaugh et al. (2007) acknowledge the tension in the care of psychiatric inpatient populations, or "the need to find a balance between maintaining patient safety while at the same time preserving patient rights and dignity." The researchers add, "Although we know that institutional measures of safety and control are common and are often perceived as frightening and/or humiliating by patients, we recognize that it may not always be feasible to completely eliminate these measures." It would seem that the very staff that can harm is also considered to be the frontline defense against abuse in institutional settings—but only if strict boundaries are observed. The Royal College of Physicians (RCP) says that the prevention of any boundary crossing or abuse in care settings is based on the recognition of incidences and the comprehension of the myriad factors that are part of the etiology of inappropriate sexual behavior. The RCP (2007) has stated that it is critical to "devise principles of good practice, training, supervision and other solutions to prevent it."

Regardless of the healthcare setting, there is a common thread in the medical literature that "difficult" patients are frequently the targets of abuse. This is especially true in psychiatric settings in which patients may behave in ways that do not correspond to social norms. The RCP (2007) notes, "They may be more aggressive, more passive or more disinhibited than usual and approach others, including staff, inappropriately." The RCP emphasized that staff, being in a position of power in relation to the patient, must exercise this authority with care, "always being thoughtful about the possible consequences of attitudes, words and actions." The RCP (2007) has added that "The staff member needs to be emotionally close enough to patients to allow disclosure of intimate personal material and for patients to feel they have been listened to and understood; however, staff need to retain the skill of clinical detachment and the ability to recognize and examine their own feelings in the interaction."

There is a danger, the RCP says, that psychiatric patients become the objects of staff members' curiosity, and that their work can become abusive or voyeuristic unless staff keep their motivations and intentions in check. Because of the stressful nature of psychiatric healthcare, the RCP advises that boundary-keeping is aided by giving staff "a safe and containing space in which they are able to acknowledge possible lack of skills or knowledge, and to voice anxieties and concerns about their own feelings and potential behavior, the behavior of patients and, if necessary, the behavior of other staff members."

Of particular concern is when staff and patients are pitted against each other when a patient has a complaint of abuse. The RCP (2007) refers to a culture in hospitals where patients are routinely disbelieved, and notes, "While false allegations do occur, the possibility of staff abuse, including by senior doctors, must be borne in mind." Internal investigations of abuse allegations are made even more challenging by the nature of psychiatric healthcare and the difficulty of repeated questioning of patient complainants. The RCP (2007) advises institutions to clearly outline standards indicating what kind of behavior is and is not acceptable under boundary maintenance efforts already inherent in healthcare provision. These standards must also include "supportive whistle-blowing policies so that staff, regardless of their status, can safely report concerns about other staff's behavior." In the event of an allegation of sexual harassment or assault, the RCP (2007) says that staff should "appropriately support the complainant while investigating the allegation."

As we will see in Chapter 6, proper preemployment screening is essential to weeding out healthcare providers with abusive or criminal histories in the first place, and it is particularly important in psychiatric healthcare settings. The RCP (2007) opined that some sexual abuse incidents could be prevented if sufficient healthcare personnel recruitment practices were used, including preemployment vetting: "All staff…should be checked if they have potential access to patients. If it is necessary to use agencies, only those that have police-checked their workers should be used." And once psychiatric healthcare professionals have been hired, the RCP (2007) has stated that it is imperative for institutions to conduct ongoing education and training on abuse and violence prevention: "Staff members who spend the most time in direct contact with patients and therefore exposed to serious psychopathologies for the longest are those who need to be highly trained and to be the most experienced. This must be supported by senior management, so that priority may be given to training in the prevention, recognition and management of abusive and potentially abusive situations." The RCP adds that boundary maintenance and other ethical issues should be part of all training efforts.

At the heart of abuse prevention is identification of the early signs of violence. As the RCP (2007) explains, "If the possibility of abuse…has not been considered, then staff will be more likely to miss or dismiss the signs that an abusive situation has arisen. Complaints by patients of sexual abuse or harassment can easily be dismissed as delusions or exaggerated fears. Staff needs to listen to their patients and to be vigilant." Investigations in recent years have uncovered common themes that can serve as indicators of situations where abuse is more likely to occur in institutional settings such as psychiatric healthcare. These include a dominant staff member who is usually older and longer-serving than the rest of the staff, harassment of staff and patients, low staff morale, substance abuse by staff, patients who are more isolated than others, lack of monitoring of procedures such as bathing, and poor record-keeping (RCP, 2007). Awareness of these indicators may enable managers, other healthcare professionals, and authorities to detect abuse or to prevent it before it occurs.

And while psychiatric healthcare professionals must stay on the lookout for signs of abuse at the hands of their colleagues, they must monitor constantly their own attitudes toward sexual abuse. As the RCP (2007) has noted, "In dealing with acutely disturbed and possibly vulnerable patients, staff need to consider procedures that relate to intimate contact, particularly during physical examination and restraint. Staff expected to do this must be properly trained in these procedures and must ensure that they regularly update their skills." Staff may need to be involved in the most intimate of personal care for some patients, and the opportunity for both abuse and detection of abuse presents itself at this time. The RCP (2007) also notes that, "Where possible, same-sex caregivers should undertake…personal care. Sexual abuse should be considered if a patient has bruising on the inner thighs, blood on underwear, sexually transmitted disease, frequent infections or genital or urinary irritation. The patient may try to hide part of the body on examination or show fearfulness with a particular member of staff, unusual clinging, weeping or sobbing, or seeking attention or protection."

Abuse can occur in psychiatric healthcare institutions, and victimization can occur in long-term alternative care settings, where there is even less visibility and oversight. Many vulnerable adults, including those with a chronic mental illness, intellectual disability, or dementia, are now looked after in group homes in the community. The RCP (2007) cautions, "The opportunities for abuse and ill treatment of these people may be even greater than in hospital settings. Many homes are isolated, with only infrequent visits from managers, registration inspectors or social workers." Among the psychiatric patient population, there are subgroups that are more vulnerable than others. The RCP (2000) asserts that older people with mental and physical disabilities are the most likely to be abused, and adds, "Abuse of such people is under-recognized and under-reported. Probably this is most true of sexual abuse, because of the nature of the acts."

It is easy to understand why these patients are an easy mark for abuse. As the RCP (2007) explains, "In institutions, older people are in a position of dependency and so may represent easily targeted victims who will not cause much trouble. In the younger staff, this situation of unequal power may stimulate sexual or sadistic responses…whatever the provocation, there are no circumstances in which a sexual response is appropriate." Complicating matters is the difficulty with which some elderly psychiatric patients may have with communicating their abuse. The RCP (2007) explains that in cases of abuse, patients may be able to describe very clearly what was done to them, but elect not to report the abuse due to shame or fear of repercussions. The RCP states that any appearance or accusation of sexual impropriety with a patient "must be taken seriously, and staff supported appropriately through an investigation, which may or may not find evidence of wrong-doing." As with the elderly, those with intellectual disability who require psychiatric care are in an imbalance of power with their care providers. As the RCP (2007) has said, "This makes it more likely both that abuse will occur and that it will go unreported. Many require help with personal care, such as bathing, which may give opportunities for physical and sexual abuse. Difficulties with communication may hinder the reporting of abuse."

Elderly Patients

Burgess et al. (2000) have stated that the physical and sexual abuse of nursing home residents is a serious problem with potentially devastating consequences. Nursing home residents have suffered serious injuries or, in some cases, have died as a result of abuse, despite the fact that nursing homes are required to protect their residents from harm by training staff to provide proper care and by prohibiting abusive behavior. The institutionalized elderly comprise a significant portion of the patient population; according to 2002 U.S. Census data, there are nearly 17,000 nursing homes in the United States with a total of 1.6 million residents, and those numbers are expected to quadruple to 6.6 million residents by 2050. Additionally, an estimated 900,000 to 1 million persons live in approximately 45,000 residential care facilities, also known as personal care homes, adult congregate living facilities, domiciliary care homes, homes for the aged, and assisted living facilities.

According to Hawes (2002), those facilities "have been plagued with reports suggesting widespread and serious maltreatment of residents, including abuse, neglect, and theft of personal property." Hawes (2002) indicated further that the elderly in residential long-term care settings are particularly vulnerable to abuse and neglect, which some evidence suggests as being serious and widespread. As we have seen with the disabled patient population, many elderly patients have limitations in their physical and cognitive functioning and are thus dependent on others for assistance in the most basic daily activities—leaving them exposed to abuse and neglect. Hawes (2002) added, "These individuals are extremely vulnerable, largely unable to protect themselves, and dependent for their care on the kindness of strangers."

The prevalence of institutional elder abuse is staggering. An Internet search using the term "elder abuse" brings up hundreds and hundreds of pages of news headlines and references in the medical literature. Hawes (2002) point to a survey conducted by an ombudsman program that interviewed 80 residents in 23 nursing homes and found that 44 percent reported that they had been abused, while 48 percent reported that they had been treated roughly. In addition, 38 percent reported that they had seen other residents being abused, and 44 percent said they had seen other residents being treated roughly. Another survey of 577 nursing home staff members from 31 facilities found that 36 percent had witnessed at least one incident of physical abuse during the preceding 12 months. Such incidents included excessive use of physical restraints; pushing, shoving, grabbing, or pinching a resident; slapping or hitting; throwing something at a resident; and kicking or hitting with a fist or object. Ten percent of the staff members surveyed reported they had committed such acts themselves. A total of 81 percent of the staff reported they had observed and 40 percent had committed at least one incident of verbal or psychological abuse during the same 12-month time period (Hawes, 2002). Nerenberg (2002) stated:

> The forms of elder abuse found in nursing homes mirror those found in domestic settings; they include homicide, physical and sexual assault, neglect, inappropriate restraint, financial abuse, isolation, verbal threats and intimidation. In addition, nursing home abuse includes institutionalized practices that result in chronic neglect, sub-standard care, overcrowding, authoritarian practices, and failure to protect residents against untrained, troubled or predatory workers, or against abusive residents or visitors. Subtle forms of abuse that have been explored include denying residents the right to exercise personal choice in such matters as when they want to eat, get up or go to bed; pressuring residents to participate in activities; and "labeling" troublesome individuals, resulting in depersonalized treatment and exclusion.

According to the National Center on Elder Abuse (NCEA), elder abuse refers to any knowing, intentional, or negligent act by a caregiver or any other person which causes harm or a serious risk of harm to a vulnerable adult. Although laws vary from state to state, abuse may consist of physical abuse, emotional abuse, sexual abuse, exploitation, neglect, or abandonment. The National Research Council defines *elder mistreatment* as intentional actions that cause harm or create a serious risk of harm (whether or not harm is intended) to a vulnerable elder by a caregiver or other person who stands in a trust relationship to the elder, or failure by a caregiver to satisfy the elder's basic needs or to protect the elder from harm (Wood, 2006). The Administration on Aging (AOA), in its instructions to long-term care ombudsmen, defines *abuse* as "the willful infliction of injury, unreasonable confinement, intimidation or cruel punishment with resulting physical harm, pain, or mental anguish or deprivation by a person, including a caregiver, of goods or services that are necessary to avoid physical harm, mental anguish, or mental illness." Physical abuse is generally thought to include hitting, slapping, pushing, or striking with objects. In nursing homes, other types of actions have been included, such as improper use of physical or chemical restraints. Physical abuse also typically includes sexual abuse or nonconsensual sexual involvement of any kind, from rape to unwanted touching or indecent exposure. In residential long-term care settings, it also includes verbal or psychosocial abuse. This is generally thought of as "intentional infliction of anguish, pain, or distress through verbal or non-verbal acts" and includes threats, harassment, and attempts to humiliate or intimidate the older person. Clarke and Pierson (1999) define *elder neglect* as "the refusal or failure of a caregiver to fulfill his or her obligations or duties to an older person, including ... providing any food, clothing, medicine, shelter, supervision, and medical care and services that a prudent person would deem essential for the well-being of another."

Elder abuse can be readily defined, but the ability to create a clear picture of the incidence and prevalence of elder abuse in the United States is frequently elusive. One way to quantify the incidence of elder abuse is to examine data from the National Ombudsman Reporting System (NORS). The Older Americans Act requires states to collect long-term care complaint data and requires the state ombudsman to report the aggregate data to the AOA. In 1995, the AOA implemented NORS, which consists of 128 complaint categories for long-term care facilities such as nursing homes. One category of NORS accounts for abuse, gross neglect, and exploitation, with additional subcategories of abuse: physical abuse, sexual abuse, verbal/psychological abuse, financial exploitation, gross neglect, resident-to-resident physical or sexual abuse, and other. The kind of abuse addresses what is considered to be the "willful mistreatment of residents by facility staff, management, other residents or unknown or outside individuals who have gained access to the resident through negligence or lax security on the part of the facility or for neglect which is so severe that it constitutes abuse" (Wood, 2006).

A report from the Office of the Inspector General (OIG) of the Department of Health and Human Services (DHHS) consisting of state long-term care ombudsman data showed the number of abuse complaints as escalating from approximately 13,450 in 1996 to approximately 15,000 in 2000. The report also found that complaints of physical abuse were included in the top ombudsman complaints for that same time period. In 1996, physical abuse complaints numbered 4,321 and ranked seventh; and in 2000 such complaints numbered 4,350 and ranked eleventh (Wood, 2006). Hawes (2002) reported that an estimated 10 percent of complaints received by ombudsmen in just 1 year involved allegations of abuse, gross neglect, or exploitation; however, it is well known that formal complaints provide an underestimate of the actual instances of abuse or neglect, because residents and families are often unwilling to file a formal complaint. Residents and family members report fear of retaliation and a belief that complaining would be futile as common reasons for not reporting incidents.

In 2001, the U.S. House of Representatives' Committee on Government Reform issued a report asserting that abuse of residents "is a major problem in U.S. nursing homes" (U.S. House, 2001). This report analyzed data from the nursing home complaint database covering all surveys and complaint investigations during a 2-year period, and made a number of conclusions, including that nearly one-third of all certified facilities had been cited for some type of abuse violation that had the potential to cause harm or had actually caused harm to a nursing home resident. In addition, the report found that 10 percent of nursing homes were cited for abuse violations that caused actual harm to residents or placed them in immediate jeopardy of death or serious injury. The cases involving abuse included physical and sexual abuse as well as verbal abuse involving threats and humiliation. After reviewing data from multiple studies of nursing home residents and staff, Hawes (2002) indicated that as many as one-half of residents self-report being abused or roughly handled, and about one-third self-report witnessing abuse of others. Approximately one-half of staff self-reported committing psychological or verbal abuse of residents, and 10 percent to 17 percent reported using some form of excessive restraint or engaging in physical abuse of residents.

There is an assumption that abuse occurs only in shabby, dark nursing homes filled with indigent patients. Higher rates of abuse can occur at facilities that are less staffed and resourced, making for more dangerous conditions, but abuse can happen among more upscale facilities. In 2010, Faturechi reported on the trial of a 21-year-old man charged with seven counts of elder abuse and one count of torture allegedly conducted at an assisted living facility in the affluent community of Calabasas, California. Prosecutors say the former caregiver beat and body-slammed several residents and encouraged two others with dementia to fight. Coworkers say they saw the man severely mistreating residents, some of whom would have been too dementia-ridden to alert anyone to the alleged abuse. If convicted, he faces a possible life sentence in prison. Faturechi (2010) wrote: "The state attorney general's office has called elder abuse in nursing homes a serious problem. In a 12-month period between 2007 and 2008, there were 85 elder abuse convictions in California, according to the state Department of Justice. Many cases go undetected or unreported, authorities say."

On March 23, 2010, healthcare reform legislation signed into law included bill language instructing the secretary of the DHHS to develop a national system for conducting criminal background checks of prospective healthcare providers who engage in direct-care activities in long-term care facilities or in private homes (NCEA, 2010). We will discuss this issue in greater depth in Chapter 6.

Who Are the Abusers: The Victimizers

Physicians

As discussed in Chapter 1, physicians are bound by the Hippocratic Oath, but as Dehlendorf and Wolfe (1998) pointed out, it has only been in the last several decades that sexual contact with patients has been clearly condemned by the medical profession:

> In 1973, the first code of ethics of the American Psychiatric Association (APA) explicitly condemned sexual contact with patients. In 1993, the APA's ethics code stated, presumably based on the growing recognition that the power imbalance of the physician–patient relationship endured even after treatment had been terminated, that "sexual activity with a current or former patient is

unethical." In 1986, the Council of Ethical and Judicial Affairs of the American Medical Association (AMA) first issued an opinion on physician sexual misconduct that stated, "Sexual misconduct in the practice of medicine violates the trust the patient reposes in the physician and is unethical." In 1992, the Council updated this opinion to explicitly define sexual misconduct, stating that all sexual contact with current patients constitutes sexual misconduct, and "sexual or romantic relationships with former patients are unethical if the physician uses or exploits trust, knowledge, emotions, or influence derived from the previous professional relationship."

If perpetrators of sexual misconduct had a common visage, they would be male, with an average age of 53, and have been in practice an average of 25 years, according to Bloom et al. (1999). Across medical specialties, Enborn and Thomas (1997) indicated that most sexual misconduct complaints were filed against physicians practicing in family medicine, obstetrics/gynecology, and psychiatry. Gabbard (1989) classified sexually abusive physicians into four categories based upon underlying psychodynamics: the "lovesick" physician who is looking for human contact, the "limitless physician" who is looking to cross ethical boundaries, the "predatory physician" who is a sexual deviant, and the "psychotic physician" who suffers from a significant psychopathology. Gross (2008) pointed to studies indicating that physician sexual misconduct is increasing: Winn (1993) reported that from 1990 to 1993, a respective 2.6 percent, 3.6 percent, and 3.9 percent of reported violations involved sexual misconduct; by 1996, that figure had risen to 4.4 percent according to Dehlendorf and Wolfe (1998); and Morrison and Wickersham (1998) reported that from 1996 to 1998, the percentage of complaints against physicians that included sexual misconduct had risen to 10 percent.

Dehlendorf and Wolfe (1998) sought to determine the frequency and severity of discipline against physicians who commit sex-related offenses and to describe the characteristics of these physicians. They analyzed a national database of disciplinary orders taken by state medical boards and federal agencies and found that 761 physicians had been disciplined for sex-related offenses from 1981 through 1996. They found that the number of physicians disciplined per year for sex-related offenses increased from 42 in 1989 to 147 in 1996, and the proportion of all disciplinary orders that were sex related increased from 2.1 percent in 1989 to 4.4 percent in 1996. Discipline for sex-related offenses was more severe than for non-sex–related offenses, with 71.9 percent of sex-related orders involving revocation, surrender, or suspension of medical license. Of 761 physicians disciplined, the offenses committed by 567 involved patients, including sexual intercourse, rape, sexual molestation, and sexual favors for drugs. Almost 40 percent of physicians disciplined for sex-related offenses between 1981 and 1994 were licensed to practice. They also found that compared with all physicians,

physicians disciplined for sex-related offenses were more likely to practice in the specialties of psychiatry, child psychiatry, obstetrics and gynecology, and family and general practice than in other specialties and were older than the national physician population, but were no different in terms of board certification status. The key conclusion of the work by Dehlendorf and Wolfe (1998) is that a substantial proportion of physicians disciplined for sexual abuse are allowed to either continue to practice or return to practice. A more detailed look at physician discipline relating to sexual misconduct is undertaken in Chapter 6.

Psychiatrists

Plaut and Foster (1986) have explained that a therapeutic relationship between a professional and a patient requires a certain level of trust, intimacy, and vulnerability that can be confusing: "It is not unusual for a health professional to feel sexually attracted to a patient. Such feelings need not be of concern if they are acknowledged and if the practitioner continues to relate to the patient in a professional manner. When a practitioner yields to the tendency to exploit such a relationship, the welfare of the patient and the level of trust in the profession are threatened." Some do not take such a permissive view of sexually related incidences. Schwartz (undated) states that "Sex between patients and psychotherapists is now uniformly deplored and unequivocally branded as wrong and unacceptable. The most comprehensive recent survey of psychiatrists reported that 98 percent of those responding felt sexual contact between psychotherapist and patient while the patient is in treatment is always inappropriate. A similar number stated that such contact is usually or always harmful to the patient. Moreover, the American Psychiatric Association flatly states that 'sexual activity with a patient is unethical.'"

Psychiatrists have been particularly diligent in examining and analyzing the occurrence of sexual contact with patient. Consequently, the majority of existing studies on physician–patient sexual contact examine sexual contact between psychiatrists and their patients. Studies of psychiatrists indicate that between 5 percent and 10 percent reported having sexual contact with patients (McMurray et al., 1991). Gross (2008) points to the fact that among medical specialties, psychiatrists were the eighth most frequently visited physician, accounting for 28,125,000 visits (or 9.7 per 100 persons per year) in 2005, the latest year for which data were available. With such high utilization, the opportunity for sexual misconduct rises in proportion. The challenge is that while not sexual assault or abuse, relationships with patients represent an ethical slippery slope. It is a very fine line between boundary violations and sexual misconduct. Therapist risk factors for violations include the therapist's own life crises, a tendency to idealize a "special" patient or an inability to set limits, and denial about the possibility of boundary problems. Factors exacerbating patient vulnerability include overdependence on the therapist, seeking therapy to find a relationship, and the acceptance by childhood abuse victims of an abusive therapy relationship.

Experts point to boundary issues as being some of the most significant causes of medical malpractice actions against providers. As Norris et al. (2003) have said, "Despite broad agreement in psychiatry that sexual misconduct and other boundary violations can cause notable harm to patients, some of our most senior and accomplished practitioners and teachers continue to find themselves embroiled in these difficulties.... We continue to see a steady stream of boundary violations, both sexual and nonsexual, in all psychiatric contexts" (pp. 517–522).

Prevalence of abuse perpetrated by psychiatrists was the focus of several groundbreaking studies from the 1980s. In a nationwide survey of U.S. psychiatrists, Gartrell et al. (1986) found that 7.1 percent (1,057) of the male and 3.1 percent (257) of the female respondents acknowledged sexual contact with their own patients. Eighty-eight percent of the sexual contacts occurred between male psychiatrists and female patients. All offenders who had been involved with more than one patient were male. Forty-one percent of the offending psychiatrists sought consultation because of their sexual involvement with patients. Herman et al. (1987) surveyed 1,423 practicing psychiatrists and found that the overwhelming majority of the respondents (98 percent) said that therapist–patient sexual contact is always inappropriate and usually harmful to the patient. However, 29.6 percent said that such contact after termination of therapy might sometimes be acceptable. Psychiatrists who acknowledged having had sexual contact with one or more patients differed markedly from their peers in their attitudes; the majority (74 percent) of these offenders believed that sexual contact could be appropriate after termination, as many apparently rationalized their behavior in this manner.

In its Code of Conduct, the Association of State and Provincial Psychology Boards (ASPPB, 2005) addresses sexual relationships between psychologists and patients by stating, "Psychologists do not engage in sexual intimacies with current clients. Psychologists do not engage in sexual intimacies with individuals they know to be close relatives, guardians, or significant others of current clients. Psychologists do not terminate the professional relationship to circumvent this standard. Psychologists do not accept as therapy clients persons with whom they have engaged in sexual intimacies." The code does not address sexual misconduct as a criminal matter. Even though they know it is wrong, some psychiatrists, physicians, and healthcare professionals are sexual addicts and find fulfillment in seducing their patients. Irons (1995) observed, "The healing potential in the professional–patient relationship is facilitated by inherent disparity in position, education and power. Yet, since its origin in prehistory, the healing profession has been shadowed by abuse of privilege. Sexual misconduct and offense are among the most common and egregious forms of abuse." Irons said that despite codes of conduct and ethics, healthcare professionals "sometimes fail to remain god-like and perfect in their discharge of duties, despite being held to these higher moral and ethical standards, for they are human and subject to the same maladies and shortcomings as the patients they serve."

Dentists

Dentists and dental hygienists have been convicted of sexual assaults on patients while they were under general anesthesia or sedation. Seldin (2008) noted, "Dental patients place themselves in an intimate and potentially vulnerable position during a dental visit. If even one case breaches the public trust in health care professionals, action is required, because these violations can cause irreparable harm to the victims." Seldin (2008) added: "While victims and perpetrators of sexual abuse can be of either gender, profiles show that the majority of offenders in dental settings are men, while the majority of adult victims are women." As Plaut and Wilson (2008) state: "We may tend to underestimate the vulnerability of our patients and often don't realize the level of power we have over them in the clinical setting, not only during the time of a professional relationship, but even for a time after a professional relationship has ended." Guidelines proposed recently by the American Association of Dental Examiners (AADE) underscore that concept:

> The position of power in the dental care practitioner–patient relationship is inherently unequal. In order to receive dental treatment, the patient surrenders certain personal liberties and authorities to the practitioner. The patient discloses private health information and cooperates with treatment conditions that render the patient physically and mentally vulnerable. The patient lies in a reclined position while receiving treatment that is provided with the practitioner(s) in close physical proximity to the patient. The patient permits touching of the oral cavity and its adjacent structures, succumbs to procedures that may be stressful and painful, and may be given pharmacological agents designed to produce analgesia, sedation, and/or anesthesia. These patient concessions position the practitioner as the more powerful party in the dental practitioner–patient relationship. Consequently, it is incumbent upon dental care practitioners to respect sexual boundaries and to ensure that nonprofessional considerations do not intrude into the practitioner–patient relationship. (Plant and Wilson, 2008)

The American Dental Association's (ADA) Code of Professional Conduct advises against personal relationships with patients and states, "Dentists should avoid interpersonal relationships that could impair their professional judgment or risk the possibility of exploiting the confidence placed in them by a patient" (Plant and Wilson, 2008). Seldin (2008) reported that at a recent annual meeting, the AADE approved new guidelines for state dental boards addressing unprofessional conduct involving sexual boundary violations. In addition, Seldin (2008) states that the ADA is expected to address the issue and that this "flurry of recent policy-making activity indicates that standards for appropriate behavior may be changing. Programs designed to treat dentists, dental hygienists, and registered dental assistants who may have violated boundaries could help to prevent some from crossing the line and becoming sex offenders."

All states have established laws prohibiting sexual misconduct in the practice of dentistry, and medical boards have provided for the discipline of a licensee found guilty of this criminal act, which frequently surfaces as one of the most common complaints filed against dentists, dental hygienists, and registered dental assistants. Sfikas and George (2004) have confirmed that states uphold laws that criminalize assaults, abuse, and batteries of a sexual nature, and that dentists are as subject to these laws as any other member of the public. They say that some states demand that any criminal convictions involving licensees be reported to licensing boards, and that other states, through their dental practice acts, allow dental licensing boards to take disciplinary action against licensees for convictions under these criminal laws. Sfikas and George (2004) add that "Licensing boards are charged with protecting the public. A review of the state practice acts shows that criminal violations, typically a felony or misdemeanor involving 'moral turpitude,' can serve as a basis for imposing discipline on dental professionals in virtually every state."

Some medical boards are taking sexual abuse of patients more seriously than others. Seldin (2008) reported that in June 2007, California Governor Arnold Schwarzenegger signed legislation preventing registered sex offenders from being licensed to practice dentistry in California. This law requires the Dental Board of California to deny an application, revoke a license, or deny the renewal of a license for registered sex offenders. The legislation's author, Senator Sam Aanestad, who also is an oral surgeon, declared in a statement, "Registered sex offenders should not be providing dental services for adults or children under any circumstance. Consumer protection is the most important service that the Dental Board can provide, and it needs the tools that will allow it to respond quickly when a patient's health or safety is put at risk" (Seldin, 2008). Other than California, no state has a specific exclusion from practice for registered sex offenders. And lest medical board action seem harsh or restrictive, Plaut and Wilson (2008) have noted that "An attorney who served as counsel to state licensing boards once pointed out that 'when we accept a license to practice, we give up certain personal freedoms in return for upholding the standards of our profession.'"

Pediatricians

The American Academy of Pediatrics (AAP, 1999) observed, "Physicians and the public recognize the need for high moral standards and accountability in medicine." It stated further that "physicians must exercise substantial care in nonprofessional relationships with patients and families to promote the highest possible degree of trust in the doctor–patient–family relationship." The AAP (1999) has also noted that "It is difficult to find reliable data on the prevalence of sexual contact between physicians and their patients or their patients' family members. Position papers about psychiatrists and obstetricians comment on the lack of well-conducted reliable studies on professional boundary violations by physicians. Attention to the subject, in the form of complaints against practitioners and publications in professional journals, has been more prominent among psychiatrists and obstetrician–gynecologists."

The AAP (1999) noted:

> Because pediatricians provide counseling services for patients and families, the concerns closely parallel those faced by mental health professionals. Pediatricians who feel sexually attracted to children may put patients at risk of sexual abuse or exploitation. More likely, however, pediatricians may be misunderstood when they first discuss sexual maturation and sexuality with patients. Similarly, examination of an adolescent's maturing genitals or breasts during an office visit may be distressing or misunderstood by the patient, especially if a parent or chaperone is not in the examining room. Pediatricians should develop and follow clear and consistent office policies about the presence of a chaperone during parts of the physical examination, taking into account local customs, families' religions and cultural traditions, and the need for patient privacy.

Because of the very nature of the pediatric population, the AAP emphasizes that,

> There is an inherent risk of exploitation for patients or family members who depend on the knowledge and authority of the physician, especially in cases involving non-routine health care. The success of the doctor–patient or doctor–parent relationship depends on the ability of the patient or family member to trust the physician completely. Patients and family members legitimately expect to feel physically and emotionally safe in professional relationships with physicians. They should not feel vulnerable to romantic or sexual advances while receiving medical care for themselves or their children. In addition, children should be free from concern that their treatment may be compromised by a nonprofessional relationship between a parent and their physician.

It is a slippery slope for pediatricians wanting to put their young patients more at ease. As the AAP (1999) has noted,

> Physicians usually prefer warm, friendly relationships with their patients. The need to avoid untoward personal intimacy should not lead to a cold, indifferent manner in their interactions with patients or family members. Many cultures expect physical expressions of care and concern in times of personal crisis, including sickness. Physicians might well be seen as unsympathetic and excessively remote if they avoid handshakes or other socially approved touching during emotional encounters with families. In most social groups in the U.S., interaction with children is likely to involve appropriate physical contact, such as hugging.... It may be helpful to recognize that some kinds of touching may be confusing or offensive to children, depending on their stage of physical and emotional maturation.

One of the most egregious cases of a pediatrician accused of sexual assault and videotaping his criminal acts is that of Earl Bradley, 56, a Lewes, Delaware, physician indicted by the Sussex County Grand Jury in February 2010 for 103 rapes of children he had treated between 1998 and 2009. Delaware Attorney General Beau Biden said the 471-count indictment contains charges of first- and second-degree rape, sexual exploitation of a child, first- and second-degree unlawful sexual contact, continuous sexual abuse of a child, second-degree assault, first-degree reckless endangering, and first-degree attempted rape. In a statement, Biden said, "We will prosecute this case to the fullest extent of the law. As a prosecutor, I am bound by certain rules that limit what I can say in the midst of an active investigation. I cannot say certain things that I am feeling, and I am feeling a great deal. I am determined to see that this defendant will never, ever be in a position again to hurt another child."

The indictment is based on video evidence seized by law enforcement during the execution of search warrants at the defendant's home and office in December 2009. The many video files seized show the defendant in the act of assaulting his victims. The indictment alleges that 103 individual children were victimized. If convicted as charged, the defendant faces a mandatory sentence of life in prison without the possibility of parole. This indictment is the result of a year-long investigation. In December 2008, Delaware State Police responded to allegations of sexual abuse against Bradley by opening an investigation, which remained open and active throughout the remainder of 2008 and 2009, until they arrested him on December 16, 2009 and executed a search warrant at his medical practice. After Bradley was arrested, search warrants were executed at his home and office which uncovered the evidence that resulted in the indictment. During the course of the ongoing investigation, the Delaware Department of Justice, working with the Delaware Child

Predator Task Force, Delaware State Police, and other agencies reviewed and analyzed the substantial amount of evidence that was seized, including more than 13 hours of video files, computers, hard drives, and other digital storage media, and more than 7,000 of the defendant's individual patient files. Biden explained that a team of national experts on child sexual abuse has been assembled to assist parents, victims, and community members, and to assist in the investigation. The Delaware Department of Justice sent more than 3,000 letters to parents and guardians of Bradley's current and former patients, notifying families of the criminal investigation. Barrish (2010) reported that the case against Bradley is believed to be one of the most heinous allegations of patient sexual abuse made against a doctor in American history.

Nursing Assistants and Aides

One of the most challenging healthcare environments a provider may find himself or herself in is a long-term care nursing facility or nursing home. The person most often charged with day-to-day caring for America's institutionalized elderly is the certified nursing assistant (CNA) or the uncertified nursing aide, who assists residents with their activities of daily living, including dressing, eating, bathing, and toileting. DeHart and Cornman (2009) has pointed out that according to the U.S. Department of Labor (2006), these jobs typically require only a high school diploma and, depending on the state requirements, about 75 additional hours of training. These aides are subjected to low pay, significant physical workloads, continuous emotional demands, and limited opportunity for advancement, even as they work with residents who can be confused, combative, or uncooperative. DeHart, Webb, and Cornman (2009) cited Goodridge et al.'s (1996) observation that CNAs experience "multiple stressors that underscore the highly interpersonal nature of caregiving," and note that other factors include being assaulted on the job by residents (Goodridge et al., 1996) and lacking skills to manage workplace conflict properly (Braun et al., 1997). DeHart, Webb, and Cornman (2009) noted, "It is also possible that CNAs lack understanding of power differentials, boundaries, and privacy issues that come into play in coping with perceived 'problematic' resident behavior" (Clough, 1999; Nerenberg, 2002).

Numerous studies of aides working in nursing homes reflect abhorrent incidences of abuse and neglect. Hawes (2002) pointed to a survey of nursing home CNAs in which 17 percent of CNAs reported they had pushed, grabbed, or shoved a resident; 51 percent reported they had yelled at a resident in anger during the last year; and 23 percent had insulted or sworn at a resident. MacDonald (2000) (from Hawes, 2002) interviewed 77 CNAs from 31 nursing facilities and reported that 58 percent had seen a staff member yell at a resident in anger; 36 percent had seen staff insult or swear at a resident; and 11 percent had witnessed staff threatening to hit or throw something at a resident. They also reported witnessing incidents of rough treatment and physical abuse of residents by other staff. Twenty-five percent of the CNAs witnessed staff isolating a resident beyond what was needed to manage his or her behavior, 21 percent witnessed restraint of a resident beyond what was needed, and 11 percent saw a resident being denied food as punishment. CNAs also reported witnessing more explicit instances of abuse. For example, 21 percent saw a resident pushed, grabbed, shoved, or pinched in anger; 12 percent witnessed staff slapping a resident; 7 percent saw a resident being kicked or hit with a fist; 3 percent saw staff throw something at a resident; and 1 percent saw a resident being hit with an object. Pillemer and Moore (1990) conducted interviews with 577 nurses and aides and found that 10 percent had committed one or more acts of physical abuse in the past year, and 40 percent admitted to psychologically abusing residents. The researchers found that the most common forms of physical abuse were restraining patients beyond what was needed to ensure their safety; pushing, grabbing, shoving, or punching; hitting the patient with an object; and throwing something at the patient. The most common forms of psychological abuse were yelling, swearing, or insulting residents; denying them privileges; or threatening to hit or throw something. More than one-third of these healthcare providers had witnessed other employees physically abuse residents, and 81 percent had observed at least one incident of psychological abuse in the last year.

Neglect can be as devastating as abuse. Hawes (2002) said that "because there is no federal reporting system and state systems are highly variable, it is impossible to generate useful estimates of neglect in residential care." MacDonald (2000) reported that the kinds of things residents and CNAs identified and reported as neglect included residents being left wet or soiled with feces; residents not being turned and positioned, which can lead to pressure ulcers; staff shutting off call lights without helping the resident seeking assistance; residents not receiving enough help at mealtimes; staff failing to perform prescribed range of motion and other physician-ordered therapies to prevent residents from developing contractures; and staff failure to respond to residents' requests or need for something to eat or drink. Johnson and Kramer (1998) also reported instances of neglect as lack of or denial of nutritional support to maintain proper body weight, pressure ulcer care, prevention of contractures, pain management, and personal assistance. Kayser-Jones and Schell (1997) found that many facilities were so understaffed that although trays were taken into rooms, residents who needed help were not fed.

In 2002, Hawes noted:

> Although there has been only minimal research on the causes of abuse and neglect in residential long-term care settings, there is remarkable consensus across diverse studies and surveys of stakeholders. Three factors are generally viewed as causing or significantly contributing to abuse and neglect in nursing

homes. They are: Staffing shortages that cause neglect and create stressful working conditions in which abuse is more likely to occur; staff burn-out, often a product of staffing shortages, mandatory overtime, and the fact that many staff must work two jobs to survive financially; and poor staff training, particularly about the impact of dementia and how to interpret and manage challenging behaviors among residents.

As discussed, CNAs face challenging work environments and workloads. Also contributing to their tendencies to abuse is chronic staffing shortages. Hawes (2002) reported that state survey agency directors, managers of state nursing assistant registries, residents, family members, ombudsmen, and CNAs working in nursing homes agree unanimously that inadequate staffing was the major preventable cause of abuse and neglect. Hawes (2002) also reported that low wages paid to CNAs made it difficult or impossible to hire and retain good staff, thus exacerbating staffing shortages and turnover. A staffing study conducted by the Centers for Medicare and Medicaid Services (CMS) concluded that most long-term care facilities were understaffed, with a significant number dangerously understaffed. Hawes (2002) conducted focus group interviews in which CNAs explained why staffing shortages caused or contributed to abuse and neglect. CNAs said that when they were understaffed, there was not inadequate time to meet all of the residents' needs. Hawes (2002) reported strong agreement among the CNAs that the first things to be neglected were range of motion exercises and other types of restorative activities, as well as nursing care, keeping residents hydrated, and giving residents enough time and assistance with eating activities. CNAs also described the way in which the abuse was more likely to occur; they would be "required" to work all or part of a second shift, leading to exhaustion and frayed tempers. Or, they might have 20-plus residents to care for on a busy day shift; during night shifts, a single CNA might have 30-plus residents for which to care.

It is a reminder that not all caregivers in the long-term care environment are intent on causing harm. Nerenberg (2002) stated, "Most studies assume that abusive nursing home employees are not acting in a malicious, premeditated manner, but rather, are responding to the highly stressful nature of the work, which is attributed to insufficient staffing and time to complete tasks, interpersonal conflict and aggression by residents." Nerenberg (2002) tells of an investigator who observed that within a single month, the majority of nursing aides surveyed had been sworn at or insulted and that they had experienced some form of physical aggression. Other sources of nursing aides' duress included aggression by supervisors and residents' family members.

It is important to examine for a moment the interaction between caregiver and patient. Nerenberg (2002) explained that predictors of abuse involve many variables: "Structural variables include societal, cultural or economic factors such as the low esteem in which the elderly are held and the insufficient labor force of workers. Environmental factors refer to the nursing home setting and include staffing levels, staff turnover, management and ownership status." The characteristics of the caregiver and the patient also come into play. Nerenberg (2002) noted, "Some have assumed that patients with cognitive and physical impairment ... are at greater risk for abuse and neglect, although these assumptions have not been substantiated. Patient aggression has been shown to be a particularly significant predictor of both physical and psychological abuse. Not only do staff strike back against aggressive residents, but severely confused and aggressive residents are more likely to be denied opportunities for personal choice."

Nerenberg (2002) also found that attitudes toward the elderly play a significant role in the potential for abuse: "Psychologically abusive staff is more likely to view patients as...children who sometimes need to be disciplined. Employees' burnout, which is described as a progressive physical and emotional exhaustion resulting from prolonged involvement with people, has been found to be strongly associated with physical and psychological abuse." Shaw (1998) suggested that workers' personality traits and circumstances influence their ability to cope with patients' aggression and determine whether they will respond negatively. According to Shaw, certain healthcare providers develop a tolerance for aggression displayed by residents; however, many caregivers lack the resiliency required to do this and eventually succumb to the fatigue that the stressors of the healthcare environment create.

Reporting, Regulating, and Prosecuting Abuse

Once a boundary has been crossed by a healthcare professional, it sets into motion a complex chain of events impacting the patient and the caregiver; however, documenting, reporting, and prosecuting the alleged abuse is an altogether challenging process. Underreporting and delayed reporting pose a significant obstacle to abuse investigations in nursing homes. In a 2002 report, the General Accounting Office (now known as the General Accountability Office) observed that allegations of physical and sexual abuse of nursing home residents frequently are not reported promptly and that local law enforcement officials indicated they are seldom summoned to nursing homes to immediately investigate allegations of physical or sexual abuse. Some of these officials indicated that they often receive such reports after evidence has been compromised. And although abuse allegations should be reported to state survey agencies immediately, they often are not (GAO, 2002).

The GAO's review of state survey agencies' physical and sexual abuse case files indicated that about half of the notifications from nursing homes were submitted two or more days after the nursing homes learned of the alleged abuse, thus compromising the quality of available evidence and hindering investigations. Another factor contributing to delayed reporting, according to the GAO, is the reluctance on the part of residents or family members to report abuse for fear of retribution (Hodges, 1998), while still others may be uncertain about where to report abuse. According to one law enforcement official the GAO interviewed, family members are sometimes fearful that the resident will be asked to leave the home and are troubled by the prospect of finding a new place for the resident to live. What's more, the GAO report (2002) noted that few allegations of abuse are ultimately prosecuted. Because so many state survey agencies follow different policies when determining whether to refer allegations of abuse to law enforcement, these authorities were sometimes either not apprised of incidents or received referrals only after long delays. When referrals were made, the GAO found that criminal investigations and, thus, prosecutions were sometimes hampered because witnesses to the alleged abuse were unable or unwilling to testify. Delays in investigations, as well as in trials, reduced the likelihood of successful prosecutions because the memory of witnesses often deteriorated.

The GAO (2002) found that safeguards to protect residents from potentially abusive individuals are insufficient at federal and state levels. There is no federal statute requiring criminal background checks of nursing home employees, and the Medicare program does not require them. As we will see in Chapter 6, this is a controversial issue. Some states require background checks to screen potential nursing home employees, but they do not necessarily include all nursing home employees, and they are not always completed before an individual begins working. They also only focus on individuals' criminal records within the state where they are seeking employment and do not catch perpetrators crossing state lines. Even more troubling is the fact that although nursing homes are expected to protect their residents, many state survey agencies seldom, if not rarely, recommended that certain sanctions, such as civil monetary penalties or terminations from federal programs, be imposed. For example, the GAO (2002) reviewed more than 150 case files and found that 26 nursing homes were cited for deficiencies related to abuse; the survey agencies recommended a civil monetary penalty for just one nursing home, and the remaining 25 facilities faced less punitive sanctions such as a requirement to develop corrective action plans.

It is an unacceptable state of affairs, considering that most nursing homes participate in the federal Medicare and Medicaid programs, which dole out billions of dollars for what is presumed to be high levels of abuse-free resident care. State survey agencies are compelled to perform facility surveys at least every 12 to 15 months to assess nursing homes' compliance with federal and state laws and regulations. These surveys are designed to determine whether nursing homes are complying with Medicare and

Medicaid standards; nursing homes that are out of compliance are cited with deficiencies that, depending upon their severity, can result in monetary penalties or other enforcement actions, including termination from federal programs. In addition to periodic surveys, state survey agencies investigate complaints of inadequate care, including allegations of physical or sexual abuse. Complaints may be submitted by residents, family members, friends, physicians, nursing home staff, and long-term care ombudsmen. State survey agencies must investigate all allegations, determine if abuse occurred, and identify appropriate corrective actions. The Medicare and Medicaid programs require nursing home administrators to notify state survey agencies of allegations of abuse in their facilities immediately, and they are also required to conduct internal investigations and submit their findings in written reports to the state survey agency within five working days of the incident. Depending on the severity of the circumstances, the state survey agency may visit the nursing home to investigate the incident or wait until the facility submits its report. Depending on the content of the facility's report, the survey agency may request the home conduct additional work or the agency may investigate further on its own. If the agency opts not to investigate further, it may still review the manner in which the home conducted its investigation during the agency's next scheduled survey of the home (GAO, 2002). Local police departments may conduct criminal investigations if they learn of suspected instances of resident abuse, but many cases involve reporting to the nursing home administrator only. The GAO (2002) interviewed one long-term care ombudsman who noted that residents and family members do not always view the abuse as a criminal matter, and that nursing homes are usually not compelled to notify local law enforcement when they learn of such reports. There is no federal requirement that they contact police, although some states have instituted such a requirement.

The consequences for individual perpetrators have typically been termination from employment or disciplinary action. Although successful prosecutions are difficult to achieve in many cases of institutional abuse, Saveman et al. (1999) noted that when individual healthcare providers are prosecuted, the sentence they are most likely to receive is probation (68 percent), with 23 percent serving time in jails or prison. Individuals convicted of sexual abuse are more likely than other offenders to receive prison sentences.

References

Acierno R, Hernandez-Tejada M, Muzzy W, and Steve K. "National elder mistreatment study." U.S. Department of Justice. March 2009.

American Academy of Pediatrics (AAP). "Appropriate boundaries in the pediatrician–family patient relationship." *Pediatrics.* 104(2): August 1999. (Accessed October 24, 2010, at: http://aappolicy.aappublications.org/cgi/content/full/pediatrics/3B104/2/334.)

Association of State and Provincial Psychology Boards (ASPPB). "Code of Conduct." 2005. (Accessed at: http://asppb.net/i4a/pages/index.cfm?pageid=3353.)

Associated Press (AP). "Workers indicted in patient abuse." *The New York Times.* November 4, 1983.

Baladerian N. Sexual abuse of people with developmental disabilities. *Sexuality and Disability.* 9(4):323–335. 1991.

Baladerian N. *Interviewing Skills to Use with Abuse Victims Who Have Developmental Disabilities.* Washington, DC: National Aging Resource Center on Elder Abuse. 1992.

Barrish C. "Grand jury indicts Dr. Earl Bradley in rapes of 103 child patients." *The News Journal.* February 22, 2010.

Bloom JD, Notman MT, and Nadelson CC, eds. *Physician Sexual Misconduct.* American Psychiatric Publishing. 1999.

Braun KL, Suzuki KM, Cusick CE, and Howard-Carhart K. Developing and testing training materials on elder abuse and neglect for nurse aides. *J Elder Abuse Neglect.* 9(1):1–15. 1997.

Brown H, and Stein J. Sexual abuse perpetrated by men with intellectual disabilities: A comparative study. *J Intell Dis Research.* 41(3):215–224. 1997.

Burgess AW, and Hartman CR, eds. *Sexual Exploitation of Patients by Health Professionals.* New York: Praeger. 1986.

Burgess AW, Dowdell EB, and Prentky RA. Sexual abuse of nursing home residents. *J Psych Nursing.* 38(6). June 2000.

Clarke ME, and Pierson W. Management of elder abuse in the emergency department. Emerg Med Clin North Am. 17(3):631–644. August 1999.

Clough R. Scandalous care: Interpreting public enquiry reports of scandals in residential care. *J Elder Abuse Neglect.* 10(1/2):13–27. 1999.

Cusack KJ, Frueh CB, and Brady KT. Trauma history screening in a community mental health center. *Psychiatr Serv.* 55:157–162. February 2004.

DeHart D, Webb J, and Cornman C. Prevention of elder mistreatment in nursing homes: Competencies for direct-care staff. *J Elder Abuse Neglect.* 21(4):360–378. October 2009.

Dehlendorf CE, and Wolfe SM. Physicians disciplined for sex-related offenses. *JAMA.* 279:1883–1888. 1998.

Department of Health and Human Services. Office of Inspector General. "Resident abuse in nursing homes. Understanding and preventing abuse." Report OEI-06-88-00360. Washington, DC. 1990.

Enborn JA, and Thomas CD. Evaluation of sexual misconduct complaints. *Am J Obstet Gynecol.* 176:1340–1346. 1997.

Faturechi R. "Brutal abuse at Calabasas retirement home described in testimony." *The Los Angeles Times.* March 30, 2010.

Federation of State Medical Boards of the United States. (FSMB). "Addressing sexual boundaries: Guidelines for state medical boards." Undated.

Furey EM. Sexual abuse of adults with mental retardation: Who and where. *Mental Retardation.* 32:173–180. 1994.

Gabbard GO. *Sexual Exploitation in Professional Relationships*. Washington, DC: American Psychiatric Press. 1989.

Gartrell N, Herman J, Olarte S, Feldstein M, and Localio R. Psychiatrist–patient sexual contact: Results of a national survey, prevalence. *Am J Psychiatry*. 143:1126–1131. 1986.

General Accounting Office. "Nursing homes: More can be done to protect residents from abuse." GAO Report 02-312. Washington, DC. 2002.

Goodridge DM, Johnston P, and Thomson M. Conflict and aggression as stressors in the work environment of nursing assistants: Implications for institutional elder abuse. *J Elder Abuse Neglect*. 8(1):49–67. 1996.

Gross B. As Hippocrates forewarned: Sexual misconduct by physicians. *Annals Am Psych Assoc*. March 22, 2008.

Grubaugh AL, Frueh BC, Zinzow HM, Cusack KJ, and Wells C. Patients' perceptions of care and safety within psychiatric settings. *Psych Services*. 4(3):193–201. August 2007.

Hawes C. "Elder abuse in residential long-term care facilities: What is known about prevalence, causes and prevention." Testimony before the U.S. Senate Committee on Finance. National Academy of Sciences Report. June 18, 2002.

Herman JL, Gartrell N, Olarte S, Feldstein M, and Localio R. Psychiatrist–patient sexual contact: Results of a national survey, II: Psychiatrists' attitudes. *Am J Psychiatry*. 144:164–169. 1987.

Hodges PD. National law enforcement programs to prevent, detect, investigate and prosecute elder abuse and neglect in healthcare facilities. *J Elder Abuse Neglect*. 1998.

Hudson, B. Ensuring an abuse-free environment: A learning program for nursing home staff. *J Elder Abuse Neglect*. 4(4):25–36. 1992.

Irons R. Sexually addicted healthcare professionals. In: *Breach of Trust: Sexual Exploitation by Health Care Professionals and Clergy*. Gonsiorek JC, ed. Thousand Oaks, CA: Sage. 1995.

Jewkes R, Abrahams N, and Mvo Z. Why do nurses abuse patients? *Soc Sci Med*. 47(11):1781–1795. 1998.

Judd A. "Federal judge rejects plan for Georgia's mental hospitals." *Atlanta Journal Constitution*. September 30, 2009.

Judd A, and Miller A. "A hidden shame: Death in Georgia's mental hospitals." *Atlanta Journal Constitution*. January 7, 2007. (Accessed at: http://www.ajc.com/health/content/health/stories/hiddenshame.html.)

Lakin KC, Bruiniks RH, Hill BK, and Hauberg FA. Turnover of direct care staff in a national sample of residential facilities for mentally retarded people. *Am J Mental Deficiency*. 87:64–72. 1982.

Lumley VA, and Miltenberger RG. Sexual abuse prevention for persons with mental retardation. *Am J Mental Retardation*. 101:459–472. 1997.

MacDonald P. "Make a difference: Abuse/neglect pilot project." Project Report to the National Citizens' Coalition for Nursing Home Reform. 2000.

Mansell S, Sobsey D, and Calder P. Sexual abuse treatment for persons with developmental disabilities. Cited in Petersilia et al. (2001), *Crime Victims with Developmental Disabilities: Report of a Workshop*. Washington, DC: National Academy Press. 1992.

Seldin H. Protecting patients from predators. *AGD Impact.* January 2008. (Accessed October 24, 2010, at: http://www.agd.org/support/articles/?ArtID=2699.)

Sfikas PJ, and George LA. Statutes and regulations relating to sexual misconduct in the practice of dentistry. *J Am Dent Assoc.* 135(8):1169–1171. 2004.

Shaw MM. Nursing home resident abuse by staff: Exploring the dynamics. *J Elder Abuse Neglect.* 9(4):1–21. 1998.

Sobsey D. *Violence and Abuse in the Lives of People with Disabilities: The End of Silent Acceptance?* Baltimore: Paul H. Brooks. 1994.

Sobsey D, and Doe T. Patterns of sexual abuse and assault. *Sexuality and Disability.* 9(3):243–259. 1991.

Sobsey D, and Varnhagen C. Sexual abuse and exploitation of disabled individuals. In: *Child Sexual Abuse: Critical Perspectives on Prevention, Intervention and Treatment.* Bagley CR, and Thomlinson RJ, eds. Toronto: Wall & Emerson. 1991.

Sorensen D. The invisible victims. *Prosecutor's Brief: California District Attorneys Associations Quarterly Journal.* 2002.

Strand et al. 2003. Cited in Hockley C. Staff violence against those in their care. In: *Workplace Violence: Issues, Trends, Strategies.* Bowie V and Fisher BS, eds. Cullompton, England: Willan. 2005, pp. 75–96.

Sullivan PM, and Knutson JF. *Child Abuse Neglect.* 24(10):1257–1273. October 2000.

Sullivan PM, Vernon M, and Scanlan JM. Sexual abuse of deaf youth. *Am Annuals Deaf.* 132:256–262. 1986.

Turk V, and Brown H. Sexual abuse of adults with learning disabilities. Cited in Petersilia et al. (2001), *Crime Victims with Developmental Disabilities: Report of a Workshop.* Washington, DC: National Academy Press. 1992.

Valenti-Hein D, and Schwartz L. *The Sexual Abuse Interview for Those with Developmental Disabilities.* Santa Barbara: James Stanfield. 1995.

U.S. House of Representatives, Committee on Government Reform. "Abuse of residents is a major problem in U.S. nursing homes." July 30, 2001.

Wilson C, and Brewer N. The incidence of criminal victimization of individuals with an intellectual disability. *Australian Psych.* 27(2):114–117. 1992.

Winn JR. Medical boards and sexual misconduct. *Federation Bulletin.* 80:90–97. 1993.

Wood EF. "The availability and utility of interdisciplinary data on elder abuse." A White Paper for the National Center on Elder Abuse. American Bar Association Commission on Law and Aging for the NCEA. May 2006.

Gabbard GO. *Sexual Exploitation in Professional Relationships*. Washington, DC: American Psychiatric Press. 1989.

Gartrell N, Herman J, Olarte S, Feldstein M, and Localio R. Psychiatrist–patient sexual contact: Results of a national survey, prevalence. *Am J Psychiatry*. 143:1126–1131. 1986.

General Accounting Office. "Nursing homes: More can be done to protect residents from abuse." GAO Report 02-312. Washington, DC. 2002.

Goodridge DM, Johnston P, and Thomson M. Conflict and aggression as stressors in the work environment of nursing assistants: Implications for institutional elder abuse. *J Elder Abuse Neglect*. 8(1):49–67. 1996.

Gross B. As Hippocrates forewarned: Sexual misconduct by physicians. *Annals Am Psych Assoc*. March 22, 2008.

Grubaugh AL, Frueh BC, Zinzow HM, Cusack KJ, and Wells C. Patients' perceptions of care and safety within psychiatric settings. *Psych Services*. 4(3):193–201. August 2007.

Hawes C. "Elder abuse in residential long-term care facilities: What is known about prevalence, causes and prevention." Testimony before the U.S. Senate Committee on Finance. National Academy of Sciences Report. June 18, 2002.

Herman JL, Gartrell N, Olarte S, Feldstein M, and Localio R. Psychiatrist–patient sexual contact: Results of a national survey, II: Psychiatrists' attitudes. *Am J Psychiatry*. 144:164–169. 1987.

Hodges PD. National law enforcement programs to prevent, detect, investigate and prosecute elder abuse and neglect in healthcare facilities. *J Elder Abuse Neglect*. 1998.

Hudson, B. Ensuring an abuse-free environment: A learning program for nursing home staff. *J Elder Abuse Neglect*. 4(4):25–36. 1992.

Irons R. Sexually addicted healthcare professionals. In: *Breach of Trust: Sexual Exploitation by Health Care Professionals and Clergy*. Gonsiorek JC, ed. Thousand Oaks, CA: Sage. 1995.

Jewkes R, Abrahams N, and Mvo Z. Why do nurses abuse patients? *Soc Sci Med*. 47(11):1781–1795. 1998.

Judd A. "Federal judge rejects plan for Georgia's mental hospitals." *Atlanta Journal Constitution*. September 30, 2009.

Judd A, and Miller A. "A hidden shame: Death in Georgia's mental hospitals." *Atlanta Journal Constitution*. January 7, 2007. (Accessed at: http://www.ajc.com/health/content/health/stories/hiddenshame.html.)

Lakin KC, Bruiniks RH, Hill BK, and Hauberg FA. Turnover of direct care staff in a national sample of residential facilities for mentally retarded people. *Am J Mental Deficiency*. 87:64–72. 1982.

Lumley VA, and Miltenberger RG. Sexual abuse prevention for persons with mental retardation. *Am J Mental Retardation*. 101:459–472. 1997.

MacDonald P. "Make a difference: Abuse/neglect pilot project." Project Report to the National Citizens' Coalition for Nursing Home Reform. 2000.

Mansell S, Sobsey D, and Calder P. Sexual abuse treatment for persons with developmental disabilities. Cited in Petersilia et al. (2001), *Crime Victims with Developmental Disabilities: Report of a Workshop*. Washington, DC: National Academy Press. 1992.

McMurray RJ, Clarke OW, Barrasso JA, Clohan DB, Epps CH, Glasson J, McQuillan R, Plows CW, Puzak MA, Orentlicher D, and Halkola KA. Sexual misconduct in the practice of medicine. *JAMA*. 266:2741–2745. 1991.

Meddaugh DI. Covert elder abuse in the nursing home. *J Elder Abuse Neglect*. 5(3):21–23. 1993.

Morrison J, and Wickersham P. Physicians disciplined by a state board. *J Am Med Assoc*. 279:1889–1893. 1998.

Mullan PB, and Cole SS. Healthcare providers' perceptions of the vulnerability of persons with disabilities. *Sexuality and Disability*. 9(3). 1991.

National Center on Elder Abuse (NCEA). "Elder Justice Act signed into law." E-newsletter. 12(10). April 2010.

Nerenberg L. "Abuse in nursing homes." National Center on Elder Abuse (NCEA) Newsletter. May 2002. (Accessed at: http://ncea.aoa.gov/ncearoot/main_site/library/statistics_Research/Research_Reviews/Abuse_In_Nursing_Homes.aspx.)

Neufeldt AH, and Mathieson R. Empirical dimensions of discrimination against disabled people. *Health Human Rights J*. 1(2):174–189. 1995.

Norris DM, Gutheil TG, and Strasburger LH. Boundary problems and sexual misconduct in the psychotherapy relationship. *Psychiatr Ser*. 54:517–522. April 2003.

Paton RN, Huber R, and Netting FE. The Long-Term Care Ombudsman Program and complaints of abuse and neglect: What have we learned? *J Elder Abuse Neglect*. 6(1):97–115. 1994.

Payne BK, and Cikovic R. An empirical examination of the characteristics, consequences and causes of elder abuse in nursing homes. *J Elder Abuse Neglect*. 7(4):61–74. 1995.

Payne BK, and Fletcher LB. Elder abuse in nursing homes: Prevention and resolution strategies and barriers. *J Crim Justice*. 33(2):119–125. 2005.

Pillemer K, and Moore DW. Highlights from a study of abuse of patients in nursing homes. *J Elder Abuse Neglect*. 2(1/2):5–29. 1990.

Plaut SM, and Foster BH. Roles of the health professional in cases involving sexual exploitation of patients. In: *Sexual Exploitation of Patients by Health Professionals*. Burgess AW and Hartman CR, eds. New York: Praeger. 1986. (Accessed October 24, 2010, at: http://www.questia.com/PM.qst?a=o&docId=27609450.)

Plaut SM, and Wilson MB. How intimate can I be with my patients? *AGD Impact*. January 2008. (Accessed October 24, 2010, at: http://www.agd.org/support/aricles/?ArtID=2699.)

Powers JL, Mooney A, and Nunno M. Institutional abuse: A review of the literature. *J Child Youth Care*. 4:81–95. 1990.

Royal College of Psychiatrists (RCP). "Institutional abuse of older adults." Council Report CR84. 2000.

Royal College of Psychiatrists (RCP). "Sexual boundary issues in psychiatric settings." College Report CR145. 2007.

Saveman B, Astrom S, Bucht G, and Norber A. Elder abuse in residential settings in Sweden. *J Elder Abuse Neglect*. 10(1/2):43–60. 1999.

Schwartz HA. "Sexual abuse of patients by healthcare professionals." Matthew Bender & Co. Undated. (Accessed at: http://www.stanford.edu/group/psylawseminar/Sex.htm.)

Fraud and Theft

4

At the time of this writing in early 2010, the U.S. Congress passed sweeping legislation that was designed to significantly overhaul the present healthcare system. Although implementation of this hard-won reform will not come easily or quickly, the process has refocused attention on a problem that has plagued healthcare for decades—fraud. *Fraud* is frequently defined as deceit or breach of confidence perpetrated for profit or to gain some unfair or dishonest advantage; Fabrikant et al. (2006) said it traditionally involves "a knowing misrepresentation or omission of fact," and added that healthcare fraud cases "often involve complex issues of law and regulatory interpretation, financial and economic policy, and medical and clinical decision-making." For the purposes of this work, fraud applies to financial theft and scheming as well as medical identity theft.

Extent and Impact of Medical Fraud

In 1993, then U.S. Attorney General Janet Reno declared healthcare fraud to be the "No. 2 crime problem in America" after violent crime, something Sparrow (2008) called "a remarkable status for a category of white-collar crime" (pp. 1151–1180). Medical fraud is a crime akin to shifting sands; no one seems to be able to affix a definitive price tag on it. The Agency for Healthcare Research and Quality (AHRQ) estimated that $24 million per hour is attributed to waste, fraud, and abuse in the U.S. healthcare system, and that because of fraud, healthcare costs continue to escalate at 15 percent or more per year. The U.S. Attorney's Office reported that in 2006, the latest year for which results were available, healthcare fraud accounted for $2.75 billion of the $3.1 billion collected in fraud settlements and 58 of the 96 major fraud cases that year (Sparrow, 2008).

Sparrow (2008) explained the appeal of the healthcare system in which to commit fraud: "All sorts, apparently, find attractive opportunities in healthcare fraud. But why steal from the healthcare system? Perhaps because, at least in the United States, that's where the money is! No other nation on Earth spends as much on healthcare as the United States" (pp. 1151–1180). Sparrow (2008) asserted that reliable data on the extent of the problem are nonexistent, even as healthcare professionals continue to swindle the system. The problem, according to Sparrow, is that each incidence of fraud can be regarded as either the work of a few bad apples or the tip of the iceberg:

"Each stakeholder group can choose whichever interpretation it prefers, and the majority prefer not to consider the possibility that the integrity of major public programs, such as Medicare and Medicaid, each of which now consume more than $400 billion in public funds each year, has been severely undermined by criminal enterprise."

In testimony in 2009 before the Senate Finance Committee, Senator Patrick Leahy observed, "The scale of healthcare fraud in America today is staggering. Our nation spends more than $2.2 trillion dollars a year on healthcare, and federal and state governments make up more than $800 billion of that spending. According to conservative estimates, about 3 percent of the funds spent on healthcare are lost to fraud—that totals more than $60 billion a year. In 2008, for the Medicare program alone, the General Accountability Office (GAO) estimates that more than $10 billon was lost to fraud just last year. Unfortunately, this problem appears to be getting worse, not better."

The 3 percent figure is the one used by the National Health Care Anti-Fraud Association (NHCAA), according to Louis Saccoccio, executive director of the organization, who added, "It's not a statistical analysis, but rather it comes from a consensus of our membership, based on the experience of fraud investigators and health insurance companies. This figure addresses strictly fraud, without including waste and abuse. In the early 1990s the GAO said it could be as high as 10 percent, and the Federal Bureau of Investigation (FBI) gives a range of 3 percent to 10 percent; any of that is an educated estimation based on experience, as opposed to hard numbers anyone can point to."

Fraud expert Malcolm K. Sparrow, professor of public management at Harvard University, Cambridge, Massachusetts, in his May 20, 2009, testimony before Congress, quipped, "The units of measure for losses due to healthcare fraud and abuse in this country are hundreds of billions of dollars per year. We just don't know the first digit. It might be as low as $100 billion. More likely two or three. Possibly four or five. But whatever that first digit is, it has 11 zeroes after it. These are staggering sums of money to waste, and the task of controlling and reducing these losses warrants a great deal of serious attention" (pp. 1151–1180).

The NHCAA (2009) estimated that between $67 billion and $224 billion is stolen from the American public through healthcare fraud annually. To put the size of the problem into perspective, $224 billion is higher than the Gross Domestic Product (GDP) of 138 countries. Lanny Breuer, assistant Attorney General in the Criminal Division of the U.S. Department of Justice, who also testified before Congress on May 20, 2009, framed the situation this way: "National healthcare spending in the United States exceeded $2.2 trillion and represented 16 percent of the nation's GDP in 2007. The federal government financed more than one-third of the nation's healthcare that year; federal and state governments collectively financed 46 percent of U.S. healthcare costs.... Over the next 10 years, U.S. healthcare spending is projected to double to $4.4 trillion and to comprise more than 20 percent of the national GDP. In short, healthcare fraud is an enormous problem that we cannot allow to continue."

Breuer (2009) emphasized that addressing healthcare fraud was especially critical in light of the news in mid-2009 that the Medicare Trust Fund will pay out more in benefits than Medicare would collect that year, and that the Hospital Insurance Trust Fund will be depleted by 2017. "It is therefore vitally important that the Departments of Justice (DOJ) and Health and Human Services (HHS) do everything possible to prevent, detect and prosecute healthcare fraud and abuse in order to return stolen Medicare dollars to the Trust Fund," Breuer said in his testimony. The depletion is significant because Medicare and Medicaid are extremely large programs; federal and state spending on both programs collectively exceeds $800 billion annually. In fiscal year (FY) 2008, the federal government devoted $1.13 billion for program integrity activities and healthcare fraud enforcement, and the Barack Obama Administration requested in the FY 2010 budget that Congress provide an additional $311 million in 2-year funding to enhance federal program integrity and antifraud enforcement work, of which $29.8 million is designated for the Department of Justice. Breuer (2009) said the additional funding will help extend the strides already made in fraud detection and prevention: "In 2008, the DOJ filed 502 criminal healthcare fraud cases involving charges against 797 defendants and obtained 588 convictions for healthcare fraud offenses—record high numbers of criminal healthcare fraud prosecutions since Congress established the Health Care Fraud and Abuse Control (HCFAC) program in 1996. Moreover, the department has obtained more than $14 billion in total recoveries, including criminal fines and civil settlements, since 1997."

Healthcare's Complexity Encourages Fraud

The inherent weaknesses in the healthcare system help to undermine it and open the door to fraud and abuse, according to the NHCAA (2009). For example, there is a lack of effective controls in public and private healthcare programs, particularly when attempting to identify fraud prior to the payment of a fraudulent claim. In addition, one small segment of the healthcare system can generate hundreds of millions of dollars in fraudulent claims from just a few healthcare services. And there is a need for improved information sharing and cooperation between public agencies, including law enforcement, and the private health insurance industry.

Sparrow (2008) enumerated some of the structural features of the U.S. health system that can contribute to fraud:

- *Fee-for-service structure*: Reimbursement for medical providers is mostly on a fee-for-service basis. Bills are presented to insurers by healthcare providers, their staff, or billing agents; the veracity of these claims is generally assumed, in the absence of any obvious indication to the contrary.
- *Highly automated claims-processing systems*: The majority of healthcare claims are now submitted electronically and processed automatically by computerized, rule-based systems. If the claims satisfy the criteria encapsulated within the edits and audits built into the system, then automatic payment follows, generally without any human involvement. Most claims paid, therefore, are not subject to any human scrutiny.
- *Processing accuracy emphasized over verification*: Claims-processing systems, designed with honest but possibly overworked and error-prone physicians in mind, do little or nothing to check that services billed were actually provided, or necessary, or that patients' diagnoses are genuine.
- *Postpayment audits focus on medical appropriateness, not truthfulness*: A small proportion of claims paid may be selected later by insurers for postpayment utilization review (PPUR), and fraud perpetrators can generally beat such audits by fabricating medical records to match their fictitious claims. (pp. 1151–1180)

There is a significant opportunity for fraud, given the immense size and complexity of the U.S. healthcare payor system, which is composed of federal programs such as Medicare (a federally sponsored healthcare program for the elderly and disabled), Medicaid (the federal- and state-government-sponsored healthcare program for low-income Americans), and hundreds of insurance companies supporting employer-sponsored health plans and self-purchased plans. According to the Agency for Healthcare Research and Quality (AHRQ, 2003), Medicare and Medicaid were billed for 58 percent of all hospital stays; private insurance was billed for 35 percent of stays; and 5 percent of stays were uninsured. Other payor sources were billed for approximately 3 percent of all stays in U.S. hospitals. The NHCAA (2009) reported that more than 4 billion health insurance claims were processed in the United States in 2007. Those big numbers contribute to the complexity of healthcare. "The industry processes billions of claims every year," Saccoccio said. "Then consider that all of those claims are spread across hundreds of thousands of providers. There are millions of patients and hundreds of health insurance carriers, plus Medicare and Medicaid, so it is a complex system and it is very easy to hide in that system."

Fabrikant et al. (2006) have stated that the complexity of regulations in the healthcare system is exacerbated by several conditions unique to the industry, including the fact that healthcare regulations change more often than in most other industries, as well as because a single provider interacts simultaneously with a number of third-party providers and is subject to a "myriad of inconsistent rules and regulations promulgated by each." An easy out for a healthcare provider caught engaging in fraud would be to point out that he or she simply did not understand or was unaware of the regulations that govern billing and reimbursement. Fabrikant et al. (2006) also said that healthcare fraud is frequently hidden within an organization, which is especially true as fraud schemes grow in complexity and sophistication.

Unique to healthcare, unlike property and casualty lines of insurance, according to Saccoccio, is that there is no all-claims database. "Say you have a group medical practice in Phoenix, with 10 physicians working there; no one has data as to what the claims for that practice might look like across all payors." Saccoccio continued:

> So, for example, Blue Cross/Blue Shield of Arizona only knows about the claims they receive from that practice; they can analyze them to see if there are issues respective to fraud or abuse. Likewise, Aetna receives their claims, Medicare receives their claims. But no one sees all of the claims that this Phoenix medical practice is generating in the course of a year. They may have contracts in a network with several health insurance companies and they may be out of network with others, and they are billing Medicare and Medicaid. But no one has the bigger picture, just slices of it. That lends itself to making fraud easier to conduct in healthcare. No one has all the data in one place to be able to analyze the claims and detect when something is amiss based the claims information. (Interview with author.)

And also unlike property and casualty insurance, which is fairly limited in scope, the healthcare system is driven by a complicated battery of diagnosis codes in which conditions, illnesses, and injuries are categorized for claims payment. "It's an incredibly detailed system for billing purposes, which makes it challenging to determine if a provider is up-coding or actually providing the services for which they are billing," Saccoccio said.

Another contributing factor, according to Saccoccio, is the healthcare system's prompt-pay law:

> Almost every state has a law that says health insurance companies must pay claims within a certain period of time, usually 30 days, and if you don't and you're audited, there are fines that come into play," he said. "So, based on those prompt-pay laws, there's a strong push to pay claims in a timely manner, which

is a good thing generally; the vast majority of healthcare providers who are providing legitimate services deserve to get paid. But from the fraud detection and prevention perspective, that makes it more of a challenge. A lot of fraud work is the pay-and-chase mode; you paid it and now you have to chase it to get it back. (Interview with author.)

"There also is an understandable reluctance on the part of fraud investigators to be seen as interfering with the relationship between the patient and the healthcare provider," Saccoccio added. He continued:

Healthcare insurance companies are part of the healthcare delivery system, and providers and healthcare facilities are necessary parts of the insurers' networks. Health insurers see the delivery of timely healthcare services as an integral part of their mission. As a result, anti-fraud efforts on the health insurance side traditionally have not been as aggressive as those of property and casualty insurers. And this is true in the government, too; Medicare's primary mission is to ensure the delivery of health services to the elderly. So, the system is designed to adjudicate and pay claims quickly. No one wants to be accused of unfairly denying claims. You don't want anti-fraud efforts to be seen as interfering with the delivery and payment for valid and necessary healthcare services. (Interview with author.)

As Sparrow (2008) observed, "The core task of healthcare systems is to deliver healthcare, not to carry out fraud control. The crime control imperative comes along later as an uninvited guest, and the rest of the system would rather not hear about it, or hear from it, at all. The awkwardness of the fraud control setting is particularly acute within the healthcare industry, for a variety of reasons." Sparrow (2008) explains that the act of defrauding insurance companies or government programs does not inspire much sympathy, and in fact, could even be socially acceptable by segments of the public that view stealing from insurers as "a natural form of revenge, either against ruthless and heartless businesses, or against wasteful, inefficient, or incompetent government agencies." The kicker, of course, is that this attitude not only harms insurers but is passed on to consumers who pay premiums. As Sparrow (2008) points out, "the real victims of fraud turn out to be the patients, subscribers and taxpayers" (pp. 1151–1180).

Investigating healthcare fraud makes people squeamish, Sparrow (2008) says, because "society holds medical practitioners in high esteem, recognizing the rigor and intensity of their training." Sparrow added that medical societies lobby hard to prevent their members' actions from being scrutinized, especially from a financial perspective. The medical establishment is quick to point out that the vast majority of fraud investigators do not possess knowledge or skills that qualify them to understand or make judgments about treatment decisions. According to Sparrow (2008), "Investigators frequently encounter medical practitioners as arrogant and condescending, counting on their professional status to afford them protection or immunity. Even when investigators persist and make their case, prosecutors may be reluctant to pursue cases that rely in any material way on questions of medical appropriateness or necessity" (pp. 1151–1180).

Another challenge of investigating healthcare fraud is that "medical professionals display an extraordinary reluctance to condemn the most egregious acts of their peers," according to Sparrow (2008), who adds, "Even when a physician or other provider is convicted of outright criminal fraud, and even when their actions have had profound adverse consequences for patients' health, their professional associations scarcely ever speak out against their conduct" (pp. 1151–1180).

This societal trust extends by association to ancillary provider groups "not subject to the same rigor in training and not bound by stringent codes of professional ethics," Sparrow (2008) asserts. He said that many fraud investigators consider entities such as medical equipment suppliers and home health agencies as for-profit businesses tempted to engage in illicit billing operations. The problem, Sparrow (2008) states, is that payors "treat such groups in basically the same way as physicians, accepting the claims they submit as true, and paying them on trust without any routine validation that the services billed were necessary or were actually provided" (pp. 1151–1180).

Perhaps one of the biggest challenges is that the current highly automated claims-processing environment "emphasizes efficiency and timeliness, not caution and risk control," according to Sparrow (2008), who adds that claims-payment systems are largely geared toward the honest, well-intentioned provider who is given the benefit of the doubt. The system's obligation to pay quickly is exploited by healthcare con artists who count on its consistency and predictability; as Sparrow (2008) explained, "if it pays one claim without a hiccup, then it will reliably pay 10,000 similar claims for other patients exactly the same way. If a fraud perpetrator bills 'incorrectly' and receives a denial, then the system explains the mistake and teaches how to fix it. And even when the system denies a lot of claims from one provider, it does not become suspicious. Provided the claims submitted are fashioned to reflect medical orthodoxy, then there is very little risk of encountering a human being at all, let alone a criminal investigator" (pp. 1151–1180).

There are many ways by which the U.S. healthcare system is defrauded. Perpetrators create fictitious physicians, secure a list of patient names, and then submit bills to Medicare or Medicaid and other health insurers for services rendered. Because the payment process is so slow, by the time payors realize that they have been duped, the perpetrators are gone. In another scheme, patient recruiters target people who are insured and who are willing to receive care they do not need in exchange for cash or for cosmetic surgery. As Sparrow (2008) states, "The predominant forms of fraud, given this combination of factors, consist of overprovision of services based on false or exaggerated diagnoses, and billing for services that were not actually provided" (pp. 1151–1180).

Examples of medical fraud include the following:

- Making false and intentionally misleading statements to patients.
- Submitting false bills or claims for service.
- Falsifying medical records or reports.
- Lying about credentials or qualifications.
- Providing unnecessary medical treatment or drug prescription.

The schemes are impressively creative, too. In phantom billing, perpetrators add charges for services never performed, or they fabricate claims. Perpetrators do this either by using genuine patient information, sometimes obtained through identity theft, to fabricate entire claims or by padding claims with charges for procedures or services that did not take place. Upcoding involves billing for more expensive services or procedures than were actually provided or performed, which often requires inflation of the patient's diagnosis code to a more serious condition consistent with the false procedure code. Doctor shopping involves the perpetrator bouncing from one physician to another to obtain multiple prescriptions for controlled substances. Unbundling means charging separately for procedures that are actually part of a single procedure. What's worse, unlicensed perpetrators have resorted to masquerading as licensed healthcare professionals, and they have resorted to medical identity theft to impersonate patients by using their health insurance card or other personal health information.

Perpetrators of Fraud

Perpetrators of healthcare fraud can be divided into two groups: individuals or small groups that are disorganized; and the organized crime groups.

Individuals

The intriguing aspect of medical fraud is that the majority of it is committed by a small minority of dishonest healthcare providers, and these perpetrators "take advantage of the confidence that has been entrusted to them in order to commit ongoing fraud on a very broad scale" (NHCAA, 2009).

"There are always a number of healthcare providers who maybe aren't in organized crime groups but who have decided they are going to come up with a way to defraud the system," Saccoccio said. "We saw that in Southern California with a so-called 'rent-a-patient' scheme, where an ambulatory surgery center recruited patients around the country to provide services that were not necessary and then bill for them."

In this case, a patient recruiter at Unity Outpatient Surgery Center was sentenced to 8 years in state prison for recruiting more than 250 healthy patients to undergo unnecessary surgeries in exchange for money or low-cost cosmetic surgery to fraudulently bill medical insurance companies. According to the Office of the Orange County District Attorney, at $154 million and involving more than 2,800 patients, it is the largest medical fraud prosecution in the nation to date. Olga Lilia Toscano pleaded guilty to the court to 98 felony counts, including conspiracy, capping, insurance fraud, grand theft, tax evasion, and sentencing enhancements for aggravated white-collar crime and loss exceeding $2.5 million. Administrators Tam Vu Pham, Huong Ngo, and Lan Nguyen, pleaded guilty to performing the same roles in the scheme. Pham, the primary perpetrator, was sentenced to 12 years in state prison. Toscano personally recruited more than 245 patients; the insurance companies were billed more than $10 million and paid more than $2.5 million for the unnecessary procedures performed on "patients" recruited by Toscano. Toscano was paid $770,000 for recruiting these patients.

The Unity Outpatient Surgery Center scheme was a joint investigation by the California Department of Insurance and Orange County District Attorney's Office with assistance from the California Franchise Tax Board (CFTB). Of the 19 defendants charged in the Unity case, 13 were indicted by a criminal grand jury. The Orange County Grand Jury examined 1,054 exhibits and heard testimony from 56 witnesses over 28 days, resulting in a 70-page indictment. The indicted defendants include an attorney, accountant, three doctors, and patient recruiters known as "cappers." The recruitment of patients, or "capping," is illegal in California; insurance companies paid out more than $20 million during a 9-month period, according to the Office of the Orange County District Attorney. Six other defendants in the Unity case pleaded guilty prior to the indictment and have been sentenced. Including Toscano, four of the indicted defendants pleaded guilty. The remaining nine defendants were scheduled for jury trial in the fall of 2009. Senior Trial Counsel Todd Spitzer and Deputy District Attorney Rick Welsh of the Healthcare Insurance Fraud Unit prosecuted this case.

The Unity cappers were accused of targeting employees from businesses in 39 states who were covered by preferred provider organization (PPO) insurance plans, affecting more than 1,000 employers whose employees became involved in this scheme. They were accused of arranging transportation for the patients, scheduling the surgeries, and coaching the healthy "patients" on what to say. In exchange for undergoing surgery, the patients received a cash payment, usually between $300 and $1,000 per surgery, or credit toward a free or discounted cosmetic surgery. The cappers who have been convicted had no medical training, recruited patients with PPO insurance, scheduled surgical procedures, and coached patients to correctly describe symptoms for the unnecessary surgical procedures. They assisted patients in filling out surgery center paperwork, including having them sign a false affidavit stating that they had not been offered compensation and had not received any compensation in exchange for using Unity's services. For Unity capping, they were paid directly and through corporations they had individually set up. They have been ordered to pay restitution and back taxes for personal and corporate taxes to CFTB; a restitution hearing for all of the convicted cappers was scheduled for late fall of 2009.

The three doctors charged in this case were accused of participating in medical insurance fraud for performing unnecessary medical procedures on healthy people with the knowledge that the patients were being recruited. Physicians Michael Chan, William Wilson Hampton, and Mario Rosenberg were accused of performing more than 1,000 procedures resulting in insurance billings exceeding $30 million for the facilities' fees alone. Unity received more than $5.1 million in payment as a result of the surgeries performed by these doctors, who were also accused of ignoring basic medical protocols, such as patients receiving surgeries on consecutive days instead of while under one anesthesia, not meeting the patients prior to their surgeries, not following up with patients after the procedure was completed, and not obtaining necessary medical information. The NHCAA (2009) explained that in conceiving fraud schemes, perpetrators enjoy access to a vast range of variables with which to plot their wrongdoing, including the entire U.S. population of patients; the entire range of potential medical conditions and treatments on which to base false claims; and the ability to spread false billings among many insurers simultaneously, including public programs such as Medicare and Medicaid, increasing fraud proceeds while lessening their chances of being detected by any single insurer.

In another remarkable scheme, healthcare providers in New York state were billing Medicaid for services provided to dead patients; New York's Medicaid program is the nation's largest, with anticipated expenditures of more than $50 billion in the next fiscal year. Campanile (2010) reported that a state audit found that 66 healthcare professionals, including pharmacists and physicians, billed Medicaid for services provided to 287 patients who were admittedly "deceased at the time of service" when confronted by state Medicaid inspector general James Sheehan's office. In one case, it was discovered that Bellevue Hospital accepted a cadaver for its organs and then sent a bill to Medicaid for "treatment." According to Campanile (2010), Sheehan said Bellevue "received the body of a deceased Medicaid patient to harvest organs for transplant but billed Medicaid as though they were treating the live patient."

In testimony at the New York state capitol presented by Sheehan on February 9, 2010, he reported that the Medicaid inspector general's office

(OMIG), together with Centers for Medicare and Medicaid Services (CMS), conducted an examination of the Medicaid program through a random sample to determine the extent of improper payments of claims based upon the patient records submitted by providers. Sheehan also reported that the OMIG has begun a series of initiatives designed to address significant gaps between the requirements of law, proper medical and billing practices, and the practices of some providers. As Sheehan (2010) explained,

> One example of our new initiatives is our deceased patients project, which began with an open letter to providers that we would be targeting claims for patients at the time the service was allegedly performed. We selected the month of October 2009, and identified 290 claims for services to patients who were, according to our records, deceased. On Dec. 1, we sent letters to each provider, asking for information within 15 days about who provided the service, which billed the service, and whether the patient was actually deceased. A number of providers responded, identifying errors they had made (wrong service date, billing for a dead twin instead of a live one, billing from a roster of scheduled patients instead of upon performance of the service). Over 150 providers claimed that the patients were still alive at the time of the service. We are currently obtaining death certificates from DOH's Vital Statistics Office to confirm the date of death.... In one pharmacy, the patient's prescription was picked up two days after her death by a family member. In another, the patient's physician requested delivery of the patient's prescription to his office after she died. One dead patient's Medicaid number visited three different dentists in a week. A family accepted delivery on a new bed paid for by Medicaid after the patient's passing. A major teaching hospital received the body of a deceased Medicaid patient to harvest organs for transplant, but billed Medicaid as though they were treating the live patient.

Sheehan added, "New Yorkers must trust that we as a state are doing everything possible to assure that Medicaid dollars are well-spent, and that the providers who receive those dollars are appropriately accountable."

Organized Criminal Groups

Healthcare fraud is not just committed by dishonest healthcare providers. The NHCAA (2009) noted,

> So enticing an invitation is our nation's ever-growing pool of healthcare money that in certain areas—Florida, for example—law enforcement agencies and health insurers have witnessed in recent years the migration of some criminals from illegal drug trafficking into the safer and far more lucrative business of perpetrating fraud schemes against Medicare, Medicaid and private health insurance companies. In South Florida alone, government programs

and private insurers have lost hundreds of millions of dollars in recent years to criminal rings—some of them based in Central and South America—that fabricate claims from non-existent clinics, using genuine patient-insurance and provider-billing information that the perpetrators have bought and/or stolen for that purpose. When the bogus claims are paid, the mailing address in most instances belongs to a freight forwarder that bundles up the mail and ships it offshore. (pp. 1–22)

"With the larger organized groups, many of them are not licensed healthcare providers," Saccoccio said. "Sometimes organized crime groups convince licensed healthcare providers to join forces with them to set up clinics and businesses through which to bill fraudulently. The organized groups see healthcare as an easy target because of the complexity of the system. And as crime goes, it has been a relatively low-risk kind of crime to commit. Unlike smuggling illegal drugs, for example, it's fairly safe and it's immensely lucrative." In fact, in 1995, then-FBI director Louis Freeh testified that cocaine traffickers in Florida and California were switching from drug dealing to healthcare fraud, because these criminals had discovered that healthcare fraud was safer, easier, and more lucrative than the drug trade, and carried a smaller risk of detection. Freeh, in testimony before Congress, observed, "No segment of the healthcare delivery system is immune from fraud … all types of recipients, providers and business people are committing fraud" (Freeh, 1995).

A third type of perpetrator is someone a patient or payor may least suspect of fraud—the community general or family practitioner who could be feeling alienated from the system he or she serves. Saccoccio said,

On any given day, you can have a healthcare provider who, if economically the practice isn't doing too well and there's a chance to up-code here and there, there's a very strong temptation to do that…. They think, 'Well, it's just the insurance company or it's just the government and they're already getting me somewhere else, so I'll get them here.' And there are cases where physicians may feel they are doing what's necessary for their patient. In those cases, they may think, 'I am providing this service and it's not technically covered under the patient's health plan but I'm going to call it something else so that the patient can get the service he or she wouldn't be able to pay for it otherwise.' It's almost like a Robin Hood concept where they think they are taking from the rich to give to the poor. (Interview with author.)

Victims of Fraud

In an annual report, the NHCAA (2009) acknowledged the impact of healthcare fraud:

Whether you have employer-sponsored health insurance or you purchase your own insurance policy, healthcare fraud inevitably translates into higher premiums and out-of-pocket expenses for consumers, as well as reduced benefits or coverage. For employers—private and government alike—healthcare fraud increases the cost of providing insurance benefits to employees and, in turn, increases the overall cost of doing business. For many Americans, the increased expense resulting from fraud could mean the difference between making health insurance a reality or not. However, financial losses caused by healthcare fraud are only part of the story. Healthcare fraud has a human face, too. Individual victims of healthcare fraud are sadly easy to find. These are people who are exploited and subjected to unnecessary or unsafe medical procedures. Or whose medical records are compromised or whose legitimate insurance information is used to submit falsified claims. Don't be fooled into thinking that healthcare fraud is a victimless crime. (pp. 1–22)

The NHCAA (2009) added,

The toll of healthcare fraud on patients whose bodies are risked for personal gain is both obvious and severe, but even less obviously harmful forms of healthcare fraud can have subtle effects that may not reveal themselves for years after the fraud is committed. For example, if a healthcare provider alters a patient's medical record in order to support reimbursement for a more expensive treatment than is warranted (whether or not the treatment is actually provided), this false diagnosis becomes part of the patient's documented medical history. Such an erroneous medical history can have serious, unseen consequences: the victim may unknowingly receive the wrong medical treatment from a future provider; he may have difficulty obtaining life insurance or individual health insurance coverage or may find coverage much more expensive; or he may fail a physical examination for employment because of a disease or condition wrongly recorded in his medical record. In addition to having one's medical records altered, patients can often become the victims of medical identify theft. Untangling the web of deceit spun by perpetrators of medical identity theft can be a grueling and stressful endeavor. The effects of this crime can plague a victim's medical and financial status for years to come. The seriousness of the threat and the enormity of the challenge posed by healthcare fraud cannot be overstated. (pp. 1–22)

Sheri Farrar, executive director of the Special Investigations Department of Health Care Service Corporation (HCSC) the largest customer-owned health insurance company in the nation, and a member of the board of directors of the NHCAA, detailed the impact on patients during testimony before the Senate Judiciary Committee on May 20, 2009:

Healthcare fraud, like any fraud, demands that false information be represented as truth. An all too common healthcare fraud scheme involves perpetrators who exploit patients by entering into their medical records false diagnoses of medical conditions they do not have, or of more severe conditions than they actually do have. This is done so that bogus insurance claims can be submitted for payment. Unless and until this discovery is made (and inevitably this occurs when circumstances are particularly challenging for a patient) these phony or inflated diagnoses become part of the patient's documented medical history, at least in the health insurer's records. Patients who have private health insurance often have lifetime caps or other limits on benefits under their policies. So every time a false claim is paid in a patient's name, the dollar amount counts toward that patient's lifetime or other limits. This means that when a patient legitimately needs his or her insurance benefits the most, they may have already been exhausted.... Shockingly, the perpetrators of some types of healthcare fraud schemes deliberately and callously place trusting patients at significant risk of injury or even death. It's distressing to imagine, but there have been many cases where patients have been subjected to unnecessary or dangerous medical procedures simply because of greed. (pp. 1–22)

Investigations and Antifraud Programs

Fabrikant et al. (2006) have observed that most white-collar crimes are difficult to investigate and prove: "Victims of assaults know immediately when they have been assaulted, but victims of fraud may never know they have been defrauded. One reason that fraud may go undetected is the fact that the perpetrator usually is in a position of trust to the victim. Because of this relationship, a fraud victim may have no reason to suspect criminal activity, even when circumstances occur that would otherwise make a reasonable person suspicious." Fabrikant et al. (2006) said that the voluminous amount of paperwork inherent to the healthcare system helps cover perpetrators' tracks and makes investigations exceedingly challenging: "This paper trail is especially arduous in the healthcare field because of the complexity and density of medical record-keeping and the extraordinarily convoluted billing and reimbursement mechanisms in place."

Successful investigation and prosecution of healthcare crime are certainly not unattainable. Fabrikant et al. (2006) state that what may make prosecution of healthcare fraud more likely to succeed is the presence of patients as victims of fraud:

The victim of many white-collar crimes—often a corporation, conglomerate, governmental entity or businessperson—is often perceived by the public or a jury as just as greedy and ruthless as the defendant. In short, the victim of many white-collar crimes does not engender much sympathy. By comparison, all too often the victim of the fraudulent healthcare provider is not only the third-party payor that lost money, but also the patient who, by definition, is ill and who perhaps received inadequate, incompetent or unnecessary medical services. In circumstances where it is possible and appropriate to include the patient as a victim in the theory of the case, prosecutors may gain substantial leverage in negotiating or trying claims of healthcare fraud. (pp. 24–25)

In 2009, a number of steps were taken to address this stealthy kind of crime. As noted previously, on May 20, 2009, the Senate Committee on the Judiciary, Subcommittee on Crime and Drugs held a hearing, "Criminal Prosecution as a Deterrent to Health Care Fraud," and heard from a number of fraud experts. In February 2009, Senator Patrick Leahy, chairman of the Senate Judiciary Committee, introduced legislation to address financial fraud, and in May, President Barack Obama signed the Leahy-Grassley Fraud Enforcement and Recovery Act (FERA) into law to combat mortgage and financial fraud. In late 2009, as Congress was contemplating healthcare reform legislation, Leahy and a number of other members of Congress were working to include in this landmark legislation provisions to strengthen enforcement of healthcare fraud, as with mortgage and financial fraud.

So as the nation adjusts to the provisions of the new federal health reform legislation, the country's antifraud agencies have continued their efforts. In his May 2009 testimony, Leahy noted that in 1997, the Clinton administration created the Health Care Fraud and Abuse Control (HCFAC) program to provide a framework for a coordinated attack on healthcare fraud. "The HCFAC program has proven to work, having provided vital resources for the Justice Department, the FBI and the Inspector General's Office at HHS to fight fraud. And like so many fraud enforcement programs, the HCFAC program pays for itself many, many times over, as last year it returned more than $1.8 billion to the federal government and led to savings of more than $30 billion in avoided healthcare costs and payments."

However, Leahy emphasized the need to push for even stronger and more effective enforcement: "We need to deter fraud with swift and certain prosecution, as well as prevent fraud by using real-time internal controls that stop fraud even before it occurs. We need to make sure our enforcement efforts are fully coordinated, not only between the Justice Department and other agencies, but also between federal, state and private healthcare fraud investigators. Much has been done to improve enforcement since the late 1990s, but we can and must do more."

That mandate came to fruition in May 2009, when Attorney General Eric Holder and HHS Secretary Kathleen Sebelius announced a new interagency effort, the Health Care Fraud Prevention and Enforcement Action Team (HEAT) to combat healthcare fraud in public programs and to specifically "marshal significant resources to prevent waste, fraud and abuse in the Medicare and Medicaid programs," according to the program's multifaceted mission statement. Holder and Sebelius also announced the expansion of the joint DOJ, CMS, and HHS Medicare Strike Forces operating in South Florida and Los Angeles to also include Houston and Detroit. Fraud prevention efforts, such as the HEAT program, are highlighted in President Barack Obama's proposed FY 2010 budget, which reflects a 50 percent increase from 2009 funding to strengthen program integrity activities within the Medicare and Medicaid programs. In total, these recent actions seem to indicate a renewed political will to dedicate increased resources to combating healthcare fraud.

The HEAT program followed a successful year in 2008, in which officials from the DOJ, the HHS Office of the Inspector General, and the CMS worked together through the criminal and civil systems to secure 588 criminal convictions and obtain 337 civil administrative actions against perpetrators of Medicare fraud. And as of early 2010, the strike force teams have obtained indictments of more than 800 individuals and organizations that collectively have falsely billed the Medicare program for more than $2.2 billion.

The HEAT program also meant the expansion of federal strike forces to a number of large metropolitan areas; the use of new state-of-the-art technology to fight fraud; increased compliance training for providers to prevent honest mistakes and help stop potential fraud before it happens; expansion of the provider audit program to help state Medicaid officials conduct audits, monitor activities, and detect fraud; and a commitment to expanded data sharing and improved information sharing procedures between HHS and DOJ in order to get critical data and information into the hands of law enforcement to track patterns of fraud and abuse, increase efficiency in investigating and prosecuting complex healthcare fraud cases, and turn off funding and profits to those who may be defrauding the system. In addition to the HEAT program, the President's 2010 budget for HHS contains funding for antifraud efforts over 5 years which are estimated to save $2.7 billion by improving overall oversight and stopping fraud and abuse within the Medicare Advantage and Medicare prescription drug programs. It also invests $311 million to strengthen program integrity in Medicare and Medicaid, with particular emphasis on greater oversight of Medicare Advantage and Medicare prescription drug programs.

States also are playing an important role in combating medical fraud through its Medicaid Fraud Control Units (MFCUs) administered through state attorneys general offices. MFCUs are federally funded criminal law enforcement agencies that are responsible for investigating and prosecuting providers that defraud the Medicaid program. In addition, the MFCUs can investigate complaints of abuse or neglect against residents in long-term care facilities, board-and-care facilities, and other Medicaid-funded healthcare institutions. According to the National Association of Medicaid Fraud Control Units (NAMFCU), in the last decade, MFCUs have increased their aggregate number of convictions and financial recoveries. For example, in FY1996, MFCUs collectively obtained 871 convictions and recovered $147.6

million in court-ordered restitution, fines, civil settlements, and penalties; in FY2006, MFCUs obtained 1,226 convictions and recovered more than $1.1 billion. NAMFCU provides new MFCU employees with the investigative and prosecutorial techniques to conduct Medicaid fraud and resident abuse investigations, a course of study that is deemed mandatory training in many state attorneys general offices. All MFCUs work closely with the U.S. Attorney and HHS/OIG offices in their respective states, along with other federal law enforcement agencies. In many states, MFCU staff return the favor by training local law enforcement to recognize, investigate, and prosecute resident abuse cases. MFCUs also sponsor training programs, while other MFCUs educate healthcare professionals, state long-term ombudsman, and adult protective services staff. Individual MFCUs also offer training for healthcare workers in residential care facilities, group homes, and hospitals, and for home healthcare aides to recognize and report resident abuse and neglect.

In January 2010, Sebelius and Holder joined private-sector leaders, law enforcement personnel, and healthcare experts for the first-ever National Summit on Health Care Fraud, part of the Obama Administration's coordinated effort to fight healthcare fraud. In a news release, Holder remarked, "Healthcare fraud affects all Americans and demands a coordinated, national response. HEAT has proven that better collaboration is the key to combating these crimes, recovering stolen resources and protecting essential Medicare and Medicaid dollars. We welcome the private sector's participation in this work—together, I'm confident we can make great strides in identifying, preventing and punishing healthcare fraud." Also providing comment was Sebelius, who noted, "Building on the work we have accomplished through HEAT, the President's FY 2011 budget ... will include historic support for anti-fraud efforts that will save billions over 10 years. He will call for increased investments in programs that have a proven record of preventing fraud, reducing payment errors and returning funds to the Trust Funds."

Issues addressed during the summit included use of technology to prevent and detect healthcare fraud and improper payments; the role of states in preventing healthcare fraud; the development of effective prevention policies and methods for insurers, providers, and beneficiaries; effective law enforcement strategies; and measuring healthcare fraud, assessing recoveries, and determining resource needs. Summaries of the workgroup discussions will be compiled in a publicly available report that will help strengthen the federal government and private-sector's work to deter healthcare fraud.

"Healthcare fraud isn't just a government problem. Criminals don't discriminate and they are stealing from Medicare, Medicaid and private companies at an unacceptable rate," said Sebelius. "We have a shared interest in stopping these crimes and today's summit brought us together to discuss how we can all work together to fight fraud."

The summit comes at a time when Sebelius and Holder announced an even tougher stance on healthcare fraud. In addition to prosecuting fraud, Sebelius said the administration is intensifying efforts to prevent it, including issuing more stringent controls over providers of durable medical equipment, requiring third-party reviews to ensure the providers are licensed properly, and requiring that these durable medical equipment providers who bill Medicare post a $50,000 bond, so that if they do perpetrate fraud, the government is able to recover some portion of the amount.

Crime and Punishment, Deterrence and Prosecution

Why has medical fraud persisted for as long as it has? Because it is easy, said fraud expert Malcolm Sparrow, who, in his May 2009 congressional testimony, noted, "Criminals who are intent on stealing as much as they can and as fast as possible, and who are prepared to fabricate diagnoses, treatments, even entire medical episodes, have a relatively easy time breaking through all of the industry's defenses. The criminals' advantage is that they are willing to lie. And provided they learn to submit their bills correctly, they remain free to lie. The rule for criminals is simple; if you want to steal from Medicare or Medicaid or any other healthcare insurance program, learn to bill your lies correctly. Then, for the most part, your claims will be paid in full and on time, without a hiccup, by a computer, and with no human involvement at all."

Fabrikant et al. (2006) state that healthcare fraud has a hybrid nature consisting of criminal and civil aspects:

> Although criminal sanctions always are in the background of any fraud and abuse investigation, many healthcare cases are pursued through civil processes at the state and federal level.... Despite the specialized setting, healthcare fraud and abuse cases share many important characteristics with other types of fraud litigation. For example, proof of fraud often rests with circumstantial evidence regardless of the criminal or civil nature of the forum. Proof of a high degree of culpability—namely, proof that an actor perpetrated fraud knowingly or with reckless disregard for the truth—is required not only in the criminal forum, but in the civil forum for some causes of action and whenever punitive damages are sought. (p. 18)

If caught, perpetrators of healthcare fraud may find themselves guilty of a federal criminal offense, according to provisions in the Health Insurance Portability and Accountability Act of 1996 (HIPAA). According to the NHCAA (2009), Congress indicated a federal prison term of up to 10 years in addition to significant financial penalties, per U.S. Code, Title 18, Section 1347. The federal law also provides that should a perpetrator's fraud result in the injury of a patient, the prison term can double to 20 years; and should it result in a patient's death, a perpetrator can be sentenced to life in federal prison. According to Breuer (2009), the DOJ's prosecutions have had a deterrent effect. In May 2009 testimony before Congress, Breuer noted, "Our inter-agency DOJ and HHS enforcement efforts in South Florida…contributed to estimated reductions of $1.75 billion in durable medical equipment (DME) claim submissions and $334 million in DME claims paid by Medicare over the 12 months following the Strike Force's inception, compared to the preceding 12-month period. The average prison sentence in Miami Strike Force cases was 48.8 months, which exceeded by nearly one year the overall national average healthcare fraud prison sentence of 37.4 months."

"The Feds are starting to put people away for long prison sentences for fraud now and I think that sends a message," Saccoccio said. "You are never going to do away with fraud, there's just too much money and the temptation is just too great. People will always come up with new schemes and they will migrate from one geographic area to the next, so you will always be chasing it, but fraud may no longer be seen as a piece of cake to perpetrate. Instead, perpetrators may ask themselves if fraud is worth the risk of 10 to 15 years in prison if they are caught."

Even though prosecution might be the best deterrent, Breuer (2009) noted, "Our criminal and civil enforcement efforts have taught us some important lessons. In the criminal arena, we have learned to identify criminal claim trends and track systemic weaknesses so we can stop false claims before they occur. We have also learned that quick apprehension and punishment of these criminals is critical to deterring others. But we have also learned that we cannot prosecute our way out of this problem. Instead, we must prevent criminals from accessing Medicare, Medicaid and other healthcare programs in the first place." According to Breuer (2009), in criminal enforcement actions during 2008, DOJ prosecutors opened 957 new criminal healthcare fraud investigations involving 1,641 defendants; conducted 1,600 criminal healthcare fraud investigations involving 2,580 potential defendants pending at the end of the fiscal year; and filed criminal charges in 502 healthcare fraud cases involving charges against 797 defendants and obtained 588 convictions for the year. Another 773 criminal healthcare fraud cases involving 1,335 defendants were pending at the end of FY 2008.

Some experts who say that rhetoric can only do so much to curtail and prevent medical fraud advocate for a more aggressive approach. Sparrow, in his May 2009 testimony, proposed criminal prosecution as a deterrent to healthcare fraud and supported effective punishment for white-collar crimes, particularly those that involve an abuse of the public's trust and diversion of public funds. Sparrow (2009) pointed to criminologists' deterrence theory, in that the magnitude of a deterrent effect depends on a potential perpetrator's assessment of three factors: the likelihood of getting caught, the probability of being convicted once detected, and the severity of the punishment if eventually convicted. In terms of healthcare fraud, Sparrow (2009) believes that healthcare fraud control is weakened by perpetrators not being easily deterred by being caught, convicted, and imprisoned. He characterizes the resources available for fraud detection and control in healthcare as inadequate and of the wrong scale in comparison to the credit card industry, for example. In terms of fraud losses, this industry's threshold for acceptable business risk is one-tenth of 1 percent. By contrast, estimates of healthcare fraud losses range from 3 percent to 10 percent. Sparrow (2009) notes,

> Measurement is normally step one in any effective fraud control operation. Without reliable information regarding the scope of the problem, everyone is free to guess what the loss rate might be, and they will guess high or low depending on their interests.... For any invisible problem, effective control begins with valid measurement. For healthcare fraud, control breaks down at this very first hurdle. No one knows quite how bad the situation has become, and industry practices seem to reflect a broad reluctance to find out. Exposing the scale of the problem might involve a dose of very bad news; but such bad news is easier to swallow at the beginning of an administration than at the end of one. I believe we have an important opportunity, now, to correct this defect and establish more appropriate levels of control based in a rational way on valid measurement of the loss rates.

Sparrow (2009) has stated that there is an extremely low probability of healthcare fraud perpetrators being prosecuted even when their false claims are detected. "There is accumulating evidence that existing control strategies are missing important opportunities to shut down major false-billing scams." Sparrow (2009) explains further,

> The last 10 years has seen an extraordinary series of reports produced by the OIG for the HHS. According to OIG reports, several different categories of patients, none of whom should be getting treatment under these programs, have been showing up in significant numbers within paid Medicare and Medicaid claims. The most obvious embarrassment involves treatments rendered to patients who were already dead on the date they were supposedly treated. In March 2000, the OIG published its investigation into provision of medical services to Medicare beneficiaries after their dates of death. They quickly found $20.6 million in such claims, paid in 1997. A significant volume of the claims showed new treatments for a patient, beginning more than a month after they had died. Dead patients also showed up in Medicaid claims around the country. An OIG report in 2006 summarized findings from 10 different states, revealing $27.3 million in Medicaid payments for services after death.... In July 2008, another group came to light, adding to Medicare's public embarrassment. The Senate Permanent Subcommittee on Investigations revealed the presence of dead doctors within Medicare's paid claims. From

2000 to 2007 between $60 million to $92 million was paid for medical services or equipment that had been ordered or prescribed by dead doctors. In many cases, the doctors had been dead for more than 10 years on the date they supposedly ordered or authorized treatments.

When implausible and potentially fraudulent claims are detected, Sparrow (2009) says payors must ask themselves how these obviously fictional claims get generated and why they were paid. According to Sparrow (2009), the OIG should focus on the business practices that generate fake claims, because they are not error-prone, they are clearly fraudulent, but that the way the agency deals with implausible billings "reflects more of a concern with payment accuracy than with crime control."

The Future and Recommendations for Fighting Fraud

Sheri Farrar of HCSC and the NHCCA sums up the challenge ahead: "Healthcare fraud cases are some of the most complex white collar crime cases handled by prosecutors, necessitating dedicated staff who develop an expertise in understanding how health claims are processed and paid by both private insurers and the government and the intricacies of proving the necessary criminal intent. In many jurisdictions limited prosecutorial resources impact the ability to dedicate staff accordingly. Additionally, healthcare fraud cases compete with other investigative programs that are often deemed higher priority. While we continue to refer the most egregious healthcare fraud matters to law enforcement, we recognize that many will ultimately not be prosecuted" (Farrar, 2009).

Sparrow (2009) has made several suggestions for how to combat medical fraud, including reinstating the requirement that the OIG provide an independent audit of the Medicare overpayment rate on an annual basis, and then require the OIG, as it designs the audit protocols for this overpayment measurement, to use a rigorous fraud-audit methodology. Sparrow has indicated that a fraud audit must include steps to verify with the patient or with others that the diagnosis was genuine and that the treatments actually occurred. It should also include contextual data analysis sufficient to identify any suspicious patterns of patient referrals, diagnostic biases, or padding of claims or treatments consistent with patterns of fraud. Additionally, Sparrow believes that there should be a review of the adequacy of the Medicare and Medicaid programs' operational responses to questionable claims. Sparrow (2009) also notes, "Auto-rejection of claims involving dead patients, dead doctors or previously deported persons is a terribly weak response, and actually helps perpetrators perfect their billing scams. The detection of such claims ought to trigger a presumption of the presence of serious criminal enterprise, and that presumption should then be tested through appropriate criminal investigation and law-enforcement response."

Farrar (2009) has suggested other remedies: "When resource constraints and/or the facts of a case do not support a prosecution, we seek other means to address billing practices that result in inappropriate payments to providers. Other remedies include seeking a voluntary repayment through negotiations with the provider. In these situations, we incorporate education of proper billing practices into the discussion in an effort to mitigate future risk as well as to eliminate any future defense that the provider was unaware their practices were inappropriate." Other strategies, according to Farrar (2009), include evaluating the factors that enabled the fraudulent claims to be successfully paid and recommending claims-processing system fixes, medical policy or processing procedure modifications, and contract enhancements to reduce our future risk to similar schemes. Another effective strategy is making referrals to state licensing agencies and other professional regulatory agencies and boards, as appropriate.

Farrar (2009) is realistic about the challenge of preventing fraud: "There is no one fix to address healthcare fraud. Healthcare fraud schemes are constantly changing and evolving as new medical procedures and new healthcare technology are developed, and as the perpetrators of healthcare fraud adjust their billing practices to defeat actions taken by the government and private insurers to mitigate risk."

Experts agree on the importance of information sharing in the fight against healthcare fraud. As Farrar (2009) explains, "Staying one step ahead of those who are intent on committing healthcare fraud requires continual information sharing and collaboration among law enforcement and prosecutorial agencies, regulatory agencies and private health insurers." A lynchpin in the communication and collaboration effort is the NHCAA, formed in 1985 by private health insurers with government agencies responsible for the investigation of healthcare fraud. The NHCAA's primary purpose is to serve as a forum and catalyst for the sharing of information about healthcare fraud investigations and emerging healthcare fraud schemes. NHCAA's 80-plus corporate members and 70 federal, state, and local law enforcement and regulatory agencies share information through NHCAA's Special Investigation Resource and Intelligence System (SIRIS) database, in-person information-sharing meetings, electronic fraud alerts, and various work groups focusing on major healthcare antifraud initiatives. For example, recently the NHCAA held a meeting in Florida which brought together representatives of private insurers, FBI headquarters and 10 FBI field divisions, CMS, OIG, the Justice Department, the Miami U.S. Attorney's Office, and local law enforcement to address the healthcare fraud schemes that have emerged in South Florida and are beginning to spread to other areas of the country. The details of the emerging schemes, investigatory tactics, and the results of recent prosecutions were discussed with the goals of preventing additional losses in South Florida and preventing the schemes from spreading and taking hold in other parts of the country.

According to Farrar (2009), "This information sharing is critical to the success of national healthcare anti-fraud efforts. Those perpetrating fraud against the healthcare system do so indiscriminately across the range of government healthcare programs and private health plans. Without effective information sharing, broad schemes targeting multiple payors of healthcare become nearly impossible to detect.... Too often, however, information sharing in healthcare fraud cases is a one way street with the private sector regularly sharing vital information with the public sector without reciprocal information sharing to bolster the fraud-fighting efforts of the private sector. This inequity works counter to a coordinated fraud-fighting effort because the private sector plays an important role in safeguarding our nation's citizens against healthcare fraud."

In May 2009, testimony before the Senate Judiciary Committee, Sean Dilweg, Insurance Commissioner for the State of Wisconsin, announced that the National Association of Insurance Commissioners (NAIC) had developed a set of recommendations that urge the inclusion of fraud and regulatory gaming prevention tools in any federal healthcare reform proposal. Dilweg, who worked with the NAIC to develop these recommendations, outlined the salient points:

- Establish a privilege and a statutory structure for confidential coordination and exchange of information among federal agencies and state insurance regulators.
- Include provisions reaffirming state insurance regulators' authority to protect consumers.
- Include a provision enabling the federal administrating agency to issue regulations or orders establishing that a person engaged in the business of insurance is subject to the laws of the states regulating the business of insurance and to foreclosing the use of federal law as cover for fraudulent health plan schemes or for schemes to exploit regulatory gaps.
- Include provisions establishing a coordinating body to focus on health insurance fraud schemes and schemes to exploit regulatory gaps.
- Support criminal and civil penalties for operators, and those who assist operators, of a health plan that falsely represents itself as exempt from state insurance regulatory authority.
- Include provisions for adequate staff and funding for regulatory enforcement.
- Include provision for adequate staff and funding for an effective consumer education program.

The key to preventing fraud is prepayment review. As the NHCAA (2009) explains,

> Many of the problems with healthcare fraud arise from a key fact about the healthcare system that holds true for both public and private programs: payment to providers is essentially built on the honor system, and various laws require both public programs and private health insurers to pay claims quickly or face penalties. This 'honor system' derives from the combination of state-law based 'prompt pay' requirements and the enormous volume of healthcare claims. While data analysis systems are improving (and may be improved even more as additional healthcare information moves into electronic data), most claims are not reviewed until after they are paid, if at all. Therefore, a key means of improving the fight against fraud is to both enhance the current efforts to share information—so that information about fraudulent providers can be distributed more efficiently—and to provide additional payment leeway to private and public programs in resolving suspected fraudulent claims. While hundreds of millions of dollars have been recovered in healthcare fraud enforcement efforts, this 'pay and chase' mentality—where claims are paid and subsequent investigations are conducted—will never sufficiently address fraudulent providers, particularly the kind of 'phantom provider' who simply can take their fraudulent financial windfall and disappear. (pp. 1–22)

The NHCAA (2009) also points to a substantial lack of effective controls for entry and reentry into the system:

> The healthcare system is also subject to access by unscrupulous providers, sometimes with little or no scrutiny. Providers can easily enter the system and begin submitting claims so long as they have what appears to be a valid license and a tax ID number. For example, in South Florida, front companies were being created to enter the system and submit claims, only to move on and go through the process all over again to re-enter the system under a new name and tax ID number. In fact, CMS took the significant step of decertifying all of the DME providers in the area and requiring them to seek re-entry into the Medicare system. It has also had to take similar action for home healthcare providers for the same reasons. In addition to these initial licensing issues, state medical boards are inconsistent in their license suspension and revocation actions arising from fraudulent activities on the part of the providers they are responsible for licensing. These state boards—intended to be a frontline in the protection of healthcare consumers—often do not act effectively when confronted with healthcare fraud by licensed healthcare professionals. For example, in 1998 the Coalition Against Insurance Fraud published a report that examined the disciplinary actions of state medical boards against providers convicted of insurance fraud. The study examined records of medical providers convicted of felony charges related to insurance fraud in 12 states and compared those individuals with adverse licensing actions taken by state medical boards. The report found that 'licensing boards often fail to take any

actions against those licensees who commit felony offenses related to insurance fraud.' This lack of action, particularly when patient harm is a possible concern, is perplexing, particularly when state medical boards have several remedies at their disposal short of revocation of a medical license: reprimand, probation, suspension, sanctions, etc. (pp. 1–22)

Although the Healthcare Integrity and Protection Data Bank (HIPDB), which was established by HIPAA, was designed to capture information regarding licensing actions, civil judgments, criminal convictions, and exclusions from federal and state healthcare programs, it has not been as successful as it needs to be at ensuring that unscrupulous providers do not reenter the system. According to the NHCAA (2009),

> In order to curb the ease with which convicted providers (or phantom providers) re-enter the healthcare system, public programs could consider implementing safeguards such as provisional participation and mandatory background checks. Private health insurers often do have policies in place that address the exclusion of providers from their networks in response to actions taken by medical boards to impair the licenses of convicted providers. For instance, an insurer may require that a provider be eliminated from its network so long as the medical license is probated, and then allow the provider to apply to be reinstated after a certain amount of time following the probationary period. (pp. 1–22)

It may be nearly impossible to completely eradicate healthcare fraud, but a few simple changes can make antifraud efforts more effective in controlling costs and protecting patients, said the NHCAA (2009). To this end, the organization has assembled a number of principles it feels should be included in healthcare reform legislation to address healthcare fraud and ensure proactive information sharing between the government and private health insurers to combat it. The NHCAA's guidelines include these tenets:

- Ensure appropriate recognition that fraudulent activity in the healthcare system can affect both public- and private-sector health plans, and that the investigation and prosecution of fraud against private health plans is integral to the overall effort to combat healthcare fraud.
- Ensure appropriate encouragement is given to private health plans to provide information concerning suspected healthcare fraud to the Department of Justice and other agencies participating in the Coordinated Health Care Fraud Program whenever possible, as well as information concerning useful investigative resources and services developed or offered by particular private plans or associations of private health care payors.

- Whenever practicable, authorized by law, and consistent with ongoing law enforcement activities, the Department of Justice and other participating agencies will make their best efforts to include private health plans in local, regional, and national healthcare fraud task forces, and in task force activities.
- The participating agencies will provide general information concerning healthcare fraud to private health plans, and specific information concerning specific healthcare fraud to those private health plans that the participating agencies believe likely are affected by the fraud, whenever such an exchange is practicable, permitted by law, and will not jeopardize ongoing law enforcement activities.
- Victims of healthcare fraud have a right to receive restitution as part of the federal criminal law enforcement process, and the Department of Justice and other participating agencies will make available to private health plans relevant investigative information including, but not limited to, information concerning the nature and scope of the fraud, the outcome of the investigation, the nature of any enforcement action, the assets of the parties charged, and the procedures for an affected victim to make a claim for restitution. (pp. 1–22)

As the NHCAA (2009) emphasized, "The return on investment realized when resources are dedicated specifically to healthcare anti-fraud efforts is significant. Accordingly, we believe it's most prudent and responsible to invest in proven success and therefore, we encourage federal and state governments to appropriate more resources to support healthcare anti-fraud work. These resources could help expand investigative and/or prosecutorial efforts. For example, the statutory establishment and funding of a unit (not just an attorney) in each U.S. Attorney's Office to increase the capabilities and visibility of existing healthcare anti-fraud efforts coordinated by the DOJ. So while we recognize and appreciatively acknowledge the intent expressed in recent months by President Obama and Congress to lend greater focus to the healthcare fraud issue, we strongly encourage any new investments to be significant and sustainable so that a true impact can be made on the problem."

Four Faces of Fraud

There are a few unique types of healthcare fraud that warrant closer examination; these include *white-coat* crime, elder financial abuse, medical identity theft, and drug diversion by healthcare professionals.

Fraud 1: White-Coat Crime: The Medical Criminals

The common thread of this book is that the very professionals in which patients place their trust are the perpetrators of medical malfeasance. When physicians commit crime, there is usually an underpinning of financial gain or abuse of power. Jesilow et al. (1985) pinpointed the underlying factor of physician-perpetrated fraud—a "basic structural conflict that to this day marks the position of physicians in the United States; they are at one and the same time scientists engaged in a vital humanitarian endeavor and free enterprise merchants operating in a capitalistic marketplace where their skills and knowledge can be of enormous financial value" (pp. 149–165).

Physician power is an important correlate of medical crime. Jesilow et al. (1985) pointed to the observations of Sir William Osler, who, it is said, "had the greatest contempt for the doctor who made financial gain the first object of his work" (Cushing, 1940, cited in Jesilow et al., 1985). Jesilow et al. (1985) said that Osler "located what he believed to be one of the primary sources of medical crime—the isolation and arrogance that can accompany medical practice unattended by leavening influences." Osler once observed, "No class of men needs friction so much as physicians; no class gets less. The daily round of a busy practitioner tends to develop an egoism of a most intense kind, to which there is no antidote. The few setbacks are forgotten, the mistakes are often buried, and 10 years of successful work tend to make a man touchy, dogmatic, intolerant of correction and abominably self-centered" (Cushing, 1940). Jesilow et al. (1985) asserted that, "The conflict between service and self-serving behavior, the autonomy and power, and the structural form of medical practice all contribute to the nature and extent of medical violations."

Offenses committed by physicians are verboten because of the respect, power, and trust that the profession engenders; Jesilow et al. (1985) added, "In addition, there is little systematic investigative or social science work on the range of illegal medical acts. In part, this results because access to information is difficult to obtain, as the strength of the profession has served to protect it from close scrutiny. Moreover, doctors are essential for the public well-being and there is an understandable reluctance to antagonize a group upon whom all of us depend" (pp. 149–165).

Detecting white-coat crime is challenging, because, as Jesilow et al. (1985) noted, "The violations are often extraordinarily difficult to detect, and intent is almost impossible to demonstrate to the satisfaction of the law" (pp. 149–165). Jesilow et al. (1985) pointed to an estimate by the Federation of State Medical Boards that at least one physician in 20 is a severe disciplinary problem, and that as many as 20,000 practitioners are repeatedly guilty of practices unworthy of the profession. Jesilow et al. (1985) said that these figures are too conservative.

There are a number of ways that physicians engage in fraud. Prescription violations are frequent; federal statistics show that as much as 90 percent of prescription drugs diverted to illegal markets originate from individuals with prescriptive and dispensing powers.

Physician self-referrals are another way in which physicians can defraud the system. In 2008, the CMS issued a final rule adopting payment and policy changes for inpatient hospital services paid under the Inpatient Prospective Payment System (IPPS) for discharges in FY 2009. The final rule also adopts a number of important changes and clarifications to the physician self-referral rules, designed to prevent potential program and patient abuse resulting from physician referrals to certain healthcare entities with which they have financial relationships. CMS says the new rules also help make the relationships between physicians and the entities to which they refer Medicare business more transparent. The physician self-referral law prohibits physicians from referring Medicare and Medicaid patients for 11 designated health services (DHS) to an entity with which the physician or a member of the physician's immediate family has a financial relationship, unless an exception applies. The DHS list includes clinical laboratory services; radiology and certain other imaging services (including magnetic resonance imaging [MRI] services, computed tomography [CT] scans, and ultrasound); durable medical equipment and supplies; orthotics and prosthetics; physical therapy, occupational therapy, and speech-language pathology services; outpatient prescription drugs; home health services and supplies; inpatient hospital services; and outpatient hospital services.

Fee-splitting, the practice of sharing fees with professional colleagues for patient or client referrals, is yet another fraudulent practice. Despite being illegal in many states, it is a widespread practice that usually involves a kickback of some kind, usually to a general practitioner, who refers patients to a specialist. The most alarming aspect of this practice is that some physicians who engage in fee-splitting tend to send their patients to the specialist who will split the largest fee rather than the specialist who will provide the best patient outcome. As Jesilow et al. (1985) explained, "Besides lowering the quality in the performance of operations, and tending to increase those that are unnecessary, fee-splitting obviously raises the cost of medical care. It restricts competition, militates against excellence, inflates health costs, and increases the number of unneeded operations, inevitably maiming and killing some patients.... A patient can be merely a pawn in such arrangements, involved for the purpose of enriching both physicians" (pp. 149–165).

Driving much of this physician bad behavior is the nation's fee-for-service structure of the benefit programs, based on typical medical payment procedures. Jesilow et al. (1985) said this "makes it easy to overcharge, double-bill for services, ping-pong (send patients to other physicians for additional treatment), family gang (request to see members of a patient's family, even though unnecessary), prolong treatments, and carry out additional fraudulent schemes. Fee-for-service can contribute to the disintegration of ideals and altruism among physicians" (pp. 149–165). Some experts suspect that the method of payment of physicians may affect their clinical behavior. Although payment systems may be used to achieve policy objectives such as cost containment or improved quality of care, little is known about the effects of different payment systems in achieving these objectives. Gosden et al. (2000) sought to evaluate the impact of different methods of payment (capitation, salary, fee-for-service, and mixed systems of payment) on the clinical behavior of primary-care physicians (PCPs). The researchers reviewed randomized trials, studies, and analyses of interventions comparing the impact of capitation, salary, fee-for-service, and mixed systems of payment on PCP satisfaction with working environment, cost and quantity of care, type and pattern of care, equity of care, and patient health status and satisfaction. The researchers looked at four studies involving 640 PCPs and more than 6,400 patients and found considerable variation in study setting and the range of outcomes measured. Fee-for-service resulted in more primary-care visits and contacts, visits to specialists, and diagnostic and curative services but fewer hospital referrals and repeat prescriptions compared with capitation. Compliance with a recommended number of visits was higher under fee-for-service compared with capitation payment. Fee-for-service resulted in more patient visits, greater continuity of care, and higher compliance with a recommended number of visits, but patients were less satisfied with access to their physician compared with salaried payment. The researchers concluded that although there is some evidence to suggest that the method of payment of PCPs affects their behavior, further evaluation is needed, especially in terms of the relative impact of salary versus capitation payments.

At the heart of the fee-for-service system is what Jesilow et al. (1985) characterized as "the conflict created by the physician's role as both healer and entrepreneur." Decades later, physicians are still fighting for fees that reflect the services provided. In the 2010 physician fee schedule, the CMS proposed modest increases in the average Medicare pay for primary-care physicians but larger reductions in average pay for some other specialists. Federal officials are phasing in refinements to Medicare relative value units starting in 2010 which they say will establish more equitable payment rates for primary-care services; however, these specialists will see reductions even before taking into account 2010's scheduled 21.2 percent across-the-board cut (CMS, 2009). These kinds of cuts, and government interference in medicine, can alienate physicians, providing greater temptation to defraud the system. Jesilow et al. (1985) asserted that the fee-for-service system creates a conflict between the "dictates of government regulation and the desire to remain autonomous." Essentially, physicians believe that no one, especially the government, can begin to appreciate the financial and operational pressures to which they are subjected regularly and that the government interferes with their ability to treat patients. Conversely, government officials believe that their requirements provide the necessary measure of accountability. Jesilow et al. (1985) said that "doctors prefer private healthcare where the marketplace and their own interests operate more freely."

The challenge with white-coat crime is that most physicians have an uncanny ability to operate under the radar, so to speak. Jesilow et al. (1985) stated that many of the same issues that hamper efforts to control white-collar crime apply to physician violations: "The transgressors are usually highly intelligent and able to manipulate the system cleverly for their own gain" (pp. 149–165). Also in their arsenal is the ability to hire superb legal representation if they are facing a criminal conviction. And because so many of their clinical actions are above reproach, it is challenging to demonstrate, to the satisfaction of the law and beyond a reasonable doubt, that any suspicious financial actions were conducted with criminal intent. According to Jesilow et al. (1985), "Juries are often reluctant to convict doctors, particularly in small towns where they may have built up a grateful clientele.... In the government healthcare field, criminal sanctions have been imposed only in the most egregious cases, such as those involving injury or death, many cooperative witnesses, and a paper trail that implicates the doctor beyond any possibility of rebuttal" (pp. 149–165). Providing greater recourse are civil judgments; however, many legal experts consider them to be less punitive than criminal proceedings.

Despite the long list of offenses, including professional incompetence, overcharging, needlessly prolonging care, fee-splitting, and the ordering of unnecessary and expensive tests, physicians are still regarded differently than many other offenders. As Jesilow et al. (1985) explained, "The status of doctors precludes the rough and insensitive treatment often accorded to street offenders. As a federal agent has noted U.S. attorneys are extraordinarily kind to doctors, because even if they are crooks, theoretically they're still providing some useful services for the community" (pp. 149–165).

Fraud 2: Financial Abuse of Vulnerable Populations

Financial abuse of vulnerable populations, particularly the elderly, in home care and in healthcare institutions is another aspect of fraud and theft. Elder financial abuse costs older Americans more than $2.6 billion per year and is most often perpetrated by caregivers and family members, according to a report from the MetLife Mature Market Institute (MMI, 2009). The 2006 National Survey of State Adult Protective Services revealed that as many as 1 million older Americans may be targeted yearly, and related costs such as healthcare, social services, investigations, legal fees, prosecution, and lost income and assets reach tens of millions of dollars annually. The alarming statistic is that for each case of abuse reported, there are an estimated four or more that go unreported (MMI, 2009).

Both researchers and practitioners acknowledge that estimates of elder financial abuse represent only the most overt cases, thus significantly under-estimating the incidence of financial abuse of elders living in the community. Even less definitive information is available about the prevalence of financial abuse in residential long-term care settings. Estimates of the occurrence, prevalence, and impacts of elder financial abuse vary considerably. For example, the 1996 National Incidence Study conducted by the National Center on Elder Abuse found that elder financial abuse constituted 30.2 percent of 70,942 substantiated cases of elder abuse. The U.S. Senate Special Aging Committee addressed elder financial abuse through a series of committee hearings held between June 2001 and May 2006. Testimony was provided by federal and state agency officials, criminal justice representatives, state attorneys general, representatives from the financial sector, consumer organizations, academic institutions, and victims and perpetrators of elder financial abuse. According to U.S. Senate sources and the National Elder Abuse Incidence Study, only 16 percent of all elder abuse cases are reported, and 30 percent of all reported cases involve financial abuse, a number close to the incidence of news reports involving elder financial abuse found in this study.

The U.S. Senate Committee on Aging reported that nearly 40 percent of America's seniors rank fear of fraud ahead of their concern for healthcare and the crisis attendant to it and even higher than terrorism. In all, Americans in general are estimated to lose $40 billion per year to telemarketing fraud and over $50 billion to identity theft. The U.S. Special Committee on Aging cited Privacy Rights Clearinghouse estimates that over 700,000 Americans are victims of identity theft each year, with several thousand being elders. Reported incidents among those aged 60 years and older skyrocketed by 218 percent from 1,821 victims to 5,802 victims between 2000 and 2001.

The National Adult Protective Services Association (NAPSA) suggested that the "typical" victim of elder financial abuse is between the ages of 70 and 89, white, female, frail, and cognitively impaired. She is trusting of others and may be lonely or isolated, although reports show that there is a very diverse population of victims. According to the National Center on Elder Abuse, elder financial abuse is the illegal taking, misuse, or concealment of funds, property, or assets of a vulnerable elder at risk for harm by another due to changes in physical functioning, mental functioning, or both. The terminology used in the 2006 Older Americans Act is *exploitation*, defined as "the fraudulent or otherwise illegal, unauthorized, or improper act or process of an individual, including a caregiver or fiduciary, that uses the resources of an older individual for monetary or personal benefit, profit, or gain, or that results in depriving an older individual of rightful access to, or use of, benefits, resources, belongings, or assets." Elder financial abuse takes many forms, including, but not limited to, fraud (coupon, telemarketing, mail); repair and contracting scams; "sweetheart scams"; false/fraudulent advice from loan officers, stock brokers, insurance salespersons, accountants, and bank officials; undue influence; illegal viatical settlements; abuse of powers of attorney and guardianship; identity theft; Internet "phishing"; failure to fulfill contracted healthcare services; and Medicare and Medicaid fraud (MMI, 2009).

Numerous cases of financial abuse have arisen in the media in the last several years:

- One physician is responsible for more than $11 million in Medicare/ Medicaid fraud. He performed unnecessary surgeries on 865 older adults aged 65 and older after reportedly diagnosing them with cancer. In one case, the doctor diagnosed a piece of chewing gum as a cancerous growth when the patient's biopsy tissue was lost. Despite a finding that tissue slides in his office were not indicative of cancer, he diagnosed virtually every patient who came into his office with cancer, and would perform surgery, removing four or more layers of skin. This allowed him to charge Medicare and Medicaid higher amounts.
- An 85-year-old woman was being cared for by a middle-aged home health aide. Between August 2005 and March 2008, the aide "borrowed" $80,000, giving different reasons for the loan each time. It was discovered that she had used the money to gamble. She is charged with financial exploitation of the elderly.
- A female caregiver had stolen more than $200,000 from an elderly man who died a month after the perpetrator was arrested, and because his wife suffers from dementia, she was unable to testify. The caregiver for this man and his wife convinced them that the poor care she was providing was all that was keeping them out of a nursing home. She effectively isolated them from friends and family, and in February 2007, prior to his being admitted to the hospital, the caregiver arranged for the elderly man and his wife, who had dementia, to sign over one-third interest in their home. Within 2 months, she had also gotten them to sign a power of attorney and was posing as their stepdaughter. By the time she was arrested, she had taken out a $150,000 mortgage against the home and run up more than $75,000 in additional credit card debt in the name of the couple (ID theft). The caregiver was sentenced to 15 years in prison for elderly exploitation.
- A case was reported of a 72-year-old woman who was found dead, and whose daughter is charged in her murder. She had moved in with her 55-year-old daughter in 2006, at which time she had more than $40,000 in the bank. At the time her daughter was arrested, there were no funds in the bank, and the conditions under which

the older woman had been living made it clear that the money had not been spent on her care. For example, the older woman broke her leg. Her daughter, who is a nurse, treated it by dosing her mother with antibiotics and cornstarch, and wrapped the leg in a diaper and taped it, rather than get proper care for the injury.

- An assistant nursing home administrator in Berkeley, California, stole more than $50,000 from six elderly patients before complaints were made about her to the state Attorney General's Office. Authorities say the administrator kidnapped an 85-year-old patient with dementia from the facility and kept her at home for almost a year to collect her Social Security checks. The administrator falsified the victim's transfer to a licensed facility to cover the kidnapping; the patient was not hurt and was moved to a licensed care home.

  The DOJ discovered that the administrator had transferred funds from the bank accounts of five other patients to her own account. The administrator faces one count each of kidnapping to commit another crime, false imprisonment, and elder abuse, and six counts of theft from elder or dependent adults by a caretaker. If convicted, the administrator could receive a sentence of up to 12 years in prison.

As discussed in Chapter 3, certain populations are more vulnerable to abuse than others, and this trend applies to financial abuse and fraud of the elderly, who suffer cognitive and physical challenges that place them at greater risk. As age advances, some people experience cognitive decline and increases in instances of chronic disease. Decreased cognitive functioning, in turn, affects their decision-making capacity, leaving them potentially susceptible to people looking to defraud or deceive them. For example, women in need of some caregiving may experience theft of their valuables or cash by their paid caregiver. The caregiver may intercept their patient's mail, obtain credit card numbers and bank information, and use this information to commit identity theft. Vulnerability to undue influence could lead to a patient changing the beneficiary of a trust or will. It could also induce an agent into changing a power of attorney document. In both situations, the elderly individual forfeits his or her legal rights to another person. Even if this were discovered and reversed, it may prove difficult to impossible to ever recover any assets transferred to the unscrupulous individual.

In a review of all media-covered cases of elder financial abuse studied between April 2008 and June 2008, the media reported a total dollar value of elder financial abuse of approximately $396 million, with the largest percentage of cases involving close associates of the victim—families, friends, caregivers, and neighbors—as the perpetrator of the abuse, accounting collectively for almost 40 percent of reported cases. The largest single category included a variety of financial professionals, attorneys, and fiduciary agents.

Non-agency-based caregivers represented 10.9 percent of all cases, agency-based caregivers represented 9.3 percent of all cases, skilled nursing facility/assisted living staff represented 7.5 percent of all cases, and Medicare/Medicaid fraud represented 6.7 percent of all cases. A large proportion of perpetrators are unrelated to their elderly victims and frequently are neighbors, apartment managers, home health aides, ministers, those with power of attorney, and guardians. They initially extend helping hands to the elders and gradually are overcome by greed: contractors and handymen who ripped off the elders with bogus charges, phony financial planners and professional con artists who provided "free" services for elders to gain their trust and then defrauded them later, and others who befriended the elders to take advantage of them.

One trait perpetrators of elder financial abuse have in common is that they exhibit excellent persuasion skills. They are very good at cultivating relationships and convincing older adults that they are worthy of their trust and money. In general, perpetrators are not bound by conventional norms or business ethics, and they rationalize their criminal and abusive behavior. Individuals involved in exploiting older adults may use "undue influence"—the substitution of one person's will for the true desires of another. In these cases, the perpetrator uses his or her role and power to exploit the trust, dependency, or fear to gain psychological control over the older adult's decision making, usually for financial gain. Some are career professionals in the business of defrauding others, and others are initially in a position of trust and apparently are overcome by greed. They encourage their elderly victims to make an immediate decision or commitment to purchase products or services, which effectively limits the opportunity for consultation with others.

Although elder financial abuse has been poorly understood, there are some compelling reasons to believe its occurrence has increased over the past decade due to the following:

- More elders in the population means more potential for elder financial abuse. The population of elders generally is increasing; in 1900, adults aged 60 and older constituted about 6 percent of the population, but in 2006, elders aged 60 and older constituted almost 17 percent of the population, and by 2030, elders 60 years of age and older are projected to compose nearly 25 percent of the U.S. population.
- Older Americans are financially well off and are obvious targets for financial abuse. The older population owns the largest proportion of wealth in the United States. People over 50 years of age control at least 70 percent of the net worth of the nation's households.
- Diminished cognitive abilities create greater vulnerability to elder financial abuse.

- While the aging population overall is growing, the oldest-old (those aged 85 and older) are the fastest-growing segment of the older population. For many, with advanced age come changes in physical and mental functioning. For those with decreased abilities, decision-making capacity may be compromised, and they thus may fall prey to elder financial abuse without fully understanding the situation. Changes in cognitive abilities make elders dependent on others for help; these "helpers" may have access to homes and assets, and may exercise significant influence over the elder.
- Changes in families alter responsibility and oversight for providing care, which increases the potential for elder financial abuse. Families still provide the majority of caregiving to elders, although they look far different than they did in previous generations. More than half of women are in the workforce and are thus unable to be the sole providers of care for elders in their homes. The family structure, and thus perceptions of who is responsible to provide care, are altered due to divorce, alternate living arrangements, and stepfamilies. There are approximately 3.3 million long-distance caregivers, and their number is expected to double over the next 15 years. Nonfamily members, paid and unpaid, are providing more care as well.

A Word about Home Healthcare

In any discussion of victimization of the elderly, it is essential to address fraud that occurs in home healthcare. As Payne and Gray (2001) have noted, "With changes in healthcare administration, a new crop of offenses that confront fraud investigators have become problematic—offenses in the home health-care industry. With the increased use of home healthcare, caused partly by the growing number of older persons in the United States, the number of violations occurring in the home healthcare system has increased significantly." Payne and Gray (2001) point to three aspects of malfeasance in the home healthcare field that require clarification: "First, the precise nature of these offenses is unclear. Second, the characteristics of employees who commit these offenses are unknown. Third, the process used to detect, investigate and prosecute these offenses is not well understood" (pp. 209–232).

Just like healthcare in general, home healthcare encompasses tens of thousands of providers and agencies, and it represents more than $20 billion as an industry. Payne and Gray (2001) note that even though home healthcare represents a key way to meet the needs of a specific patient population, it is rife with fraud and abuse—government reports have suggested that up to 40 percent of home healthcare bills submitted to Medicare were fraudulent or in error.

The National Association of Attorneys General (NAAG) produces the Medicaid Fraud Report 10 times annually and summarizes the various fraud cases prosecuted by Medicaid fraud control units throughout the United States. Payne and Gray (2001) studied 247 of these cases and created a composite of the average perpetrator and crime committed. They found, for example, that nearly 60 percent of those accused of committing fraud in the home healthcare industry were female, and more than two-thirds were home health aides or personal care attendants. Other perpetrators included nurses, physicians, and home healthcare agency owners and operators. Payne and Gray (2001) found that these individuals engaged in eight kinds of offenses, including falsified billing, forgery, direct theft from clients, kickbacks, substituting provision of services, overcharging, double billing, and *criminal neglect*. This last offense, defined as intentionally failing to provide for the care of the client, can be particularly heinous in the home setting; Payne and Gray (2001) point out one case in which an aide kept a quadriplegic in a 10-foot-by-10-foot tent in the backyard for up to 10 days during which time the temperature ranged from 42 degrees to 84 degrees. Most worrisome is that the majority of home healthcare fraud tends to be committed over an extended period of time of at least several years before detection. Payne and Gray (2001) noted that at that point, fraud control officials would have been notified about the case by some concerned individual, either directly or by way of another agency that received the complaint.

Investigators looking into home healthcare fraud cases have encountered a wide range of schemes, including aides who billed clients while incarcerated, or home healthcare agencies who billed Medicaid for care provided to clients who had died or moved out of state. And as for prosecution of these kinds of cases, Payne and Gray (2001) explained that most cases that have clear-cut evidence, a "smoking gun" so to speak, were resolved through some admission of guilt on the part of the perpetrator. Sanctions received by offenders ranged from community services, fines, and probation, to jail time and prison sentences, and punishment was meted out according to the severity of the offense. For example, Payne and Gray (2001) found that forgerers received jail sentences much of the time, while those who stole from clients outright usually received fines and probation. As a side note, Payne and Gray (2001) also noted the need for a better system of background checks for individuals working in home healthcare—an issue examined in greater detail in Chapter 6.

Fraud 3: Medical Identity Theft

Medical identity theft is a growing threat, and it takes several forms. "One is the individual identity theft where person A steals person's B health insurance card and is paid the benefits, or person B allows person A to use their health insurance information or paid benefits," explains Louis Saccoccio of the NHCAA. "Another method of identity theft we see often is the wholesale theft of medical identities to bill claims. Someone on the inside at a health-care facility will steal the insurance health claims of a series of individuals, sell them, or pass them on to someone who will set up a clinic and will bill that information for a few months. They will close down once the money stops because someone looks into the fraudulent billing. For these organized groups, they are not so much assuming identities but they are stealing the information in order to make claims and then quickly move on."

As Day and Kizer (2009) have noted, "Safeguarding protected health information against unauthorized or unjustified disclosure is a fundamental duty in healthcare that derives from the basic concept of 'first do no harm.' These safeguards protect patients from embarrassment, stigma, and discrimination, among other things, and demonstrate respect for personal dignity. Protecting patient privacy is essential to the trust that is the foundation of the physician-patient or other caregiver-patient relationship upon which health-care is based."

The Federal Trade Commission (FTC) released a survey in 2007 showing that 8.3 million American adults, or 3.7 percent of all American adults, were victims of identity theft in 2006. Of the victims, 3.2 million, or 1.4 percent of all adults, experienced misuse of their existing credit card accounts; 3.3 million, or 1.5 percent, experienced misuse of non-credit-card accounts; and 1.8 million victims, or 0.8 percent, found that new accounts were opened or other frauds were committed using their personal identifying information. Medical identity theft is also becoming a significant crime perpetrated by healthcare professionals. Toporoff (2009) indicates that as many as 9 million Americans have their identities stolen each year, and that medical identity theft happens when a person seeks healthcare using someone else's name or insurance information. A survey conducted by the FTC found that close to 5 percent of identity theft victims have experienced some form of medical identity theft. Theft of electronic medical records is on the rise as well. In a 2008 survey of identity theft victims, the Identity Theft Resource Center found that 67 percent of respondents had been charged for medical services they never received, and 11 percent were denied health or life insurance due to unexplained reasons. Dixon (2006) noted that there have been 19,428 complaints regarding medical identity theft to the FTC since January 1, 1992, the earliest date the FTC began recording such complaints. Dixon (2006) adds that medical identity theft is "deeply entrenched in the healthcare system. Identity theft may be done by criminals, doctors, nurses, hospital employees and increasingly, by highly sophisticated crime rings."

"I am definitely starting to see an increase in identity theft cases," says Joseph Bellino, CHPA, HEM, president of the International Association for Healthcare Security and Safety (IAHSS). "The good news is that patients are becoming more astute about HIPAA and they are watching over their medical identity and their credit more closely. The bad news is that identity theft-related cases are persisting; as a common example, people try to switch identities during a department of transportation physical in which a urine sample is required. People will attempt to swap their identity with another person who already exists in the system. We're seeing an uptick in identity theft as part of the national trend of medical fraud."

Despite the harm it poses to its victims, medical identity theft is "the least studied and most poorly documented of the cluster of identity theft crimes," according to Dixon (2006), who adds, "It is also the most difficult to fix after the fact, because victims have limited rights and recourses. Medical identity theft typically leaves a trail of falsified information in medical records that can plague victims' medical and financial lives for years" (p. 5).

Dixon (2006) explained that

> Medical identity theft occurs when someone uses a person's name and some-times other parts of their identity—such as insurance information—without the person's knowledge or consent to obtain medical services or goods, or uses the person's identity information to make false claims for medical services or goods. Medical identity theft frequently results in erroneous entries being put into existing medical records, and can involve the creation of fictitious medical records in the victim's name. As the healthcare system transitions from paper-based to electronic, this crime may become easier to commit. Victims may find it more difficult to recover from medical identity theft as medical errors are disseminated and re-disseminated through computer networks and other medical information-sharing pathways. (p. 5)

Victims of medical identity theft may experience consequences such as loss of credit, harassment by debt collectors, and inability to find employment. Dixon (2006) pointed to a Colorado man whose Social Security number, name, and address were stolen, and who discovered he was a victim of medical identity theft when a bill collector wrote to demand the $44,000 he owed to a hospital for a surgery he never had. The victim did not have insurance and endured a lengthy procedure to clear his name, a process that is ongoing after more than 2 years. Dixon (2006) noted, "But unlike purely financial forms of identity theft, medical identity theft may also harm its victims by creating false entries in their health records.... Sometimes the changes are put in files intentionally; sometimes the changes are secondary consequences of the theft. The changes made to victims' medical files and histories can remain for years, and may not ever be corrected or even discovered." Because of medical identity theft, victims may receive the wrong care or may exhaust their health benefits prematurely, or may become virtually uninsurable. As Dixon (2006) asserts, "It is nightmarish that patients' medical records may include information about individuals who have stolen their identities for the purposes of using the victims' insurance or for dodging medical bills."

Medical identity theft can be difficult to uncover. Dixon (2006) explains that this type of fraud is commonly well concealed in electronic payment systems and databases, and that it may not be revealed through credit reports. Compounding matters is that perpetrators are sophisticated in their ability to hide their fraud, a situation that makes detection extremely difficult. Dixon (2006) states that there is the potential for medical identity theft "to be happening substantially more frequently than anyone has documented to date."

Victims of medical identity theft are frequently left with little to no recourse. Dixon (2006) observes,

> Recovery for victims of medical identity theft may be difficult or impossible because of the lack of enforceable rights, and because of the dispersed and often hidden nature of medical records. Victims of financial identity theft can depend on rights such as the ability to see and correct errors in their credit report, the ability to file fraud alerts, the right to obtain documents or information relating to transactions involving their personal information, and the right to prevent consumer reporting agencies (such as credit bureaus) from reporting information that has resulted from identity theft. But victims of medical identity theft do not have a similar complete set of rights or redresses. They do not have the blanket right to correct errors in their medical files. In some cases, victims have not been allowed to even see the compromised files. And victims of medical identity theft do not have the right to prevent healthcare providers, medical clearinghouses or insurers from reporting and re-reporting information that has resulted from identity theft. (p. 8)

Further complicating the challenges of medical identity theft is the push to make patient medical records electronic and place patient information in a National Health Information Network (NHIN). The digitizing of health records in general and the national network is a process related to an overall transition from paper records to electronic records. Dixon (2006) observed, "Currently, the mantra is that digitization of patient records will improve healthcare, reduce fraud, reduce medical errors and save lives. But this does not account for the challenging reality of medical identity theft and the substantial problems it can introduce into such a system. Many other questions and problems with medical information networks also remain unexplored."

Although transition from a paper system to an electronic system is inevitable, it creates two significant problems in the context of medical identity theft, according to Dixon (2006): a national network may make individuals more vulnerable to medical identity theft by making personally identifiable health information more accessible to criminals who have already learned how to work inside the healthcare system to steal digitized information that is much more portable and lends itself to rapid transmission. Additionally, the national network may perpetuate and transmit errors in medical charts and documents arising from medical identity theft which would percolate through a nationwide system. Dixon (2006) noted, "The implementation of new technologies in health care need not be a negative development for patient privacy and security. Conversely, neither is the implementation of new technologies a solution that will automatically resolve all problems with medical identity theft. This is especially true when the nature and scope of medical identity theft have not been rigorously studied or acknowledged as a problem. The digitization and wider availability of patient health records without adequate understanding and risk assessment could pose many difficulties."

Dixon (2006) goes on to say that medical identity theft victims need an expanded right to correct their medical files in order to recover from this crime, and need more specialized consumer education that is focused on correcting the specific harms of medical identity theft. The World Privacy Forum, a nonprofit public interest research and consumer education group founded in 2003, asserts that

- Individuals' rights to correct errors in their medical histories and files need to be expanded to allow them to remove false information from their files.
- Individuals should have the right to receive one free copy of their medical file.
- Individuals should have expanded rights to obtain an accounting of disclosures of health information.
- Studies are needed to determine what the incidence of medical identity theft is, how and where it is occurring, and how it can be detected and prevented.
- Notification of medical data breaches to consumers has the potential to save lives, protect health, and prevent losses.
- All working prototypes for the NHIN need comprehensive risk assessments focused on preventing medical identity theft while protecting patient privacy.

There have been some steps toward curtailing identity theft in general. In September 2008, President George W. Bush signed into law a bill that filled the gaps in previous identity theft laws by ensuring that victims can recover the value of the time lost attempting to repair damage inflicted by identity theft, criminalizing additional acts of identity thieves, and expanding the definition of aggravated identity theft. In October 2008, FTC chairman William Kovacic announced the release of a report from the President's Identity Theft Task Force on progress the federal government has made in addressing identity theft since the Task Force's Strategic Plan was released in April 2007. That plan outlined 31 recommendations the federal government should undertake to help prevent the theft and misuse of consumers' personal information, help consumers detect and recover from identity theft, and increase the prosecution and punishment of identity thieves. Following the release of the Strategic Plan, Task Force members worked with others in the public, private, and nonprofit sectors to implement the recommendations. The 2008 report indicated progress in the expansion of the Task Force's data security and identity theft business and consumer education campaigns, exploring means of improving consumer authentication processes to prevent the use of stolen information to commit identity theft, launching new initiatives to help identity theft victims recover, and improving law enforcement tools to investigate and prosecute identity thieves.

In late 2009, with an eye toward establishing a stronger and more transparent bond between healthcare consumers and trustworthy health information, the American Health Information Management Association announced the establishment of a Health Information Bill of Rights as a model for protecting the personal health information of the nation's 300 million-plus healthcare consumers. In a statement, AHIMA president Vera Rulon said that the bill of rights was made necessary by "repeated abuses of access, accuracy, privacy and security of the most basic rights of individuals whose trust has been betrayed and dignity compromised." These protections include the right for consumers to:

- Know who provides, accesses, and updates their health information, except as precluded by law or regulation.
- Expect healthcare professionals and others with lawful access to their health information to be held accountable for violations of all privacy and security laws, policies, and procedures, including the sharing of user IDs and passwords.
- Expect equivalent health information privacy and security protections to be available to all healthcare consumers regardless of state or geographic boundaries or the location (jurisdiction) of where the treatment occurs.
- Have private legal recourse in the event of a breach of one's health information that causes harm.

Healthcare providers have new obligations to prevent medical identity theft under the newly issued "Red Flag" rules from the FTC. Toporoff (2009) explains that as of November 1, 2009, certain businesses and organizations, including many doctors' offices, hospitals, and other healthcare providers, were required to develop a written program to spot the warning signs—or "red flags"—of identity theft. Toporoff (2009) said that every healthcare organization and practice must review its billing and payment procedures to determine if it is covered by the Red Flags Rule, and added that healthcare providers may be subject to the rule if they are considered to be "creditors." The law defines *creditor* to include any entity that regularly defers payments for goods or services or arranges for the extension of credit. Toporoff (2009) explained that a facility or practice is a creditor if it regularly bills patients after the completion of services, including for the remainder of medical fees not reimbursed by insurance. Similarly, healthcare providers who regularly allow patients to set up payment plans after services have been rendered are creditors under the rule. Healthcare providers are also considered creditors if they help patients get credit from other sources (for example, if they distribute and process applications for credit accounts tailored to the healthcare industry). On the other hand, healthcare providers who require payment before or at the time of service are not creditors under the Red Flags Rule. In addition, if a facility or practice accepts only direct payment from Medicaid or similar programs where the patient has no responsibility for the fees, it is not a creditor. *Covered account* is defined as a consumer account that allows multiple payments or transactions or any other account with a reasonably foreseeable risk of identity theft. The accounts that a facility opens and maintains for patients are generally "covered accounts" under the law. If a healthcare organization or practice is a "creditor" with "covered accounts," it must develop an identity theft prevention program to identify and address the red flags that could indicate identity theft in those accounts.

An example of a red flag includes suspicious documents, which encompasses everything for a potentially falsified identification card or a document that is inconsistent with other patient information, such as an inconsistent date of birth or a chronic medical condition not mentioned elsewhere. Toporoff (2009) notes that "If a patient provides information that doesn't match what you've learned from other sources, it may be a red flag of identity theft. For example, if the patient gives you a home address, birth date, or Social Security number that doesn't match information on file or from the insurer, fraud could be afoot." Another red flag is suspicious activities, such as mail returned repeatedly as undeliverable, even though the patient still shows up for appointments, or complaints from patients about receiving a bill for a service that he or she did not receive. Although there are no criminal penalties for failing to comply with the rule, violators may be subject to financial penalties, according to Toporoff (2009), who noted that even more importantly, compliance with the Red Flags Rule assures patients that facilities are doing their part to fight identity theft.

Fraud 4: Substance Abuse and Drug Diversion

As discussed in Chapter 1, stress and workplace violence are two significant factors in the lives of healthcare professionals. Complicating the issue for many providers is substance abuse, which some may engage in to combat their occupational stressors. This abuse is a driver of drug diversion in healthcare institutions, a unique form of fraud. The Drug Enforcement Administration's (DEA) Office of Diversion Control asserts that the abuse of prescription drugs—especially controlled substances—is a serious social and health problem in the United States, and adds, "People addicted to prescription medication come from all walks of life. However, the last people we would suspect of drug addiction are healthcare professionals—those people trusted with our well-being. Yet healthcare workers are as likely as anyone else to abuse drugs."

Hospitals are smorgasbords for substance abuse possibilities. The substances most often abused are sedatives (such as barbiturates and benzodiazepines), analgesics/opiates (such as heroin, morphine, codeine, propoxyphene, oxycodone, hydrocodone, and hydromorphone), stimulants (such as cocaine, benzedrine, dextroamphetamine, crystal methamphetamine, and methylenedioxymethamphetamine), and hallucinogens (such as LSD or ketamine). Like kids in the proverbial candy store, healthcare professionals with substance abuse problems find temptation all around them. Trinkoff and Storr (1998) observed that "Substance use among health professionals is a problem that threatens professional standards and the delivery of quality services and, if left unchecked, can lead to grave consequences for healthcare consumers. Significant numbers of professionals experience substance use problems that affect their ability to practice. Many have sought treatment, while others may continue to practice undetected" (pp. 581–585). Studies have shown that as many as 13 percent of physicians and as many as 8 percent of nurses will develop a substance abuse at some point in their career; many more of these impaired practitioners may be functioning below healthcare institutions' radar.

Physicians

Cicala (2003) found that 8 percent to 12 percent of physicians were estimated to develop a substance use problem at some point during their career; emergency medicine physicians and anesthesiologists are at the highest risk. At any given time, as many as 7 percent of practicing physicians—roughly 1 in 14—are active substance abusers. Cicala said that despite the prevalence, the subject of substance abuse is rarely discussed and receives limited coverage in medical training. He said that in the majority of cases, physicians with substance abuse problems remain undetected by their colleagues for several years before any intervention is made. Cicala (2003) said this is possible when the impaired physicians "work hard to keep their problem invisible" and avoid colleagues who might notice the effects of their abuse. What's more, Cicala (2003) has stated that the abusing physician will often leave a job rather than risk being identified as impaired. The other challenge is that according to Cicala (2003), most physician abusers continue to function quite well until the problem is far advanced. "Because their work provides either the income for drugs or access to drugs, physicians are very likely to protect their performance at work until the disease has neared end stage."

Cicala (2003) said that 90 percent of physicians referred for substance abuse treatment are male. Physicians most at risk include individuals with high stress and long work hours, occupational access to controlled substances, and those who have a self-medicating or self-prescribing behavior. Detection is difficult, because, as Cicala (2003) explains, "Physicians with substance abuse problems rarely exhibit the obvious symptoms of intoxication, such as slurred speech, pinpoint pupils or bizarre behavior. Somnolence occurs with certain drugs but is easily explained as exhaustion from being on call or working long hours. Because they have access to … needles, physicians who are intravenous substance abusers will rarely have obvious needle marks."

Most physicians are detected when the signs and symptoms of abuse are present, along with the requisite changes in behavior or attitude, and the physician is caught in diversion. These things create a reasonable degree of suspicion but might not clearly prove misbehavior. These things should be reported to a proper authority so that an investigation can take place. Cicala (2003) notes, "Many states have a legal requirement that a physician must report any suspicions that a colleague may be practicing while impaired to the proper authorities. Failure to do so could theoretically result in sanctions against the physician who does not make such a report." Cicala adds that if further investigation reveals evidence that a substance abuse problem is indicated, a referral to a state medical society–sponsored program dedicated to the identification, treatment, and support of physicians with substance abuse can be made. "Typically, as long as the physician remains in compliance with the wellness committee, no action will be taken by the state medical board, and the interaction remains protected by confidentiality laws" (p. 43). Does treatment work? Cicala (2003) reports that physicians coming out of treatment programs have long-term success rates of more than 70 percent.

Nurses

The American Nurses Association (ANA) estimates that 6 percent to 8 percent of nurses use alcohol or drugs to an extent that is sufficient enough to impair professional performance. Trinkoff and Storr (1998) said, "For some, substance use is the primary problem, while for others, the substance use may have begun as treatment for another condition, such as back pain or depression. Healthcare professionals with both kinds of problems need to be identified early, before they inflict harm on themselves or their patients." Having said that, however, Trinkoff and Storr (1998) acknowledged that some studies indicate that nurses may have no higher risk of substance use than the rest of society; they add, "Nevertheless, within the profession there may be subgroups of nurses that are particularly vulnerable, owing to the presence of certain risk factors for substance use (inadequate preparation for demanding aspects of the position, burnout). Some nurses may also believe that they are immune to the negative consequences of drug use because they are so familiar with drugs."

Trinkoff and Storr (1998) conducted an investigation where substance use was studied among nurses. Thirty-two percent of 4,438 respondents indicated some substance abuse. They were asked about use of marijuana, alcohol, cocaine, prescription drugs, and nicotine. The prevalence of past-year substance use for all substances combined was 32 percent. For marijuana/cocaine use, it was 4 percent; for prescription-type drugs, it was 7 percent; and for cigarette smoking, it was 14 percent. Binge drinking was reported by 16 percent of the nurses. The researchers found that oncology nurses reported the highest past-year prevalence for all substances combined (42 percent), followed by psychiatry (40 percent) and emergency and adult critical care (both 38 percent). Emergency and pediatric critical care nurses had the highest prevalence of marijuana/cocaine use (7 percent), followed by adult critical care nurses (6 percent). Use of prescription-type drugs was highest among nurses working in oncology, rehabilitation, and psychiatry. Copp (2009) described a survey of 300-plus nurses' attitudes toward and experiences of addiction. Fifty-nine respondents said they had worked or are working with impaired nurses. Twenty respondents admitted they had experienced addiction, and most said they had been treated and were in recovery for a number of years. Seventy-six respondents indicated they thought impaired nurses had hurt patients at their facilities by diverting pain medications, by failing to recognize changes in patient assessments, and by making medication errors. When asked what causes nurses to become addicted, the majority of respondents indicated stress from personal and professional obligations to be the culprit; others said that being surrounded by controlled substances set them up for addiction. When asked what kept them from reporting an impaired nurse, respondents cited fear of losing one's license, job, and livelihood, and the lifelong stigma attached to this loss.

Why do so many healthcare professionals succumb to substance abuse? There are several explanations. One study indicates that some healthcare professionals possess a proclivity for thrill-seeking behavior. Trinkoff and Storr (1998) reported that critical care and emergency nurses were more likely than other clinicians to report using marijuana or cocaine. The researchers add that healthcare professionals who work in high-stress hospital departments are more likely to possess sensation-seeking personality traits that attract them to crisis situations. Beyond genetics, Trinkoff and Storr (1998) attributed substance abuse by healthcare professionals to other factors, such as dealing with death, heavy workloads, and fairly easy access to controlled substances.

This access is certainly a contributing factor. Dunn (2005) said that healthcare professionals are at risk for drug abuse "because of the availability of medications in the workplace and the cultural acceptance within nursing that pharmacologic agents provide a desirable method to cure one's ills." Dunn (2005) proposes that because healthcare professionals have been indoctrinated that medications solve problems, they are not averse to self-medicating to alleviate burnout, anxiety, or other uncomfortable feelings. Due to daily exposure to controlled substances, Dunn (2005) believes nurses are more likely to indulge, believing they will not become addicted to the narcotics they are using and potentially abusing.

Substance abuse can also be a coping mechanism; in their study, Trinkoff and Storr (1998) reported high overall substance use rates and binge drinking among nurses. Dunn (2005) also cited stress in the workplace as another explanation for why some nurses abuse substances: "Increased workloads, decreased staffing, double shifts, mandatory overtime, rotating shifts, and floating to unfamiliar units all contribute to feelings of alienation, fatigue, and, ultimately, stress. Substance abuse may be a way of coping in jobs perceived as alienating. Nurses may deal with these issues because they have no choice or because they are workaholics." Dunn (2005) points out that a healthcare professional may be driven to substance abuse like any other individual coping not only with the demands of one's work, but also sleep deprivation, a lackluster social or family life, and financial problems. Quite frequently, healthcare professionals who drink excessively or do drugs are bright, ambitious, driven, and highly skilled. As Dunn (2005) observed, "Evidence demonstrates that nurses who abuse alcohol tend to be achievement-oriented people who strive to be 'super nurses' at work and 'superwomen' elsewhere."

Healthcare practitioners working while impaired is not as uncommon as one would think. Sullivan et al. (1990) conducted a survey of 300 U.S. nurses recovering from alcohol and other drug dependency to describe the effect of drug use on job performance and related disciplinary actions. Subjects admitted experimentation with or dependence on a variety of drugs, and although many visible effects on job performance were reported, just 23 percent reported disciplinary action against their nursing licenses.

Even though licensing boards and most states have laws that require healthcare professionals to report addicted or impaired colleagues, the challenge is noticing impairment in the first place. Dunn (2005) states that choosing to report abuse or to remain silent has significant consequence for patient safety: "Nurses should understand that if addicted nurses are not helped, they are in danger of harming patients, the facility's reputation, the nursing profession, and themselves. The consequences of not reporting concerns can be far worse than reporting these issues." The most alarming aspect is that in most cases, by the time the impairment is noticed and reported, the practitioner's harmful work habits have escalated to the point of posing a hazard to patients and colleagues. Dunn (2005) implores nurses to break their complicit code of silence that permeates nursing units, and advises healthcare institutions to "create systems that allow for reporting and tracking substance-abuse incidents and provide education and support to help nurses participate in rehabilitation and avoid placing patients in harm's way."

As discussed in Chapter 1, healthcare professionals have an ethical and a legal obligation to report questionable practice of a potentially impaired colleague. Dunn (2005) noted, "In some states, remaining silent can result in charges against the nurse who knew something but did nothing because this nurse supported an environment that permitted a colleague's negligence or malpractice. Remaining silent violates a nurse's ethical duty to safeguard patient care." In Chapter 6, we will examine the problems of whistle-blowing more closely. As with substance abuse or patient abuse, healthcare professionals make daily decisions about which actions merit reporting and which do not. They take into consideration the severity of the action, the level of harm inflicted, and the overall character and integrity of the healthcare provider in question. Dunn (2005) outlined several reasons why healthcare professionals will not report suspected substance abuse. First, the loyalties associated with friendship prevent many from recognizing and addressing deviant nursing practice. Second, an occupational subculture dictates that bending the rules is acceptable when there are shared personal or professional concerns they understand. Third, healthcare professionals are loath to report for fear of being branded as a snitch and suffering repercussions of their reporting. Fourth, many healthcare professionals may feel uncertain about what they see, and this self-doubt fosters an environment that enables an abusing healthcare provider to continue and prevents colleagues from documenting and reporting the suspicion. Fifth, many healthcare professionals are afraid of not being believed by their supervisor, or being sued for their reporting. Dunn (2005) adds, "Compounding these issues is the fact that the law is not very forgiving. A nurse can be a good nurse for 25 years, but if he or she makes one serious mistake, the board of nursing may call it incompetence, which could culminate in the nurse losing his or her license. If the end result could be a termination of employment, arrest or prosecution with prolonged loss of license, nurses will be less inclined to report an impaired colleague." For healthcare professionals, the stigma of being reported—or being the whistle-blower—has lasting impact on one's livelihood, career, and home life. In studies, nurses report feelings of shame and suffering of social and familial isolation, whether they were reported or they did the reporting.

Weber and Ornstein (2009) found that healthcare providers routinely practiced while intoxicated, stole narcotics from patients, and falsified records to cover their tracks. And even when these cavalier practitioners were caught, reported, and sanctioned, an allegedly lax system of treatment has not sufficiently rehabilitated impaired healthcare professionals. They note that since the inception of California's impaired nurse treatment program in 1985, more than half the nurses who have entered the program have not completed treatment, and that some who fail treatment are "deemed so incorrigible that the board labels them 'public safety threats.'" Based on a review of all nurses who faced disciplinary action since 2002, Weber and Ornstein (2009) identified more than 80 of these kinds of nurses. In the summer of 2009, California Governor Arnold Schwarzenegger replaced the majority of the nursing board and demanded reform after *The Los Angeles Times* and investigative group ProPublica reported that it took more than 3 years on average to investigate and discipline impaired or law-breaking nurses. Weber and Ornstein (2009) reported that the program's director said the program, which nearly 1,400 nurses have completed since 1985, had a graduation rate of 59 percent in 2008. The program does not track the number of relapsing nurses.

Substance abuse and drug diversion is a double-edged sword used against patients; impaired healthcare professionals can harm patients, and their drug habits force them to steal the narcotics patients need to ease their pain. Cifaldi (2009) defines *diversion* as "the unlawful channeling of regulated pharmaceuticals from legal sources to the illicit marketplace." Methods for diverting controlled substances vary and can include outright theft, substitution, and forgery of prescriptions. Yarin (2006) said that drug diversion in hospitals can involve physicians who sell prescriptions to drug dealers or abusers, pharmacists who falsify records and subsequently sell the drugs, employees who steal from facility inventory, executives who falsify orders to cover illicit sales, prescription forgers, and individuals who commit armed robbery of pharmacies and drug distributors.

Yarin (2006) notes: "Mostly, the problem lies in criminal activity of physicians and pharmacy personnel. Healthcare providers are one of the leading sources of diverted drugs, given the types and quantities of drugs purchased, the number of people routinely involved in the purchase and distribution of drugs, and the incorrect use of automated storage and dispensing units."

There are many ways healthcare professionals can get their hands on controlled substances.

Substitution

With substitution, a healthcare professional removes a narcotic from a syringe or bottle and replaces it with saline or water. One of the worst recent cases of drug diversion occurred in Colorado when a surgical technician, Kristen Diane Parker, 27, stole the sedative fentanyl from the medical center's surgery carts, used the syringes on herself, refilled them with saline, and returned her hepatitis C–contaminated syringes to the carts (see Case Study 4.1). Parker, an admitted drug addict, claimed to have been unaware that she was infected with hepatitis C. She swapped the syringes while working at Rose Medical Center in Denver and Audubon Surgery Center in Colorado Springs. The job of a surgical technologist includes preparing the operating room and the sterile field for surgical procedures by preparing sterile supplies, instruments, and equipment using sterile technique. As many as 6,000 patients were forced to undergo testing for this incurable disease; to date, 18 infections have been linked to Parker's actions. In late 2009, Parker pleaded to five counts each of tampering with a consumer product and obtaining a controlled drug by deceit, and she was sentenced on February 24, 2010, to 30 years in federal prison.

Another recent case in Washington state involved registered nurse Drea Lynne Gibson, who was sentenced to a year in prison and 3 years of supervised release for product tampering. Gibson pleaded guilty in mid-2009 to replacing doses of Demerol, a narcotic pain medication, with epinephrine at the surgery center where she worked. At sentencing, U.S. District Judge Ricardo Martinez said, "This is an extremely serious offense. Using Demerol for herself is one thing, stealing it is another. But replacing it with something else takes it to another level. Replacing the Demerol with epinephrine shows she was willing to put other people in pain and even at risk of death to treat her own pain." According to filings in the case, Gibson fed her addiction by stealing vials of Demerol from a locked case and then completing records indicating the drugs were being administered to patients. As her addiction worsened, Gibson would break open and consume the contents of Demerol ampoules, refilling those ampoules with saline solution, and then super-gluing the ampoules back together, and returning the ampoules to the Demerol box. On multiple occasions, anesthesiologists administered the tampered ampoules to patients recovering from surgery under the belief that they were administering Demerol. When patients complained that their pain was not being relieved, the anesthesiologist switched pain medications and administered fentanyl. Previously, Gibson had been sanctioned by the Washington State Nursing Commission for removing a patient's prescription for oxycodone and attempting to fill that prescription for herself at a local pharmacy. In requesting a prison sentence for Gibson, Assistant U.S. Attorney Patricia Lally wrote to the court, "Drea Gibson's on-going conduct put many unsuspecting patients at risk. Not only did some patients unnecessarily experience pain during surgical procedures because they were injected with saline instead of the prescribed anesthetic but these same patients were placed at risk of infection from Gibson's non-sterile handling of the tampered ampoules."

Forgery

A common diversion tactic is theft from medication carts and fabrication of entries in the medical record. Healthcare professionals have stolen prescriptions for controlled substances or forged prescriptions in order to obtain narcotics. They may also ask a colleague to cosign the narcotics record to show that a controlled substance was destroyed without witnessing the drug's disposal.

Partial Administration

They also may divert drugs by administering a partial dose to a patient and saving the rest for themselves. As Fernandez (2007) explains, "Drug diversion … can occur when patients receive medications on an as-needed basis. Part or none of the medication is given to the patient exactly on schedule during the shift, but a nurse documents that the maximum amount of the medication was administered. Numerous instances of this have been reported."

One method of drug diversion deterrence is through technology. Fernandez (2007) states that hospitals are combating drug diversion by installing medication management machines such as the Pyxis® systems from CareFusion Corporation (San Diego, California) that track medication dispensing to thwart theft. The system issues an alert if more medications than normal are dispensed. Pedersen et al. (2006) reported that in the 2005 American Society of Health System Pharmacists' survey of dispensing practices, 71.8 percent of all hospitals use automated dispensing cabinets (ADCs) in their drug distribution systems, and that 92.5 percent of hospitals with more than 399 beds have these systems. Through a nationwide survey of hospitals, Crowson and Monk-Tutor (2005) investigated how the use of automated controlled substance cabinets (ACSCs) for storage and distribution of narcotics can provide the documentation necessary to identify and detect drug diversion. The researchers found that more than 80 percent of respondents indicated that their institution used an ACSC, and 62 percent provided data to calculate a diversion detection of 0.36 per 100 beds preautomation and 1.12 per 100 beds postautomation. Out of the 19 percent of institutions not using ACSCs, 60 percent provided the necessary information to calculate a diversion detection rate that was determined to be 0.76 per 100 beds. All respondents reported having policies and procedures related to the diversion of controlled substances; however, they varied significantly regarding drug screening practices and specific conditions for the rehire of staff that were detected diverting drugs. The researchers concluded that when used properly, with effective checks and balances, ACSCs have the capability to improve detection of narcotic diversion and may help to decrease diversion of controlled substances by healthcare professionals.

Although hospitals are resorting to the use of automatic dispensing units, Cifaldi (2009) said facilities should be on the look-out for the following signs of diversion:

- Fictitious user names are created and deleted to gain access to automatic dispensing devices.
- Employees make drug transactions during off shifts or unscheduled times.

- Patients complain of poor pain management, and their record shows erratic pain relief.
- Narcotics are pulled for excessive numbers of patients or for larger doses than ordered.
- Excessive amounts of leaking IV bags are returned to the pharmacy.
- Excessive patterns are seen of broken vials and ampoules.
- Narcotic waste is thrown into the general trash where it is later picked up by the diverter.
- Changes in patterns of narcotic-use quantities are detected.
- Returned capsules are missing powder or broken tablets are returned without all of their pieces.
- Diluent is substituted for active injectables for narcotics in IV bags.
- Look-alike drugs are substituted as narcotics in pharmacy storage.

O'Neal and Siegel (2007) outline the different opportunities for drug diversion in hospitals:

- A pharmacy purchasing manager could order more narcotics than are needed to refill the pharmacy's controlled substance vault; when the order arrives, the purchaser intercepts the delivery and refills the vault to its maximum par levels, while keeping the excess product. By ordering more products than are needed, the purchaser is less likely to draw attention than if he or she diverted product that may be needed by the pharmacy, thereby resulting in a stock outage. O'Neal and Siegel (2007) recommend that hospitals prohibit the same employee from ordering and receiving controlled substances, as well as periodically audit and reconcile records of controlled substances received into the vault against purchase orders.
- A healthcare professional could attempt to withdraw extra narcotics that never make it to the patient. Dispensing systems can foil would be diverters in that the transaction will be flagged as a discrepancy if the exact amount of narcotics or the number of vials or syringes is not received on the unit from the pharmacy vault. O'Neal and Siegel (2007) advise hospitals to review daily all transactions involving movement of controlled substances out of the pharmacy to an ADC to ensure that diversion did not take place between the pharmacy and the end destination. The most commonly used automated vaults feature reports that automatically reconcile transactions to rapidly identify discrepancies in need of further investigation.
- A pharmacist could attempt to divert from multidose vials used to prepare intravenous bags or other controlled substances in bulk. For example, a pharmacist could prepare a 20 mg drip for a patient; he or

she removes a 40 mg per 20 mL multidose vial from the vault and prepares the admixture, leaving 20 mg of the controlled substance in the vial. When the pharmacist receives another order for an IV drip of the same controlled substance, rather than remove the remaining 20 mg from the previously opened multidose vial, the pharmacist withdraws a new vial from the vault to prepare the admixture and pockets the previously opened vial. O'Neal and Siegel (2007) recommend that hospitals have auditing procedures in place to ensure that the potential for diversion associated with these practices is minimized.

- A pharmacist or nurse could pocket an expired controlled substance that is scheduled to be destroyed in what medical professionals call a "wasting," and then the perpetrator could falsify the signature of a nonexistent witness. Pedersen and Siegel (2007) advise hospitals to closely monitor waste procedures, and add, "Inevitably, there will be controlled substances that are not used and must be wasted while in the pharmacy's control. Whether the pharmacy wastes expired or unused items, or hands these products to an expired returns company for destruction, the final destination of these products is one that should not go unmonitored by the pharmacy." (pp. 145–148)

Personal use of diverted drugs by pharmacists and healthcare professionals is starting to be compounded by the problem of healthcare providers stealing high-cost narcotics to sell on the street. O'Neal and Siegel (2007) noted, "Escalating pharmaceutical costs and the emergence of unscrupulous small volume wholesalers have led to a new type of diversion for hospital pharmacists to tackle. Several high-profile cases of diversion have involved high-dollar chemotherapeutic agents, growth factors and human growth hormone. The willingness of some wholesalers to purchase and re-sell these products can potentially entice pharmacy employees to divert. Lack of adequate security in the pharmacy may enable this problem." O'Neal and Siegel (2007) emphasized that locked vaults and locked refrigerators (for more perishable controlled substances) are essential, as is a security system in which a hospital employee must identify himself or herself to gain access, and cameras are directed at the storage units. They also suggest that pharmacy managers consider adoption of policies that ban personal belongings such as backpacks from being taken into drug-storage areas. But nothing is as effective as simple risk management. As O'Neal and Siegel (2007) noted, "Controlled substance vaults and ADCs have certainly made the pharmacy manager's job easier through positive identification, secured storage, and automated reporting. Unfortunately, the responsibility for preventing and detecting controlled-substance diversion does not end with the purchase of this technology" (pp. 145–148).

Yarin (2006) suggest the following steps be taken to investigate, detect, and prevent drug diversion:

- Review, reconcile, and properly secure DEA-222 forms used for ordering Class II controlled substances.
- Reconcile drug orders to drug receipts, and then to drug stocking.
- Secure the delivery process when drugs are moved from the pharmacy to individual floors or units.
- Limit, secure, and monitor access to the pharmacy vault in which controlled substances are stored, including reviewing the use history of the vault to find access by unauthorized personnel or questionable access at certain dates or time of day.
- Investigate and review discrepancies on a timely basis.
- Train employees on the proper way to use ASDUs, including procedures for opening and closing drawers and fixing jammed doors, and use of system screens and software.
- Review and track key data produced by ASDU systems. Look for a high frequency of discrepancies by certain individuals or service areas (including the pharmacy), more than usual waste of certain drugs, and questionable transactions. This may mean a higher than expected use of a controlled substance on a particular floor or unit. In certain instances, a review of related medical records may be needed to confirm both the physician order of the drug and administration to the patient.
- Limit the number of individuals with access to controlled-substance ASDU bins.
- Limit the number of personnel with "super user" status in the ASDU system.
- Establish more frequent inventory counts.
- Develop written policies and procedures required by state and federal agencies for disposing unused drugs, handling accidental spills, destroying expired drugs, and reporting and resolving discrepancies.
- Educate relevant employees on identifying, detecting, and reporting potential drug diversion.

CASE STUDY 4.1: A DRUG DIVERSION

Colorado hospitals seemingly have experienced a mini epidemic of drug diversions in the last several years. The Kristen Parker case is just one of many that have come to light; a review by *The Denver Post* of state health department records showed drug diversion and substitution by healthcare providers occurring more than 100 times in the last 3 years at 22 Colorado hospitals, putting thousands of patients at risk.

Included among the incidents are the following:

- A staffing agency worker was found dead at home, with hospital syringes scattered throughout the apartment; the individual's death followed patient complaints that they were not receiving their medication.
- A surgical nurse at a hospital stole large amounts of fetanyl and refilled the vials with water.
- A medical center employee was fired on suspicion of stealing Percocet and other drugs as well as vials of fentanyl from locked cases.
- Hospital employees noticed that a patient's IV bag of fentanyl was empty hours before it should have been; they found the employee responsible for caring for the patient in a bathroom with blood-spattered clothes and a plastic catheter wrapped around the employee's arm.
- A hospice nurse was accused of writing forged prescriptions for more than 4,000 pain pills.
- A member of the emergency department staff at a hospital was seen withdrawing morphine for a patient who did not need it; an investigation showed a similar withdrawal had occurred for two other patients, and the staff member failed a drug test.
- A medical center employee who was supposed to deliver an IV bag could not account for the drip's whereabouts; an investigation showed the same worker had other situations when it could not be shown that medication had been delivered.
- A hospital employee was found to have taken an unusually large amount of narcotics from an automated dispensing machine; an investigation showed the worker took out a larger dose than the patient needed, gave the patient what was needed, and kept the rest.

Prompted to action by the Kristen Parker case, the Colorado Hospital Association's safety task force is reviewing potential reforms, including the establishment of a database for the reporting of nonlicensed professionals such as surgery technicians; a better system of reporting problematic former employees to prospective new employers; improved preemployment screening; and expansion of employee drug testing to include controlled substances such as fentanyl. In addition, Colorado State Representatives Sara Gagliardi and Debbie Benefield introduced legislation in April 2010 that would require surgical techs to register with the state's Department of Health and Department of Regulatory Agencies (DORA), as well as require healthcare institutions to report by name techs who are fired or disciplined for reckless behavior and check the state's database of names to ensure potential hires have not been flagged due to past disciplinary actions.

"Cases like the one involving Kristen Parker are disturbing because it offers us a glimpse into how quickly our lives can be changed by a reckless act," Gagliardi said. "The medical field is expansive and often complex, and it's difficult for investigators to play catch-up and determine how something like these infections came about in the first place. It's much easier if we can impede or stop those who would abuse the system before they begin. Especially when we are dealing with infectious disease and the lives of the innocent, prevention is immensely important. We're creating this registry to help keep patients safe. We have no illusions of stopping addicts altogether, but this bill is a great deterrent, and it prevents re-hiring of those who have been involved in dangerous activities."

State law varies on what it demands of surgical techs. Currently, Colorado law does not require surgical technologists to be competent, qualified, or credentialed; however, most of the employers for which they work are regulated. All hospitals and ambulatory surgery centers are licensed by the Colorado Department of Public Health and Environment (CDPHE), and this agency, through the State Board of Health, has promulgated rules that require hospitals to have policies that identify the scope of the services to be provided by various personnel, the lines of authority and accountability, and the qualifications of the personnel performing those services. Elsewhere, surgical technologists must be registered in Washington state; and in Indiana, Texas, South Carolina, and Tennessee, surgical technologists must be graduates of accredited surgical technology programs and certified by a nationally accredited credentialing organization. Legislation related to the regulation of surgical technologists is pending in several more states, according to the Association of Surgical Technologists (AST), but interestingly enough, a Colorado regulatory agency does not back legislative change.

In January 2010, Colorado's Department of Regulatory Agencies (DORA)'s Office of Policy, Research, and Regulatory Reform released a sunrise review examining the need for state regulation of surgical technologists. A sunrise review is required when any interested party proposes state regulation of a currently unregulated occupation or profession. Sunrise reviews determine whether the public is being harmed by the unregulated practice of an occupation or profession and whether there are less burdensome alternatives. These reviews are presented to the General Assembly to better enable it to evaluate the need for the regulation and to determine the least restrictive regulatory alternative consistent with the public interest.

A sunrise application was filed requesting licensure or certification of surgical technologists. The functions of surgical technologists are dictated, in large part, by the training and experience of the individual surgical technologist, the policies of the facility employing that individual, and the functions delegated to the surgical technologist by the licensed personnel in the operating room. The 2010 sunrise review found no evidence of widespread competency-related harm caused by surgical technologists. Additionally, the review found that the current model, where employers determine the qualifications and competencies of the surgical technologists they employ, is sufficient to protect the public health, safety, and welfare. Consequently, the review recommended no regulation of surgical technologists.

Driving this request for the sunrise review was the nonprofit group Family Voices of Colorado, which says either licensure or certification for surgical technologists is the appropriate level of regulation to protect the public. The group says that because surgery is inherently dangerous and the risk of physical harm or death due to intraoperative mistakes is so high, only properly educated and examined individuals should be allowed to practice. The group acknowledges that many techs have been practicing successfully in Colorado for many years, but it asserts the need exists to create standardization for the occupation and maintains that the general public does not have the opportunity to evaluate technologist qualifications and must depend on varying standards set by employers. Additionally, Family Voices of Colorado asserts that the state cannot prevent a tech from practicing after he or she has proven to be "erroneous, incompetent, unqualified or guilty of negligent error."

In its sunrise report, DORA (2010) stated, "It is incumbent upon the facility employing surgical technologists to ensure that the people it employs as such are qualified and perform within certain, predetermined parameters. Additionally, licensed facilities are routinely surveyed for compliance with a variety of laws, and as part of that survey process, personnel files are reviewed to ensure that the particular facility is complying with its own policies."

The DORA report (2010) also addresses the Kristen Parker case as it explores the questions of "whether the unregulated practice of the occupation or profession clearly harms or endangers the health, safety or welfare of the public, and whether the potential for harm is easily recognizable and not remote or dependent on tenuous argument."

DORA weighed the same facts that have been in the public domain since news of the Parker case broke in 2009: Parker had previously worked in hospitals in New York, where she was discharged for poor performance due to having a bad attitude, problems labeling specimens, and problems keeping track of instruments, as well as worked in Texas (Griffin and Booth, 2008). Parker moved to Colorado and began working at a Denver area hospital in October 2008. At some time prior to her start date, Parker was given a drug test and a physical evaluation. The drug test came back clean, but there were some indications that Parker carried the hepatitis C virus. It was suggested she seek medical attention, but such status did not disqualify her from employment. Part of Parker's job involved retrieving fentanyl, a highly addictive pain medication, and delivering it to the operating room. Over the next several months, Parker diverted fentanyl by removing some of the drug from its vials with needles she previously used to inject herself with previously diverted drugs, and replacing the diverted fentanyl with a saline solution (Booth and Sherry, 2009). By April 2009, Parker's employer became aware of the drug diversion and terminated her employment. The employing hospital informed the CDPHE that it had terminated an unnamed employee for drug diversion, in keeping with standard practice and nothing exceptionally unusual was noted; the hospital also notified authorities (The Denver Channel.com, 2009). By May, Parker had secured employment at an ambulatory surgical center in Colorado Springs, where she again diverted pain medications. She worked there until June 2009, at which time the details of her actions became more widely known. All told, Parker deprived approximately 5,700 patients (4,700 in Denver and 1,000 in Colorado Springs) of their pain medications.

Considering this information about Parker, the DORA Report (2010) stated:

> While this example is certainly illustrative of deplorable conduct, it is less clear that any kind of regulatory structure could have prevented this surgical technologist from harming these patients. Regulation is an inherently weak response to criminal activity. The deterrent value of administrative discipline pales in comparison to the possibility of imprisonment. If jail time is insufficient to deter someone from diverting drugs, the threat of losing a license to practice certainly will not stop that person. Additionally, regulation is ineffective at preventing intentional conduct. Regulation, such as a licensing or certification program, serves to ensure a minimal level of competency in order to help reduce the occurrence of negligence. Therefore, it is reasonable to conclude that the licensing program proposed by (Family Voices of Colorado) would not have prevented this situation from occurring. On the other hand, however, even a minimal regulatory system, such as a registration program, could have provided the Denver employer a vehicle through which to file a complaint against the person, thereby, at a minimum, starting the administrative investigatory process, rather than simply complying with its general duty to report the drug diversion to CDPHE and law enforcement.

DORA (2010) seemingly shifted responsibility onto healthcare institutions by remarking, "The marketplace appears to be taking a proactive stance on this issue.

The Colorado Hospital Association has created a 75-member task force to study a variety of safety issues and to share best practices. The goal of this task force is to develop proposals to improve safety and procedures related to medication. These proposals are expected sometime in mid- to late-2010. Therefore, it is reasonable to conclude that if there are systemic problems, the hospitals, as the employers of surgical technologists, and thus ultimately liable for the acts of those surgical technologists, will identify any problems and correct them through this process."

Sidebar References

Booth M, and Sherry A. Hospital officials look to fix lapses. *The Denver Post*. July 16, 2009.

Brown J, and Booth M. Colorado hospitals fight inner demons. *The Denver Post*. July 16, 2009.

Department of Regulatory Agencies Press (DORA). Press release: 2010 Sunrise Review of Surgical Technologists. January 26, 2010. (Accessed at: www.dora.state.co.us/dora_pages/newsreleases/SurgeryTechniciansSunrise ReleaseFinal.pdf.)

DORA Office of Policy, Research, and Regulatory Reform. 2010 Sunrise Review: Surgical Technologists. January 25, 2010.

Griffin G, and Booth M. Rose surgery tech previously fired in New York. *The Denver Post*. July 17, 2009.

TheDenverChannel.com. Timeline in hepatitis C scare. (Accessed at: www.thedenverchannel.com/print/20008580/detail.html.)

References

Agency for Healthcare Research and Quality (AHRQ). "Procedures in U.S. hospitals." 2003.

American College of Fraud Examiners (ACFE). "Report to the nation on occupational fraud and abuse." 2008.

Anthony J, Eaton W, and Trinkoff A. The prevalence of substance abuse among registered nurses. *Nurs Research*. 40(3):172–175. 1991.

Breuer L. "Criminal prosecution as a deterrent to healthcare fraud." Testimony before the Committee on the Judiciary, Subcommittee on Crime and Drugs. May 20, 2009. (Accessed October 23, 2010, at: http://judiciary.senate.gov/pdf/09-05-20BreuerTestimony.pdf.)

Centers for Medicare and Medicaid Services (CMS). Payment policies under the physician fee schedule and other revisions to Part B for CY 2010. *Federal Register*. October 30, 2009.

Cicala RS. Substance abuse among physicians: What you need to know. *Hosp Phys*. 39(7):39–46. 2003.

Cifaldi AJ. "Drug diversion in the hospital." PowerPoint Presentation. 2009. (Accessed October 23, 2010, at: http://pharmacy.ruters.edu/files/Drug/20Diversion/20in/20the/20Hospital.pdf.)

Copp MB. Drug addiction among nurses: Confronting a quiet epidemic. *RN*. April 2009.

Crowson K, and Monk-Tutor M. Use of automated controlled substance cabinets for detection of diversion in U.S. hospitals: A national study. *Hosp Pharm*. 40:977–983. 2005.

Day G, and Kizer KW. "Stemming the rising tide of health privacy breaches." A report by Booz Allen Hamilton Inc. McLean, VA. 2009.

Dilweg S. Testimony of Sean Dilweg before the Senate Judiciary Committee Subcommittee on Crime and Drugs. May 20, 2009. (Accessed October 23, 2010, at: http://judiciary.senate.gov/hearings/testimony.cfm?id=3860&wit_id=7952.)

Dixon P. "Medical identity theft: The information crime that can kill you." World Privacy Forum Report. May 2006.

Drug Enforcement Administration (DEA). "Drug addiction in health care professionals." Undated.

Dunn D. Substance abuse among nurses: Defining the issue. AORN J. October 1, 2005. (Accessed October 23, 2010, at: http://findarticles.com/p/articles/mi_mOFSL/is_4_82/ai_n15754444.)

Fabrikant R, Kalb PE, Hopson MD, and Bucy PH. *Healthcare Fraud: Enforcement and Compliance.* pp. 24–25. New York: Law Journal Press. 2006.

Farrar S. "Criminal prosecution as a deterrent to healthcare fraud." Testimony before the Committee on the Judiciary, Subcommittee on Crime and Drugs. May 20, 2009.

Federal Trade Commission (FTC). "Identity theft survey report." November 2007.

Fernandez J. Hospitals wage battle against drug diversion. *Drug Topics.* February 19, 2007. (Accessed October 23, 2010, at: http://drugtopics.modernmedicine.com/drugtopics/article/articleDetail.jsp?id=405412.)

Freeh LJ. Healthcare fraud, hearings before the Senate Select Committee on Aging. U.S. Senate, 104th Congress. March 21, 1995.

Gagliard Sara. Personal communication. April 1, 2010.

Gosden T, Forland F, Kristiansen I, Sutton M, Leese B, Giuffrida A, Sergison M, and Pedersen L. Capitation, salary, fee-for-service and mixed systems of payment: Effects on the behavior of primary care physicians. *Cochrane Database of Systematic Reviews.* Issue 3. 2000.

Health and Human Services. Press release: "Secretary Kathleen Sebelius and Attorney General Eric Holder Convene National Summit on Healthcare Fraud." January 28, 2010. (Accessed October 23, 2010, at: http://www.hhs.gov/news/press/2010press/01/20100128a.html.)

Jesilow PD, Pontell HN, and Geis G. Medical criminals: Physicians and white-collar offenses. *Justice Quarterly.* pp. 149–165. June 1985.

Lally P. (Accessed October 23, 2010, at: http://www.stopmedicarefraud.gov/innews/washington.html.)

MetLife Mature Market Institute (MMI). "Broken trust: Elders, family and finances." March 2009.

National Health Care Anti-Fraud Association (NHCAA). "Fighting healthcare fraud: An integral part of healthcare reform." pp. 1–22. June 2009.

O'Neal B, and Siegel J. Prevention of controlled substance diversion: Scope, strategy and tactics. *Hospital Pharmacy.* 42(2):145–148. 2007.

Payne BK, and Gray C. Fraud by home health care workers and the criminal justice response. *Crim Justice Rev.* 26:209–232. 2001.

Pedersen CA, Schneider PJ, and Scheckelhoff DJ. ASHP national survey of pharmacy practice in hospital settings: Dispensing and administration. *Am J Health Syst Pharm.* 63:327–345. 2006.

Sheehan JG. Joint Legislative Budget Testimony, New York State Office of the Medicaid Inspector General. Albany, NY. February 9, 2010. (Accessed October 23, 2010, at: http://docstoc.com/docs/26641945/Testimony-Present-by-James-G-Sheehan-New-York-State.)

Sobel MG. A comprehensive guide to preventing controlled-substance diversion. *Pharm Pur Products.* 2(6):16–18. 2006.

Sparrow M. Fraud in the U.S. healthcare system: Exposing the vulnerabilities of automated payments systems. *Social Res.* 75(4). 2008.

Sparrow M. Malcolm Sparrow testifies before the Senate Subcommittee on Criminal Prosecution as a deterrent to healthcare fraud. May 22, 2009. (Accessed October 23, 2010, at: http://www.hks.harvard.edu/news-events/news/testimonies/sparrow-senate-testimony.)

Sullivan EJ, Bissell L, and Leffler D. Drug use and disciplinary actions among 300 nurses. *Substance Use & Misuse.* 25(4):375–391. 1990.

Toporoff S. "The red flags rule: What healthcare providers need to know about complying with new requirements for fighting identity theft." Federal Trade Commission. 2009.

Trinkoff AM, and Storr CL. Substance use among nurses: Differences between specialties. *Am J Public Health.* 88:581–585. April 1998.

Weber T, and Ornstein C. "Drug diversion and impaired healthcare workers." ProPublica.com. July 25, 2009.

Yarin D. "Detecting and preventing drug theft." Hospitals and Health Networks Online. March 21, 2006. (Accessed October 23, 2010, at: http://hhnmag.com/hhnmag-app/jsp/articledisplay.jspdcrpath=HHNMAG/pubsNEWSArticle/data/2006March/ 060321HHN_Online_Yarin&domain=HHNMAG.)

Suspicious Death and Homicide

5

As discussed in Chapter 4, the sheer number of patients and procedures provides many places to hide in the massive U.S. healthcare system. Thunder (2003) said that the number of employees who have routine access to patients is well over 4 million people. And there is ample opportunity to create medical mischief. According to the Agency for Healthcare Research and Quality's (AHRQ) report, "Procedures in U.S. Hospitals, 2003," close to 60 percent of all patients received a procedure during their hospital stay, which means a significant opportunity for healthcare professionals to gain access to patients during bedside procedures. Some moments are more advantageous than others in the healthcare environment for a practitioner wishing to cause harm to a patient, such as when changing dressings, changing IVs, and administering narcotics. As we will see, hospitals are rife with opportunities for committing murder.

Healthcare Serial Killers: An Overview

Would you be surprised to learn that some of the most prolific killers have been healthcare professionals? And that there is no certainty how many more victims these murderers had outside of the crimes for which concrete evidence was available? A number of individuals have attempted to take inventory of perpetrators and victims, although there is no definitive number of each. Thunder (2003) noted, "At least 18 people in the United States have been charged with quiet killings in medical facilities in the past 25 years. Twelve have been convicted of two attempted murders and 66 counts of murder or manslaughter, with three more having 20 counts of murder or manslaughter pending against them. The 18 are suspected of having killed more than 370 others, for a total of about 455."

A seminal paper on serial murder by healthcare professionals by Yorker, Kizer et al. (2006) examined 90 criminal prosecutions of healthcare providers for serial murder of patients and found that between 1970 and 2006, 54 of the 90 were convicted for serial murder, four were convicted for attempted murder, five pled guilty to lesser charges, and others are awaiting trial or outcomes have not been reported. Of these perpetrators, nursing personnel comprised 86 percent. The number of deaths resulting in murder convictions is 317, and the number of suspicious deaths by the convicted 54 healthcare workers is 2,113.

The paper by Yorker, Kizer et al., in which these killers' characteristics, motives, methods, and legal outcomes were catalogued, at the time was considered to be one of the most thorough examinations of healthcare serial killers. Yorker, Kizer et al. (2006) reported that there were 10 healthcare serial murder cases in the 1970s, 21 in the 1980s, 23 in the 1990s, and 40 from 2000 to 2006. By profession, registered nurses carry the day, with 60 percent of perpetrators (or 54 out of 90 prosecutions) being RNs, seven being licensed practical nurses, and 16 being nurses aides. Almost 49 percent were women, and 94 percent were Caucasian. Yorker, Kizer et al. (2006) also found that 72 percent of the majority of deaths occurred in hospitals' medical/surgical units or intensive care units (ICUs) on the evening or night shifts; 20 percent of the perpetrators worked in long-term care. Most of the perpetrators were first suspected of murder and following termination found another position where the killing resumed. Their victims were almost always female, critically ill, very old, very young, or otherwise more vulnerable than the rest of the patient population. The perpetrators' favorite method of killing was mostly lethal injection of narcotics such as epinephrine, insulin, KCL, anectine, pavulon, digoxin, and lidocaine; on occasion, perpetrators created air embolus or induced suffocation. Many liked to trigger cardiac arrests, and blood samples collected during the code event revealed elevated levels of potassium, or low blood glucose/high serum insulin for a planned insulin overdose. Most of the perpetrators seemed to get their kicks out of killing certain patients, and many enjoyed predicting which individuals would die under their care.

Yorker (2008) updated the healthcare serial killer count to a total of 307 patient deaths that resulted in convictions for murder, and noted, "In most of the incidents the caregiver was suspected of being linked to many more deaths than for what were actually prosecuted. The total number of suspicious deaths associated with the 53 convicted healthcare providers was 2,081. This may be a significant undercount. In addition, there were 130 patients who survived an injection and the healthcare provider was convicted for attempted murder or assault."

In 2010, the primary authors of that 2006 paper on healthcare serial killers updated their study of the issue to continue questioning the priority of efforts among healthcare institutions and policy makers to address and prevent medical murder. As Kizer and Yorker (2010) reported, "Since 1975, at least 35 healthcare workers in the U.S. have been formally charged with serial murder of patients. Additional persons have been investigated for such crimes but have not been prosecuted because of problems with the evidence needed for indictment and prosecution." They acknowledge the difficulty of assembling concrete data: "Studying healthcare serial murder is especially difficult because the events are rare, there is no disease classification code or other specific method to identify such deaths, the events are not generally required to be reported to public health agencies, and there is no centralized source of information about such occurrences. Law enforcement statistics are not helpful because they do not routinely distinguish murder victims at healthcare facilities according to whether they are patients, staff or visitors" (pp. 186–191).

Despite these challenges, Kizer and Yorker (2010) offer one of the most comprehensive, contemporary efforts to define and analyze the problem of medical murder: "A review of 90 healthcare professionals prosecuted for healthcare serial murder between 1970 and 2006 identified more than 100 instances of suspicious deaths. Reported instances were from 21 countries and 22 states in the U.S., with the United States accounting for 40 percent of the incidents.... More than 1,050 suspicious deaths have been linked to persons charged with healthcare serial murder in the U.S. since 1975, giving an average of 30 such deaths per year. However, the circumstances of many of the convicted healthcare serial murderers suggest that additional killers have not been recognized, so the actual number of patients harmed by these acts may be higher. The number of healthcare workers charged with HCSM has increased in each of the past four decades, with more than four times as many such occurrences being reported worldwide during 2000–2009 than 1970–1979. The number of such instances reported in the U.S. suggests an increase but the trend is less clear than for the number of such occurrences worldwide" (pp. 186–191).

Kenneth W. Kizer, M.D., has spent much of his life dedicated to improving public health and healthcare, and especially encouraging stakeholders of the healthcare system to embrace quality improvement and patient safety strategies. Among his myriad accomplishments, Kizer served as the founding president and chief executive officer (CEO) of the National Quality Forum (NQF), a Washington, D.C.–based not-for-profit organization whose mission is to improve American healthcare through endorsement of national voluntary consensus standards for measuring and reporting healthcare quality. Established in 1999, pursuant to a recommendation of a presidential commission, Kizer developed a unique public–private partnership of more than 300 organizations representing all aspects of the healthcare industry and whose aggregate membership is estimated to include more than two-thirds of Americans. Kizer is well acquainted with the issue of intentional harm of patients at the hands of healthcare professionals due to several key public-sector appointments he held during his career, including his tenure as director of the California Department of Health Services from 1985 to 1991, where he oversaw licensure of all healthcare facilities in the state (at the time, some 5,300 facilities in 18 different categories) and had to repeatedly deal with instances of sexual assault, patient abuse, and other types of intentional harm, especially in long-term care facilities.

However, it was Kizer's 5 years serving as Under Secretary for Health in the U.S. Department of Veterans Affairs that exposed him to healthcare serial murder. In this role at the Veterans Administration (VA), Kizer was CEO of the veterans healthcare system, the largest healthcare system in the nation, and the highest-ranking physician in the federal government. Kizer explained:

> My interest in healthcare serial murder, in particular, was spurred by my experience and direct involvement with two well-known cases while I was at the VA—the Richard Williams case at the Columbia, Missouri. VAMC and the Kristen Gilbert case at the Manchester, New Hampshire, VAMC.... In the course of these cases I also became very familiar with the Michael Swango case, since a VA hospital was one of the sites where Swango practiced. Given the apparent rarity of these events, having to deal with two such instances is highly unusual and probably unique. My interest in trying to increase awareness about and otherwise address healthcare serial murder stems, in part, from my frustration with the lack of information and resources available to me when having to handle these cases. In dealing with the cases at the VA, I sought information and assistance from the Federal Bureau of Investigation and the Department of Justice, the American Hospital Association, the Joint Commission, the Centers for Disease Control and Prevention, the Department of Health and Human Services and multiple other entities, and was unable to find any source of information or assistance. I also encountered a clear reluctance to even talk about or acknowledge the issue from all the healthcare-related entities. This stands in marked contrast to other similarly rare safety-related conditions. For example, in the course of my career, I have also studied and written about dog bites and shark attacks. Fatalities from both of these causes are much less frequent than deaths from healthcare serial murder, but based on the amount of information available, the number of studies that have been conducted and the apparent public interest in these safety problems, one might conclude that as a society we care more about getting eaten by a shark than being murdered in a hospital. (Interview with author.)

The Medical Murder Hall of Shame

Holmes and Holmes (1993, p. 16) defined a *serial killer* as someone who murders at least three people over a period longer than 30 days. Ramsland (2007) said, "Healthcare serial killers may be any type of employees in the healthcare system that use their position to murder at least two patients in two separate incidents, with the psychological capacity for more killing" (p. xi). To understand the etiology of medical murder, it is helpful to review some of the most high-profile cases of serial murder by healthcare professionals.

Physicians

Harold Shipman

British physician Harold Shipman had been suspected of killing at least 215 of his patients while under investigation from 1974 to 1998. In 2000, he was convicted of 15 murders, and he died in prison in 2004. Most of his victims were elderly women, and his preferred method of killing was by lethal injection.

Michael Swango

American physician Michael Swango had been convicted of poisoning his coworkers and served 2 years in prison. He traveled extensively, falsifying his credentials and using aliases to practice medicine again, and left a trail of questionable illnesses and death behind him. He was arrested in 1997 and was arraigned in 2000 when he pleaded guilty to fatally poisoning several patients in 1993 at a New York hospital. He received three consecutive life sentences without parole. His preferred method of killing was using a paralyzing drug in intravenous solution.

Nurses

Beverly Allitt

In 1993, British pediatric nurse Beverly Allitt was convicted of murdering four children, attempting to murder three, and causing grievous bodily harm to six, and was given 13 life sentences. Allitt is among a handful of nurses who are suspected of operating under a factitious disorder, in which perpetrators garner attention for feigning illness or injury, using innocent patients as their proxy.

Richard Angelo

In 1989, American nurse Richard Angelo was convicted of two counts of second-degree murder, one count of second-degree manslaughter, one count of criminally negligent homicide, and six counts of assault, and he was sentenced to 61 years to life in prison. His preferred method of killing was using paralyzing drugs.

Charles Cullen

American nurse Charles Cullen, who had a disturbingly long history of job dismissals, was quoted by the prosecutor as boasting that he had killed 30 to 40 patients in his 16-year career to alleviate their pain and suffering. In 2006, Cullen received 18 consecutive life sentences. His preferred method of killing was using digoxin and other drugs.

Robert Diaz

American nurse Robert Diaz was convicted in 1984 for murdering 12 patients in a 26-day period at two California hospitals in 1981. His preferred method of killing was injecting patients with large doses of lidocaine.

Vickie Dawn Jackson

In 2002, American nurse Vickie Dawn Jackson was charged with killing four elderly patients from 2000 to 2001 by injecting them with lethal doses of the muscle relaxant mivacurium chloride.

Kristen Gilbert

American nurse Kristen Gilbert was convicted in 2001 of four murders and two attempted murders at a VA hospital. Her preferred method of killing was administering an overdose injection of epinephrine. She was sentenced to life imprisonment for having fatally injected three of her patients with a stimulant to mimic heart attacks.

Gwendolyn Graham and Catherine Wood

American nurses Gwendolyn Graham and Catherine Wood were convicted in 1988 of suffocating five elderly women in a nursing home in 3 months. They were lesbian lovers who obtained sexual gratification through their killing.

Genene Jones

American pediatric nurse Genene Jones was convicted in 1984 for murdering a 15-month-old infant by injection with muscle relaxant succinylchlonine chloride. She was sentenced to 99 years in prison. In 1983, a grand jury convened to investigate 47 suspicious deaths of children at a medical center where Jones had worked previously; while evidence suggested Jones was implicated in as many as 20 murders, she was not convicted for these potential crimes.

Orville Lynn Majors

American nurse Orville Lynn Majors was convicted in 1999 of six murders and was suspected of having committed 150 killings by lethal injection of potassium chloride between 1993 and 1995. He was sentenced to 360 years in prison.

Filipina Narciso and Leonora Perez

In 1975, 35 patients at a VA hospital in Michigan suffered 51 cardiopulmonary arrests. A grand jury indicted American nurses Filipina Narciso and Leonora Perez for conspiracy to commit murder, five counts of murder, and 10 counts of poisoning. They were convicted in 1977.

Terri Rachals

In 1996, American nurse Terri Rachals was acquitted of six murders but found guilty of one count of aggravated assault for injecting a patient with potassium chloride. She was suspected of injecting 20 patients in a series of mercy killings.

Mary Rose Robaczynski

In 1979, prosecutors dropped charges for three murders against American nurse Mary Rose Robaczynski, who had been suspected of separating patients from their respirators. The case ended in a mistrial on one of the counts, and prosecutors concluded that the legal definition of death in the state of Maryland was too ambiguous to secure a definitive ruling.

Kimberly Saenz

In 2009, Texas dialysis nurse Kimberly Saenz turned herself in to local authorities and was booked on one count of capital murder, as well as five counts of aggravated assault for allegedly injecting 10 dialysis patients with bleach, which caused five deaths. A grand jury indicted her on the charges of capital murder and aggravated assault; she could face the death penalty if convicted. Texas state and federal health officials were notified in April 2008 about a cluster of four patient deaths at a dialysis clinic; an investigation found that 19 patients died at the clinic in a 5-month period that ended in April. A break in explaining the cluster of deaths came when two patients at the clinic told staff that they saw Saenz injecting bleach into the dialyzer lines. In May 2008, Saenz was charged on two counts of aggravated assault for allegedly injecting patients with bleach. Those two patients survived, but police had reason to believe she was responsible for the deaths of at least four other patients at the time. The state of Texas suspended Saenz's nursing license in May 2008 due to the bleach-injecting allegations, as well as a complaint that she had stolen painkillers from a hospital she worked at in August 2005. She voluntarily surrendered her nursing license. Tubing, blood samples, and other medical equipment of the affected patients were preserved to be used as evidence against Saenz. Testing on the equipment showed bleach had been used in the syringes and dialysis lines.

Richard Williams

In 2002, American nurse Richard Williams was charged with 10 murders at a VA hospital via lethal injection with succinylcholine. He pleaded innocent. An investigation by the FBI and the Office of Inspector General in the Department of Veterans Affairs determined that 41 people died between May and August 1992 while Williams was on duty. Investigators concluded patients were 20 times more likely to die while Williams was working than while 11 other nurses were on duty. However, the charges were dropped in August 2003 after newer science called the succinylcholine results into question.

Allied Healthcare Providers

Donald Harvey

American nurses assistant Donald Harvey pleaded guilty in 1987 to killing 37 patients at hospitals in two states by using cyanide, arsenic, and suffocation. He was sentenced to three concurrent life terms in prison.

Efren Saldivar

In 2002, American respiratory therapist Efren Saldivar pleaded guilty to six counts of murder in exchange for life imprisonment instead of the death penalty; he received six consecutive life sentences and 15 additional years for attempted murder. He was suspected of murdering more than 40 to 50 patients from 1989 to 1998 by reducing the ventilated patients' oxygen flow or administering a lethal injection of the muscle relaxants pavulon or succinylcholine chloride.

Kizer and Yorker (2010) reported, "The types of healthcare workers involved have included nurses (68 percent), nursing aides (18 percent), physicians (12 percent) and allied health professionals (2 percent). Physicians have been involved with a relatively small percentage of the incidents but have accounted for a disproportionately large number of deaths" (pp. 186–191).

Much has already been written about these healthcare serial killers elsewhere; what is left to ponder is the number of perpetrators who literally have gotten away with murder. As Thunder (2003) noted, "It is probable that quiet killings in medical facilities have occurred but investigators have thus far been unable to identify the perpetrators." The unsettling aspect of serial murder by medical professionals is the number of cases in which employers and investigators could not secure enough evidence or prosecutors could not obtain a conviction. As Thunder (2003) explained, "In some instances, investigators have evidence that a crime has occurred and may have evidence identifying the perpetrators, but there is lack of sufficient evidence to win a criminal case. In such instances, there may be sufficient evidence to suspend a professional license or to obtain money damages in a civil suit."

The Mechanics of Medical Murder

Let us take a closer look at the elements that come into play.

The Victims: Why They Are Marked for Murder

In the majority of cases, healthcare serial killers selected patients who were helpless or in some way more vulnerable than others, either because they were in a coma, on a respirator, or incapacitated in some way so that they could not resist, raise an alarm, or summon help. Feldman and Eisendrath (1996) noted that patients who were victimized were physically compromised, critically ill, elderly, or very young. Thunder (2003) observed, "The victims are quiet. Indeed, we may not even know that they are victims for a long time. They are dead but we do not know they are victims of a homicide. They made no announcements beforehand asking to die—at least there are no witnesses to such other than perhaps the perpetrator." Thunder (2003) continues, "Who are these victims? They may be too sick, too old, or too young to be capable of communication. They may be older persons. They may be terminally ill. Since they are in medical facilities, they are typically sick or injured or in need of medication. In any case, they are vulnerable and depend on medical personnel for food, water, care and treatment.... The killings are quiet. They are not obviously violent. Neither guns nor knives are the weapons of the perpetrator. The means are often painless; there are no screams. There are no obvious signs of a struggle. There are no wounds or blood."

Although a victim typology of a sort emerges from the study of healthcare serial killers, not all patients are targeted for specific reasons; some experts believe it could be a random process. Feldman and Eisendrath (1996) stated, "Contrary to the vast majority of homicides and assaults, which are acts of violence directed toward specific individuals, the victims of serial murder are generally simply in the wrong place at the wrong time. Serial murder has an underlying compulsive psychological drive, whereas other forms of murder are usually motivated by anger, revenge, money or jealousy" (p. 166).

The Methods of Their Madness: How They Kill

Healthcare serial killers seem to favor a variety of ways to commit murder; Yorker (2008) noted that common methods include the administration of medications such as potassium chloride, digoxin, epinephrine, insulin, lidocaine, and a host of respiratory paralyzing agents. In a look at 99 cases, Yorker (2008) reported that injection was used to kill 51 times, suffocation 11 times, water in lungs four times, air embolus three times, oral medications three times, equipment tampering one time, and poisoning one time, with an unknown method used 25 times. Researchers seem to concur that the preferred method of killing among healthcare serial killers appears to be lethal injection, most often leading to the patient's medical "code blue" before death. As Kizer and Yorker (2010) noted, "The most common method of healthcare serial murder has been intravenous injection of a non-controlled medication such as epinephrine, succinylcholine, concentrated potassium chloride, digoxin or insulin. Narcotics are rarely used by healthcare serial killers in the U.S. (in contrast to assisted suicide or euthanasia), and then mostly by physicians. Other methods have included suffocation (e.g., smothering with a pillow), drowning (e.g., by pouring large quantities of water into a patient's mouth), intravenous injection of air (air embolus), and tampering with medical equipment" (pp. 186–191).

Feldman and Eisendrath (1996) noted that 20 percent of known serial killers in the United States are nurses charged with causing epidemics of patient cardiopulmonary arrest. Kent and Walsh (2004) observed that "In all cases found, clinicians were believed to have intentionally inflicted life-threatening distress upon their victim patients." Hockley (2005) emphasized that practitioners have access to drugs powerful enough to kill unobtrusively through intravenous lines that access the patient's bloodstream. Advances in medical technology have made it easier for healthcare serial killers to kill, at least in terms of the lowly syringe; it has become one of the most effective tools of the trade for many medical murderers. Kaplan (2009) said that improvements to the syringe in the 1850s made the administration of potent narcotics a reality and said "this coincided with the refinement of opium into morphine, a product of great potency that could not only provide rapid relief from pain but just as easily kill by respiratory arrest with a minute increase in dose." With the advent of intravenous lines, healthcare serial killers can simply inject a narcotic into the line's port and do away with the need to inject into the patient's vein, leaving a telltale needle mark.

Trestrail (2007) acknowledge the challenge of detecting a criminal poisoner: "Homicide by poisoning is one of the most difficult types of cases to prove, both for the death investigator and medical expert. It has been stated that poisonings occur rarely, accounting for only about 3 percent to 6 percent of homicides. In this statement, we should add the word 'known' before homicides, as I believe that they do not rarely occur, but rather are rarely detected. The main problem is that in poisonings, the investigator often has no visible signs of trauma to indicate that the death is other than natural. Bullets leave holes, knives leave cuts, clubs leave bruises, but the poisoner covers the murder with a blanket of invisibility. As poisons are offensive weapons, not defensive weapons, often the crime scene may seem nonexistent" (p. xvi). To this end, Trestrail (2007) recommended that to ascertain whether a death was committed by the use of poison, an investigator should ponder the following questions:

- What substance was found in the victim that should not be there?
- Is the substance in a toxic amount?
- Were observed symptoms consistent with the substance and the amount? (compare to witness description or autopsy findings)
- How and when did the substance get into the victim? (by what route and at what time?)
- Who would gain from the victim's death?
- Who had access to the victim and to the toxic substance? (p. 75)

Poisoning has been a staple of the murderer's arsenal, and it has achieved new heights in the cases of medical murder. There is still much to be understood about those who commit homicide via poisoning, as Westveer et al. (2004) have noted that "Other than a few published reviews of some famous historical poisoning cases, the authors found little written material on the characteristics of poisoners and their victims. A further probe of the international forensic literature also failed to reveal any previously published epidemiological studies dealing with criminal investigative analyses, or psychological 'profiles' of the homicidal poisoner."

What is known, however, is that the act of poisoning another individual requires skill and daring. As Glaister (1954) observed, "Poisoning, of course, differs considerably from many other crimes, frequently committed in uncontrolled passion and in the heat of the moment. The innate character of the crime of homicidal poisoning demands subterfuge, cunning and, what is equally important, usually a period of careful planning, and also not infrequently the repetition of the act of administering poison…its characteristic being one of premeditation, it is a method of murder, which, therefore, cannot be the subject of extenuation as some other forms of killing can" (p. 184).

Steck-Flynn (2007) stated, "Poisoning is a unique type of crime. It is strangely 'accepted' as less of a crime than a homicide involving physical violence. But this dastardly crime takes cunning and planning and causes its victims suffering beyond comprehension. Investigators must be ever-vigilant in their efforts to detect homicidal poisoning and bring its toxic perpetrators to justice."

As we have seen, vulnerable patients are the perfect targets of poisoning. Steck-Flynn (2007) said: "The terminally ill, mentally incapacitated, drug addicts, the elderly and the very young are at highest risk of poisoning. The offender is usually personally involved with the victim and is often in the role of caregiver. Poisoners often position themselves as an individual trying to 'nurse' the victim back to health. Why do they do it? Poisoners often derive pleasure from seeing their victims suffer, frequently staying to watch their target experience the poison's effects. The thrill of the poisoner's power over the victim is what motivates the perpetrator to serially offend." Steck-Flynn (2007) adds, "Today, perpetrators of homicidal poisonings are often employed in the medical or care-giving fields. Though there are no proven theories to explain this phenomenon, perhaps their behavior is similar to that of pedophiles, who often take on roles in positions of trust over children, such as coaches, clergy and other professions, in order to gain access to their victims. Poisoners, in some cases, take on jobs that give them access to poisonous substances, and having poisons (drugs) in ready reach and extensive knowledge of their effects may be what tempts perpetrators to use them in a crime."

Steck-Flynn (2007) says that investigators should ask themselves the following questions when attempting determine a possible homicidal poisoning:

- Was the death sudden?
- Has the caregiver been associated with other illnesses or death?
- Did the victim receive medical treatment and appear to recover, only to die later?
- Did the caregiver have access to restricted drugs or other chemicals?
- Was the victim isolated by the caregiver? Did the caregiver position himself or herself to be the only one with access to the victim's food or medications?

Healthcare serial killers know that to escape detection, the poisons they use must be as untraceable as possible. Steck-Flynn (2007) described the ideal poison for committing a homicide as being odorless, tasteless, difficult to detect, and mimics the symptoms of naturally occurring diseases, and adds that "there are literally thousands of substances perpetrators can choose from to commit homicidal poisoning. It is much easier to detect these substances today thanks to modern scientific methods and advances. However, unless the death is unexpected or the circumstances questionable, it is unlikely extensive testing for more exotic substances will be performed."

Forensic toxicologists screen for the presence of poisons and toxins in the victim's urine, blood, and tissue. Although toxicological testing is done in some cases, many drugs pass through the body quickly, and unless suspicion at the time of the adverse event is strong enough to warrant immediate testing, the window of opportunity for detection will close. Steck-Flynn (2007) states, "The sudden death of an otherwise healthy adult also is cause for suspicion. Autopsies routinely screen for some toxins, but it should be determined in advance if the caregiver or spouse had access to unusual substances. This is particularly important if the persons with access to the victim can readily obtain uncommon medicines."

Injections into patient's intravenous lines are a significant cause of patient distress and eventual death. As Kerrigan and Goldberger (2006) have explained, "Intravenous (IV) drug administration provides maximum drug delivery and rapid onset of effects. The injection of a drug bypasses the body's natural safeguards. Intravenous administration is complete and not affected by gastrointestinal absorption or intramuscular or subcutaneous absorption. In addition, IV drug administration also avoids the liver and is transported directly to the site of action without being inactivated by liver enzymes."

Ramsland (2007) cited Yorker who noted, "The high-tech healthcare environment almost invites sociopaths to (kill).... It is too easy to kill a patient when you don't even have to stick their skin with a needle. You simply put a needle in their IV line with ordinary, soluble, everyday medication. You just need to put in a milliliter or two more. The brink between toxic and therapeutic doses of what are usually therapeutic medications is so imperceptible."

Because IVs are implicated in so many healthcare serial killer cases, it is imperative for investigators on the scene to identify and collect any evidence of syringes, vials, ports, and dressings that may have been touched in the act of the IV tampering. It is also important for investigators to collect biological samples from medical devices such as urinary catheters, to help determine the cause of the patient's illness or death. As Kerrigan and Goldberger (2006) stated, "Appropriate selection, collection, preservation and storage of biological evidence are essential during a toxicological investigation. Delays in specimen collection can also have a profound impact on the toxicological outcome."

The Methods of Their Madness: When They Kill

A number of nursing experts emphasize the importance of observing patterns of time-specific and care-related mortality on hospital wards. As Hockley (2005) explained, "It is easier to target certain victims by the circumstances of location (in bed and out of sight of nursing stations), time and lack of supervision (evening and night shifts), and ease of administration (intravenous therapy). For example, a registered nurse while working on night duty in an aged-care facility secluded a resident in his room for a number of hours during the night." There have been cases in which healthcare serial killers have been able to use the darkness and stillness of night as a cover for their medical murder. Although most hospitals still are quite lively with activity during the evening and night shifts, the same cannot be said for many nursing homes, which become much quieter and are much less staffed at night.

Hickey (1991) and Stark et al. (2001) stated that higher risk is associated with the delivery of intravenous fluids, with being in a bed out of sight of a nursing station, and with evenings or nights. And as Kent and Walsh (2004) have observed, "The strongest victimization numbers were seen on the 11 P.M. to 7 A.M. shifts. Some of the more obvious cases revolved around the ICUs, but more research is needed to identify prevalence in specific units within the various hospital pavilions."

Some nursing experts, including Barber (2001), believe that the change of shift at hospitals provides a window of opportunity for medical malfeasance. As Sullivan (2006) explains:

> For example, staff members who are getting off duty, especially after a busy shift, may disengage from responsibilities too early, leaving loose ends and incomplete reports. Documentation and oral reports often take precedence

over hands-on care activities, increasing the risks for omissions or duplication of tasks, medication administration or specifically timed one-on-one checks on patients.... Social interactions may take precedence over professional communications when shift workers merge. Patients as well as visitors are aware of the confusion and chaos that may occur at change of shift, and some may take advantage of these opportunities to engage in behavior not conducive to the health and welfare of patients on the unit. Those caregivers who have ideas other than providing healthcare on their minds will also realize that the change of shift provides an optimum time for inappropriate, illegal or otherwise dangerous behavior. (pp. 559–561)

The Methods of Their Madness: Where They Kill

As Kizer and Yorker (2010) reported, "Most reported instances of apparent healthcare serial murder have occurred in countries having technologically advanced healthcare and generally in healthcare settings employing sophisticated technology. These events most often have occurred in acute-care hospitals (70 percent), followed by nursing homes (20 percent) and outpatient settings (10 percent), with the perpetrator often murdering in more than one healthcare setting and/or multiple geographic locations."

The intensive care unit (ICU) of a hospital is a common place for medical murder. As Park and Khan (2002) explain, "The ICU is a place of technology, unusual drug formularies and rapid decision-making, all designed to help critically ill patients get better. However, these same factors can create an environment where a healthcare worker might systematically harm a patient without fear of detection or punishment. Such allegations are difficult to substantiate because evidence is so difficult to obtain and thus criminal prosecutions are rare."

Park and Khan (2002) pointed out that one of the most notorious cases involving the ICU was that of Texas nurse Genene Jones in the late 1970s. After being dismissed from two previous posts, she was hired to work at a pediatric ICU; during the first year of her employment, Jones was accused by her supervisors of errors in drug administration and equipment use, as well as emotional overinvolvement with her patients. Over the course of 3 years, Jones' supervisors began to notice an unusual pattern of deaths occurring in children whose conditions were not necessarily considered as critical, during the evening shift; the deaths also occurred with greater-than-expected frequency in those being cared for by Jones. Although Jones' nursing colleagues and supervisors dismissed their initial suspicions related to unexpected deterioration in patients' conditions, an investigation was launched, and nursing staff were also asked by the ICU's medical director to take extra precautions with drug administration and equipment settings. Jones was eventually convicted for infant deaths, and the case stands out as an example of how changes in the conditions of the most vulnerable patient populations should be monitored. Park and Khan (2002) also note that the inherent nature of the ICU and the frequent occurrence of death—expected or not—make "a murder allegation an occupational hazard of nursing the critically ill." Park and Khan (2002) add, "By its very nature, critical care medicine attracts people who thrive in such an environment and who tend to have a black sense of humor, which could be misconstrued if taken out of context. The patients they care for also tend to be the most unstable, so clusters could occur simply by chance leading to a crime of just 'being there' or 'having a bad run.'"

The Methods of Their Madness: Why They Kill

There is no definitive explanation for medical serial murder, although there are many theories. Sullivan (2006) asserts:

> There are several contributing causes to this type of caregiver malfeasance. The reality is that most medical facilities across the country are in a crisis mode when it comes to who provides hands-on patient care and how well it is accomplished. In hospitals across the U.S., units are filled to capacity and those patients are sicker. A high patient census with equally high acuity levels combined with fewer licensed registered nurses (RNs) to share the workload makes for a dangerous situation. Rarely do RNs have time to help each other because of their own workloads and supervisor positions have been cut back in efforts to downsize. Additionally, some applicants are not always completely honest with background histories, and screening efforts do not always catch the discrepancies. Further, there is an overall failure to discipline or terminate marginal employees, and because of short staffing it is often felt that a 'warm body' is better than nobody showing up for work. These all contribute to setting the stage for those who may have something other than the best intentions of patients in mind. History has certainly shown that individuals such as former nurse Gilbert and many other former licensed healthcare professionals who have been successfully prosecuted for criminal acts against patients have taken advantage of these dynamics. (pp. 559–561)

As Park and Khan (2002) observe:

> People join the caring professions for a variety of reasons; equally, the motives for harming patients may be just as diverse. Trust forms the basis of all healthcare. Carers who harm are so far outside this that it is commonly believed that such people must be mentally ill. In fact, only one nurse has pleaded insanity as a defense. Beverly Allitt, a pediatric nurse from the U.K., suffered from Munchausen's syndrome by proxy. This syndrome describes a person who fabricates signs of illness in another (usually a dependant) leading to secondary

gain for the perpetrator. It is believed that healthcare workers who suffer from this share many of the characteristics of other groups diagnosed with the condition such as a previous history of abuse and self-harm. (pp. 621–623)

Factitious disorders as an explanation for medical murder will be discussed later in this section.

That the healthcare profession has at its core a focus on life and death can be a powerful attraction for would-be killers. Does healthcare turn individuals into killers, or do killers simply use the healthcare environment to its full advantage? We may never know, but as Ramsland (2007) has said, "A few healthcare serial killers enter the profession as predatory angels of death, alert to the opportunities for murder in a clinic or hospital, where the administration of medication is easy and some deaths are already expected; however, many transform into killers on the job. After killing once, usually out of pity, they learn that they enjoy it and so they continue."

Stark and Paterson (2001) as well as Kinnell (2000) have also suggested that the incidence of serial homicide among physicians may indicate a pathological interest in the power of life and death. However, Stark and Paterson (2001) state that their analysis of serial killers in nursing suggests an alternative interpretation, in that while all walks of life have people who possess the potential to murder, the key difference may be opportunity. As Stark and Paterson (2001) explain, "The difference between nurses and doctors may be that doctors also control the means of disposal; in the case of ... Shipman, he also provided the death certificate. The reason for the difference in the number of reported deaths may simply relate to doctors' greater opportunity to remain undiscovered."

Serial murder expert Katherine Ramsland, an associate professor of forensic psychology at DeSales University in Pennsylvania, who has been widely published on this topic, said:

People who become healthcare serial killers might not be attracted to it until they actually find themselves in a situation where they can exercise some power.... And then there are others who are the psychopaths who see the easy victims in patient populations. As for someone like Charles Cullen, I don't believe he went into this thinking he was going to start killing people. There were a number of factors influencing his life at the time, as well as the anger issues he had, and these began to eat away at him when he was in certain situations. For example, he would do things like work in the hospital burn unit, where some of the most critical patients were, so he had access to very vulnerable patients during periods of personal stress. He would work longer hours than anyone else, which made him seem to be caring and trustworthy, which in turn gave him greater freedom to exploit the availability of medications and the decreased supervision. The truth is, there are many complex factors involved in the development of a serial murderer in the healthcare profession, but nevertheless, more simplistically, those who are already predators who already have anti-social traits stemming from childhood look for careers in which they know people can be their victims without necessarily being caught. They will tend to gravitate toward young victims such as infants who can't say, "so-and-so came in here and gave me a shot," or elderly people who are expected to die who aren't listened to, or the worst cases like people who are burn patients who are comatose and who hardly know what's going on around them. That's an easy population of people to begin to exploit.

That being said, some of those people are truly mentally ill, not simply psychopaths, but they may have Munchausen Syndrome by Proxy or some other personality disorder that makes it more of a compulsion, and I don't see that as quite the same dynamic as an outright anti-social immoral predator. I see healthcare serial killers as a subcategory of serial murderers, but even within that subcategory, there are different reasons why someone begins to develop this behavior. I don't see them as insane either, as I don't think they could get into their positions if they were actually psychotic. (Interview with author.)

Motives for murder can be as individual as the crimes healthcare serial killers commit.

Dalrymple (2001) asked, "Do the nurses who behave like this have a deep-seated personality trait or a motive in common? It is natural to assume that they must have characteristics that distinguish them from others of their profession (after all, mass murder by nurses is still very uncommon) that would enable them to be identified in advance, and therefore tragedy to be averted." Dalrymple (2001) noted further, "Some of the nurses who kill are thought to want to be present at real life-and-death dramas, as if they were inhabiting a television soap opera. Moreover, by reviving the people whose hearts and breathing they have stopped, they cast themselves in a heroic light. Their fantasy is made flesh: but in the process, of course, a certain number of participants, that is to say patients, pay the ultimate price. The motive remains a mere hypothesis, since people like Beverly Allitt rarely confess or confide their thoughts to anyone. But in any case, it is clear that other nurse-murderers have other motives: One motive does not fit all."

No discussion of healthcare serial killers is complete without mention of the difficulties that mercy killing present; are these cases as clear-cut as murder? Are "mercy killings" considered to be serial murder? Dalrymple (2001) stated:

Nurses kill because they believe in euthanasia. The great majority of the victims of nurse-murderers are at the extremes of life. In Austria, a country with a great tradition of mercy-killing, some nurses unilaterally decided that their geriatric patients would be better off dead, and duly liberated more than 40 of them from their travails. A recent survey among American intensive-care nurses, conducted to ensure anonymity among the respondents, suggested that about one-fifth of them had actively killed (or claimed to have killed) at least one patient, taking the initiative into their own hands. The survey was criticized for being unrepresentative, but it clearly demonstrated that the killing of patients by nurses was not confined to a mere psychopath or two.… Orville Lynn Majors—who was convicted of injecting six of his elderly patients to death, and who prosecutors alleged killed over a hundred—was said to view old people with contempt and even hatred. In a culture as fixated on youth as our own, old age is seen in itself as something terrible, cruel, pointless, and even obscene. In the circumstances, it would not be surprising if the suffering that mercy killers sought to relieve was their own rather than their patients'. Compassion easily slides into contempt. The helpless are often not very appealing: It is all too easy to think the world would be better off without them.

Healthcare professionals can be some of the stealthiest killers, due to the comfort and familiarity of their surroundings, their inside knowledge of drugs and mechanisms for murder, and the ability to create the most opportune moments for their mischief. As Thunder (2003) put it, "The perpetrators are quiet. They do not make announcements before, or after, about their deeds. There is no talk around the hospital bed of the time, place or manner of death so that others may hear. The perpetrators are not like Jack Kevorkian seeking publicity to change the law."

There is no definitive reason why healthcare professionals commit serial murder. Motivation is as personal as a fingerprint; some have cited power or revenge, others sexual gratification, while still others maintain they simply desired to "help" their patients. Some healthcare serial killers have claimed various medical conditions as the impetus for their killing sprees; in court, Charles Cullen's defense counsel argued that he suffered from a disassociative disorder. Stark and Paterson (2001) have suggested that the incidence of serial homicide among doctors may indicate "a pathological interest in the power of life and death" and that although all occupations have individuals with the potential to murder, the key difference with health professionals is that they have the opportunity as well.

Healthcare serial killers seem to defy generalization as to their motives, and some experts believe it's important to resist profiling them. Ramsland (2007) states, "There is no way to provide a generic profile of healthcare serial killers because each case, while exhibiting common behaviors and contexts, is nevertheless unique. Some experts believe that attempting a profile based on a psychological and behavioral blueprint is risky, as it could result in selective attention to stereotypical details, and neglect of distinctive indicators, but others believe there is sufficient overlap in these cases to at least devise a reasonable risk assessment." Ramsland (2007) adds, "Healthcare serial killers are usually predators, whether due to having an evil character or a less malignant personality disorder. As such, they learn how to use the most subtle means of murder and gain access to pharmaceuticals without being detected. Unless some specific behavior triggers suspicion, they may effectively hide their crimes for quite a long time.… Healthcare serial killers generally use some sort of overdose, equipment tampering or smothering, and they are quick to claim when apprehended that their motives were mercy or compassion. In most cases, evidence undermines this claim."

Ramsland confirmed:

> It is always risky to do prospective profiling. No risk analysis is going to offer a formula that's going to be 100 percent accurate. This is really at the stage where it is still an art, not a science. So the best tools that you have are lists of traits and behaviors that crop up consistently in these cases. The fact that someone prefers a night shift is not enough; you must have a collection of these traits and behaviors that over time are consistent. Obviously, the downside is that during this time, patients are at risk. But when you start seeing the same kind of suspicious behavior, such as deception and attention-getting activities, you can start tightening surveillance at the very least. For example, in the Efren Saldivar case, the supervisor heard enough to say, "I'm going to start watching this guy more closely," and that was helpful. Rather than just dismiss some of the things people were saying, such as there are suspicions that patients are dying on his shift, attention was paid to watching behavioral trends. It's important that people are trained to know what to look for, to keep this in their heads and when they begin to spot those behaviors, they start to put a little more surveillance and effort into it. I think that the prospective profile in that regard, which really is just risk analysis assessment, will help people document things in order to develop a case. (Interview with author.)

Ramsland (2007) outlines a number of motives:

- Wanting to be a hero: Some healthcare serial killers turn a medical emergency such as a drug-induced cardiac arrest into the opportunity to "save" the patient and to earn accolades from coworkers and supervisors.
- Wanting attention: Some healthcare serial killers with factitious disorders achieve attention by harming themselves or their patients. And some killers, such as Charles Cullen, Efren Saldivar, and Donald Harvey, enjoyed discussing their crimes with investigators.
- Wanting to experiment: Some healthcare serial killers such as Michael Swango used patients for their experimentations with drugs and other therapies.
- Wanting the thrill of the kill: Some healthcare serial killers, such as Michael Swango and Kristen Gilbert, achieved sexual arousal or heightened states of being by committing murder, respectively.

Many killers become addicted to a rush of adrenaline that comes from anticipating the act or the act itself.

- Wanting power over life and death: Some healthcare serial killers enjoy the opportunity to dominate their patients, frequently seen as retribution for a childhood spent in submission to a domineering parent. Some killers also have exhibited disdain for their patients to feed a need for superiority, as exhibited by Harold Shipman.
- Wanting relief from boredom, tedium, or personal conflict: Some healthcare serial killers have used killing as a way to distract themselves from ongoing turmoil in their personal or professional lives. Charles Cullen, Donald Harvey, and Beverly Allitt were among those who channeled their personal demons into medical murder.
- Wanting to be compassionate: Many healthcare serial killers see themselves as the proverbial "angels of mercy" and convince themselves that their murderous deeds are actually acts of compassion, perverted as it may seem.
- Wanting to dispose of problematic patients: Some healthcare serial killers, such as Efren Salvidar, admitted that their crimes had less to do with mercy and more to do with ridding themselves of bothersome or demanding patients. (Interview with author.)

If nothing else, the stressors of healthcare, as discussed in Chapter 1, can contribute significantly to a motive for murder. "In many ways it's a stress-related disorder and we certainly have a high amount of stress in our culture today," said Ramsland. She continues:

I teach a class on mass murderers and serial killers and one day recently I said to my students that I thought we would be seeing much more violence, as the conditions are ripe for it. Sure enough, we saw mass murders taking place nearly every week as the economy soured and people's stress levels elevated. I think the conditions are also ripe for healthcare serial killing. We do see them pop up in other countries; not here as much but they continue to be detected. The problem is, a lot of these people are like Charles Cullen who went undetected for 16 years! There are definitely people killing in healthcare institutions today, but they haven't been found out yet. I do believe the cause is not limited to just being predatory but it's often spiked by stress, the need for attention, certain types of mental illness—those things are already present and they are exacerbated by stress. People who are mentally ill absorb the culture's stresses not only from their own lives but from society at large. Additionally, there is an emphasis on healthcare reform and reducing costs, so hospitals will become increasingly overburdened and their employees will feel those pressures. (Interview with author.)

Serial murder by healthcare professionals is still the exception to the rule, but incidence has been significant enough for forensic psychiatrist Robert Kaplan to coin the term "clinicide" to describe the death of multiple patients in the course of treatment by a physician. Kaplan (2009) notes, "Medical murders are appalling but unusual crimes. It is a paradox, considering the extraordinary effort, discipline and devotion that it takes to become a doctor when throughout history medicine has been regarded as a sacred calling." Kaplan (2009) adds, "That some doctors become killer says much about human nature, society and the practice of medicine. But it should be remembered that very, very few members of a great profession follow this path. The practice of medicine is an inherently good activity, and it is to the credit of the profession that there are so few killers.... In a setting where medical practice is defensive and insecure, to say the least, there are any number of opportunities for the psychopathic doctor. And the reckless treatment killer, driven by mania, narcissism or hubris, can find any number of cracks in which to insert themselves in the medical edifice."

Kaplan (2009) divided clinicide into three categories: medical serial killing, treatment killing, and the sufficiently explanatory mass murderers. We have come to know medical serial killing as the murder of two or more patients in a short amount of time. Kaplan defines *treatment killing* as multiple patient deaths in which it is not immediately obvious that the doctor intended the patient to die. As Kaplan (2009) explains, "A separate category is merited because the question of intentionality (motivation) and self-awareness of the harmful nature of the action is blurred in these cases." Ramsland (2007), in citing Kaplan's theory on serial-killer physicians, says that as predators, they are attracted to medicine because it allows them to pursue their interest in life and death, and that initially ordinary physicians become serial killers because they learn how to do it, become proficient at it, and find it easy because they have the means to do it.

Most experts would agree that healthcare serial killers are psychopaths. Ramsland (2007) stated that most psychopaths are "narcissistic, impulsive and callous, with a tendency to divert blame from themselves to others." Ramsland (2007) adds,

> From brain scan studies, it appears that they fail to process the emotional content of situations, such as empathy, concern or alarm, and tend to seek arousal. Their offenses are more brutal than those of other criminals, more aggressive and more diverse. They also represent a high percentage of repeat offenders. They're resistant to therapy and intolerant of frustration. It doesn't matter whom they hurt; what matters is that they get what they can for themselves. They find victims easily because they are glib, charming and predatory, while their victims are generally trusting, vulnerable and naïve. Psychopaths don't suffer from fear of consequences because unless it's immediate and severe, the idea of punishment has little impact on them. (Interview with author.)

As Kaplan (2009) notes,

> Serial killing is the hallmark of the psychopath, a character incapable of remorse, lacking empathy for other people's feelings and driven solely by the desire to reward his or her own needs. What is not recognized is that there are varying degrees of psychopathy and some individuals combine a high intelligence with an ability to manipulate others to advance their career. A certain degree of ruthlessness, after all, is no handicap in climbing the academic or clinical ladder, and the authoritarian and hierarchical nature of medicine is nothing but encouraging for the career development of such individuals. However, unleashed psychopathic drives can easily turn to seeking the ultimate sensation for emotionally numb individuals: the power over life and death, the all-too-frequent opportunities provided by medicine to usurp this power for personal thrill—first by chance, then by experimentation, finally by compulsion to re-experience a sensation that requires constant killing. (p. 24)

Citing the work of psychiatrist Robert Jay Lifton, Ramsland (2007) posits that healthcare serial killers have personality mechanisms known as "doubling" that help allow them to kill: "According to Lifton, a person is capable of existing as two independently functioning wholes so that a 'part-self' can act as an entire self, each part surfacing according to the demands of the situation. This is no disassociative identity disorder in which the person has two functional personalities, nor a schizophrenia psychosis. Doubling is instead an adaptive mechanism that under certain conditions can assist any of us to survive, but it can also serve nefarious purposes."

Lifton coined the term the *protean self*, named after the Greek Sea God Proteus who could take on many forms. As Lifton (1993) explains, "The protean self emerges from confusion, from the widespread feeling that we are losing our psychological moorings. We feel ourselves buffeted about by unmanageable historical forces and social uncertainties...we readily come to view ourselves as unsteady, neurotic or worse. But rather than collapse under these threats and pulls, the self turns out to be surprisingly resilient." According to Lifton (2000), it is the opposing self that can win dominance over an individual: "In doubling, one part of the self 'disavows' another part. What is repudiated is not reality itself...but the meaning of the reality." Lifton (2000) added, "Doubling is an active psychological process, a means of adaptation to extremity.... The adaptation requires a dissolving of 'psychic glue' as an alternative to a radical breakdown of the self." Lifton (2000) also goes on to explain that "Doubling is the psychological means by which one invokes the evil potential of the self. That evil is neither inherent in the self nor foreign to it. To live out the doubling and call forth the evil is a moral choice for which one is responsible, whatever the level of consciousness involved."

Ramsland (2007) relates Lifton's theory to healthcare professionals: "Doctors or nurses who double in order to kill use their clinical distance as a way to redistribute their sense of morality to accommodate their killing. To some extent, they're aware of what they're doing but they fail to consider the meaning of their deeds…they possess no sense of integrity and each part of the doubled self acts according to its own situational demands and opportunities. In fact, many healthcare serial killers are quick to claim they're being victimized." Ramsland (2007) adds, "The doubled self is responsible for what it does, and if murder becomes necessary in their minds, or desirable, then it can be misinterpreted in such a way as to ensure that it be repeated. Doubled doctors or nurses can view themselves as compassionate and humane, yet still go out and kill." According to Ramsland (2007), Lifton describes three types of *doubling*: "The limited doubler kills only under certain permissible circumstances. Such as financial or personal need; the conflicted doubler feels guilty but still kills; and the enthusiastic doubler is pleased to know that he can kill, get away with it, and still function normally. Lifton states that only psychopathic individuals can double for long periods without emotional harm and it is the psychopathic individuals who are enthusiastic doublers. In fact, psychopaths suffer no remorse and have no trouble killing to achieve their personal goals as often as they can."

Another theory is that healthcare serial killers may have what psychologist Al Carlisle terms as a "compartmentalized self," as Ramsland (2007) explains, "a public persona that appears to others to be adaptive and a darker side that allows murderous fantasies free reign." Ramsland (2007) adds:

> As with Lifton's doubler, the compartmentalized killer allows the expression of unacceptable impulses, desires and aspirations to become an equal with his or her more appropriate persona. Then as normal life grows more boring, frustrating or disappointing, the powerful and unrestricted fantasy life becomes more attractive. Eventually, with mental rehearsal, the brutal dimension gains greater substance and unrestricted fantasy feeds an unquenchable habit.… Acting out the fantasy can feel powerful or satisfying as it displaces remorse, self-hate or guilt. With no effective inhibitions, the hunt for victims begins again. When it becomes overly compulsive, it can psychologically overwhelm the killer, leading to decompensation, carelessness and mistakes. Many healthcare serial killers grow bolder and more daring, taking greater risks and thus often they make the mistakes that alert others to their spate of murders. (p. 163)

Factitious Disorders and Healthcare Professionals

As discussed, some experts believe that healthcare professionals exhibit symptoms of factitious disorder or Munchausen syndrome by proxy (MSBP), mental conditions that allow them to twist reality to justify their deeds. The term *factitious disorder* (FD) refers to the psychiatric condition in which an individual presents with an illness that is deliberately produced or falsified for the purpose of masquerading as medically afflicted. The most common ways of faking illness include making false claims about one's medical history, combining this factitious history with falsified physical manifestations of symptoms, and blending a factitious history with behaviors that actually induce illness or injury. Healthcare professionals with FD feign or exaggerate their symptoms; healthcare providers with FD by proxy feign or exaggerate symptoms in their patients. As difficult as this may be to believe, some healthcare professionals see the act of harming their patients as the perfect vehicle through which to achieve the attention they crave. As Leamon et al. (2004) explained, "Factitious disorder is characterized by a person intentionally fabricating or inducing signs or symptoms of other illnesses solely to become identified as 'ill' or as a 'patient.' The concept became firmly established in modern medical thinking in 1951 when Richard Asher (1951) described what has since been classified as a subtype of factitious disorder, Munchausen syndrome."

In 1995, the fourth edition of the *Diagnostic and Statistical Manual of Mental Disorders* included a definition for *factitious disorder by proxy*, which is now the accepted psychiatric category for MSBP: "Intentional production or feigning of physical or psychological signs or symptoms in another person who is under the individual's care. The motivation for the perpetrator's behavior is to assume the sick role by proxy. External incentives for the behavior, such as economic gain, avoiding legal responsibility or improving physical well-being, are absent."

Some experts believe there is a connection between this controversial FD affecting mothers who intentionally harm their children, and a compulsion by some healthcare providers to harm their patients. In 1977, British pediatrician Samuel Roy Meadow rose to fame for an academic paper he wrote to document a new form of child abuse; he named it MSBP after the syndrome that first had been reported by Asher. He believed that "one sudden infant death is a tragedy, two is suspicious and three is murder until proved otherwise" and this axiom became known as Meadow's Law (Fish et al., 2005).

Repper (1995) said that although knowledge about the incidence of this syndrome is widespread, less is known about healthcare providers who manifest the behavior: "It was not until the Beverly Allitt case in the United Kingdom in 1993 that this syndrome was used to explain the behavior of a healthcare worker who harmed people in his/her care. However, a review of available details of previous healthcare workers accused of murder reveals that five shared some of the distinctive features of MSBP. Although care must be taken when applying diagnoses, in view of the risk of morbidity and mortality which MSP poses for the people involved, it is important that healthcare workers become more informed and involved in understanding and detecting MSBP." Allitt is not alone in the ranks of healthcare professionals with MSBP; as Feldman and Eisendrath (1996) pointed out, "Genene Jones, the Texas nurse, has been described as having a history of self-injurious behavior, a desperate craving for attention, a need to be in control, and an intense attraction to the world of healthcare. Jones exhibited the same dualities seen in the FDP mothers—personal feelings of disdain and triumph over the baffled physicians and a coexisting, almost obsequious dedication to the healthcare team."

Yorker (2006) addressed the fact that maternal MSBP has crossed over to professional factitious disorder by proxy in healthcare professionals:

> Meadow (1977) listed having a previous history of feigning or inducing one's own illness as a risk factor in individuals who later develop MSBP. Of the unusual cluster of adverse patient outcomes associated with the presence of a nurse, at least five of the nurses convicted of murder have a history that suggests they showed signs of having a factitious disorder. Although the term MSBP has traditionally been reserved for family caretakers, there is now sufficient anecdotal evidence to suggest using a child or helpless dependent as a "proxy" for fabricated or induced illness is not isolated to familial caregivers and can occur in professional settings. (pp. 82–86)

Rosenberg (1987, cited in Yorker, 2006) discovered that some maternal perpetrators with MSBP had nursing training or were medical office workers. Feldman and Eisendrath (1996) noted, "Babysitters, foster mothers and other caregivers have been perpetrators in some FDP cases. People in these roles are the logical extensions of mothers who perpetrate. It is less clear in the individual cases of healthcare professionals—nurses, physicians and nurses aides—whether they are compelled by the usual dynamics of FDP or whether they are simply serial murderers who perpetrated in the course of employment" (p. 163). Feldman and Eisendrath (1996) observed further:

> Meadow (1994) has stated that the term Munchausen syndrome by proxy can be appropriately applied when illness in the child is invented by a parent or other caregiver; the child is presented for medical assessment and care, usually persistently, often resulting in multiple medical procedures; the perpetrator, at least initially, denies inventing or causing the child's illness; and the signs and symptoms diminish greatly or cease when the child separated from the perpetrator. If the term 'dependent person' is substituted for child, then indeed all these criteria are met in many cases of nurses convicted of serial murder: the nurse invents the patient's illness; the patient typically experiences multiple cardiac arrests and resuscitations; the nurse initially denies any wrongdoing; and the epidemics cease when the culpable nurse is removed from the patient-care area. (p. 164)

Feldman and Eisendrath (1996) pointed to several examples of FDP behavior in healthcare professionals. In one case, the Illinois Board of Nursing had previously suspended the license of a nurse convicted in Florida because she had stabbed herself with scissors and had required treatment for Munchausen. This information never made it across state lines, and she was able to pass a background check and obtain a Florida nursing license. She was observed to be an exemplary nurse at her job at a nursing home, but then suddenly seven patients died within 10 days. Then suddenly five more patients died within hours of each other. This nurse reported being stabbed by a prowler, but the next day she was fired from her position after it was determined that the injury had been self-inflicted. The state department of health noted that the death rate for the month at the nursing home had been 25 percent, a significant increase. A criminal investigation was launched when a patient who had been critically ill had to be treated for an unexplained insulin shock. The investigation revealed that this nurse had been on duty during seven of the shifts on which a terminal event began, and that she had been on duty 4 to 8 hours before the onset of four other terminal events. The story of her life began to unfold when it was discovered that she had overdosed with psychotropic medications her young son on three separate occasions and that the child had almost died from one overdose, thus triggering action from child protective services. Her ex-husband had reported issues with her mental stability. The nurse's medical records revealed that she had been hospitalized for broken limbs, surgeries, and ulcers, and had made a claim to worker's compensation for an on-the-job injury.

In another case study, a male nurse in California with a history of factitious illness and the obsession with becoming a physician, was particularly excited during codes—other nurses described him as getting an emotional high from it. He received a great deal of satisfaction from being in charge and predicting which patients would die and when. The nurse had worked at several hospitals and nursing homes when a supervisor detected too many unexplained codes, clustered around the times when the nurse was on duty. Bodies were exhumed, and investigators found lidocaine concentrations in tissue that was too large to have been accidental. In the trash bags of units on which the nurse worked were syringes of lidocaine, labeled by the nurse. As many as 27 deaths were linked to his care; he was found guilty of 12 deaths in two hospitals and was sentenced to death.

Feldman and Eisendrath (1996) pointed to several themes that emerge among nurse-induced epidemics, including denial upon confrontation: "Though literature on FDP describes varied reactions of mothers when confronted, the usual reaction is one of denial...whereas there were occasional confessions, with statements such as 'I was only trying to help the patients' or 'I just needed to appear competent,' confrontation is most notable for continued emphatic denial, even while the nurses are serving jail sentences. The nurses who continue their denial are similar to mothers with FDP who blame hospital staffs for their children's ongoing difficulties. Both convicted nurses and mothers have claimed to be scapegoats for shoddy medical diagnostics or iatrogenic patient incidents" (p. 171).

Feldman and Eisendrath (1996) also asserted that there are similar personality traits exhibited by those with FDP: "Mothers with FDP have been described as exploitive, sadomasochistic, attention-seeking, and wildly erratic in their attitudes toward and relationships with others. The same descriptors have often been used to apply to nurses convicted of serial murder." This attention-seeking is a common thread, something that Feldman and Eisendrath (1996) called "the overriding feature that links the FDP literature with the nurses and other healthcare professionals accused of serial murder" (p. 171).

Lest one think that healthcare professionals with factitious disorder or MSBP are incompetent or insane, Yorker (2006) asserted, "There has been no evidence of psychosis or decreased mental competence in persons diagnosed with Munchausen syndrome ... factitious disorders are conceptualized in the literature as predominantly consciously motivated, carefully and intelligently crafted, and quite believable until diagnostic technology shows inconsistencies that could not occur unless deliberate interference took place" (pp. 82–86).

Nursing, forensic criminology, and law expert Beatrice Crofts Yorker, JD, MS, RN, dean and professor at the College of Health and Human Services at California State University Los Angeles, said she believes "most healthcare serial killers have classic personality disorders." Yorker added, "People like this are going to kill in their homes, in the workplace, and anywhere that they have relationships. What we've found in our research of serial killers in healthcare is that they do perpetrate in their personal world as well."

There is some disagreement among contemporary experts as to the reasons why healthcare professionals kill their patients. Former nurse Paula Lampe, who has studied healthcare serial killers and the case of Lucy Quirina de Berk, a nurse in The Netherlands who was charged with 18 counts of murder and attempted murder at four hospitals (and was convicted in 2003 of the murders of three elderly women and a child), believes de Berk is a victim of what she calls the Mother Teresa syndrome—when caregivers become addicted to the feeling of being needed. As Ramsland (2007) explains, "This syndrome ranges from excessive self-sacrifice to outright aggression, all in the name of meeting one's personal need for love and attention. Those who suffer from Mother Teresa syndrome are typically loners or meticulous workers, and are reliable and competent. After saving a patient, they experience an emotional high, and some nurses then start putting patients at risk so they can achieve the adrenaline rush again."

Yorker states,

> I think the vast majority of people who go into the caring profession give of themselves in a very selfless way. I think that the people who cross the line are people who were personality-disordered to begin with, and it's not the caring that pushes them over the edge. Now, Paula Lampe, in her Mother Theresa syndrome, would not agree with that. Paula and I agree to disagree. I believe that these people are bad, they are not mad, as in insane, and yes, they can blame trauma, violence or neglect from their childhood, but there are lots of people who can say they have that and they ended up not hurting others as a result of their backgrounds. So I consider them to be bad, not mad, and that it's any one of a variety or mixture of personality disorders, from psychopathic, sociopathic, narcissistic, borderline or disassociative. They are very organized, calculated and shrewd. I have worked with psychotic murderers and child abusers, and they are horrified when they realize what they have done; they admit doing what they've done and I think Andrea Yates is a classic example of somebody who truly was mad, not bad, and made no attempt to hide what she did. (Interview with author.)

In 2001, Texas housewife Yates drowned her five children in a bathtub, and in 2002 she was convicted of first-degree murder and subsequently sentenced to life in prison with a possibility of parole after 40 years. Her conviction was overturned after winning an appeal, and in 2006 she was sent to a Texas state hospital after being committed by the court system.

Yorker says that remorse is not a reliable assessment of a perpetrator's guilt or innocence, and it is not a way to ascertain a healthcare serial killer's state of mind either at the time of the murder or after its occurrence. "How do you actually assess remorse?" Yorker asks. "I have worked with people who have cried alligator tears of remorse, but the remorse is that they got caught. The remorse is the sadness over how their life has been destroyed once they are caught and punished. Some perpetrators require a 12-step type of intervention to get them to admit that they are 100 percent to blame, no one else is to blame, that they are the ones who got themselves in prison, and that there are other people that they have hurt way more than they are hurting."

Detection of Medical Murder: Suspicious Deaths and Mortality Patterns

Kizer and Yorker (2010) explain the epidemiology of medical murder:

> Healthcare serial murders share common characteristics of setting, circumstance and psychopathology that differentiate them from other homicides or

serial murders, including: the murders, or attempted murders, are of patients in a healthcare setting; the perpetrator of the crime is employed by the medical facility where the incident occurs; the malicious acts occur consequent to the healthcare worker's duties; two or more patients are affected in separate incidents that span a period of time that is almost always longer than 30 days; and the perpetrator has the psychological capacity for committing additional malicious acts affecting patients. The last characteristic is usually determined during the investigation of a suspicious incident.

Detection of medical murder is challenging in part because, as we have seen, healthcare is a convoluted, chaotic environment with plenty of places for perpetrators to hide. Ramsland (2007) states that certain conditions in healthcare lend themselves to providing a safe haven for murderers; these include the following:

- Disbelief or denial that a serial murderer could be preying on patients.
- Lack of cooperation from hospital administration or law enforcement.
- Murder weapons that are challenging to detect.
- Readily available narcotics in doses and mechanisms that can kill.
- Lack of personnel or time with which to conduct detailed analysis of mortality patterns.
- Lack of supervision or oversight on some shifts or in some units.
- Lack of training in identifying red flags or suspicious behaviors.
- Lack of training in evidence collection, preservation, and documentation.
- Punishment of whistle-blowers.
- Superficial nature of background checks.
- Reluctance of facilities to share poor performance reviews with healthcare professionals' prospective employers.
- Lack of central reporting databases for problematic nurses.

Some of these issues will be explored more fully in Chapter 6.

All of these factors notwithstanding, why do murderous epidemics go undetected? The answer is that they can be surprisingly difficult to detect, if healthcare institutions do not know or do not heed the warning signs. Murder of patients is not an everyday expected occurrence, and few healthcare institutions are prepared for this situation. There is the added danger of apathy toward medical murder. For the very reason that it is not an everyday occurrence, there may be the assumption that it is not something to worry about. After all, in hospitals every day, patients are more likely to experience medication errors, contract an infection, or experience some other adverse event, rather than have an attempt taken on their life. However, it would be all too easy to pretend that murder in hospitals does not exist. It is these "quiet killings" that deserve greater attention. As Thunder (2003) stated, "Quiet killings have occurred, and are occurring, in our medical facilities. Quiet killings make headlines, but then they recede from our memory. They do not seem to have prompted any sustained public discussion. Apparently, as a nation we are blithely confident that these cases are fairly idiosyncratic, but there is no justification for this confidence."

As Ramsland (2007) has noted, "We need to deal with these cases in a pre-emptive fashion, not after the fact, and we can. But to do so means erasing some of the institutional self-protective devices that have given these people shelter and assistance. Admitting that medical institutions are vulnerable to the invasion, and even the making, of a predator is a fact; only if we accept that fact and work to change it will we ensure that we make healthcare serial killers either less effective in the future or less likely to exploit the medical system" (p. 129).

As Kizer and Yorker (2010) note, "Based on the relatively small number of deaths known to be caused by HCSM one might reasonably conclude that it is not a significant healthcare problem compared to many others, which probably explains why so little has been done to address the problem" (pp. 186–191). Thunder (2003) adds that society can be complacent about medical murder; he points to the official report on Shipman that blithely observed, "Everything points to the fact that a doctor with the sinister and macabre motivation of Harold Shipman is a once-in-a-lifetime occurrence." The truth is that "There have been outbreaks of nursing murder in many different hospitals in the last quarter of a century," Dalrymple (2001) observed, adding, "They are often surprisingly difficult to detect. Indeed, many may have gone completely undetected. During the 1980s, the *New England Journal of Medicine* and the *Journal of the American Medical Association* published several articles about epidemics of unexpected cardiopulmonary arrest in hospital intensive care units, usually coming to the cryptic conclusion that patients were 47.5 times as likely to have had a cardiopulmonary arrest while a certain nurse (who could not be named for obvious legal reasons) was on duty as when any other nurse was on duty."

Sometimes other medical reasons can masquerade as the appearance of medical murder. Winnowing murder as a cause of death from numerous other plausible explanations is a challenge for medicolegal and law enforcement experts. As Dalrymple (2001) notes:

> One of the most notorious outbreaks occurred in Toronto in 1980 and '81, in the cardiology ward of the famous Hospital for Sick Children. The death rate suddenly increased by four times in Ward 4A. High levels of digoxin were found in the blood of four of the deceased children, and it was estimated that, during the epidemic of sudden and unexpected death, the children in Ward 4A were 64.5 times as likely to die when Nurse A was on duty as when any

other nurse was on duty. She was arrested but released 45 days later for lack of evidence. The police, however, sought no other suspect. In fact, Nurse A may have been innocent, and the deaths may have been no murder. The high digoxin level found after the deaths of the children may have been an artifact of the methods used to detect the drug. In those days, the rubber in syringes and other medical apparatus was manufactured using a potentially toxic substance that could have killed the children, either directly or by allergic reaction to it. To this day, therefore, the deaths at the Hospital for Sick Children have not been satisfactorily explained, and these doubts (which are similar to those that accompany several other such epidemics in hospitals) have been used to suggest that the very concept of mass murder by nurses is a reversion to the medieval witch mania or to the Salem trials of the 1690s. American courts have ruled that epidemiological evidence—that an excess of deaths in a hospital ward when a particular nurse was on duty—is not sufficient to convict, even when there is also evidence that a fatal substance was administered.

In their review of 37 U.S. healthcare serial killers, Kent and Walsh (2004) point out, "It was common for older victims to fall through the cracks of our death investigation and reporting systems, mainly because all of these healthcare victimizations were initially recorded as 'natural' deaths, primarily because they occurred in a hospital and/or under the active care of a physician." That is exactly why Harold Shipman, the British doctor, was able to continue his killing spree for so long. As O'Neill (2000) notes, "Like many single-handed doctors, Harold Shipman had over 3,000 patients in his care.… Until the suspicions began to gather that eventually led to his prosecution, few concerns were raised about his clinical competence."

In so many of the healthcare serial killer cases, the perpetrators were able to carry out their dastardly deeds for a shockingly long time before suspicion was ever raised. As Kizer and Yorker (2010) point out, "Episodes of healthcare serial murder have often spanned prolonged periods of time (sometimes decades), involved large numbers of victims before being recognized, were perpetrated by the same individual in multiple settings and/or geographic locations, and were suspected by co-workers long before any formal investigation was undertaken. These characteristics highlight significant vulnerabilities in health care safety systems, including problems in sharing information about potentially problematic healthcare workers, delayed recognition and inadequate investigation of suspicious incidents, inconsistent or ineffective methods of monitoring and evaluating important care-related adverse events, and an incomplete understanding of the causes of these occurrences."

The implicit trust that people have in healthcare professionals is most likely the reason why investigations are not launched until so much damage is already done. And much of the murdering can be accomplished under the guise of medical care and treatment, further obfuscating the crime. One of the most common aspects of medical murder is the issuance of a falsified or

vague certificate of death to deflect the real cause of death and the acceptance of such a certificate by the medical examiner or coroner. As O'Neill
(2000) notes, "Having murdered these patients, Shipman issued a certificate of the cause of death, which in every case was accepted by the registrar. Should his crimes have been detected at this stage? Doctors attending
patients during their last illnesses must issue a certificate giving the cause
of death to the best of their knowledge. The information on death certificates is often not accurate, especially when compared with information
from necropsy. Many patients die of chronic disease and characterizing the
immediate cause of death might require investigations that seem meddle-
some. An underlying acceptance of the limits of accuracy when certifying
the cause of death is one factor that allowed Shipman to go undetected for
so long. None of the deaths with which Shipman was charged was reported
to the coroner. Coroners make their own rules on the categories of death
they require to have reported to them, and the registrar of births, marriages
and deaths is the only person with a legal duty to report deaths to the coroner. It has repeatedly argued that although in practice doctors do report
deaths directly to the coroner, a statutory duty should be placed on them
to do so in specified circumstances and that these circumstances should be
defined and agreed nationally. Similar duties should be imposed on nurses
and undertakers if they suspect that the death warrants investigation."

Smith (2002) notes that the Harold Shipman case "sent shock waves of
revulsion and disbelief though UK society" and that,

> The notion that a doctor could repeatedly, systematically and callously mur-
> der patients in his care shattered the assumptions that many held about
> healthcare professionals. As terrible as Shipman's actions were, they raised
> quite fundamental questions about how a doctor could kill patients over such
> a long period without being detected and stopped. As such, Shipman served
> to surface a much wider sense of malaise within the health service.... What
> the Shipman murders do illustrate, along with a number of other events con-
> cerning problem doctors, are the difficulties facing a health service that, until
> the turn of the millennium, had failed to adequately address the problems
> of rogue doctors. Shipman proved to be one of a number of trigger events
> that illustrated the fragility of the regulatory system that was in place to deal
> with medicine and, more importantly, it illustrated the importance of societal
> assumptions in the generation and incubation of that crisis. (pp. 55–74)

At the time Shipman was convicted for his crimes, authorities and medical leaders in the United Kingdom were debating the efficacy of its death
investigation system. As O'Neill (2000) explains,

> There are safeguards, to detect crime, when a body is cremated, but their
> effectiveness is questionable. For deaths not being investigated by the coroner,

permission to cremate must be applied for. The doctor who issued the death certificate must complete a form and a second doctor who has been registered for at least five years must sign a confirmatory certificate. Both doctors must see the body and the second doctor must discuss the circumstances of the death with the first. These forms are then inspected by crematorium medical referees who must be satisfied that the cause of death has been definitely ascertained. No specific training is required either for the second doctor or for crematorium referees. (pp. 329–330)

O'Neill reported that a task force that previously reported on death certification and the coronial system, recommended abolishing these safeguards because it doubted their necessity, a move opposed by the British Medical Association. But as O'Neill (2000) has pointed out, "It is tempting to think that Shipman may have been detected sooner if all those who died at his hand had undergone (autopsy); indeed, Shipman made determined efforts to avoid (autopsies). Nevertheless, (autopsies), though likely to raise questions, may not have revealed the cause of the deaths unless suspicion was high. In only 5 percent of hospital deaths can necropsy show findings that are incontrovertibly incompatible with life" (pp. 329–330).

Under the U.S. medicolegal death investigation system, any violent, sudden, or expected/suspicious death requires further investigation, as does any death that may be due entirely or in part to any factor other than natural disease. Timmermans (2006) reported that about 75 percent of U.S. deaths take place in hospitals or nursing homes, and that "about 20 percent of people die in suspicious circumstances, meaning out of place and time." Timmermans (2006) adds, "The social institutions and professionals taking care of the dying did not anticipate the death, which generates an anomalous, potentially threatening situation.... Was a traumatic death due to criminal activity?... Because of the tight medical control surrounding most terminal events, death becomes suspicious not only when crime is involved, but also when the passing escapes a medical prognosis: when people die without medical records, when they die unexpectedly under medical care, or when they die because of trauma in a medical setting" (p. 3). It is an imperfect science in the United Kingdom as well as in the United States, the latter which allows both medical personnel and laypersons to act as coroners—although many medicolegal experts prefer a transition to an all medical examiner system staffed by specially trained and uniquely qualified forensic pathologists. Regardless of this title and training differential, Lynch (2006) states, "Their responsibility is to determine the cause and circumstances of death, provide a comprehensive scene investigation, request a post-mortem evaluation as required, and notify the next of kin. This requires a systematic and methodical approach to confirm or rule out events disclosed prior to, during and immediately after death occurs. A miscarriage of justice often results where specific knowledge related to the medical, legal and social aspects of death investigation does not exist."

Most deaths occurring in hospitals are the result of a natural, expected disease progression or from trauma received outside of the healthcare institution but treated in the hospital emergency department. However, the focus of this chapter is the death that is suspected to have been committed at the hands of the healthcare professional. Determining whether or not there is a medical serial killer in a healthcare institution requires time and diligence on the part of clinical investigators, and it is a process that can be hampered by the healthcare machine. As Yorker (2006) states, "Factors that contribute to prolonged epidemics with no criminal convictions include the difficulty in establishing clusters of adverse outcomes in a timely fashion, the prevalence of temporary agency staff, the lack of sophisticated forensic toxicology input, a general reluctance on the part of healthcare professionals to suspect a provider as the cause of an epidemic, and the need to obtain evidence before making accusations" (pp. 83–86). (In another section, we will look at treating the hospital room as a crime scene.)

One of the key indicators of the presence of a medical murderer is curious morbidity and mortality patterns on a particular unit or ward. As both Yorker (1994) first surmised and as Kent and Walsh (2004) explained, "Several recent cases were brought to light purely through analytical examination of historical mortality figures that identified the exact shift and precise department where the abnormally high patient-deaths were occurring. Since hospitals no longer routinely perform autopsies, the only method of raising legitimate suspicion was by the linkage between the out of proportion mortality data that clustered by ward and time of day. Rate ratios and relative risk appraisals have been employed to ascertain the frequencies at which patients seized while the various nursing complements were on duty, compared to when each worker was off duty" (pp. 103–111). And as Yorker (2006) observed, "studies have concluded that the presence of a specific healthcare provider was associated with increased numbers of deaths and cardiopulmonary arrests. Additionally, toxicology studies performed following resuscitative efforts revealed the presence of lethal levels of medication commonly found on hospital units" (pp. 83–86).

The cases of physician murderers Harold Shipman and Michael Swango got the medical community wondering if monitoring mortality rates in healthcare institutions could be one way to detect patterns of behavior more quickly. Guthrie et al. (2008) pondered whether mortality rate monitoring could be shown to be workable in detecting a future mass murderer in general practice. Researchers conducted an analysis of routine general practice data combined with estimation of control chart effectiveness in detecting a medical murderer in a simulated dataset. Practice stability was calculated from routine data to determine feasible lengths of monitoring. A simulated data set of 405,000 patients was created, registered with 75 practices whose underlying mortality rates varied with the same distribution as case-mix-adjusted mortality in all Scottish practices. The sensitivity of each chart to detect five and 10 excess deaths was examined in repeated simulations. The sensitivity of control charts to excess deaths in simulated data, and the number of alarm signals when control charts were applied to routine data were estimated. Monitoring mortality over 3 years, charts were most sensitive but only reliably achieved a little more than 50 percent successful detection for 10 excess deaths per year and generated multiple false alarms (less than 15 percent). Guthrie et al. (2008) concluded that at best, mortality monitoring can act as a backstop to detect a particularly prolific serial killer when other means of detection have failed. They say policy should focus on changes likely to improve detection of individual murders, such as reform of death certification and the coroner system.

Aylin et al. (2003) also sought to investigate if by use of data on annual deaths a problematic physician or clinician could be detected. The researchers looked at whether using cumulative sum charts (a type of statistical process control chart) could be used to create a workable monitoring system. On such charts, they asserted, thresholds for deaths can be set, which, if crossed, may indicate a potential problem. They selected thresholds based on empirical calculations of the probabilities of false and successful detection after allowing for multiple testing over physicians or practices. Of 1,009 family physicians in the United Kingdom, 33 (including Harold Shipman) crossed the alarm threshold designed to detect an increase in standardized mortality, with 97 percent successful detection and a 5 percent false-alarm rate. Aylin et al. (2003) stated that poor data quality, plus factors such as the proportion of patients treated by these physicians in nursing homes or hospices are likely explanations for most of these additional alarms, but if used appropriately, such charts represent a useful tool for monitoring deaths in primary care. However, improvement in data quality is essential.

Whether or not monitoring mortality data can help detect a serial killer, the fact remains that many deaths are simply not investigated as they should be, especially depending on the type of healthcare institution. Oversight of nursing homes, up until very recently when the Centers for Medicare and Medicaid Services (CMS) launched its databank of nursing homes to create greater transparency for the public, was not perceived as stringent in many states. Gruszecki et al. (2004) pointed out that despite death being one of the most common reasons for discharge from a nursing home, fewer than 1 percent of nursing home resident deaths are autopsied. Gruszecki et al. (2004) conducted a retrospective review of all decedents in an Alabama county in 2001 in which death certificate data indicated that 995 deaths occurred in nursing homes. Of those 995 deaths, 119 (12 percent) were reported to the county coroner's or medical examiner's office.

The researchers report that jurisdiction was accepted in five cases in which the circumstances already made clear that the death was a nonnatural event. In the remaining 96 percent of nursing home deaths reported to the medical examiner, the statements of the reporting person were taken to be true concerning the expected nature of the death. An independent scene evaluation was provided by a police officer or paramedic in 82 percent of the cases reported to the medical examiner's office. As Gruszecki et al. (2004) stated, "Elderly individuals, as a group, are expected to die, but the death of a particular elder may or may not be expected. In our jurisdiction, only 12 percent of all nursing home deaths are reported to our office, and only 4 percent of reported deaths are actively investigated. Actively investigating each nursing home death would overwhelm the resources currently available to our office. We advocate the study and development of criteria to aid in determining whether the death of an individual elder is sudden and unexpected" (pp. 209–212). If mortality data and surveillance do not turn up a medical serial murderer, Yorker said it is the right thing to do to help uncover other adverse events. "Hospitals should conduct surveillance and examine their mortality patterns anyway," Yorker said, "even if they are not looking for healthcare serial killers because they should have dashboard indicators of trends in risk management in general. And if they are good at that in the first place, they will be very proactive in catching any potential pattern caused by a human being." She added, "I actually think serial murder by healthcare professionals is on the wane in the United States, and I think that it is because hospitals have better surveillance."

Kent and Walsh (2004) emphasized the importance of recognizing an epidemic for what it is in a timely fashion: "In one southern U.S. Air Force base hospital 32 infants barely survived near-lethal lidocaine attacks that left each with neurological damage. Top military brass never invited the CDC or FBI to assist them and ultimately allowed the enlisted technician off the hook, despite having to pay $ 27 million in injury claims.... In spite of the insidious lack of official cooperation by some hospital administrators, federal epidemiologists from the CDC were usually successful in identifying the cause of a mysterious epidemic as having resulted from the intentional acts of a staff caregiver" (pp. 103–111).

Once clinical investigators ascertain that morbidity and mortality figures indicate an inordinately elevated death incidence, epidemiologists should start their search for the source and cause. As Kent and Walsh (2004) explained, "The first indicator is usually a suspicious cluster of patient deaths that can be associated with one particular shift. Elderly patients with do-not-resuscitate chart entries and those experiencing multiple codes are generally at elevated risk. In a few cases studied, the average monthly mortality may have been about 2.5 deaths by unit, yet administrators and front-line managers were reluctant to cry out when the monthly average jumped between 10 to 15 ICU deaths" (pp. 103–111). There have been numerous suspicious death clusters that emerged upon investigation of some of the most notorious cases of medical serial murderers. Kent and Walsh (2004) inventoried these incidents, which include 35 patients in Michigan who stopped breathing on 51 occasions in just 6 weeks, as well as 67 patient deaths in a 5-month period in Indiana which averaged out to be one death for every 23.1 hours the suspect worked; in this case, patients were 49.2 times more likely to die when the suspect was on duty.

Thunder (2003) points to the case of Orville Lynn Majors, in which the death rate in an intensive care unit shot up from an average of 26 per year to 101 in 1994: "The director of the intensive care unit of Vermillion County Hospital, on her own initiative, started tracking mortalities and shifts. A nurse in the intensive care unit independently started to mark the deaths on her personal calendar. Similarly, in the case of Gilbert, staff members became suspicious based on the number of deaths on the evening shift. People die suddenly and unexpectedly, yet autopsies reveal no natural cause of death."

Of course, concrete evidence is a must in order to raise and investigate suspicions. As Park and Khan (2002) observe,

The British legal system so far has refused to declare guilt by association; that is, a person is guilty if, on the basis of probability, they were involved at the time of a major change in a patient's condition more often than could be explained by chance alone. This sort of case control study has been used to support other evidence, but of itself, it is considered circumstantial. One of the first of these was undertaken by the CDC in response to a series of deaths in a children's cardiology ward where the epidemiological evidence showed that the relative risk of a 'terminal deterioration' was 8.2 for the nurse who was charged with murder. There was a relative risk of 64.6 for a second nurse, who has never been charged, again emphasizing the way in which the courts have viewed such epidemiological evidence. If this type of analysis can only be conducted retrospectively, how can a train of suspicious events be identified? (pp. 621–623)

Yorker (1988) identified a number of helpful factors that clinical investigators should look for, including the following:

- A significant increase in cardiopulmonary arrests or deaths, or both, particularly in patients not thought to be in immediate danger.
- An unusually high rate of successful resuscitation.
- Multiple events in the same patient.
- Events occurring more often in a particular shift. (pp. 1327–1328)

There is no guarantee that surveillance can catch all medical murderers. As O'Neill (2000) asserts,

> Deficiencies have long been recognized in the legal systems surrounding death and more rigorous procedures for certification and registration, and should at least make detection more likely and investigation more efficient and straightforward. Trust in doctors, fundamental to an effective relationship with patients, has been undermined by this case. The profession must respond robustly to show that trust is well founded. Nevertheless, although lessons can be learned and procedures tightened up, no guarantees can be given that any doctor, nurse or other clinician could not if sufficiently determined and perverse repeat Shipman's crimes. In the investigation following the Allitt murders the Clothier Committee concluded that "a determined and secret criminal may defeat the best regulated organization in the pursuit of his or her purpose." It is difficult to envisage any set of laws or regulations that will guarantee that the acts of a criminal as experienced, knowledgeable, cool, and determined as Shipman can be prevented in the future. (pp. 329–330)

In the wake of the Shipman case, Dyer (2000) reported that "Changes expected to follow include closer monitoring of general practitioners—particularly single-handed practitioners—by health authorities; greater controls to prevent the stockpiling of drugs (Shipman had enough diamorphine to kill 1,500 patients); more stringent requirements on general practitioners who countersign other doctors' cremation certificates; and wider powers for coroners."

In terms of what action should be taken if a healthcare provider is suspected of harming patients, Park and Khan (2002) note,

> Legally, responsibility for the investigation of suspicious deaths rests with the coroner and the police; however, it is the healthcare professionals who will be the first to raise suspicion. An awareness of those features that might indicate foul play is needed. They should make detailed records about the nature of the event and the persons present, take great care to preserve potential evidence such as infusion sets and consider taking specimens for later toxicological analysis. From an institutional perspective, the issues may be different; there is the concern of damage limitation in respect to not only patients, but also the institution itself and to other members of staff. (pp. 621–623)

Park and Khan (2002) stated that a postinvestigation report on the Beverly Allitt case

> …Suggested that people working with vulnerable patients should undergo pre-employment screening to detect those who were felt to pose significant risk—particularly mental health problems. However, mental illness is not thought to be a major factor in those cases currently in the public domain and

therefore the positive predictive value of such information is limited. Such strategies discriminate against people with any mental illness; even if it is not relevant in the day-to-day performance of a job. The best way to deal with this seems to be prevention; an awareness of the possibility and improving practices such as the use of nurse-controlled and dangerous drugs, two staff signatures for every potentially harmful treatment and a willingness to react rapidly to any concerns. New technology will also reduce the risk—such as patient-controlled analgesia systems to give intermittent bolus doses of morphine rather than having syringes at the end of the bed. Such measures should also raise standards of care generally and thereby minimize the chance of a genuine mistake. Healthcare workers who harm patients intentionally are rare, although the practice of euthanasia may be relatively common. Anyone who is sufficiently determined can circumvent the detection and investigation procedures. The best strategy is to implement procedures that improve the quality of care and will minimize harm to patients. The intensive care nurse who murders a patient is exceedingly rare, but there is great scope for this type of accusation in this environment. (pp. 621–623)

Complacency can be a hospital's worst enemy in the identification of medical serial murderers, and the Genene Jones case is one of the best examples of this. King (1983) reported that physicians and staff members at a hospital under investigation for possible multiple infant homicides were aware of a significant increase in infant deaths for as long as a 2-year period. From November 1981 to February 1983, Bexar County Medical Center conducted three inquiries into the deaths in its pediatric intensive care unit, suspecting that its own employees might be responsible. King (1983) reported,

Despite the concern, no report of any suspicious or unexplained death was ever made to the county medical examiner, as the law would require, according to Dr. Vincent DiMaio, the Bexar County medical examiner who initiated the grand jury investigation. A nurse who left the hospital in March 1982 with what she termed a "great" job recommendation and took a job as a nurse in a pediatrician's office was indicted on murder and other charges after seven children treated by the pediatrician last year suffered seizures, said to have been caused by the injection of drugs. One of these children died. Dr. DiMaio said in a telephone interview that he resigned a year ago from the faculty of the University of Texas Health Science Center at San Antonio to protest what he described as a general failure of doctors to report to him any unexplained or suspicious deaths at the hospital, which is used as a teaching hospital by the Health Science Center. Jeff Duffield, a hospital spokesman, said the obligation to report unexplained deaths lay with individual physicians and not with the hospital itself, and that no such deaths had been brought to the hospital's attention. He also said, however, that the second of the hospital's three internal inquiries was "triggered by a particular doctor's complaint" that "there had been a child who died and he could not explain why."

King (1983) reported further that "DiMaio said he had made physicians at the hospital aware that state law required deaths to be reported when the cause was not certain, 'but it was just hopeless.'" Jones worked in the pediatrics intensive care unit of the hospital in the period under investigation, and was eventually indicted for injecting infants with the muscle relaxant succinylcholine, which, in excessive doses, causes respiratory failure by attacking the nervous system. Succinylcholine is very difficult to detect, and its presence is not revealed in a routine autopsy.

The Importance of the Index of Suspicion

The use by healthcare professionals of powerful, untraceable drugs such as succinylcholine against their patients underscores the need for alertness in healthcare institutions. Among nurses, this sense of intuition or knowing when something is awry is sometimes called a nurse's index of suspicion. Sullivan (2006) said this type of suspicion or intuition "involves the use of a sound, rational, relevant knowledge base in situations that, through experience, are so familiar that the person has learned how to recognize and to act on appropriate patterns. This intuition often materializes in situations where patients who are unable to communicate—those who are sedated, ventilated, etc., and they are deteriorating—the nurse's intuition can pick up on subtle, nuanced changes. Many have a forensic antenna."

The index of suspicion is most acute among a special breed of nurses, known collectively as forensic nurses, or more specifically, as clinical forensic nurses, who are specially trained in medicolegal investigations. There is a justification for the presence of forensic nurses in today's hospitals not only for the detection of medical serial murder, but, as Christ et al. (2000) found, there are a number of forensic issues that pop up in hospitals, including abuse and neglect, assault, suicide, homicide, medication or delivery system tampering, equipment tampering, and improper medication delivery, thus necessitating a hospital's emphasis on merging forensic nursing with quality management and risk management. As Sullivan (2006) explains, "The clinical forensic nurse is an essential part of any hospital team and has responsibilities that include monitoring and studying adverse events through a root cause analysis process. Adverse patient events range from accidents and therapeutic errors to the willful abuse and neglect of patients" (pp. 559–561). Sullivan (2006) added, "Recognition of both overt and subclinical abuse and neglect, as well as situations where artificial means are used to create illnesses (i.e., Munchausen's syndrome by proxy), is often obscured by the mindset of the healthcare provider who is focused on 'natural' illnesses. The astute forensic nurse practicing in a clinical setting is able to maintain a professional balance between the nursing assessment of 'natural' illness and the willingness to consider all possibilities, no matter how distasteful" (pp. 559–561).

Winfrey and Smith (1999) stated that nurses increase their suspiciousness factor and hone their intuition even while they incorporate forensic principles and practice into clinical practice. And as Sullivan (2006) added, "The importance of the rapidity of nursing response inherent in intuition cannot be overlooked or dismissed, especially as it pertains to potential forensic cases. This intuition results in definitive action and timely nursing intervention." Sullivan (2006) states that clinical forensic nurses can respond to codes and clinical deaths, often the events that can herald foul play. This nurse monitors the event and accounts for all actions taken during the code. As Sullivan (2006) noted, "The nurse ensures that ECG strips are preserved along with the sequential records of medications, airway management and other interventions such as defibrillation. In addition, all circumstances that immediately preceded the code are documented, including the names of family members and staff members present before and during the code. A standard set of laboratory specimens are typically collected, especially if the patient does not survive the resuscitation attempt. This information is archived and if a suspicious trend is later identified, more complete information is available for root cause analysis or other investigation processes."

In the event of a clinical death, the clinical forensic nurse can be on the scene to investigate. Sullivan (2006) notes, "At times, caregivers or family members may choose to hasten death as a way to end suffering, perhaps by administering a medication to depress respirations enough to cause death. This is an example of what a clinical forensic nurse may evaluate when looking at circumstances of any given death." Sullivan (2006) adds,

> Ideally, upon each death a standard set of laboratory work is collected and circumstances surrounding the patient's demise are documented. The laboratory specimens that would yield the most helpful information are blood gases, complete blood counts with differential, pertinent drug levels and EEG/ECG as well as whatever would be appropriate for the circumstance. Notations are made of the last physician order changes, medication and treatments received in the last 24 hours, any visitors and other pertinent data.... If the death is suspicious or completely unexpected, the clinical forensic nurse may opt to "freeze" the scene until further consultation with the supervisor or law enforcement. Fortunately, these events happen rarely, but it is important to have someone who realizes what may be vital evidence and to assign that person to maintain the integrity of this potential crime scene. (pp. 559–561)

As discussed, mortality patterns on a hospital ward can reveal the presence of a medical murderer, as in the Kristen Gilbert case in which she was present for 37 patient deaths and half of the medical emergencies that occurred on that unit, according to Ramsland (2007). Sullivan (2006) observed, "Had a clinical forensic nurse been in a collaborative role with quality management staff, perhaps the suspicious pattern of Gilbert being on duty for half the total number of patient deaths occurring on her ward over seven years would have indeed come to the attention of administration much sooner than it did. This type of thought process, one that at least considers the suspicious or unthinkable, is routine with a clinical forensic nurse. A statistical study used by the prosecution said that the odds that Gilbert attended so many deaths simply by chance was 1 in 100 million" (pp. 559–561).

Entertaining one's suspicions and acting upon them are two entirely different thought processes. Connecting the dots between the signs of medical murder and the investigatory steps that should be taken is a delicate and distasteful task, especially when it is not obvious that a murder has actually been committed. But sometimes it is right under investigators' noses. As Thunder (2003) states,

> Although the perpetrators, victims and killings are quiet, they are not always so hidden, so secret, they are never to be discovered. Some victims have survived attempted murders. They, relatives and nurses have seen perpetrators seek to be alone with the patient. Survivors, relatives and nurses, have seen perpetrators inject medication when there were no orders for medication. Nurses have noticed syringes left in a room. At the Gilbert trial, a nurse testified she had heard a patient yell at Gilbert, "Stop! Stop! You're killing me!"— words remembered in retrospect that were not investigated at the time. Majors used potassium chloride from the inventory of the hospital. Hospital personnel had noticed drugs missing. Gilbert also used readily available, normally life-saving, epinephrine. People inside and outside a medical facility may have heard medical employees say things like "Majors said he hated old people and thought they should be gassed."

Some healthcare institutions are recognizing the importance of having a forensic nurse on staff as a frontline defense against staff-initiated crime, especially in cases where the evidence pointing to medical murder is not so clear-cut. Goll-McGee et al. (2006) observed that "Clinical forensic nursing has come of age as a means of coping with the resultant increased complexity of nursing practice, society and the law. A living forensic population, survivors of criminal or liability-related injuries that result in an investigation by a legal agency, is being recognized by healthcare professionals in varied clinical practice environments, especially in the ED. In fact, personnel frequently interface with forensic cases and therefore have the greatest potential for evaluating the associated forensic elements."

A patient becomes a forensic patient if an act of violence or abuse or injury is perpetrated against him or her. And patients with medicolegal needs require special handling. Goll-McGee et al. (2006) state, "Once a forensic patient is recognized, four overlapping clinical practice issues are addressed. These are physical evidence collection, non-physical evidence collection, meticulous documentation and crisis intervention." According to Goll-McGee et al. (2006), physical evidence is anything that has been used, left, removed, altered, or contaminated during the commission of a crime by either the suspect or victim, and add that "The ability to recognize evidence acknowledges that it has relevance and may come in varying forms and sizes. In many situations, important information ... which may not be required for patient care is nonetheless vital to later investigation and requires the patient's consent to ensure that collection of the evidence will not amount to an illegal search (or perhaps malpractice). Proper collection of evidence is imperative to avoid the compromise of its integrity. Preservation of evidence in the clinical setting requires planning, attention to detail and the guidance of agency policies and procedures."

For many nurses, the index of suspicion kicks in as a natural part of their responsibilities, a built-in radar, so to speak. Goll-McGee et al. (2006) noted that "Non-physical evidence collection suggests the use of an index of suspicion to uncover the how and why of their mechanisms of injury. This effort involves an assessment of psychosocial history, separating the injuries from the story and asking hard questions. It looks for inconsistencies in clinical presentations. Meticulous documentation provides evidence that something is done or not done, exists or doesn't exist, it provides evidence for the client, protection for the nurse and testimony for the court. Intuition research gives the forensically educated nurse permission to trust and to act upon his or her suspicions."

Yorker (2006) also believes in the power of forensic nursing in these kinds of forensic cases: "The forensic nurse examiner as a clinical investigator is an ideal resource for epidemiological surveillance and systematic study of such incidents that may later prove to be serial in nature if not handled swiftly" (p. 86).

Red Flags Associated with Medical Murder

Ramsland (2007) notes,

> From intensive study, we now know that within the medical context, serial killers tend to show the same types of behaviors, from one to another, even if driven by different motives. Thus we can collect a list of red flags that will assist their colleagues and supervisors to recognize the behavioral and personality signals. It's not easy for anyone to accept that a co-worker might actually be a killer, and it's hard to be a whistle-blower based on suspicion alone. Yet those who are prepared and who understand the need for documentation and evidence, will realize that the phenomenon of healthcare serial killers does occur;

that healthcare serial killers are not always convicted; and that the healthcare system does provide conditions that facilitate their deadly deeds. With better awareness, the conviction rate can be improved and the facilitating conditions corrected. (p. xii)

According to Yorker et al. (2006) and Ramsland (2007), the following red flags are common to medical serial murderers:

- Statistically, there is a higher death rate when the suspected person is on shift.
- The suspect deaths were unexpected.
- The death symptoms were also not expected, given the patient's illness or procedure.
- The suspect is always available to help with patients who have crashed or coded.
- The suspect is often the last one seen with the victim.
- The suspect has moved around from one facility to another.
- Other staff members give the suspect nicknames like "death angel."
- The suspect is overly interested in death.
- Other patients have complained about the suspect's treatment of them.
- The suspect likes to predict when a patient will die.
- The suspect attempts to prevent others from checking on their patients.
- The suspect makes inconsistent statements when questioned about patient incidents.
- The suspect is in possession of questionable substances in a work locker or at home.
- The suspect is secretive or has a difficult time with personal relationships.
- The suspect has a history of some form of mental instability or depression.

"The traditional red flags are as relevant as ever, because nothing has changed," says Bruce Sackman, former special agent in charge of the Office of the Inspector General, Northeast Field Office for the U.S. Department of Veterans Affairs (VA), who was involved in the investigations of two high-profile healthcare serial killers, Michael Swango and Kristen Gilbert. The challenge is that many facilities may not know what they are and certainly might not be looking for them.

"I have talked to administrators who often have not heard of the list of red flags," says Ramsland. She continues,

They often have not seen such signals and it isn't that they're protecting their hospital's reputation, they just haven't been trained to spot these perpetrators.

After all, who thinks that someone will go into the healthcare profession as a murderer? They are not even thinking about that possibility. I think they can be excused, but the lack of training in terms of what to look for is sorely lacking in many healthcare institutions. Having said that, I do think most people want to learn more about how to look for the red flags and how to document them. The fact that they are interested in learning is a good start because it means healthcare is becoming more proactive instead of remaining reactive. (Interview with author.)

Ramsland expresses the sentiments of other experts who are incredulous at the acts of healthcare professionals who commit medical malfeasance with impunity. "Who can possibly comprehend that a person who enters into a profession where trust and nurturing are essential traits is exploiting that access in order to kill for their own benefit and gratification? I don't think it's a case of insanity because so many of them invoke the motive of mercy, so they know that what they are doing is wrong. They're not doing it out of mercy, but to satisfy their deep urges and motivations. I think it's horrifying to see egregious self-centered violence in a profession where absolute selflessness is expected. And to discover that this can go on for months or years is part of what makes it so scary; it's the unsuspected trespass, the disturbing 'the-monster-is-among-us' kind of revelation."

A Word about Mercy Killing

The subject of mercy killing and euthanasia of their patients by healthcare professionals is not within the scope of this book; however, it is one potentially criminal aspect of medicine that remains controversial. As you may remember, in 2005, in New Orleans, Louisiana, following the ravages of Hurricane Katrina, several healthcare workers were accused of hastening the deaths of patients at Memorial Hospital. CNN (2010) reported that after reviewing the disputed case of a 79-year-old woman who died at the healthcare institution in the days after Hurricane Katrina, Orleans parish coroner Frank Minyard said that he could not classify her death as a homicide. CNN reported Minyard as saying that he hopes his findings on the death of Jannie Burgess would mark "the end of the Memorial Hospital hurricane situation." Burgess' manner of death is unclassified, Minyard said, and the cause of her death undetermined.

The review was initiated after an article in *The New York Times* in August 2009 quoted a physician, Dr. Ewing Cook, who reported that morphine and other narcotics were administered to patients after Katrina struck, with hospital staff knowing that it could hasten some of their patients' deaths. CNN said that Minyard thought the woman's overall physical condition led to her death more than the narcotics did; Burgess was recovering from cancer surgery but had liver and kidney failure as well as sepsis. According to CNN (2010), Cook told the *Times* that he requested a nurse to increase Burgess' morphine and give her "enough until she goes." The *Times* quoted Cook as saying, "If you don't think that by giving a person a lot of morphine, you're not prematurely sending them to their grave, then you're a very naive doctor. We kill 'em."

Regarding Burgess, the *Times* quoted Cook as noting, "I gave her medicine so I could get rid of her faster, get the nurses off the floor.... There's no question I hastened her demise." According to CNN (2010), Minyard said he does not believe that Burgess received enough morphine to kill her.

As CNN (2010) reported,

> Charles Foti Jr., who was then the state attorney general, launched an investigation after officials from Lifecare, an acute-care facility operating on the seventh floor of Memorial, reported allegations that several seriously ill, mostly elderly patients had been euthanized by medical staff at Memorial as the floodwaters rose around the hospital and

conditions inside deteriorated. In 2006, Foti ordered the arrest of Dr. Anna Pou and two nurses, Lori Budo and Cheri Landry, on preliminary charges of second-degree murder in the deaths of four of the patients. Former Orleans Parish District Attorney Eddie Jordan, who under Louisiana law was responsible for prosecuting crimes, gave Budo and Landry immunity in exchange for their testimony. In July 2007, a grand jury refused to indict Pou. Foti said his investigation revealed that the four patients were given a "lethal cocktail" of morphine and midazolam hydrochloride, both central nervous system depressants. The patients were 63, 68, 91, and 93, he said. Pou, Landry, and Budo denied the charges, and their attorneys said they acted heroically, staying to treat patients rather than evacuate.... The grand jury never heard testimony from five specialists who advised Foti that the patients were deliberately killed with overdoses of drugs after Katrina struck. All five were brought in by Foti's office to analyze the deaths and concluded that the patients were homicide victims. After the grand jury refused to indict Pou, Jordan called the case closed and said he would no longer pursue it.... The case went to the Louisiana Supreme Court, which in July sent it back to the trial court to rule on whether criminal charges in the case are reasonably anticipated. No new trial date has been set, Lori Mince, the New Orleans attorney representing the media organization, said. Hospital workers identified only as John and Jane Does have sued to block the file's release, claiming that the records are covered by grand jury secrecy rules, that they should have been considered confidential informants and that releasing the documents would violate their privacy.

REFERENCE

CNN. "Coroner: Post-Katrina hospital death not homicide." March 11, 2010.

References

Asher R. Munchausen's syndrome. *Lancet.* 1:339–341. 1951.

Aylin P, Best N, Bottle A, and Marshall C. Following Shipman: A pilot system for monitoring mortality rates in primary care. *Lancet.* 362(9382):485–491. August 9, 2003.

Barber J. "Cause of death: Change of shift." Paper presented at Forensic Nursing Clinical Update. August 2001.

Dalrymple T. Attack of the killer nurses: A look at a curious phenomenon: Nurses who kill their patients. *National Review.* May 28, 2001. (Accessed October 23, 2010, at: http://www.politicsandcurrentaffairs.co.uk/Forum/world-events/46699-nurse-guilty-killing-patients.html.)

Dalrymple T. Attack of the killer nurses: A look at a curious phenomenon of nurses who kill their patients. *National Review.* June 20, 2009.

Dyer C. Tighter control on GPs to follow doctor's murder convictions. *British Med J.* 320(7231):331. February 5, 2000.

Feldman MD, and Eisendrath SJ. *The Spectrum of Factitious Disorders.* Arlington, VA: American Psychiatric Publishing. 1996.

Fish E, Bromfield L, and Higgins D. A new name for Manchausen syndrome by proxy: Defining fabricated or induced illness by carers. *Child Abuse Prevention Issues.* 23:1–3. Spring 2005.

Glaister J. Methods and motives. In: *The Power of Poison.* New York: William Morrow. 1954, pp. 153–182.

Goll-McGee B, Couto S, Ferrandi J, Jankowski K, Lawlor P, Luciani-McGillvray I, and Robertson M. Forensic nursing process: An evaluation of forensic patients in the clinical environment. *Forensic Nurse.* 2006. (Accessed October 23, 2010, at: http://www.forensicnursingmag.com/articles/371lifedeath.html.)

Gruszecki AC, Edwards J, Powers RE, and Davis GG. Investigation of elderly deaths in nursing homes by the medical examiner over a year. *Am J Forensic Med Path.* 25(3):209–212. September 2004.

Guthrie B, Love T, Kaye R, MacLeod M, and Chalmers J. Routine mortality monitoring for detecting mass murder in UK general practice: Test of effectiveness using modeling. *Br J Gen Pract.* 58(550):311–317. 2008.

Hickey EW. *Serial Murderers and Their Victims.* Pacific Grove, CA: Brooks & Cole. 1991.

Hockley C. Staff violence against those in their care. In: *Workplace Violence: Issues, Trends, Strategies.* Bowie V and Fisher BS, eds. Cullompton: Willan. 2005, pp. 77–96.

Holmes RM, and Holmes ST. *Murder in America.* Thousand Oaks, CA: Sage. 1993.

Kaplan RM. *Medical Murder: Disturbing Cases of Doctors Who Kill.* New South Wales: Allen & Unwin. 2009.

Keeney BT, and Heide KM. Gender differences in serial murderers. *J Interpersonal Violence.* 9:383–398. 1994.

Kent DR, and Walsh PD. Modern U.S. healthcare serial killings: An exploratory study and work in progress. In: *Linking Data to Practice in Violence and Homicide Prevention: Proceedings of the 2004 Meeting of the Homicide Research Working Group.* Bunge VP, Block CR, and Lane M, eds. Chicago: HRWG Publications. 2004.

Kerrigan S, and Goldberger BA. Forensic toxicology. In: *Forensic Nursing.* Lynch VA, and Duval JB, eds. New York: Elsevier. 2006.

King W. Questions on infant deaths beset San Antonio hospital. *The New York Times.* July 2, 1983. (Accessed October 23, 2010, at: http://www.nytimes.com/1983/07/02/US/questions-on-infant-deaths-beset-San-Antonio-hospital.html.)

Kinnell K. Serial homicide by doctors: Shipman in perspective. *British Med J.* 321:1594–1597. December 23, 2000.

Kizer KW, and Yorker BC. Healthcare serial murder: A patient safety orphan. Joint Commission. *J Qual Patient Safety.* April 2010, pp. 186–191.

Leamon MH, Feldman MD, and Scott CL. Factitious disorders and malingering. In: *Essentials of Clinical Psychiatry.* Hales RE and Yudofsky SC, eds. Arlington, VA: American Psychiatric Publishing. 2004.

Lifton RJ. *The Protean Self: Human Resilience in an Age of Fragmentation.* Chicago: University of Chicago Press. 1993.

Lifton RJ. *The Nazi Doctors: Medical Killing and the Psychology of Genocide.* New York: Basic Books. 2000.

Meadow R. Munchausen syndrome by proxy. *J Clin Forensic Med.* 1:121–127. 1994.

O'Neill B. Doctor as murderer. *British Med J.* 320:329–330. February 5, 2000.

Park GR, and Khan SN. Murder and the ICU. *Euro J Anesthes.* 19(9):621–623. September 2002.

Ramsland KM. *Inside the Minds of Healthcare Serial Killers: Why They Kill.* Westport, CT: Praeger. 2007.

Repper J. Munchausen syndrome by proxy in healthcare workers. *J Adv Nurs.* 21(2):299–304. 1995.

Schreier H. Munchausen by proxy defined. *Pediatrics.* 110(5):985–988. 2002.

Smith D. Not by error, but by design: Harold Shipman and the regulatory crisis for healthcare. *Pub Policy Admin.* 17(4):55–74. 2002.

Stark C, and Paterson B. Opportunity may be more important than profession in serial homicide. *British Med J.* 322(7292):993. April 21, 2001.

Stark C, Paterson B, Henderson T, Kidd B, and Godwin M. Counting the dead. *Nursing Times.* 93(46):34–37. 1997.

Steck-Flynn K. Just a pinch of cyanide: The basics of homicidal poisoning investigations. *Law Enforce Tech.* October 2007. (Accessed October 23, 2010, at: http://ncjrs.gov/App/publications/Abstract.aspx?id242465.)

Sullivan MK. Forensic nursing in the hospital setting. In: *Forensic Nursing.* Lynch VA, ed. New York: Mosby. 2006, pp. 559–561.

Thunder JM. Quiet killings in medical facilities: Detection and prevention. *Issues Law Med.* March 22, 2003. (Accessed October 23, 2010, at: http://accessmylibrary.com/article-1G1-100112231/quiet-killings-medical-facilities.html.)

Timmermans S. *Postmortem: How Medical Examiners Explain Suspicious Deaths.* Chicago: University of Chicago Press. 2006.

Trestrail JH III. *Criminal Poisoning: Investigational Guide for Law Enforcement, Toxicologists, Forensic Scientists and Attorneys.* New York: Humana Press. 2007.

Westveer AE, Jarvis JP, and Jensen CJ. Homicidal poisoning: The silent offense. *FBI Law Enforcement Bulletin.* August 1, 2004. (Accessed October 23, 2010, at: http://www.fbi.gov/publications/leb/2004/August04/August04leg.htm#page_2.)

Winfrey ME, and Smith AR. The suspiciousness factor: Critical care nursing and forensics. *Crit Care Nurs Q.* 22(1):1–7. May 1999.

Yorker BC. Nurses accused of murder. *Am J Nurs.* 88:1327–1328. 1988.

Yorker BC. Nurse-related homicides. In: *Forensic Nursing.* Lynch VA, and Duval JB, eds. New York: Elsevier. 2006, pp. 82–86.

Yorker BC. "Forensic nursing applications: Preventing crime in hospitals." Presentation to the Southern California Association of Healthcare Risk Managers. February 19, 2008. (Accessed October 23, 2010, at: http://www.powershow.com/view/b9a9-MZIxO/Forensic_Nursing_Applications_Preventing_Crime_in_Hospitals_Southern_California_Association_of_Healthcare.)

Yorker BC, Kizer KW, Lampe P, Forrest ARW, Lannan JM, and Russell DA. Serial murder by healthcare professionals. *J Forensic Sci.* 51(6). November 2006.

Investigations, Sanctions, and Discipline

6

Much of the killing committed by medical murderers is a covert operation, as discussed in Chapter 5, thus necessitating either eyewitnesses or other evidence. In many cases of abuse or medical murder, coworkers acting as whistle-blowers have aided investigations. As Kent and Walsh (2004) noted, "When withheld care, smothering or disconnected equipment is involved, it is impossible to establish an element of proof without witnesses. Few crime laboratories can run the variety of tests necessary to screen for all those potentially toxic substances that are readily available to healthcare workers. Without informants or whistle-blowers, successful prosecutions can be highly expensive and very difficult to obtain."

"Peer nurses are usually the first to identify something is amiss because they're so close to what has transpired," says Beatrice Crofts Yorker, RN, MS, JD, dean and professor at the College of Health and Human Services at California State University Los Angeles. "These nurses are concerned about leaving their patient with someone like Orville Lynn Majors; their patient is stable when they leave for their break, and they come back to find that their patient has crashed. They report it and then they get in trouble for doing so. It was horrible how the head nurse who tried to stop Orville Lynn Majors was treated. She was harassed and she lost her job, having been fired for insubordination because she reported it to the board of nursing."

Investigations can turn healthcare providers' lives upside down, and not just the individuals being accused of harm; Yorker (2006) has pointed to whistle-blowers who experienced immense hostility from coworkers or were fired and reinstated, only to leave for extreme stress and duress and even disability, and some were never able to work again.

"Sometimes they're the very ones who get punished for reporting," confirms Katherine Ramsland, an associate professor of forensic psychology at DeSales University, Pennsylvania. She continues:

> We have certainly seen some whistle-blowers lose their jobs when they bring suspicious activity to their hospitals' attention. We had that in the Charles Cullen case; a number of nurses brought Cullen's behavior to light and then they were shut out and ignored. And now, of course, lawsuits have been initiated over this. I think co-workers who see questionable activity do tend to tell someone, but I think when you are working alongside someone, especially if there is a lot about them that you like or you get along with them, it is hard to

start thinking of them as a murderer. And even if you do, it's hard to document because the nefarious behavior can be so secretive. The thing we have to understand here is that predators always have the advantage because they're thinking in a way that most people are not. They're always looking for opportunities; they're secretive and deceptive, they're clever, and they figure out how to get away with things and how to dupe people in the process. It's challenging when you're the person potentially being duped. It makes you think, "Am I *really* seeing what I think I'm seeing?" (Interview with author.)

"In so many cases of serial killing in hospitals, it wasn't so much the nurses failed to see what was happening and to suspect something; rather, they failed to *do* anything about it," asserts forensic nursing expert Janet Barber, RN, MSN, FAAFS, a clinical nurse consultant, author, and lecturer based in Indiana. She continues:

Nobody wants to be the whistle-blower or the tattletale. Nobody wants to be the person who steps up to the plate because the first thing that happens when you say something like, "I really have concerns about this situation," is that they begin to have concerns about *you*. When I was in the Air Force, all the managers and administrators seemed to operate under the rule that if you identified a problem, you suddenly become the problem; after all, they figure that they didn't have the problem before you told them about it. They suddenly identify you as being the problem, not the problem you are reporting. It's a strange phenomenon. So nurses are very reluctant to step forward and say, "You know I really think so-and-so is spending a lot of extra time in the medicine room and we are finding more drugs disappearing on his shift." People suddenly think to themselves, "Why are you reporting this kind of thing and what's in it for you?" Or they may be thinking, "Why do you have so much time to watch what he's doing?" Nurses are good, independent workers but they are not necessarily good managers because many of them don't want to take the responsibility for other nurses' interactions with co-workers. They don't want to be the ones who get someone else in trouble. There are numerous situations where it's almost impossible to get nurses to testify about a peer because they just don't want to be involved. I don't know how we are ever going to get away from that. I think nurses are pretty aware about what each other is doing, and they know when they feel uncomfortable and when something is not quite right. But they feel they are not equipped or confident enough in their understanding of the situation that they want to report it.... All of the signs that something is wrong are there, and there are weird things happening, and sometimes everything falls into place and you can catch the perpetrator in action. But more often than not, what happens is as the net widens, the person who is doing something wrong realizes people are watching, and the perpetrator resigns and disappears. And they go on to the next hospital where the cycle is repeated. (Interview with author.)

As we will see later in this chapter, the fact that murderers are able to move on from hospital to hospital without being stopped is a significant challenge to investigators and medical license regulators. Reluctance to report over fear of legal action also creates a chilling effect, according to Ramsland:

I think what has happened is that some laws have made it difficult for them because they can be sued if they don't have good, clear evidence.... It's very difficult to secure that kind of concrete evidence, so what are they going to do? Hospital administrators may be tempted to say, "Let that person move on" and then the healthcare provider kills somewhere else. I don't think that's their intent, but they also know if they don't have a solid case, they probably don't stand a good chance of getting anything to stick. There were extensive investigations in the Cullen case and they didn't find much evidence, but now laws are beginning to be changed to accommodate suspicions and to accommodate investigations. Back in the days when Michael Swango was working, administrators preferred to hope he just moved on and became someone else's problem, so one of the people who believed Swango was a killer started calling around and saying, "Don't hire this guy," and I think he lost his job over it. I think that people try to protect their institutions and more than that, I believe they think their hands are tied. And they are afraid of consequences if they make accusations that they can't support. So hopefully we will continue to see changes in the legal arena that allow healthcare institutions to relay their concerns and suspicions to the next employer. (Interview with author.)

Although many nurses felt as though they had been mistreated during investigations, there is a moral imperative and a professional obligation for whistle-blowing. The Code of Ethics for Nurses from the American Nurses Association (ANA) states, "When the nurse is aware of inappropriate or questionable practice in the provision of healthcare, concern should be expressed to the person carrying out the questionable practice. Attention should be called to the possible detrimental effect upon the patient's wellbeing or best interests as well as the integrity of nursing practice.... If indicated, the problem should be reported to an appropriate higher authority within the institution or to an appropriate external authority." The code adds that "There should be established processes for reporting and handling incompetent, unethical, illegal or impaired practice within the employment setting so that such reporting can go through official channels, thereby reducing the risk of reprisal against the reporting nurse. All nurses have a responsibility to assist those who identify potentially the questionable practice." It also states, "When incompetent, unethical, illegal or impaired practice is not corrected within the employment setting and continues to jeopardize patient wellbeing and safety, the problem should be reported to other appropriate authorities such as practice committees of the pertinent professional organizations, the legally constituted bodies concerned with licensing of health workers and professional practitioners, or the regulatory agencies concerned with evaluating standards of practice." Also, the code states that "Accurate reporting and factual documentation, and not merely opinion, undergird all such responsible actions. When a nurse chooses to engage in the act of responsible reporting about situations perceived as unethical, incompetent, illegal or impaired, the professional organization has a responsibility to provide the nurse with support and assistance and to protect the practice of those nurses who choose to voice their concerns." The code acknowledges that reporting "may present substantial risks to the nurse; nevertheless, such risks do not eliminate the obligation to address serious threats to patient safety."

"Nurses may know they are morally and professionally obligated to report what they believe could be malfeasance when they see it, but so many of them ignore that observation or that gut-level suspicion and don't do the responsible thing," Barber says.

> I believe what prevents nurses from doing so is the fear of paying a price with their supervisor because they have created a situation that previously was not on anyone's radar. Now, armed with this knowledge, the supervisor then must do something about it, and that makes them nervous. So it's just easier for most nurses to say to themselves, "Well, I won't identify this suspicious situation or talk about it; instead I'll just keep watching it and maybe I'm wrong," and so the situation persists. However, reporting is the law of the land; in every nurse practice act it states that nurses are there to protect the patient and these nurse practice acts state very clearly that if there is anybody in your environment that you feel is engaging in malfeasance that might harm a patient, it is your obligation to report it. Many nurses will admit that they have never really read the nurse practice act and they don't realize they can be held accountable because they failed to report or refused to report. If anyone has even an inkling that there is a domestic violence case or child abuse case, they are on the hotline right away. But somehow when it comes down to reporting violence at the hands of one of their own, they tell themselves they can't get involved. (Interview with author.)

Some healthcare professionals may experience what Ulrich et al. (2007) characterized as ethics stress, an occupational stress that is the emotional, physical, and psychosocial consequences of moral distress, the consequences of which include "frustration, interpersonal conflict, dissatisfaction, physical illness and possibly abandonment of the profession. Ethics stress may be inherent in the professional role of nurses…based on their daily interactions and care for ill persons and their relationships within a complex bureaucratic healthcare system; ethics stress is also organizationally induced."

Ulrich et al. (2007) add that a healthcare institution's ethical climate has much to do with healthcare providers' job satisfaction, because employees must buy into the organization's mission statement and goals, as well as policies addressing how conflicts are managed. An ethical institutional culture also must encompass fair decision making as well as address issues of power and trust. Ulrich et al. (2007) noted that "Improving the ethical climate may be essential for addressing ethics stress, job satisfaction and turnover intentions" (pp. 1708–1719), but adds that few studies have examined importance of an organization's ethical climate to healthcare professionals.

In their study of nurses' attitudes toward their employers' ethical climate and the potential link to job satisfaction, Ulrich et al. (2007) found that the majority of respondents rated the ethical climate of their work environment to be somewhat higher than neutral, but not overtly positive with a mean score of 97.3. Most indicated they received support from their peers (90.6 percent) and managers (77 percent) and worked in an environment with competent colleagues (82.3 percent). However, only 58.3 percent reported that members of their profession and physicians respect each other, and only 55.4 percent indicated that there was trust among the respondent group and physicians. Moreover, 10.5 percent disagreed, and 19.5 percent neither agreed nor disagreed that nurses were supported and respected in their practice setting. About one out of four respondents (23.9 percent) were not sure whether patients know what to expect, although more than three-quarters (77.5 percent) said that patients' wishes were usually respected and that safe patient care was given (78.3 percent). One out of four respondents (25 percent) did not perceive that conflict was openly addressed. Finally, 39 percent of nurses reported having no organizational resource or process to assist them with their ethical concerns. Respondents reported fatigue (39.9 percent) and a sense of being overwhelmed (34.7 percent) when dealing with ethical problems and having to make ethical decisions. Nearly one-third (32.5 percent) felt powerless in dealing with others about ethical issues, and 37 percent reported that their job has become more difficult because of these issues. Physical symptoms associated with ethical problems were reported by 22 percent of respondents, 52.8 percent reported feeling frustrated or angry when they cannot resolve an ethical issue, and 68.2 percent reported being upset when others avoid ethical issues. Finally, 10.8 percent feared reprimand for their ethical decisions, and 62 percent stated there were some ethical issues they could do nothing about. Although the majority was fairly satisfied in their present work, more than one-fifth (21.9 percent) said their work situation was a major source of frustration, and a full 25 percent said they would like to leave their current position. Furthermore, 21 percent agreed that if they were starting over again, they would not choose to be nurses. Finally, 35 percent cited their level of ethical conflict as strongly influential.

So, if healthcare professionals are not necessarily the ethical watchdogs that they should be, where does the responsibility fall? Ramsland believes that patients could be some of the best possible whistle-blowers. She says:

What patients can do is report when they are being mishandled.... We know that some patients get the reputation of being whiney, but they have rights and they need to be firm about saying, "Someone came into my room, gave me an injection and I don't know what it was, but I want to know now." I used to work with cancer groups trying to help them become informed about their cases and about the questions to ask, and I do find very few people will be brave enough to ask, "Why was this done to me," or "Why did this person give me something in the middle of the night?" Even if they get a reputation as being the patient from hell, they are going to get answers and they have a right to do so as an informed patient. Family members can also be helpful in watching for questionable behavior and reporting if a caregiver is acting oddly. This happened in the Charles Cullen case; the son of a patient said that a nurse injected her with something even though she was getting ready to go home that day. She was doing fine and then all of a sudden she crashed, but nobody listened and the patient died. There can be difficulties all the way up the chain of command, but no matter who complains, that inherent difficulty shouldn't stop anyone from saying, "I don't think what happened to me was right." (Interview with author.)

Absent a coworker who comes forward with an eyewitness account of the perpetrator's actions, there is need for concrete evidence that has been properly identified, collected, preserved, and documented. Essentially, it is crucial to treat the hospital as a potential crime scene. It is helpful to this particular discussion to first understand what happens when a discovery of death in the clinical environment is made. Yorker (2006) states that "nurses are usually the first hospital staff members to identify cases of unexpected and adverse patient events that may be precipitated at the hands of a caregiver. They are also typically the first to request an investigation of suspicious events." Hospitals can be busy, frantic, chaotic places, with practitioners who are preoccupied with saving lives, not focusing on deaths. Yet it is death that demands a most careful and precise scrutiny, for suspicious circumstances may not always reveal themselves immediately. That is why Lynch (2006) has emphasized the importance of immediately identifying, securing, and preserving potentially forgotten or overlooked items that can later be considered as evidence if a patient dies or experiences harm. Two key members of the medicolegal team—the medical examiner and the crime laboratory—rely on healthcare professionals to provide an accurate and detailed description of wounds, to collect and preserve admission or postmortem blood and body fluids, and to recognize and recover trace evidence.

In the case of a suspicious death, it may not be evident at first if the deceased died at the hands of a family member, visitor, healthcare professional, or some other unknown subject. It is prudent for healthcare professionals to set aside routine postmortem care and engage in activities more conducive to a forensic investigation. As Lynch (2006, cited in Yorker, 2006) advocates, "Do not remove clothing or treatment paraphernalia, and do not wash the body. The forensic nurse examiner should distinguish those features caused from injury from those caused by life-saving intervention or medical treatment. Document those features on the patient's chart or use a skin marker on the body with medical examiner/coroner approval." Essentially, the patient's body and the patient's room become the crime scene, and must be treated as such by clinical investigators. "It is critically important that the hospital room be treated as a crime scene," Yorker emphasizes. "And that includes knowing how to maintain chain of custody of the evidence, understanding how important it is to save vials, tubing and syringes, get toxicology screens, to save records, and to document everything when anything suspicious happens."

As Standing Bear (2006) notes, "Proper crime scene processing protocol is as essential in the hospital as it would be anywhere else. In fact, a higher degree of skill may be warranted due to the sophisticated environment, technologically advanced equipment and the fast pace of certain areas of the hospital, such as the emergency department, or the complexity of the intensive care unit. Key forensic principles and practices must be followed" (p. 91). To this end, Saferstein (2006) has suggested that healthcare professionals be familiar with several key forensic principles, including Locard's Principle that states that when a person or object comes in contact with another person or object, a possibility exists that an exchange of materials will occur. This is critical, because a presence or absence of physical evidence can corroborate or disprove the events at the scene. Another principle is the chain of custody; this process documents and links every person who handles or examines a piece of evidence. This is critical to show where the evidence has been, who has touched it, and what has been done to it since its initial collection (p. 101). As Standing Bear (2006) states, "The key focus in evidence recovery is to ensure preservation of the evidence in order to maximize the capabilities of the forensic laboratory.... An important part of maintaining the integrity of the physical evidence is to ensure that the chain of custody is not broken and that the evidence is adequately identifiable from the time of recovery until the disposition of the case.... It is generally safest to recover the evidence in an uncontaminated state when possible, marking the container in which the evidence is placed with the time, date and initials of the recovering investigator" (p. 91). As Standing Bear (2006) explains further,

> The scene investigation ... must be undertaken in a systematic, sequential manner by trained and skilled investigators in order to ensure that all valuable evidence is identified, accurately documented and effectively recovered, preserved and secured so as to permit optimal laboratory or other expert examination. At the same time, the chain of custody must be obtained so that the evidence is admissible [in court]. The scene investigation ... is among the most

important initial activities in a chain of events that may significantly affect the outcome (successful suspect identification and prosecution, consideration of the victim, public safety and security) of a serious criminal offense. (p. 91)

Saferstein (2006) notes, "Forensic science begins at the crime scene.... The healthcare professional is in a unique position to facilitate evidence collection ... the clinical investigator may be the sole determiner of what evidence to collect" (p. 101). Classic forensic techniques of crime scene investigation can be reinterpreted for the healthcare environment; many of these tasks can be facilitated quickly by a clinical forensic investigator:

- Initial actions at the scene include noting the time, date, and general condition of the crime scene immediately upon arrival; scene assessment should include what is there as well as what is not there or out of place.
- Document these and all details of the scene in writing and through photography, if possible.
- Search the scene for evidence; for example, check waste cans for evidence, gather electrocardiogram (EKG) strips, and so forth, as clinically related evidence to help reconstruct what occurred.
- Have the right supplies on hand to help contain and secure and preserve evidence.
- Secure the crime scene to prevent evidence removal or tampering.
- Gather statements from the patient (if possible), family members, and other staff in the vicinity.

Kizer and Yorker (2010) note:

Law enforcement officials have repeatedly noted that the investigation and prosecution of suspicious healthcare deaths is exceptionally complicated and is often confounded by routine healthcare practices that result in potential evidence of wrongdoing being destroyed or not safeguarded in a manner that it can be used for forensic purposes. For example, bodies are customarily moved from the site of death and the site cleaned soon after the patient's demise, thereby precluding crime scene investigation. Resuscitation efforts may destroy the crime scene. Bodies may be cremated before foul play is suspected, or bodies may be embalmed and buried, complicating use of toxicological evidence because of problems interpreting data from exhumed bodies. Drugs used to commit the murder may have been used therapeutically, also complicating toxicological findings. Physician orders and hospital protocols may be vague or ambiguous in specific patient care situations. Medical records may be incomplete, unclear or even contradictory. Further, information about the death may not be readily shared because of patient privacy reasons, causing delays in recognizing foul play. (pp. 186–191)

Experts say that classic investigational and forensic techniques for crime scene processing and documentation should be modified to better fit the healthcare environment and healthcare investigations. Bruce Sackman, former special agent in charge of the Office of the Inspector General, Northeast Field Office for the U.S. Department of Veterans Affairs, asked, "Crime scene, what crime scene? By the time the investigators arrive the crime scene has long been scrubbed to surgical standards. Let's see CSI handle that one." Sackman, who was involved in the investigations of two high-profile healthcare serial killers, Michael Swango, a physician, and Kristen Gilbert, a nurse, added, "If an investigator is lucky enough to arrive with things still intact, my simple advice is to seize everything including all equipment, clothing, records from every department, videos, sign-in logs, etc. Then everyone connected with this patient's treatment, all visitors and staff must be interviewed. Inventory all drugs utilized by the staff as well. Forensic analysis includes autopsy and toxicology by forensic professionals, not just hospital staff."

As Sackman advises healthcare investigators, "Be prepared to hear a lot of medical reasons why the patient died a natural progressive death. Resist the temptation to accept the medical/scientific reasons for the patient's demise as being sufficient enough to decline an investigation. Someone in the hospital probably knows or has strong suspicions as to what exactly happened to the patient. Utilize your own medical experts such as forensic nurses to peel away the white wall of silence."

Video surveillance is an option for detection that must be handled with care. In cases of suspected factitious disorder or Munchausen by proxy syndrome, hospitals can undertake direct and indirect methods of obtaining evidence. It is a process similar to that undertaken when a parent is suspected of harming a child; in this case, it is frequently a healthcare worker who is suspected of harming a patient. According to Yorker (2008), direct methods include toxicology screens, eyewitness accounts, charting of observation of caretaker behavior, and covert video surveillance. Indirect methods include seeing if the child or patient improves when separated from the suspected caretaker, as well as seeing if a medical chart review shows multiple system involvement. Caution must be taken with these methods. In particular, covert video surveillance invokes potential violations of an individual's Fourth Amendment rights, which guard against unreasonable searches and seizures. In terms of case law and applicability, in *Katz v. United States*, 389 U.S. 347 (1967), the Supreme Court ruled that the amendment covered a person's "reasonable expectation of privacy," and not solely whether that person's property had been intruded upon. To that end, there is no reasonable expectation of privacy in a hospital room, but the courts could leave room for legal challenge. Yorker (2008) advises that hospitals have very specific protocol for surveillance, including having solid probable cause or suspicion of abuse, working closely with the healthcare institution's security department, and ensuring meticulous documentation.

According to Yorker (2006), several methods of detecting caregiver-associated incidents exist, including encouraging personnel to report their suspicions; family members may also come forward with knowledge about caregivers who act suspiciously. Yorker (2008) says that simple steps can help curb or eliminate medical malfeasance, including employing proper risk management strategies, ensuring the control of medications and narcotics, conducting routine data reviews, ensuring night and evening shift super-vision, and detecting early anything untoward or suspicious. As discussed in Chapter 5, examining mortality patterns could suggest the presence of a healthcare professional bent on medical malfeasance. Yorker (2008) also sug-gests that healthcare institutions engage in surveillance, chart review, per-sonnel tracking, and behavior documentation and step up data collection in general in a unit in which suspicions are cast. That data should be analyzed for trends and evidence of criminal activity; once probable cause of a crime exists, healthcare institutions are advised to notify law enforcement.

Yorker (2008) suggests the following steps for investigation of caregiver-related incidents:

- At any statistically significant deviation from the norm, begin surveillance.
- Is there an association between staff and adverse events?
- Does the trend reverse under obvious surveillance?
- Regardless of whether the trend reverses or not, continue to conduct surveillance and document the individual's job activity.
- Is there probable cause of a crime? If yes, notify law enforcement.
- If insufficient evidence of a crime exists, begin accounting for each dose of medication and gather postarrest equipment and statements from family and staff.
- Does additional evidence emerge? If yes, notify law enforcement. If not, continue to monitor legally.
- If a staff member resigns, engage in legally permissible references and follow-up of future employment.
- If the person leaves the jurisdiction, follow up with the national licensure board.

Evidence and eyewitness accounts can be the impetus for the launch of internal investigations by healthcare institutions, but as Thunder (2003) asks, "What degree of proof is necessary to move from suspicion, to preliminary investigation, to formal investigation, to prosecution, to conviction? Medical examiners and police are not going to give much credence to mere suspicions that a crime has occurred when sick or old or frail people die." Thunder (2003) explains that once the need for an investigation is verified, the next step is to determine the scope of the investigation, including the identification of key suspects and their motives: "For example, it was only after an involved investigation that the police in the Efren Saldivar case were able to exclude 22 of the 40 suspected members of his respiratory unit. What period of time should the investigation encompass? How far back should the investigation go? What evidence is able to be obtained and analyzed without publicity and without major expense (such as the exhumation of bodies)?"

Internal investigations are necessary to establish the facts and assess the healthcare institution's criminal-, financial-, regulatory-, and reputation-related exposures. This is especially true in cases that are eventually turned over to the authorities, or in the case of crimes occurring at Veteran's Administration (VA) hospitals such as in the Kristen Gilbert and Michael Swango cases, which triggered U.S. government investigations. As Levine (2005) explains, "The goals of an internal investigation are to learn whether the allegations are accurate…and to evaluate regulatory, civil and/or criminal exposures and defenses; determine how to deal with civil plaintiffs, government regulators, law enforcement agencies; and remedy any systemic failures that contributed to the misconduct; and levy appropriate discipline." Levine (2005) alludes to an investigation as a "battle to gain accurate information in a timely way," at least before suspicions and allegations are made public. This information is needed to assess exposures and risks, Levine (2005) has said, as once the issue gets out and possibly is reported in the media, the healthcare institution "will be placed in a pressured, reactive posture which makes methodical investigation and deliberative decision-making that much tougher." Levine (2005) adds, "It is a battle because it involves reconstructing history (what happened) through the prism of often incomplete documentation and of witnesses who have disparate memories and biases."

James and Leadbetter (1997) also emphasize the need to act swiftly, noting that swift recognition of situations that justify suspicion about a patient death or irreparable harm can help retrieve vital evidence at the crime scene and facilitate a proper investigation. "The hospital must take responsibility for the detection of covert homicide. Confidence that such deaths will be uncovered by 'routine' investigation through the existing coroner system, including postmortem examination, is misplaced" (pp. 296–298).

Healthcare Crime Investigations in the Digital Age

Although physical forensic evidence is essential to any investigation, in today's hospitals, there is an increasing focus on digital evidence. As discussed in Chapter 2, the exploitation of patients using electronics comes at a time when the forensic science and law enforcement communities are embracing digital forensics, or cyber forensics, to investigate crime in healthcare institutions and beyond. Barber (2010) has pointed to the proliferation of computers, recording devices, and numerous wireless applications that have added to the types of evidence for court proceedings and noted that "Hospitals and other healthcare agencies, insurance carriers, law enforcement and many community services realize the power of forensic evidence in cases involving violent crimes, fraud and other illegal activities."

The advent of sophisticated digital-based technology in hospitals is a giant leap forward in the detection of potential medical malfeasance. Digital evidence is considered to be any information of probative value that is stored or transmitted in a digital format on a device such as from computer hard drives, compact discs, digital audio and video recording devices, and cell phones. As Barber (2010) explains, "The analysis of data stored in these communication instruments can be recovered and analyzed to assist in determining the facts. Information derived from such sources proves relationships between perpetrators and victims, confirms identification of those involved in a crime, and confirms timelines that support or refute reported information" (pp. 97–104).

From the moment a patient enters a digitally advanced hospital, Barber (2010) said his or her treatment is recorded in some way, thus adding to the medical record to establish treatment modalities and to track all clinical actions that occur during patient-care delivery. Included in this vast, streaming digital trail are vital signs and the patient's responses to therapies administered via devices such as ventilators and IV pumps, plus the recorded movements of healthcare professionals who are tracked via radio-frequency badges or keystrokes on a computer keyboard. This data stream is critical to the reconstruction of events during an investigation should criminal activity be suspected.

The advantage of a progressive healthcare setting that uses wireless connections for many routine communications is that patients and personnel—and what they do—can be monitored everywhere they go. Barber (2010) states that few healthcare professionals are aware of the digital recording and archiving of information by medical devices and equipment. Even as patients are moved throughout the hospital, the wireless-enabled devices and equipment that accompany them continue to record healthcare professionals' interactions with them. If a malicious healthcare worker attempts to pull the plug on a device to try to hide his or her malfeasance, Barber (2010) notes that "Hospital beds, portable monitors, transport ventilators, and infusion pumps work seamlessly and memory continues, even when unplugged from their power source" (pp. 97–104).

Radio-frequency identification (RFID) systems, which track and locate people, equipment, and supplies, can aid investigators in reconstructing events leading up to a patient code or other adverse or suspicious event.

As Barber (2010) confirms, "Forensic investigators can use records stored within these systems to reconstruct events that might have led to serious injury or death, to identify caregivers who misappropriate drugs or hospital supplies. 'Footprints' of the interfaces with devices and supplies are left behind with time-stamps and event sequences preserved for discovery" (pp. 97–104).

Because so much of a hospital's equipment can communicate in real time and has archival capabilities, during routine clinical processes, records can be captured and stored in the event of an adverse patient event. As Barber (2010) points out, "It is now possible to integrate information coming from a wide array of equipment and locations and to make clinical decisions based upon the integration of the data. For example, the various physiological monitor, the bed, the infusion pumps, point-of-care testing devices and other equipment can share data used for clinical decisions.... The equipment collects the information, analyzes it, automatically initiates action and precisely documents the events in real time."

According to Barber (2010), there is also immense forensic value in hospital communication and documentation systems when it comes to medical record tampering, a frequent component of medical malfeasance:

In some situations, the medical record is altered after it is known that a case involves a legal action such as suing for damages arising from negligence, malpractice or failure of the facility, medical equipment or device. Either the prosecution or the defense may alter documentation in an attempt to improve their chances of winning a lawsuit. This may involve several types of alteration including adding false statements, changing times or dates, making additional entries or changing those of another provider, removing pages from the medical record or even completely destroying the medical record by burning or shredding.... Often there is an unnatural sequence to a patient's progress notes. The selection of words or descriptions of a disease or condition may be more elaborate than usual, with emphasis about a particular fact or situation. Writing 'later entries' in the margin of the paper, or inserting additional phrases or sentences is considered suspicious. Nursing notes that are quite detailed and lengthy (uncharacteristic for a given nurse) should alert the forensic investigator of an unusual circumstance. (pp. 97–104)

With the current transition from paper to electronic medical records, computer-based forensics can come into play in the healthcare institution. As Barber (2010) explains,

A forensic nurse expert or legal nurse consultant who is assisting in preparing a court case will scrutinize the record for unusual entries or for data which proves or disproves certain reported facts or events. Does the hospital invoice support the tests and procedures outlined in the physician's progress notes?

Are there charges that cannot be supported by the patient's clinical course? Do medication records from the pharmacy conflict with the medication administration form? Are there entries that appear to be out of chronological order? Do any entries appear to be crowded within a page? With computerized charting in place at many hospitals, often incorporating some automated documentation, there are more data points to reveal intentional alteration of records. Computers store precise information about every keystroke and this information can be extracted from the system's mainframe or one of several back-up systems for reconstruction if needed. Changes made at any time can be recovered from the electronic database since all keystrokes are recorded and stored in redundant networks. The stored information reveals removals or changes in information, and provides information about the sequence of the associated events. Given today's technology linkage that provides redundancy for various systems, it is difficult (some would say virtually impossible) to defeat or alter automated documentation of medical equipment or devices that generate real-time records of physiological and caregiver events. (pp. 97–104)

Forensic nursing and critical care expert Janet Barber said that most hospitals have not come to terms with technology and its ability to help solve crime in the healthcare environment. Barber said that several years ago, she delivered a presentation on the topic of reconstructing criminal events at the annual meeting of the American Academy of Forensic Sciences (AAFS):

The room was absolutely packed with experienced investigators and they were truly amazed—they had no idea that hospital beds and equipment such as IV pumps, physiological monitors and ventilators have embedded memory that calculates every keystroke of input and also can reveal when changes were made and who input the data. The investigators attending my talk are used to doing interviews and just talking to people and here they have a new avenue for hard data unaffected by subjectivity. Without consulting the data from this kind of equipment they have only been using a portion of all the tools afforded them while attempting to reconstruct criminal events in a hospital. They don't know this data exists and can be captured for the purposes of investigation or litigation, and neither do patients. I think we haven't tested a lot of this evidence in the courtroom yet because people have not been generally aware of its existence, including those who are prosecuting these cases. (Interview with author.)

Barber is familiar with the technology from her role as clinical nurse consultant for Hill-Rom (Batesville, Indiana), the maker of high-tech beds and other equipment for hospitals:

Some of the nurses like me who are working with the engineers and designers of this equipment are in a better position to know this than anybody. Even some of the nurses who use this kind of medical equipment daily don't have any idea that keystrokes and other instructions that are inputted are kept in memory. Most nurses don't realize that the IRRF badge that they wear to identify themselves when they come in the patient's room or when they access the Pyxis® machine is the same surveillance system that tracks them around the hospital and knows where they are located at any given moment. That information is captured by the software and usually digitally stored somewhere for a specified interval for retrieval. That's how crimes can be reconstructed, using data reported by equipment in the patient room and elsewhere. (Interview with author.)

The issue of privacy is a concern to many individuals, but Barber says it is unrealistic to expect that a healthcare employer will not be tracking a person's whereabouts and clinical tasks. "This kind of technology isn't just about tracking the location of employees, it's about the location of patients as well; are they getting out of bed when they are not supposed to? Are they unattended?" Barber notes. "Hill-Rom makes a lot of advanced equipment with a significant amount of technology embedded in it; for instance, clinicians can tell whether a bed has its side-rails up or down, or if the head of the bed is elevated 30 degrees or if it is flat. We can also tell if a specific caregiver was the last in contact with the device. People perceive this as a negative, as if Big Brother is watching them, but in all honesty, it's a protection for everybody. And in terms of crime reconstruction, being able to account for people's whereabouts is critically important."

Technology can only go so far to aid in the prevention and investigation of medical malfeasance; old-school human intelligence and investigations can never fully be supplanted by it. Barber emphasizes:

In the case of an intentional medication overdose, for example, just because you have an automatic dispensing unit doesn't mean you have a fool-proof method of narcotics dispensing.... The automatic dispensing unit can be set up wrong, or it's filled with the wrong product, or someone finds a way to outsmart the technology. So technology, if it's programmed wrong or if it falls in the hands of the wrong person, just like an IV pump, there's a margin for error or malfeasance. But the good news is that the automatic dispensing unit and the IV pump tracks that data entry and keystrokes exactly how and when it occurred and who did it. That information can greatly facilitate investigations. The challenge is that as people become increasingly savvy with technology, they find new ways to defeat it. There are people who have already learned how to override the Pyxis and who can override other hospital technology. Or they can steal someone else's badge and implicate them in wrongdoing, since what is tracked is not the person but the electronic badge. Someone can use the same digital devices we think are protecting people to actually create more perfect crimes. (Interview with author.)

Despite some of the most sophisticated means of investigations, as we have seen, some healthcare serial murderers still escape detection. As Kizer and Yorker (2010) confirm,

> When considering the mortality attributable to healthcare serial killers and the number of persons prosecuted for these crimes it should be recognized that modern healthcare provides many nearly ideal settings and circumstances for committing murder without being detected or held accountable. Patients are often disoriented, sedated, or not aware of their surroundings or what is being done to them. They may be severely weakened and unable to defend themselves. Caregivers often work alone and in private and have ready access to multiple potentially lethal agents, the use of which may not be attributable. Care may involve numerous types of technology utilized by, or invasive interventions performed by, persons unknown to the patient or other caregivers. In addition, death is a relatively frequent occurrence in healthcare facilities, so a patient's death initially may not be suspected of being due to a criminal act even when it is unexpected. (pp. 186–191)

Obstacles to Investigations

Sometimes the healthcare institution is loath to acknowledge potential malfeasance, let alone investigate it. As Yorker (2006) points out, "In many cases prosecutors found hospital administrators and physicians to be uncooperative. In some cases, they were simply stonewalling; in other cases they actually obstructed the investigation. Some reasons for the uncooperative behavior include: fear of negative publicity, civil suits for negligence, civil suits by nurses being investigated, and poor record-keeping."

Ramsland admonishes healthcare institutions to cooperate when predators are discovered:

> Numerous physicians and nurses have been inadvertently protected by administrators, and thus their compulsion to harm or kill continued. It is unfortunately a fact of bureaucracy that in order to retain customers, administrators might be tempted to hide whatever sheds a negative light on their facility, but since the paramount issue with hospitals is customer trust, effective attention to the problem of healthcare serial killers actually assists that goal. The fact that a facility has detected and stopped a predator is in its favor—especially in light of the embarrassment it will suffer if a successive facility accomplishes it and then asks why they weren't told about this person. Protecting a predator, even with nothing more than passive avoidance, actually makes a facility appear to be less safe for patients. (Interview with author.)

Ramsland continues, "While one bad employee doesn't make an entire facility unsafe or medical practice generally corrupt, media-assisted public perception can exaggerate the situation. Yet by that same token, a healthcare facility can utilize the media to improve the image. Somerset County Medical Center, in the Charles Cullen case, came out looking like both the victim to other institutions and society's hero for putting an end to Cullen's 16-year spate of patient termination."

The healthcare industry is facing its most transparent era ever, yet investigative delays or outright obstruction can still occur. As Kent and Walsh (2004) state, there is a double standard in which serial killer investigations receive full cooperation from federal, state, and local agencies, while healthcare serial killer cases frequently encounter "frustrating levels of obfuscation, disinterest, obstruction, concealment and denial," particularly in government institutions, where "near insurmountable levels of friction" can exist between investigators and delay proceedings. As an example, Kent and Walsh (2004) pointed to one VA hospital case that exceeded 10 years; congressional intervention was needed to allow state authorities to intervene after federal criminal jurisdiction had lapsed.

"Medical center management will always be questioned as to the timing of any internal investigation in any subsequent civil suit," said Sackman. "The faster management responds the better and most management officials know that. I am concerned about the quality of the inquiry, who is conducting it, and whether or not the primary goal is to undercover the truth or to protect the management. No business wants negative publicity and healthcare is no exception. An internal inquiry that fails to show any significant wrongdoing can be spun into a positive reflection on the hospital."

Despite the potential to be exonerated of any cover-ups or involvement in allowing caregiver-associated malfeasance to continue, Smith (2002) states that healthcare institutions frequently take no action because of the chain of events set off by a report of suspicions or allegations: "Except in known cases of reported homicide to the coroner or criminal acts where police are notified, staff may be unwilling to report cases of abuse outside of the organization in case they are labeled whistle-blowers and potentially lose their employment status. In addition, the organization may be reluctant to report cases of staff-initiated violence because they have an inherent aversion to litigation and publicity."

According to Smith (2002), healthcare institutions do not want healthcare consumers to know that they may have employed a serial killer, so they choose to ignore the problem, and as a result, the problematic healthcare professional moves on to a job at another hospital and is free to continue his or her illicit behavior. "For example, following an employment interview, one nurse's credentials checked out even though he was under investigation in the deaths of patients by his previous employer," Smith (2002) explains. "Such omissions show deficiencies in personnel procedures which may lead later to legal action of negligent hiring or vicarious liability. The outcome of the reluctance to report to respective authorities allows health professionals to avoid accountability and public and professional notoriety." Of great concern is the fact that these perpetrators are being unwittingly employed by other healthcare institutions, and if undetected, numerous more patients are placed in harm's way. Even though new state laws regarding licensing and discipline requirements have made it more difficult for healthcare organizations to quietly dismiss healthcare professionals with suspicious behavior and questionable backgrounds, there is nothing to stop these caregivers from resigning before an investigation of legal proceeding commences. According to Smith (2002), "The organizational challenge is to recognize and to respond to deficiencies in human resource processes such as recruitment, dismissal practices, staff development as well as professional monitoring."

Prosecution of Medical Malfeasance: Moving from Criminal to Civil

In Chapter 5, we looked at a number of cases in which healthcare professionals were convicted for their crimes. The criminal courts have resolved these cases, but civil litigation followed, as former employers of convicted killers fend off litigation by other hospitals and by families of victims. In 2004, New Jersey Supreme Court Chief Justice Deborah T. Poritz decided not to designate as a mass tort all pending and future civil litigation statewide involving the alleged actions of former nurse Charles Cullen. According to Michelle V. Perone, chief of the Civil Court Programs within the Civil Practice Division in Trenton, New Jersey, as of January 2010, there are no remaining civil cases relating to Cullen.

As discussed, Cullen admitted to the murder of more than 30 patients at five different hospitals. He pleaded guilty on April 29, 2004, to the murder of 14 patients at Somerset Medical Center in Somerville, New Jersey, and the attempted murder of two more. Cullen committed these murders via injection of various medications, including digoxin, insulin, nitropresside, norepinephrine, dobutamine, and pavulon, while on staff at these facilities. Investigation revealed that Cullen had a history of reported incidents at hospitals in Pennsylvania and New Jersey, but there was no tracking system in place and no mechanism by which his acts could be disclosed as he moved from hospital to hospital. His employment history included termination from several hospitals because of various forms of misconduct, hospitalizations for mental illness, and a criminal investigation in Pennsylvania into whether he was administering medication improperly. In an open letter published in *The New York Times* on March 14, 2004, Somerset Medical Center asserted, "Mr. Cullen worked at nine other healthcare facilities over a 16-year period. His former work history problems were not revealed to us. Nor were any state agencies or licensing boards able to provide us with accurate information about his employment history." New Jersey Senators Frank Lautenberg and Jon Corzine echoed these concerns in a January 16, 2004, letter to the Health Resources and Services Administration of the Department of Health and Human Services (HHS) that stated in part: "Mr. Cullen was investigated by three hospitals, a nursing home and two prosecutors for causing the deaths of patients, and was fired by five hospitals and one nursing home for suspected wrongdoing. Yet each time Mr. Cullen was fired he was able to continue his killing spree by finding employment at another healthcare facility. Hospital officials continued to hire Mr. Cullen time after time because they had no information regarding his job history, and those who served as a reference for him generally just confirmed his employment record, without providing information on suspensions, dismissals, or other actions taken against him."

Administrators at hospitals where Cullen had worked responded to inquiries as to why they had not divulged this negative information by stating that the possibility of lawsuits kept them from sharing information about Cullen's employment problems with subsequent employers.

In February 2008, the Associated Press reported that the families of New Jersey patients murdered by Cullen settled a lawsuit with the hospitals where he worked. The confidential settlement with five hospitals where Cullen worked was reached after court-ordered mediation between both sides, approximately 4 years after the lawsuit was filed in New Jersey Superior Court. Four New Jersey hospitals were part of the settlement: St. Barnabas Medical Center in Livingston, Warren Hospital in Phillipsburg, Hunterdon Medical Center in Flemington, and Somerset Medical Center. A Pennsylvania facility, St. Luke's Hospital in Bethlehem, was also involved in the settlement. A judge ruled in 2007 that it could be sued for failing to warn Somerset Medical Center not to hire Cullen, who left St. Luke's in 2002 after the hospital conducted an investigation into mishandling of medications and told him he could resign or be fired.

The hospitals that employed Cullen experienced their own legal battles beyond suits filed by patients' families. One legal complaint was that St. Luke's Hospital should be liable for Cullen's actions at Somerset Medical Center because St. Luke's knew or should have known that Cullen was a threat to the welfare and safety of its patients. According to a summary of the plaintiff's complaint in a memorandum of decision on motion filed by justice Bryan Garruto in August 2007, prior and subsequent to Cullen's hiring at Somerset Medical Center, St. Luke's Hospital had a legal obligation to protect patients at its facility as well as other patients at other facilities where Cullen might seek employment. Several actions could have been taken, including reporting Cullen's activities to the authorities as well as to state and other governmental agencies empowered to investigate the allegations, and responding to any healthcare facility requesting a reference or information regarding Cullen's employment at St. Luke's Hospital to determine if Cullen indeed posed a foreseeable risk of harm to patients if hired. St. Luke's Hospital asserted that it could not be held liable for negligence arising out of a failure to inform Somerset Medical Center that Cullen was not eligible for rehire or that Cullen was a potential danger to patients, because it gave Cullen a "neutral" reference that consisted of verifying Cullen's employment and dates of service. St. Luke's Hospital asserted further that this was a "routine practice" regarding former employee references.

At the time, Garruto acknowledged that New Jersey courts had not decided whether a former employer has a duty to disclose negative information about a former employee to a prospective hospital employer when the prospective employer makes an inquiry about the previous employee; however, the California Supreme Court had already considered the issue and decided "under what circumstances courts may impose tort liability on employers who fail to use reasonable care in recommending former employees for employment without disclosing material information bearing upon their fitness." Somerset Medical Center contended that St. Luke's had a duty to inform Somerset about Cullen's employment eligibility and criminal conduct, and that St. Luke's breached this duty by leaving the rehire status as essentially "blank" and thus omitting key details about Cullen's performance. St. Luke's contended that it did not have a duty to inform Somerset that Cullen was listed as a do-not-rehire employee, because the harm to patients at Somerset was unforeseeable and because no special relationship existed between St. Luke's and Somerset.

In his August 21, 2007, opinion, Garruto noted, "Instead of firing him, St. Luke's allowed Mr. Cullen to resign so that he could obtain future employment. St. Luke's cannot assert it did not foresee the risk of harm Mr. Cullen posed to patients...when its own hospital personnel were making phone calls to local area hospitals alerting them that Mr. Cullen was on the do-not-rehire list. This is evidence sufficient to support Somerset's contentions that St. Luke's had reason to believe Mr. Cullen's actions at St. Luke's could be repeated at another hospital and could lead to harm of a hospital's highly vulnerable patients."

Garruto, in an August 24, 2007, memorandum of a decision on a motion, commented on the issue of whether under New Jersey law a former hospital employer has a duty to report negative information about a former nurse to the Department of Health and Senior Services, the New Jersey Nursing Board, or the authorities. Bearing in mind that Cullen had worked for a number of healthcare facilities in fairly rapid succession, Garruto wrote, "At no time did anyone from Saint Barnabas, Warren Hospital, Hunterdon Medical Center or Morristown Memorial Hospital report any of the events to the Department of Health and Senior Services, the New Jersey Nursing Board or police. Indeed, the only incident reported to police was made by a family member and not by the hospital wherein the conduct occurred." Garruto maintained that Saint Barnabas, Warren, Hunterdon, and Morristown owed the plaintiffs and Somerset a duty to report Cullen's activities pursuant to the Health Care Facilities Planning Act, because the state law required hospitals to report any event that jeopardizes the health and safety of patients or employees. The hospitals, however, asserted that the state law did not impose upon them a duty to report Cullen's substandard professional practices. They also asserted that New Jersey's passage of the Patient Safety Act in 2004 and the Health Care Professional Responsibility and Reporting Enhancement Act in 2005 created a duty that did not exist at the time of the murders committed by Cullen. Garruto disagreed, explaining that well before the two aforementioned acts were passed, "New Jersey's strong public policy in favor of patients' rights had already been expressed in the Health Care Facilities Planning Act" passed in 1971. Garruto added that state law "places the onus on the hospital administration to determine which alleged or suspect crimes fall within the purview of the reporting requirements." Garruto continued, "To illustrate the flaws in the defendants' argument, it is important to note that even after a patient complained that Mr. Cullen injected her with an unknown substance—which ultimately resulted in her death—the hospital did not report the incident to the police. In fact, the police investigation was only commenced after the patient's family member reported the suspicious death to authorities. The law clearly places an obligation upon Mr. Cullen's former employers to report suspected or alleged crimes. It is important to note that the word 'suspected' does not require certainty."

In a position paper, the American Society for Healthcare Risk Management of the American Hospital Association (ASHRM, 2005) acknowledged that healthcare institutions fear the specter of litigation when involved in situations such as the Cullen case: "Healthcare employers are subject to suit from a myriad common law and statutory enactments, such as medical malpractice, lack of informed consent, battery, violations of the Emergency Medical Treatment and Active Labor Act and violations of the Health Insurance Portability and Accountability Act, just to name a few. Healthcare entities are justifiably afraid of litigation at this point in time." What is needed, ASHRM asserted, is "nationwide immunity from civil litigation for the provision of adverse information, disclosed in good faith, to prospective healthcare employers."

According to ASHRM, the Health Care Quality Improvement Act (HCQIA) provides some immunity for reporters of adverse information, but it does not apply to interemployer communications, and it applies only to physicians. As a protection for those providing information to professional review bodies, the act stated, "Notwithstanding any other provision of law, no person (whether as a witness or otherwise) providing information to a professional review body regarding the competence or professional conduct of a physician shall be held, by reason of having provided such information, to be liable in damages under any law of the United States or of any state unless such information is false and the person providing it knew that such information was false."

Henry (2004) has acknowledged that many employers would like to warn another prospective employer but are afraid of potential defamation suits by the ex-employee. Instead, they are forced to rely on traditional tools that can be extremely fallible, such as criminal background checks and credit reports. The shortcomings of these tools become evident when healthcare professionals who have no financial problems or criminal histories are caught and their transgressions are revealed. Henry (2004) asserts that what healthcare employers have needed for some time is "freedom of good-faith expression; the freedom to discuss candidly an ex-employee's weaknesses as well as strengths, and even suspicions that are well-founded, without fear of reprisal. Now, increasingly, that freedom is a reality."

More states have adopted laws that afford employers substantially greater protection than in years past. In 2004, in the wake of the Charles Cullen case, the U.S. Senate made an attempt at qualified immunity in Senate Bill 720, but the proposal limited it to reporting of medical errors and does not clearly articulate privilege or immunity. This bill was not reintroduced in Congress. The purpose of S.B. 720 was to promote disclosure of medical errors without fear of lawsuits. Known as the Patient Safety and Quality Improvement Act of 2004, the bill set forth a privilege for "patient safety data," defined as "data, reports, records, memoranda, analyses (such as root cause analyses), or written or oral statements" that are collected for or provided to a "patient safety organization," an entity that receives and collates information on medical errors, among other things. In the bill, patient safety data are privileged from discovery in connection with federal, state, or local civil or criminal proceedings and cannot be admitted as evidence in such proceedings. However, ASHRM (2005) asserts that the concept underlying this provision suffers from the same drawback as the proposal to expand the National Practitioner Data Bank; there was no requirement in the bill that prospective employers query the patient safety organization about applicants for direct-care positions. ASHRM (2005) says that even if such a requirement were added, this would create an additional step in the hiring process, and that there is nothing in S. 720 that permits the patient safety organizations to divulge safety data referable to applicants to healthcare providers seeking to hire nonphysician personnel. As ASHRM (2005) notes, "S. 720 is an attempt to create at least some form of immunity for communication of patient safety data at the federal level. It could therefore serve as a platform, with appropriate amendments, for nationwide immunity from civil litigation for the provision of adverse information, disclosed in good faith, to prospective healthcare employers."

Various states have passed legislation to address this issue, especially New Jersey, perhaps in reaction to the Cullen case. Its Patient Safety Act signed by then-Governor James McGreevey on April 27, 2004, requires reporting of "serious preventable adverse events" to the state's Department of Human Services, but also sets forth a limited privilege for documents concerning "serious preventable adverse events, near misses, preventable events and adverse events." Although these documents cannot be used in an "adverse employment action" and are not considered to be a public record," guidance from the courts will determine whether the language of the statute will apply to employment references. On May 3, 2005, then-Governor Richard Codey signed into law the state Health Care Professional Responsibility and Reporting Enhancement Act, which further established new reporting responsibilities for healthcare institutions as well as new protections to encourage such reporting. The reporting is required of a broad range of healthcare entities, including hospitals, public health centers, diagnostic centers, treatment centers, rehabilitation centers, nursing homes, outpatient clinics, and home healthcare agencies licensed in New Jersey, as well as health maintenance organizations (HMOs) authorized to operate in New Jersey, carriers that offer a managed-care plan regulated by state law, state or county psychiatric hospitals, state developmental centers, staffing registries, and home-care services agencies.

Specifically, the legislation requires New Jersey healthcare professionals and healthcare entities to notify the New Jersey Division of Consumer Affairs in the Department of Law and Public Safety when they have information regarding the incompetence or negligence of a healthcare worker, which would endanger patients. Healthcare entities must report if a healthcare professional has become impaired on the job or has engaged in incompetence or professional misconduct that relates adversely to patient care or safety, as well as if the healthcare provider has had full or partial privileges reduced, revoked, or suspended, has been removed from the list of eligible employees of a health services firm or staffing registry, has been discharged from the staff, or had a contract to register professional services terminated or rescinded.

The legislation also requires a healthcare entity that receives an inquiry from another healthcare entity concerning a healthcare professional to truthfully disclose whether, within the 7 years preceding the inquiry, it provided any notice about the individual. The healthcare entity must provide to the inquiring entity a copy of the form of notification and any supporting documentation that was provided with it. In addition, the healthcare entity must provide information about a current or former employee's job performance as it relates to patient care, and in the case of a former employee, the reason for the employee's separation from the entity. The legislation offers some protection to healthcare entities that report disciplinary actions, in that healthcare entities and their employees who provide information in good faith and without malice to another healthcare entity regarding a healthcare professional are not liable for civil damages in any cause of action arising out of the provision or reporting of the information. However, if a healthcare entity does not truthfully disclose information to an inquiring entity or fails to cooperate with an inquiry, it could be subject to penalties to be determined by the Department of Health and Senior Services.

The legislation also requires criminal background checks of healthcare providers who apply for licensure or license renewal in New Jersey. As ASHRM (2005) emphasizes,

> Many healthcare employers would seek reference information in the future, whereas they do not at the present time. They believe that they would not get an honest reference if they asked because they know that the previous employer would be reticent to give honest information out of fear of reprisal— of risking the liability associated with giving honest opinions about former employers without assurance of immunity. Consequently, many (if not most) prospective healthcare employers do not even ask. The suggested federal legislation would balance the rights of the respective parties. Future employers would receive honest appraisals of their new employees. Employees would be protected from having falsehoods, rumors or innuendoes spread about them, because the protection for employers would come from giving factual information. The rights of patients would be respected because they could have greater assurance that they will receive care from persons who have not been successively terminated by previous employers under very distinct clouds of suspicion.
>
> There is a pressing need for such legislation because the health and safety of the public depends upon it. While it may not be possible to prevent all homicides in healthcare, such legislation would allow problems to be contained and would help to prevent problems of the magnitude of the Cullen case. The need is pressing because healthcare services are often provided without supervision by people in whom we place the utmost trust. Recipients of healthcare services are often the most vulnerable members of society who are usually powerless to defend themselves. It is incumbent upon society to protect them to the extent that it is possible to do so. (p. 8)

Yorker believes that the civil cases could serve an important purpose in overall healthcare risk management, including putting hospitals on notice about improving their screening, hiring, and reference-checking processes. "The families of the victims of healthcare serial murderers are now suing hospitals, including big lawsuits associated with the Charles Cullen case," she said. "There are other cases triggering litigation that have not yet come to light, including cases in which plaintiffs are saying that hospitals have been negligent in hiring, but also that hospitals were negligent in not warning other hospitals or not protecting the patient. These plaintiffs charge that the hospital did not take seriously the sentinel event, and did not immediately (if at all) crack down on the employee by suspending the nurse." Yorker continues, "Many hospitals have been so vigilant and have reported malfeasance to law enforcement, but then law enforcement says, 'We can't find anything.' Well, you can't suspend somebody from work when you don't have law enforcement backing you up, and that there is some reason to suspend an employee in the first place. So hospitals are truly damned if they do, damned if they don't. I'm excited about these lawsuits because I'm thinking they will then allow hospitals to start suspending healthcare providers, even without criminal charges. With civil suits, all it takes is a preponderance of evidence."

Evasion of Detection by Health Professionals

Evasion of detection and discipline of problematic healthcare professionals appears to be a persistent problem in many areas of the United States. Investigations are conducted of some practitioners, but many more are elusive and continue to operate under the radar of investigators and medical licensure and regulatory boards. Charles Cullen was a prolific medical murderer, but he is also a poster child for the necessity of healthcare institutions conducting thorough background checks before hiring healthcare professionals. Cullen had been fired by numerous other hospitals before coming to Somerset Medical Center in Somerville, New Jersey, and every time he simply moved on to another facility. As we will see throughout this chapter, databanks, fingerprinting, and background checks are not foolproof measures with which to catch and prevent would be abusers and killers.

In California, an ongoing investigation of nurses has become symbolic of the country's ongoing problem of keeping problematic practitioners out of healthcare institutions. As Weber and Ornstein (2009a) reported, "Dozens of registered nurses who have been convicted of serious crimes including murder, sex offenses, robbery and assault have been identified by California regulators reviewing newly required fingerprints from tens of thousands of caregivers." Following a 2008 investigation into regulators' lack of knowledge about nurses' prior convictions by *The Los Angeles Times* and the nonprofit news organization ProPublica, California's state Board of Registered Nursing began expanding its review of nurses' criminal records. As Weber and Ornstein (2009a) explain,

> At the time, nurses who had received licenses before 1990 were exempt from providing fingerprints, which are used to flag arrests for regulators. Since March, the board has required those nurses to submit their fingerprints. Most of the crimes turned up are misdemeanors, such as driving under the influence,

petty theft or fraud. But the records as of November also included two murders, two solicitations for murder, an attempted murder, a manslaughter and a vehicular homicide. There also were 19 convictions for assault, including five felonies, and 39 for sex offenses, three of them felonies. The nursing board has referred at least 13 cases to the attorney general to start disciplinary proceedings against the nurses involved.

According to Weber and Ornstein (2009a), of the 1,900 conviction reports sent to the board, about 1,300 were closed without action because of the crime's age or nature. The remaining ones await further investigation. *The Los Angeles Times* and ProPublica's investigation in 2008 found more than 115 cases in which the state did not seek to discipline nurses until they had three or more criminal convictions. They add, "It also turned up cases in which nurses with felony records continued to have spotless licenses—sometimes while behind bars." Weber and Ornstein (2009a) go on to say that "In 1990, the board began requiring nurses applying for licenses to provide their fingerprints—the first nursing board in the country to do so. But nurses who already had their licenses at that time were not required to submit prints. That group now numbers 138,500. As of December 2009, nearly 64,000 nurses in that group had submitted prints. More than 400 nurses' licenses have been put on hold because they haven't complied with the new rule. The rest have not yet renewed their licenses." The background checks are part of the state board's continuing overhaul of its operations following reports by ProPublica and *The Los Angeles Times* about lengthy delays in investigating and disciplining nurses accused of wrongdoing. The fingerprinting effort is being expanded to include all licensed health professionals in California; until late 2009, each of the state's health regulatory agencies established its own requirements about who needed to submit fingerprints. Weber and Ornstein (2009a) reported that almost one-third of the state's 937,100 licensed healthcare workers had not been screened as of December 2008. Additionally, even within the state, the rules were inconsistent for different groups of health professionals.

Weber et al. (2009) reported that in August 2009, "California Gov. Arnold Schwarzenegger conceded that long-standing delays in disciplining errant health professionals were 'absolutely unacceptable' and promised broad reforms to better protect patients from dentists, pharmacists, therapists and others accused of misconduct." According to Weber et al. (2009), among the proposed changes are adding more investigative and legal staff, appointing an official to audit the boards, and seeking legislation that would allow quicker suspension of uncooperative or jailed professionals' licenses. The announcement came a month after ProPublica and *The Los Angeles Times* reported that it takes an average of more than 3 years to investigate and discipline registered nurses accused of wrongdoing, including patient abuse, neglect, and drug thefts. Also in August 2009, the state, in response to a public records request from ProPublica, released data showing that it takes more than 2 years to resolve all types of complaints against health profession-als. Schwarzenegger replaced the majority of the state Board of Registered Nursing and ordered a review of the state's other health-related boards as a result of the ProPublica/*Times* investigation.

In October 2009, county social service chiefs in California had pro-tested Schwarzenegger's plan to require prospective home health aides for the elderly and disabled to begin undergoing criminal background and fingerprint checks, saying that they were not ready to begin such a time-consuming process and that this process could mean some patients could go without care. Bailey (2009) reported that California's 376,000-plus care workers would require the new background checks by June.

Background checks can be a healthcare institution's first line of defense against hiring problematic healthcare professionals, and they can reveal some surprising details about practitioners. An observational study conducted in 2009 by Medversant Technologies, LLC (Los Angeles, California), a provider of Web-based credentials verification solutions for the healthcare industry, determined that of 29,845 healthcare practitioners with professed current medical licensure, 1.9 percent were practicing without a license, and 18.7 percent were flagged with one or more "adverse findings," including mal-practice, expired license, and credentials falsification. The Medversant study surveyed a database that included physicians, dentists, podiatrists, chiroprac-tors, physician assistants, nurse practitioners, and other ancillary personnel from 30 healthcare organizations with a state license number under which the practitioner professed to practice at the time of credentials verification. The study measured the number of practitioners with one or more adverse findings, those practicing without a license, and those with an adverse find-ing not reported by the Excluded Parties List System (EPLS) or the National Practitioner Data Bank (NPDB). Additionally, 110 flags across 13 credentials were identified, with criteria based upon credentialing standards promul-gated by the National Committee for Quality Assurance (NCQA), Utilization Review Accreditation Commission (URAC), the Joint Commission, and the Centers for Medicare and Medicaid Services (CMS).

As another example, a few years ago, then Michigan Attorney General Mike Cox and his healthcare fraud division commissioned two studies to evaluate the effectiveness of Michigan's statutes in response to a disturbing series of cases. The studies uncovered the following:

- Of the more than 5,500 certified nursing assistants (CNAs) studied, 9 percent had a total of 836 outstanding criminal warrants, and 3 percent had past criminal convictions.

- Twenty-five percent of residential-care facility employees committing crimes against residents since 2002 had past criminal convictions.
- Background checks of entire employee populations at four nursing homes across Michigan revealed 58 of 618 employees (more than 9 percent) had 101 outstanding warrants and that 68 (11 percent) of the staff had past criminal convictions.

In both studies, the criminal histories included homicides, armed robberies, criminal sexual conduct, weapons violations, drug charges, and retail fraud.

A piece of legislation in Congress now could create much-needed change in how healthcare providers such as CNAs are hired. As of January 2010, Senate Bill 631, known as the Patient Safety and Abuse Prevention Act, was sitting before the Senate Finance Committee of the 111th Congress. SB 631, which was introduced in March 2009, provides for nationwide expansion of the pilot program for national and state background checks on direct patient-access employees of long-term care facilities or providers. SB 631 directs the Secretary of Health and Human Services to establish a program to identify efficient, effective, and economical procedures for healthcare facilities to conduct background checks on prospective direct patient-access employees on a nationwide basis under similar terms and conditions as the pilot program established under the Medicare Prescription Drug, Improvement and Modernization Act of 2003. It also establishes requirements for states wishing to participate in the program, including requiring searches of neglect registries and databases; searches of any proceedings that may contain disqualifying information; searches of federal criminal history records, including a fingerprint check; and methods that reduce duplicative fingerprinting. A similar bill was introduced in the House of Representatives in March 2009 and has been referred to the House Energy and Commerce committee and the House Ways and Means committee.

Problematic nurses continue to fall through the cracks, despite background checks and fingerprinting. Sheets and Kappel (2007) reported that in 1990, the California Board of Registered Nursing became the first state nursing board to conduct criminal background checks on applicants for nursing licensure. In 1998, a policy recommendation to member boards of nursing to conduct checks was adopted by the NCSBN Delegate Assembly. And in 2005, the National Council of State Boards of Nursing (NCSBN) officially urged the member boards to integrate criminal background checks into the licensure protocol. Currently, 32 state boards of nursing require federal criminal background checks as part of the licensing process.

Ornstein and Weber (2008a) reported,

Dozens of nurses convicted of crimes, including sex offenses and attempted murder, have remained fully licensed to practice in California for years before the state nursing board acted against them, a *Los Angeles Times* investigation found. The newspaper, in a joint effort with the nonprofit investigative news organization ProPublica, found more than 115 recent cases in which the state didn't seek to pull or restrict licenses until registered nurses racked up three or more criminal convictions. Twenty-four nurses had at least five. In some cases, nurses with felony records continue to have spotless licenses—even while serving time behind bars.

By comparing the state's Megan's Law database, which lists registered sex offenders, with the state's list of registered nurses, for instance, reporters immediately found three cases in which the names and addresses of sex offenders matched those of registered nurses with clean records. Armed with additional information about the state's nurses, such as birth dates, the board might find even more matches. Reporters also matched the state's list of registered nurses against the federal government's database of healthcare providers banned from Medicare. It found four examples of banned nurses that the board has never disciplined, one of whom was found guilty of patient abuse or neglect.

Ornstein and Weber (2008b) reported that

California's failure to check the criminal backgrounds of health profession-als extends well beyond nurses, encompassing tens of thousands of doctors, dentists, psychiatric technicians and therapists. The *Times* reported this fall that regulators had not vetted about 195,000 of the state's registered and voca-tional nurses, exposing patients to caregivers with histories of violence, addic-tion, predatory behavior, or corruption. Prompted by those articles, the state Department of Consumer Affairs has identified 104,000 more professionals from all levels of medical care to add to that tally. All told, the agency now estimates that close to a third of the state's 937,100 licensed healthcare workers have not been screened through fingerprint checks. Licensing boards maintain inconsistent rules about who must be fingerprinted and when. Fingerprints are the primary tool that regulators can use to root out convictions and allow law enforcement agencies to automatically alert regulators if a licensee has ever been arrested. Those who have not been fingerprinted include almost three-quarters of psychiatric technicians; nearly half of family therapists, social workers and dentists; and 12 percent of physicians.

Ornstein and Weber (2008b) reported that the Dental Bureau of California started requiring fingerprints in 1986 but has almost none on file for any dentist licensed before then, accounting for about 16,000 practitioners. This is alarming in light of the case of former California dentist Kiyoshi Fukuda; while he has maintained a clear record since original licensure in 1969, Ornstein and Weber (2008b) discovered that he is a registered sex offender and is listed on the state's Megan's Law Web site. Fukuda was convicted in 1990 of two counts of oral copulation on a child under 16. As Ornstein and

Weber (2008b) continued, "In an interview, Fukuda said he had disclosed his conviction to the board when he renewed his license years ago and never heard anything back. He closed his private practice in January and said he recently sent a request to the dental board to cancel his license."

After the reports by *The Los Angeles Times*, which collaborated with the investigative news organization ProPublica, the state Department of Consumer Affairs moved quickly. Agency Director Carrie Lopez ordered the 20 health-related boards and bureaus she oversees, including the Medical Board of California, to collect fingerprints from any licensee who had not provided them. She also told the agencies to begin asking licensees whether they had been convicted of a crime since their last renewal. Other states' boards, including those in Arizona and Texas, already do that. The Board of Registered Nursing has received expedited approval from the state Office of Administrative Law to collect fingerprints from the 147,000 nurses licensed before 1990. In a statement, Lopez noted,

> I have and fully intend to make use of all resources to ensure that we remove threats to the public safety and well-being of Californians. I intend to make this Department and its regulatory entities the model for consumer protection and licensing in the nation and will continue to invest resources to accomplish that goal. I am committed to making continuous improvements to further strengthen consumer confidence in the services provided by our licensees. Under my watch, the Department of Consumers Affairs has instructed all of the healing arts boards and bureaus to quickly move forward with a number of administrative and policy changes to further strengthen the screening of existing licensees, initiate appropriate disciplinary actions, and create transparency for the public concerning questionable licensees.

Fingerprinting is not the silver bullet against hiring problematic practitioners, as not all of them are required to submit prints. Revoking privileges is also a strategy some hospitals use to curtail dangerous doctors, but as a watchdog group pointed out, many facilities are not participating. Although a federal law requires hospitals to report physicians who have had their admitting privileges revoked or restricted for more than 30 days, a report released in May 2009 by Public Citizen found that in addition to inadequate discipline of physicians, hospitals routinely exploit loopholes to avoid government requirements, with nearly half of all hospitals not submitting a single doctor's name to the NPDB in the more than 17 years it has existed. The failure of hospitals to adequately discipline doctors or to report cases of physician discipline to the NPDB deprives state medical boards of critical information needed for regulatory oversight and creates the potential for patient harm, Public Citizen said in the report and in a letter sent to Kathleen Sebelius, secretary of the Department of Health and Human Services (HHS).

When the database was first created, federal officials estimated that hospitals would report approximately 5,000 cases a year. But since it began in 1990, the database has averaged only 650 reports a year, Public Citizen found. "It is impossible to justify the fact that thousands of hospitals, which collectively have granted admitting privileges to hundreds of thousands of doctors, have not reported a single discipline case in 17 years," said Sidney Wolfe, MD, Public Citizen's acting president and director of its Health Research Group. "Our report shows there is an urgent need for the Obama administration to step in and hold hospital administrators accountable as well as ensure that hospital medical staffs hold their own physicians accountable for patient safety."

Pubic Citizen compiled the report by reviewing studies by the Office of the Inspector General, medical journal articles, work by the nonprofit Citizen Advocacy Center, and recommendations from an October 1996 national meeting on hospital underreporting attended by hospital administrators, government officials, medical associations, and consumer advocates, including Public Citizen. Public Citizen also analyzed the NDPB to examine the relationship between hospital reports and actions taken by state medical boards on the same physicians. The report points to two troubling factors behind the dangerously low number of hospital discipline reports: lax peer review, including a culture among doctors of not wanting to "snitch" on a colleague; and hospital administrators evading reporting requirements by doing things such as imposing discipline of less than 31 days, thereby evading the reporting requirement or giving doctors a leave of absence in lieu of suspensions.

Public Citizen makes several recommendations, including amending the Health Care Quality Improvement Act of 1986 to add fines for each instance of a hospital's failure to report, and tying compliance with the act to the hospital accreditation process and Medicare conditions of participation. "Hospital peer review has been called one of the pillars of quality assurance in the U.S. health care system," said Al Levine, the Public Citizen researcher who compiled the report. "Based on all the data and reports we analyzed, it appears to be a questionably effective form of self-regulation that needs more accountability and better oversight. We hope our report is the tipping point for action by Congress and the Department of Health and Human Services." Public Citizen's letter to Sebelius urges her to implement recommendations made long ago by the HHS Inspector General's office but never acted upon.

In August 2009, watchdog group Public Citizen sent another letter to the HHS asserting that more than 22 years after the federal government started tracking serious disciplinary actions against nonphysician health workers, the infractions—everything from fraud and abuse to improperly prescribing drugs—are still kept secret from most hospitals and many nursing homes doing background checks of potential employees. The Healthcare

Integrity and Protection Data Bank contains discipline records for more than 100,000 nurses, physician assistants, pharmacists, and other nonphysician health workers. However, Public Citizen says that HHS has failed to finalize a regulation that would implement a 1987 law that would allow access to the records to more than 5,000 U.S. hospitals and about 700 nursing homes. "Many of these workers would not have jobs in the healthcare field if their current employers knew about their checkered pasts," said Wolfe. "Keeping these records secret greatly increases the chance that patients will be injured or killed at the hands of their caretakers."

The letter to HHS Secretary Kathleen Sebelius points out that as of December 31, 2007, the healthcare database listed more than 40,000 nurses sanctioned for healthcare-related violations, including: unsafe practice or substandard care (23,551 reports); misconduct or abuse (10,930 reports); fraud/deception/misrepresentation (3,437 reports); and improper prescribing/dispensing/administering of drugs (7,526 reports). In addition, there have been more than 49,000 licensed practical nurses and nurse aides sanctioned for healthcare-related violations, such as: unsafe practice or substandard care (16,110 reports); misconduct or abuse (12,197 reports); fraud/deception/misrepresentation (4,247 reports); and improper prescribing/dispensing/administering of drugs (4,634 reports).

Weber and Ornstein (2010) reported that the names of many licensed healthcare professionals who have had serious disciplinary actions taken against them are missing from the national database created by Congress to keep dangerous and incompetent caregivers—including nurses, pharmacists, and psychologists—from crossing state lines. As part of an investigation between The Los Angles Times and ProPublica, Weber and Ornstein (2010) reported that as of March 1, 2010, hospitals will finally be able to use this database maintained by the Health Resources and Services Administration (HRSA), but that this repository lacks information on individuals who have harmed patients. Weber and Ornstein (2010) said that Mary Wakefield, the head of HRSA, acknowledged that records were missing and that the agency had launched a "full and complete" review to determine what is wrong and how to fix it, and that Wakefield and Sebelius sent a letter to the nation's governors asking for their immediate help to address gaps in the database. Weber and Ornstein (2010) added that the letter said that the federal government will begin publicly listing any state agencies that do not report properly and that the HRSA plans to hold training sessions for state officials and conduct audits to help ensure compliance.

The aforementioned media reports leave one to wonder if oversight of healthcare professionals is sorely lacking. The NPDB, the national repository for the records of doctors disciplined by their peers for unprofessional or incompetent behavior, was established by the Health Care Quality Improvement Act of 1986 to protect patients from problematic physicians.

But, as Levine and Wolfe (2009) point out, it has been handicapped by the failure of thousands of hospitals to report to the NPDB. Levine and Wolfe (2009), of watchdog group Public Citizen, asserted that as of December 2007, almost 50 percent of the hospitals in the United States had never reported a single privilege sanction to the NPDB. They explained that operated by the HRSA, part of the Department of Health and Human Services (HHS), the NPDB was designed as a searchable resource for hospitals and other medical entities to check practitioners' backgrounds and to consider taking their own action based on the information in the data bank. Prior to its launch, this function was not being provided in any systematic way. The NPDB's goal was to reduce the likelihood that disciplined doctors might continue to injure patients by relocating to another hospital or state where their reputations and track records were not known.

As Levine and Wolfe (2009) explain,

> Our review identified and focused on two factors associated with under-reporting: failure of hospitals to report and failure of hospitals to take action on questionable physicians. For example, a HRSA funded study reported in the *American Journal of Public Health* noted that, to avoid reporting, hospitals imposed disciplinary periods of less than 31 days thereby avoiding the need for reporting physicians to the NPDB; a medical board official informed Public Citizen that some hospitals avoid reporting by changing their bylaws or by having physicians take a "leave of absence." State medical board officials report that hospital clinical privilege sanctions are a valuable source of information for identifying physicians with performance or conduct problems, and many boards use this information to launch investigations that can lead to disciplinary action. However, our analysis of the NPDB Public Use File found that almost 1,000 physicians who had at least two adverse clinical privilege reports to the NPDB did not have any subsequent licensure board disciplinary action. One physician had nine adverse clinical privilege reports but no licensure board actions.

As discussed, one of the most egregious cases is that of Dr. Michael Swango. In 1993, Swango entered the VA healthcare system—the largest integrated healthcare system in the United States and serving millions of veterans—as a medical resident, although before entering the residency program he had been convicted and imprisoned for 2 years for aggravated battery against his fellow employees. Swango admitted to medical school officials that he had a prior arrest and conviction but lied about the nature of the crime. In 2000, he pleaded guilty to murdering three veterans at the VA facility located in Northport, New York, and received a sentence of three consecutive life terms without the possibility of parole. In another case in 2000 at the VA facility in Albany, New York, the VA hired a research assistant to help administer several cancer studies. The research assistant had lost his medical license because he had forged his medical credentials. Once at the VA, the research assistant allegedly falsified data that were used to qualify veterans for cancer studies, and this may have resulted in the untimely deaths of several veterans. In 2003, the researcher was indicted in federal court on charges including manslaughter, criminally negligent homicide, and fraud.

Events at VA facilities, such as in the case of Swango, raised concerns about VA's screening of the professional credentials and personal backgrounds of healthcare practitioners at its facilities. The VA had not conducted oversight of its facilities' compliance with key healthcare worker screening requirements, thus creating vulnerabilities to the extent that VA remains unaware of practitioners who could place patients at risk. The then–Government Accounting Office (GAO) (now known as the Government Accountability Office) was asked to investigate. The GAO examination (2004) revealed acceptable and adequate measures, such as verifying professional credentials, completing background investigations for certain practitioners, including fingerprinting to check for criminal histories, and checking national databases that contain reports of practitioners who have been professionally disciplined or excluded from federal health care programs. The GAO (2004) found adequate screening requirements for certain practitioners, such as physicians, for whom all licenses are verified by contacting state licensing boards; however, screening requirements for others, such as currently employed nurses and respiratory therapists, are less stringent because they do not require verification of all licenses and national certificates. Moreover, they require only physical inspection of the credential rather than the contacting of state licensing boards and national certifying organizations. The GAO (2004) noted that physical inspection alone can be misleading, as not all credentials indicate whether they are restricted, and credentials can be forged. The VA also does not require facility officials to query, for other than physicians and dentists, a national database that includes reports of disciplinary actions involving all licensed practitioners. In addition, many practitioners with direct patient-care access, such as medical residents, are not required to undergo background investigations, including fingerprinting to check for criminal histories.

In its investigation, the GAO reviewed the VA's policies and identified key screening requirements for 43 healthcare occupations; interviewed officials from VA, licensing boards, and certifying organizations; and randomly sampled about 100 practitioners' personnel files at each of four VA facilities that investigators visited. The GAO report (2004) noted,

> In the four facilities we visited, we found mixed compliance with the existing key VA screening requirements. All facilities generally checked the professional credentials of practitioners periodically for continued employment. However, they were less compliant in checking the professional credentials of applicants that they intended to hire. Furthermore, VA facilities varied

in how quickly they took action after obtaining the results of background investigations. During the site visit at one facility, we discovered returned background investigation results that were over a year old but had not been reviewed. We brought them to the attention of facility officials, who reviewed the reports and then terminated a nursing assistant who had been fired by a previous employer for patient abuse. Although VA established an office more than a year ago to perform oversight of human resources functions, including whether its facilities comply with these key screening requirements, it has not started these reviews. There is no VA policy outlining the human resources program evaluations to be performed by this office, and the resources have not been provided to support the functions of this office. (p. 2)

In its report, the GAO (2004) recommended that the VA expand its existing verification process to require that all state licenses and national certificates held by all practitioners be verified by contacting the appropriate licensing boards and national certifying organizations, expand the query of a national database to include all licensed practitioners, and fingerprint all practitioners who have direct patient-care access. The GAO also recommended that the VA conduct oversight of its facilities to ensure their compliance with all screening requirements. The VA generally agreed with the GAO's findings and said it would develop a detailed action plan to implement the recommendations.

The year 2010 witnessed a major victory in the fight against elder abuse. On March 23, 2010, 32 years after the first Congressional hearings were held on elder abuse, President Barack Obama signed into law the Elder Justice Act and the Patient Safety and Abuse Prevention Act as part of the expansive U.S. healthcare reform bill. The new healthcare legislation incorporates three related bills, including the Nursing Home Transparency and Improvement Act, the Elder Justice Act, and the Patient Safety and Abuse Prevention Act.

Elder Justice Act

The Elder Justice Act was introduced in the Senate on April 2, 2009, and the House on April 21, 2009. S. 795, known as the Elder Justice Act (EJA), was authored in the Senate by Senator Orrin Hatch (R-UT) and was coauthored by Senator Blanche Lincoln (D-AR) with original cosponsors Senator Herb Kohl (D-WI) and Senator Olympia Snowe (R-ME). On the House side, the EJA companion bill, H.R. 2006, was authored by Representative Peter King (R-NY) and was cosponsored by Representative Tammy Baldwin (D-WI), Representative Jan Schakowsky (D-IL), and Representative Joe Sestak (D-PA). According to the National Consumer Voice for Quality Long-Term Care, formerly known as the National Citizens' Coalition for Nursing Home Reform (NCCNHR),

The number of older Americans is fast growing, and so is the problem of elder abuse, neglect and exploitation. This often-invisible treatment is among the gravest issues facing millions of American families. The Elder Justice Act provides federal resources to support state and community efforts on the front lines dedicated to fighting elder abuse with scarce resources and fragmented systems. From a social perspective, elder justice means assuring adequate public–private infrastructure and resources to prevent, detect, treat, understand, intervene in and, where appropriate, prosecute elder abuse, neglect and exploitation. From an individual perspective, elder justice is the right of every older person to be free of abuse, neglect and exploitation.

The Elder Justice Coalition said that the Elder Justice Act promotes both aspects of elder justice with the following goals:

- *Elevate elder justice issues to national attention.* Key are the creation of Offices of Elder Justice at the Department of Health and Human Services and at the Department of Justice to serve programmatic, grant-making, policy, and technical assistance functions relating to elder justice; a public–private and a coordinating council to coordinate activities of all relevant federal agencies, states, communities, and private and not-for-profit entities; and a consistent funding stream and national coordination for Adult Protective Services (APS).
- *Improve the quality, quantity, and accessibility of information.* An Elder Justice Resource Center and Library would provide information for consumers, advocates, researchers, policy makers, providers, clinicians, regulators, and law enforcement and prevent "re-inventing the wheel." A national data repository also will be developed to increase the knowledge base and collect data about elder abuse, neglect, and exploitation.
- *Increase knowledge and support promising projects.* Given the paucity of research, Centers of Excellence will enhance research, clinical practice, training, and dissemination of information relating to elder justice. Priorities include conducting a national incidence and prevalence study, jump-starting intervention research, developing community strategies to make elders safer, and enhancing multidisciplinary efforts.
- *Develop forensic capacity.* There is scant data to assist in the detection of elder abuse, neglect, and exploitation. Creating new forensic expertise (similar to that in child abuse) will promote detection and increase expertise. New programs will train healthcare professionals in both forensic pathology and geriatrics.

- *Provide for victim assistance, "safe havens," and support for at-risk elders.* Elder victims' needs, which are rarely addressed, will be better met by supporting creation of "safe havens" for seniors who are not safe where they live and development of programs focusing on the special needs of at-risk elders and older victims.
- *Increase prosecution.* Technical, investigative, coordination, and victim assistance resources will be provided to law enforcement to support elder justice cases. Preventive efforts will be enhanced by supporting community-policing efforts to protect at-risk elders.
- *Provide training.* Training to combat elder abuse, neglect, and exploitation is supported both within individual disciplines and in multidisciplinary (such as public health–social service–law enforcement) settings.
- *Provide for special programs to support underserved populations including rural, minority, and Indian seniors.*
- *Model state laws and practices.* A study will review state practices and laws relating to elder justice.
- *Increase security, collaboration, and consumer information in long-term care*:

    - Improve prompt reporting of crimes in long-term care settings.
    - Require criminal background checks for long-term care workers.
    - Enhance long-term care staffing.
    - Provide information about long-term care for consumers through a Long-Term Care Consumer Clearinghouse.
    - Promote accountability through a new federal law to prosecute abuse and neglect in nursing homes.

- *Conduct evaluations and assure accountability.* Make provisions to determine "what works" and assure funds are properly spent.

The main funding provisions of the Elder Justice Act include the following:

- $400 million ($100 million per year) is authorized in dedicated funding for APS, in addition to $100 million ($25 million annually) for state demonstration grants to test a variety of methods to improve APS.
- $32.5 million (over 4 years) is authorized in grants to support the Long-Term Care Ombudsman Program, and an additional $40 million ($10 million annually) in training programs for national organizations and state long-term care ombudsman programs.

Because the funds authorized are discretionary (as opposed to mandatory), the Subcommittee on Labor, Health and Human Services and Education

Appropriations will evaluate the requests for funding authorized by the legislation (NCEA, 2010).

The legislation also establishes at the federal level the Elder Justice Coordinating Council to propose recommendations within 2 years to the secretary of the Department of Health and Human Services regarding coordination of federal, state, local, and private agency activities relating to elder abuse, neglect, and exploitation. "The healthcare reform bill will give consumers more choices about where and how they receive long-term care and services, and every long-term care setting—from one's nursing home to one's own home—will be safer when it is implemented," said Sarah F. Wells, NCCNHR Executive Director.

Nursing Home Transparency and Improvement Act

The Nursing Home Transparency and Improvement Act will require disclosure of the wide array of individuals and entities that own, operate, and finance nursing homes, and it will require nursing homes to escrow fines if they appeal violations. It also will provide consumers access to information that is now unavailable or hard to obtain, such as accurate information about staffing levels and turnover rates, sanctions against facilities, and inspection reports. The nursing home transparency provisions are the first comprehensive improvements in nursing home quality since OBRA '87. When fully implemented, the law will provide consumers a substantial amount of new information about individual facilities, most of it from resolutions passed by NCCNHR members. The legislation was sponsored by Senator Herb Kohl (D-WI), Senator Chuck Grassley (R-IA), Representative Henry Waxman (D-CA), Representative Pete Stark (D-CA), and Representative Jan Schakowsky (D-IL).

Key provisions of this legislation include the following:

- Public disclosure of nursing home owners, operators, and other entities and individuals that provide management, financing, and services to nursing homes.
- Establishment of internal procedures by nursing homes (compliance and ethics programs) to reduce civil and criminal violations and improve quality assurance.
- Collection of staffing data electronically from payroll records and other verifiable sources and public reporting of hours per resident day of care and turnover and retention rates.
- Improved public information on *Nursing Home Compare*, including staffing data for each facility that includes hours of care per resident day, turnover, and retention rates; links to facilities' survey reports and plans of correction on state Web sites; summaries of complaints

against facilities, including number, type, severity, and outcome; a standardized complaint form; and adjudicated criminal violations by facilities and their employees inside the facility, including civil monetary penalties levied against the facility, its employees, contractors, and other agents.

- Establishment of a consumer rights information page on *Nursing Home Compare*, including services available from the long-term care ombudsman.
- Improved timeliness of survey information made available to the public.
- Requirement that states maintain a Web site with information on all nursing homes in the state, including survey reports, complaint investigation reports, plans of correction, and other information that the state or Medicare considers useful.
- Improved complaint handling, including a voluntary standardized form for filing complaints with the survey agency and ombudsman; and protection of residents' legal representatives and other responsible parties from retaliation when they complain about quality of care.
- Dementia care and abuse prevention in nursing assistant training programs.
- Demonstration projects to identify best practices in culture change and information technology.

Patient Safety and Abuse Prevention Act

Perhaps most importantly, the Patient Safety and Abuse Prevention Act creates a national program of criminal background checks for persons seeking employment in nursing homes and other long-term care facilities. Sponsored by Senator Herb Kohl (D-WI), the legislation creates a national program of criminal background checks on employees of long-term care providers who have access to residents of facilities or people receiving care in their own homes. The legislation was added to the healthcare reform bill by Senator Debbie Stabenow (D-MI).

This most recent legislation is not without precedent; in 2003 Congress, through the Senate Special Committee on Aging (SSCA), called for a pilot program under the Medicare Prescription Drug, Improvement and Modernization Act (MMA) to conduct background checks on long-term care workers. Senator Herb Kohl, chairman of the U.S. Senate Special Committee on Aging, reported, "Over three years and in seven states, this pilot program prevented more than 9,500 applicants with a history of substantiated abuse or a violent criminal record from working with and preying upon frail elders and individuals with disabilities" (SSCA, 2008). This program afforded states an opportunity to expand their existing background check programs in order to screen a wide range of long-term care workers working in a variety of settings, including the home, and to incorporate FBI criminal history checks. In addition, pilot programs were charged with identifying "efficient, effective, and economical procedures" for conducting comprehensive background checks in long-term care settings. The Centers for Medicare and Medicaid Services (CMS) administered this pilot program between 2005 and 2007, allocating $16.4 million over 3 years to fund background check pilot programs in seven states: Alaska, Idaho, Illinois, Michigan, Nevada, New Mexico, and Wisconsin. (The MMA also included money for three states—Alaska, Michigan, and Wisconsin—to conduct pilot programs in abuse prevention training for frontline direct-care workers.)

A report on the program produced by the SSCA (2008) noted that it was successful in achieving its objectives:

> First and foremost, older Americans receiving long-term care services in these states are at lower risk of abuse: more than 9,500 applicants with a history of substantiated abuse or a serious criminal background have been barred from working in positions involving direct patient access. Second, better-integrated databases and electronic fingerprinting procedures have helped reduce background check processing time from several months to a few days. Third, investments in information technology, such as a "rap back" system (A rap back system is one in which any new crimes that an individual commits after an initial background check are flagged in the state's database and reported back to the employer; rap back systems can therefore avoid the cost of having to re-fingerprint individuals each time they change jobs), helped some states reduce ongoing costs associated with conducting criminal history checks. Finally, all of the pilot states chose to continue their background check programs for long-term care workers at the end of the pilot period in September 2007. Overall, the Committee concludes that the pilot program has been a success and recommends that similar background check programs be replicated in other states to reduce the risk of elder abuse in long-term care settings. (p. 6)

Discipline of Problematic Healthcare Professionals

Regarding performance standards and expectations for health professionals, Kohn et al. (2000) stated that health professional licensing bodies should implement periodic reexaminations and relicensing of doctors, nurses, and other key providers, based on both competence and knowledge of safety practices; and work with certifying and credentialing organizations to develop more effective methods to identify unsafe providers and take action.

As Kohn et al. (2000) observed:

For most health professionals, current methods of licensing and credentialing assess knowledge, but do not assess performance skills after initial licensure. Although the state grants initial licensure, responsibility for documenting continued competence is dispersed. Competence may be considered when a licensing board reacts to a complaint. It may be evaluated when an individual applies to a healthcare organization for privileges or network contracting or employment. Professional certification is the current process for evaluating clinical knowledge after licensure and some programs are now starting to consider assessment of clinical skills in addition to clinical knowledge. Given the rapid pace of change in healthcare and the constant development of new technologies and information, existing licensing and accreditation processes should be strengthened to ensure that all healthcare professionals are assessed periodically on both skills and knowledge for practice. More effective methods for identifying unsafe providers and better coordination between the organizations involved are also needed. The time between discovery of a problem, investigation, and action can currently last several years, depending on the issue and procedures for appeal or other processes. Efforts should be made to make this time as short as possible, while ensuring that practitioners have available the due process procedures to which they are entitled. States should also be more active in notifying other states when a practitioner's license is rescinded. Although unsafe practitioners are believed to be few in number and efforts to identify such individuals are not likely to improve overall quality or safety problems throughout the industry, such efforts are important to a comprehensive safety program. Finally, professional societies and groups should become active leaders in encouraging and demanding improvements in patient safety. Setting standards, convening and communicating with members about safety, incorporating attention to patient safety into training programs, and collaborating across disciplines are all mechanisms that will contribute to creating a culture of safety. As patient advocates, healthcare professionals owe their patients nothing less. (p. 135)

As we will see, there is immense variation found in professional licensure, which compounds the problem. Kohn et al. (2000) pointed to the variation inherent in the professional licensure process, which is regulated by individual state licensing boards. To compound matters, there is little coordination of information among different boards, thus making it very challenging for these agencies to share information about problematic healthcare professionals. The variation also surfaces in the rate at which a complaint is investigated and at which disciplinary action is taken. Depending upon the state, a complaint can be construed as a call to a licensing board or it can be recognized only when a formal charge is made against the healthcare professional.

It is not clear, therefore, when information can be shared: when something is filed (which may or may not lead to a charge), while it is being investigated, after there is a charge, or only if disciplinary action is taken.

Inconsistencies permit unsafe practitioners to move to different jurisdictions before a complaint can be investigated and handled.

For physicians and nurses especially, there are consequences for medical misconduct through sanctions enforced by medical boards; however, not all breaches of professional conduct are reported, not all perpetrators are reported, and many continue to cross state lines and work. Let's take a look at what is known about the discipline of these errant healthcare professionals.

Physician Discipline

There have been a number of recent attempts to characterize disciplined physicians and their offenses. Dehlendorf and Wolfe (1998) reported on the construction of database on disciplinary activity by the Public Citizen's Health Research Group, which began requesting information on all disciplinary orders that state medical boards and federal agencies had taken against physicians. By 1996, 20,914 disciplinary orders taken prior to January 1, 1995, had been entered into Public Citizen's database as 24 types in order of decreasing severity: revocation of license, surrender of license, disallowance of the right to renew a license, revocation of controlled substance license, surrender of controlled substance license, disallowance of the right to renew a controlled substance license, denial of a license, denial of license reinstatement (from a revocation or surrender), reinstatement (from a revocation or surrender), suspension, suspension of controlled substance license, emergency suspension, license probation, probation of controlled substance license, fine, license restriction, restriction of controlled substance license, reprimand, education, enrollment into an impaired physician's program or alcohol or other drug treatment program, cease and desist order, monitoring of a physician's practice, participation in community service, and exclusion from Medicare. In about one-third of the orders, state medical boards imposed more than one action in a single disciplinary order. The database also contains sex-related offenses, including any orders in which the state board or federal agency mentioned a sex offense, ranging from rape to indecent exposure, as one of the causes for action.

Dehlendorf and Wolfe (1998) also sought to determine the frequency and severity of discipline against physicians who commit sex-related offenses and to describe the characteristics of these physicians. They analyzed the aforementioned sex-related orders from a national database of disciplinary orders taken by state medical boards and federal agencies and found 761 physicians disciplined for sex-related offenses from 1981 through 1996. Dehlendorf and Wolfe (1998) found that the number of physicians disciplined per year for sex-related offenses increased from 42 in 1989 to 147 in 1996, and the proportion of all disciplinary orders that were sex related increased from 2.1 percent in 1989 to 4.4 percent in 1996. Discipline for sex-related offenses was significantly more severe than for non-sex–related offenses, with 71.9 percent of sex-related orders involving revocation, surrender, or suspension of medical license. Of 761 physicians disciplined, the offenses committed by 567 (75 percent) involved patients, including sexual intercourse, rape, sexual molestation, and sexual favors for drugs. As of March 1997, 216 physicians (39.9 percent) disciplined for sex-related offenses between 1981 and 1994 were licensed to practice. Compared with all physicians, physicians disciplined for sex-related offenses were more likely to practice in the specialties of psychiatry, child psychiatry, obstetrics and gynecology, and family and general practice than in other specialties and were older than the national physician population, but were no different in terms of board certification status. The researchers concluded that discipline against physicians for sex-related offenses is increasing over time and is relatively severe, although few physicians are disciplined for sexual offenses each year. In addition, a substantial proportion of physicians disciplined for these offenses are allowed to either continue to practice or return to practice.

Morrison and Wickersham (1998) conducted a case-control study on publicly available data matching 375 disciplined physicians with two groups of control physicians, one matched solely by locale, and a second matched for sex, type of practice, and locale. The study subjects were all disciplined physicians publicly reported by the Medical Board of California (MBC) from October 1995 through April 1997. The 375 physicians licensed by the MBC were disciplined for 465 offenses, the most frequent of which were negligence or incompetence (34 percent); abuse of alcohol or other drugs (14 percent); inappropriate prescribing practices (11 percent); inappropriate contact with patients (10 percent); and fraud (9 percent). The discipline imposed was revocation of medical license (21 percent); actual suspension of license (13 percent); stayed suspension of license (45 percent); and reprimand (21 percent). Like many other states, California invokes four levels of discipline: reprimand, probation, suspension of license, and permanent revocation of license. Of the 375 disciplined physicians, 32 (9 percent) were women; and 288 (77 percent) had been in practice at least 20 years. Of these physicians, 327 (87 percent) were involved in direct patient care; 31 (8 percent) were retired or inactive; 11 (3 percent) were in academic administrative practice; and 6 (2 percent) were resident physicians. Compared with controls matched by location, disciplined physicians were less likely to be women and were more likely to be involved in direct patient care. Compared with controls matched by location, sex, and type of practice, disciplined physicians were more likely to have been in practice more than 20 years and were less likely to be board certified. Of the self-reported specialties with sufficient numbers for meaningful comparison, only anesthesia and psychiatry appeared overrepresented among disciplined physicians, although neither reached statistical significance. Comprising nearly one-fifth of all causes for disciplinary action, issues related to physicians' health were the next most common cause for action. Overall, the data reaffirm the continuing importance of physician impairment as a cause of discipline, although physical illness appears to be a less frequent source of physician impairment than mental disorder and substance abuse. Illegal activities and other inappropriate voluntary behaviors not associated with mental disorders or substance abuse precipitated another strong minority of actions. Sexual misconduct constituted the major offense for 10 percent of disciplined physicians, although that proportion seems low considering reports that up to 9 percent of physicians admit having sex with one or more patients. Misrepresenting credentials was a principal or secondary offense of only eight disciplined physicians (2 percent). Most offenses by disciplined physicians involve some aspect of patient care (negligence or incompetence, inappropriate prescribing, sexual contact, Medicare fraud) or tend to attract attention in the context of patient care, such as substance abuse or mental impairment. Even the 11 physicians primarily involved in academics and administration had offenses in the context of patient care: negligence or incompetence in six cases, substance abuse in three, and inappropriate sexual contact with a patient in one.

The FSMB (2009b) reported that during 2009, state medical boards took 5,721 actions against physicians, an increase of 342 actions over 2008. Each year, the FSMB publishes the Summary of Board Actions, a compilation of disciplinary actions initiated by its 70 member medical boards. In addition to providing disciplinary data, the report includes information about the context in which each board operates, including standards of proof required when prosecuting cases and the healthcare professions regulated. These actions range from loss or restriction of license to formal reprimand of the physician.

While the medical profession continues to grapple with the issue of sexual abuse perpetrated by healthcare providers, the Federation of State Medical Boards of the United States, Inc. (FSMB) issued guidelines to address medical practitioners' sexual boundaries and to help provide a framework through which to handle sexual misconduct cases. State medical boards are responsible for informing licensees that sexual misconduct in any form will not be tolerated, and when sexual misconduct does occur, they are to take prompt and decisive action against any licensee found to have participated in such conduct (FSMB, 2009a).

To that end, the FSMB (2009a) emphasizes that state medical boards have sufficient statutory authority to investigate complaints and any reported allegations of sexual misconduct. It also says state medical boards should place a high priority on the investigation of complaints of sexual misconduct due to patient vulnerability unique to such cases. The purpose of the investigation is to determine whether the report can be substantiated in order to collect sufficient facts and information for the board to make an informed decision as to how to proceed. If the state medical board's investigation indicates a reasonable probability that the physician has engaged in sexual misconduct, the state medical board should exercise its authority to intervene and take appropriate action to ensure the protection of the patient and the public at large.

Upon a finding of sexual misconduct, the FSMB (2009a) says that a medical board should take appropriate action and impose a sanction(s) reflecting the severity of the conduct and potential risk to patients. It says that findings of sexual misconduct are often sufficiently egregious as to warrant revocation of a physician's medical license; however, boards may find that mitigating circumstances do exist and, therefore, stay the revocation and institute terms and conditions of probation. In determining an appropriate disciplinary response, the FSMB advises medical boards to consider a number of factors relating to the misconduct, including the extent of harm done to the patient; the severity of the impropriety committed, and the context within which impropriety occurred; the degree of culpability of the licensee; the number of patients involved; and prior professional misconduct, disciplinary history, and malpractice.

Nurse Discipline

As discussed previously, problematic nurses have escaped detection and discipline for their medical malfeasance. As Ornstein et al. (2009b) have reported, "The board charged with overseeing California's 350,000 registered nurses often takes years to act on complaints of egregious misconduct, leaving nurses accused of wrongdoing free to practice without restrictions, an investigation by the *Times* and the nonprofit news organization ProPublica found. It's a high-stakes gamble that no one will be hurt as nurses with histories of drug abuse, negligence, violence and incompetence continue to provide care across the state. While the inquiries drag on, many nurses maintain spotless records. New employers and patients have no way of knowing the risks."

Reporters examined the case of every nurse who faced disciplinary action from 2002 to 2008—more than 2,000 cases in all—as well as hundreds of pages of court, personnel, and regulatory reports. They interviewed scores of nurses, patients, families, hospital officials, regulators, and experts. Among the findings is that the board took more than 3 years, on average, to investigate and discipline errant nurses, according to its own statistics. In at least six other large states, the process typically takes a year or less. In addition, the board failed to act against nurses whose misconduct already had been thoroughly documented and sanctioned by others. Reporters identified more than 120 nurses who were suspended or fired by employers, disciplined by another California licensing board, or restricted from practice by other states—yet have blemish-free records with the nursing board. The board gave probation to hundreds of nurses—ordering monitoring and work restrictions—then failed to crack down as many landed in trouble again and again. One nurse given probation in 2005 missed 38 drug screens, tested positive for alcohol five times, and was fired from a job before the board revoked his probation 3 years later. The board failed to use its authority to stop potentially dangerous nurses from practicing. It obtained emergency suspensions of nurses' licenses just 29 times from 2002 to 2007. In contrast, Florida's nursing regulators, who oversee 40 percent fewer nurses, take such action more than 70 times each year.

Later, the state Department of Consumer Affairs, which oversees the board, sent reporters a three-page list of "process improvements." Many were mundane or incremental adjustments, such as revising disciplinary guidelines or planning expert witness training. Others seemed more directly aimed at reducing delays: adding staff, meeting with investigators about stalled cases, and using computer systems to better track complaints. The *Times* and ProPublica found more than 60 nurses disciplined since 2002 who were accused of committing serious misconduct or mistakes in at least three health facilities before the board took action. The biggest bottleneck occurs at the investigation stage, as Consumer Affairs staffers struggle to handle complaints against nurses as well as those against cosmetologists, acupuncturists, and others. The nursing board must share a pool of fewer than 40 field investigators with up to 25 other licensing boards and bureaus. Some investigators handle up to 100 cases at a time. All told, cases closed by the nursing board in fiscal 2008 took an average of 1,254 days.

Weber and Ornstein (2009b) reported that shortly after the *Times/ProPublica* investigation made it to print, Governor Arnold Schwarzenegger replaced most members of the state Board of Registered Nursing, citing the unacceptable time it takes to discipline nurses accused of egregious misconduct. He fired three of six sitting board members, including President Susanne Phillips, in two-paragraph letters curtly thanking them for their service. Another member resigned the next day. "It is absolutely unacceptable that it takes years to investigate such outrageous allegations of misconduct against licensed health professionals whom the public rely on for their health and well-being," Schwarzenegger said in a written statement.

Ornstein and Weber (2009a) reported:

After moving swiftly to replace the leadership of the Board of Registered Nursing, California officials are revamping practices that had allowed errant nurses to work for years after complaints were filed against them. For the first time, the board is prioritizing complaints, moving first to investigate nurses who pose the greatest threat to the public. In addition, top officials will this month get subpoena power to gather documents about nurses accused of wrongdoing. Before, some cases sat for months until outside investigators issued such orders. The moves come after the *Times* and ProPublica disclosed in July that the board took more than three years on average to investigate and discipline even its most troubled nurses. Some were able to move from hospital to hospital despite accusations of assault, criminal activity or on-the-job drug use. Within days, Gov. Arnold Schwarzenegger replaced the majority of the board's members and the board's longtime executive officer resigned. Three months later, statistics show early progress on the governor's pledge to reform the system. In the first quarter of the fiscal year that started in July, the board filed formal accusations seeking disciplinary action against 159 nurses, compared with 68 during the same period a year earlier, officials said. Also in the first quarter, the board obtained emergency orders to suspend the licenses of six nurses, compared with none in the same period last year. The *Times* and ProPublica had found that California used such orders to stop dangerous nurses far less often than several other states.

The Role of the Medical Boards

The Pew Health Professions Commission conducted an extensive investigation of licensure and continued competency issues, and its report identifies four places in which assessment of competency can occur: upon entry into practice, for continuing authorization to practice, reentry to practice, and after disciplinary action (Kohn et al., 2000). The report recommended increased state regulation to require healthcare practitioners to "demonstrate their competence in the knowledge, judgment, technical skills and interpersonal skills relevant to their jobs throughout their career." It also noted that considerations of competence should include not only the basic and specialized knowledge and skills, but also other skills such as "capacity to admit errors." The report asserted that the current system that relies on continuing education and disciplinary action after a problem has occurred is insufficient.

As discussed, state medical and nursing boards have come under fire for failing to identify and discipline dangerous, law-breaking, or incompetent physicians and nurses, and for being remiss in their oversight responsibilities. As discussed, numerous practitioners continue to practice with suspended or revoked licenses, or are allowed to cross state lines and to continue working despite a questionable history of infractions, violations, and convictions. A growing movement by watchdog groups and patient-safety advocates has helped to create databases that healthcare consumers can access to help close the information gap on practitioners that these boards have facilitated. In 1996, the Massachusetts Board of Registration in Medicine was the first to provide physician profiles online; since then, more than 65 of 70 member boards of the FSMB have developed Web access to at least some physician information. Only a handful of state boards provide a summary of each disciplinary action taken against a physician as well as the nature of the offense that triggered the action (Sala, 2008).

Under the protection of the Tenth Amendment, states have exercised their powers to protect the health, safety, and welfare of its citizens, and pursuant to these "police powers," states are authorized to regulate professions such as medicine, which they accomplish by delegating authority to professional licensing boards. The boards work from the provisions of the modern medical practice act, which defines the practice of medicine, establishes the requirements for medical licensure, and establishes procedures for disciplinary action against licensees, according to the Federation of State Medical Boards (FSMB, 2006). The medical practice act also establishes the state board of medicine responsible for implementing and enforcing the act's provisions through its rule-making and adjudicative powers (FSMB, 2006).

The FSMB (retrieved October 2010a) stated, "Medicine is a regulated profession because of the potential harm to the public if an incompetent or impaired physician is licensed to practice. To protect the public from the unprofessional, improper, unlawful, fraudulent and/or incompetent practice of medicine, each of the 50 states, the District of Columbia and the U.S. territories has a medical practice act that defines the practice of medicine and delegates the authority to enforce the law to a state medical board. State medical boards license physicians, investigate complaints, discipline those who violate the law, conduct physician evaluations and facilitate rehabilitation of physicians where appropriate. By following up on complaints, medical boards give the public a way to enforce basic standards of competence and ethical behavior in their physicians, and physicians a way to protect the integrity of their profession."

Medical practice acts mandate the basics of medical licensure, and some go beyond to require good moral character as well as proof of malpractice insurance coverage or a clear criminal background check. State medical boards seldom require mandatory continuing education, practice audits, or recertification, which are all concrete measures to ensure quality of practice. Instead, they are most frequently the enforcers of discipline when licensees stray from acceptable medical conduct—or at least that is the ideal. Levels of real-world oversight suggest a different story. The medical disciplinary process is launched when a complaint against a licensee is filed or a law enforcement agency files a report with the medical board. The board then investigates this complaint, and if it is valid, it may pursue disciplinary action against the individual, which could range from a reprimand to license suspension or revocation. Although grounds for discipline vary from state to state, medical practice acts allow for discipline for gross incompetence, physical or mental impairment, substance abuse, practicing without a license, or discipline against practitioners who have been subject to disciplinary action in other states. State medical boards may also take disciplinary action against what they consider to be unprofessional conduct, such as violations of codes of medical ethics, or conduct otherwise unbecoming to the medical profession.

As the FSMB (retrieved October 2010b) states,

Medical boards also monitor licensed physicians' competence and professional conduct. They review and investigate complaints and/or reports received from patients, health professionals, government agencies, health care organizations and other state medical boards about physicians who may be incompetent or acting unprofessionally and take appropriate action against a physician's license if the person is found to have violated the law. State laws require that boards assure fairness and due process to any physician under investigation. While medical boards sometimes find it necessary to suspend or revoke licenses, regulators have found many problems can be resolved with additional education or training in appropriate areas. In other instances, it may be more appropriate to place physicians on probation or place restrictions on a physician's license to practice. This compromise protects the public while maintaining a valuable community resource in the physician. Probation and restrictions of a medical license can also be in place while a physician receives further training or rehabilitation.

The FSMB (2010b) states, "The most common complaint received by medical boards is allegations a physician has deviated from the accepted standard of medical care in a state. According to board investigators, some of the most common standard-of-care complaints include over-prescribing or prescribing the wrong medicine; failure to diagnose a medical problem that is found later; misreading X-rays to identify a medical problem; failure to get back to a patient with medical test results in a timely manner, which can lead to harm to that patient; failure to provide appropriate post-operative care; failure to respond to a call from hospital to help a patient in a traumatic situation. Other complaints allege sexual impropriety or substance abuse. Even complaints about rudeness could be indicative of a bigger issue."

To see what kind of activity with which state boards must contend, let's look at one of the most active states, California, whose board is responsible for licensing and regulating some 125,000 physicians and surgeons. Sala (2008) reported that the Medical Board of California's (MBC) complaints database included 191,577 complaint cases dating from 1949—although 90 percent of cases were opened in 1991 or later. Since 2000, 78.6 percent of physicians have zero complaints on record, and 1.4 percent have five or more complaints filed against them in this period. From January 2000 through March 2008, the MBC received 68,310 complaints against licensed physicians. Of these, 42,478 (62.2 percent) originated by members of the public—patients or their families; an additional 9,875 complaints originated from medical malpractice insurers, court clerks or healthcare facility peer review bodies, as well as from physician self-reports of malpractice judgments, settlements, and criminal convictions. Since 2004, 49.5 percent of complaints received against physicians have been classified as quality of care complaints. On average, more than 80 percent of all complaint cases received annually by the MBC were terminated by its central complaint unit without disciplinary or administrative action, including more than 90 percent of public complaints. About 23 percent of complaints were referred for field investigation, and of those, between 14 percent and 25 percent were "closed without merit." Cases with strong legal and medical evidence after field investigation are referred to the Attorney General for formal charges, known as an "accusation." According to MBC data, 13 percent to 23 percent of field investigations were referred to the Attorney General from 2000 to 2007. Processing complaints is costly. Sala (2008) indicated that the average per case cost of investigating complaints is $678, and that the average cost of an Attorney General investigation is $6,094 in 2000 to 2001, or $7,529 in current dollars. The average cost of prosecutions and hearings was $14,827 in 2000 to 2001, or $18,319 in current dollars.

Perhaps indicating that there is improvement to be made within medical boards, the FSMB (2009a) observed, "Medical board investigative divisions are always looking for ways to improve how they operate. Nevada, for instance, has instituted regular health care task force meetings that include not only investigators from the medical board, but also their counterparts from the FDA, FBI, state Department of Public Safety and other government agencies, as well as special investigators from insurance companies. The goal is to facilitate information sharing among organizations with a common interest in weeding out problem doctors. By delving into complaints and digging up all the relevant information, investigators make it possible for medical boards to take action when necessary against unethical or incompetent physicians. Ultimately, both the public and the medical profession benefit when expert investigators put physician misconduct under a magnifying glass."

In April 2009, Public Citizen's annual ranking of state medical boards showed that most states, including two of the largest, are not living up to their obligations to protect patients from doctors who are practicing substandard medicine. For the first time since Public Citizen has been publishing the rankings, California and Florida are among the 10 states with the lowest rates of serious disciplinary actions. Minnesota was the worst state when it came to disciplining doctors, and along with Maryland, South Carolina, and Wisconsin, has consistently been among the worst 10 states for each of the last six rankings. Overall, the rate of discipline for doctors in 2008 was 21.5 percent lower than the peak year of 2004. In 2008, there were 2.92 serious disciplinary actions per 1,000 physicians, compared to 3.72 actions per 1,000 physicians in 2004. This means that if the higher 2004 rate of discipline were still occurring, 770 more doctors would have been subject to serious disciplinary actions in 2008 than actually were.

The annual rankings are based on data from the Federation of State Medical Boards, specifically on the number of disciplinary actions taken against doctors in 2008. Public Citizen calculated the rate of serious disciplinary actions (revocations, surrenders, suspensions, and probation/restrictions) per 1,000 doctors in each state. The number of actions in 2008 was averaged over the past 3 years to establish the state's rank. California is one of five states with the largest decrease in rank for doctor discipline since the 2001 to 2003 period, dropping from a rank of 22 to 43. The four other states with the biggest decline are Alabama (13 to 36); Georgia (15 to 42); Mississippi (20 to 48); and New Hampshire (25 to 46). All of these states had large decreases in the actual rates along with the decrease in rank.

The best states when it comes to doctor discipline, in order, are Alaska, Kentucky, Ohio, Arizona, Oklahoma, North Dakota, Louisiana, Iowa, Colorado, and Maine. The five states whose rank has improved the most since 2001 to 2003 are Hawaii (51 to 13); North Carolina (41 to 14); Maine (34 to 10); the District of Columbia (42 to 17); and Illinois (35 to 15). The progress in these states is commendable because the medical boards have figured out ways—often with legislatively mandated increases in funding and staffing—to improve the protection for patients from doctors who need to be disciplined but, in the past, were disciplined much less rigorously.

"The overall national downward trend of serious disciplinary actions against physicians is troubling because it indicates many states are not living up to their obligations to protect patients from bad doctors," said Sidney Wolfe, MD, Public Citizen's Acting President and Director of its Health Research Group. "State lawmakers must give serious attention to finding out why their states are failing to discipline doctors and then they need to take action—either legislatively or by applying pressure on medical boards. Otherwise, they will continue to allow doctors to endanger the lives and health of their residents because of inadequate discipline" (*Public Citizen*, 2009).

Wolfe said that medical boards are likely to do a better job disciplining physicians if most, if not all, of the following conditions exist:

- They have adequate funding (all money from license fees going to fund board activities instead of going into the state treasury for general purposes).
- They have adequate staffing.
- They undertake proactive investigations rather than only respond to complaints.

- They use all available/reliable data from other sources such as Medicare and Medicaid sanctions, hospital sanctions, and malpractice payouts.
- They have excellent leadership.
- They are independent from state medical societies and other parts of the state government.
- A reasonable legal framework exists for disciplining doctors (the "preponderance of the evidence" rather than "beyond reasonable doubt" or "clear and convincing evidence" as the legal standard for discipline). (*Public Citizen*, 2009)

As medical boards scramble to improve their oversight responsibilities, recidivism of disciplined healthcare professionals lingers as a pressing issue; however, there is a paucity of information on the recidivism rates for medical practitioners. Zhong et al. (2009) sought to determine what factors might affect the outcomes of remediation, including the likelihood of recidivism, among nurses who had been the subject of disciplinary action and had been put on probation by a state board of nursing in six states. A 29-item questionnaire was used to investigate the records of 207 RNs (57 percent), LPNs (36 percent), and advanced practice RNs (APRNs, 3 percent) who were disciplined and put on probation by a state nursing board in 2001, as well as to collect data on their employment settings, the boards' actions, and remediation outcomes (the presence or absence of recidivism); 491 nurses who had not been disciplined served as controls. Zhong et al. (2009) reported that of the disciplined group, 39 percent recidivated between 2001 and 2005. Three factors were shown to influence the recidivism rate: having a history of criminal conviction, having committed more than one violation before the 2001 probation, and changing employers during the probationary period. Data on their history of criminal conviction prior to state board disciplinary action were available for 112 (54 percent) of the 207 nurses. Among those 112, 35 percent had a history of criminal conviction, whereas only 3 percent of the control group reported this history. The recidivism rate among those with a history of criminal conviction (56 percent, 22 of 39 nurses) was nearly twice as high as the rate among those without such a history (33 percent, 24 of 73). Also, 33 percent of the disciplined nurses changed employers during their probation; the recidivism rate among them was more than twice the rate among the disciplined nurses who stayed with the same employer. The recidivism rate of the 45 disciplined nurses who committed more than one practice-related violation from 1996 through 2001 was twice as high as the rate of those who committed only a single violation. Forty-four percent of the disciplined nurses (82 of 186; employment information was not available for 21 nurses) were employed in long-term care facilities when the incident resulting in the 2001 probation occurred, while 35 percent (65 of 186) reported employment in hospitals at that time. According to the National Sample Survey of Registered Nurses, in 2000 an estimated 7 percent of all U.S. RNs worked in long-term care or home healthcare settings; the Zhong et al. (2009) study found that 34 percent of RNs disciplined in 2001 worked in long-term care or home healthcare settings, a proportion nearly five times greater than would be expected if those who were disciplined were evenly distributed across all employment settings. Zhong et al. (2009) emphasize that healthcare regulators and nursing employers should be aware of the association between a history of criminal conviction and the likelihood of committing a violation that requires state nursing board disciplinary action. Nurses are not the only recidivists. In their study of how physicians are disciplined by state medical boards throughout the United States, Grant and Alfred (2007) also found that there are a significantly large number of repeat offenders among physicians who have received board sanctions, indicating a possible need for greater monitoring of disciplined physicians or less reliance upon rehabilitative sanctions.

Sanctions and Legal Action

Recidivism may not be such a problem if practitioners faced stronger sanctions for their medical malfeasance, some experts suggest. As Hockley (2005) has observed, "Victims pay a high price for being targeted—emotionally, physically, psychologically, spiritually, socially and financially. One approach to redressing what has happened to the victims is through the legal system. Exposing even the most marginal of cases may eventually bring a halt to this phenomenon of staff-initiated violence against those in their care" (pp. 77–96).

Hockley (2005) states that an advantage of taking legal action is that it is "one way of making the individual and the organization accountable for their actions because of the strong legal framework in place" (pp. 77–96). Freckelton (1998) argued that criminal sanctions have "the advantage of being highly public, enabling the imposition of harsh sanctions and broadcasting in a very clear way a message to the general community as to standards of professional behavior which will not be tolerated. It is a flagship in upholding the rights of victims. However, it is dependent upon proof of criminality beyond reasonable doubt" (pp. 26–37).

But not everyone agrees. According to Smith (1998), "The criminal justice system has faced the problem of preventing and deterring deviant behavior throughout history, and we are just starting to realize that the use of the criminal courts and the imposition of judicial punishments may not be the most effective way of changing people's behavior for the better. Often, the criminal justice system acts as a rather blunt instrument which fails to deter and harms those who are caught in its net in unintended ways. The key question: Do criminal sanctions deter healthcare providers from acting illegally or are there better ways of preventing deviant conduct from occurring in the healthcare context" (p. 2)?

Healthcare providers are faced with a wide variety of legal as well as informal controls over their conduct. They have their own internalized ethical codes of conduct to follow, as well as more formal mechanisms to keep them in check. These include investigations into complaints, whether by the public health department, medical boards, or local, state, and federal law enforcement, as well as the threat of criminal charges or civil cases brought against the healthcare provider or the employer by the patient's family. As Smith (1998) explained, "In various jurisdictions of the United States, new offenses have been enacted which make certain types of professional misconduct criminal, for example, sexual contact in professional relationships. The extent to which sanctions are appropriate and effective in deterring unprofessional conduct by so-called white-collar offenders such as doctors is hotly debated and many have argued that more appropriate sanctions should be used such as adverse publicity, financial penalties or further compulsory training in ethics and professional conduct" (p. 4). Smith (1998) added, "There are also a variety of systems in place which ensure that the conduct of healthcare providers is monitored. Practitioners may be subject to peer review, auditing of their professional activities, and ongoing requirements to maintain skills through compulsory education" (p. 4).

Smith (2002) outlined a four-step model of sanctions for staff-initiated violence against those in their care; step one involves conciliation. As Smith (2002) explains, "Many countries have a statutory health complaint agency whose function it is to respond to and investigate patient complaints. At times, by conciliation the complaints may be resolved with an apology or paying a sum of money to the complainant. However, if conciliation fails, the agency may refer the complaint to the registration body for disciplinary action."

Steps two through four involve civil, disciplinary, and criminal action. Smith (2002) said that to take action in the legal sense is to seek to enforce resolution of a right, to seek redress for a wrong, to punish, or to deter: "A civil action occurs when one person seeks redress or compensation for wrongs committed by another party, such as in medical malpractice." Smith (2002) adds that "consumers of professional services who have suffered loss as a result of unprofessional conduct may commence civil proceedings for damages in negligence, trespass or breach of contract; if successful it will provide a financial sum to successful claimants, which aims to place them in the same position they would have been in, had the wrongful act not taken place. Normally, an award of damages aims at compensation rather than punishment.... A criminal action in contrast, could arise when the behavior of a person in society is considered of such a serious nature that the state uses its powers to punish or deter that behavior, such as in cases of homicide."

Some experts hold out for self-policing on the part of healthcare professionals as a deterrence measure. As Smith (1998) explains,

> In the healthcare context, both disciplinary and criminal proceedings are principally deterrence-based in that Draconian sanction such as imprisonment may be imposed upon practitioners who fail to demonstrate appropriate standards of professional conduct or who fail to comply with the provisions of the criminal law.... In order for a compliance-based system to be effective, the various motivations of the actors need to be considered. First, healthcare providers may seek to comply with...those ancient ethical precepts of the relevant profession such as those espoused in the writings of Hippocrates. Second, providers may be motivated through a sense of social responsibility in that they seek to avoid harm being inflicted on their patients through unprofessional or incompetent conduct. Thirdly, utilitarian motivations based on financial and lifestyle considerations may guide a practitioner's actions such that compliance is achieved through a self-interested fear of losing income and position. They may also try to avoid the stigma of disciplinary hearings and the attendant publicity that attracts. (p. 5)

Freckelton (1998) mused as to whether there should be special criminal offenses for "nurses or doctors who are particularly inept in their performance, thereby causing serious injury or even death, or who exploit their position of power to have sexual relations with their patients, whether adult, minor, or disabled by intellectual impairment, psychiatric illness or unconsciousness." What about negligence? Freckelton (1998) noted, "Grossly negligent behavior which results in death is a form of manslaughter. Generally, though, grossly negligent behavior which results in injury, physical or mental, does not constitute a criminal offense, so long as it does not cross the line into intentional or reckless conduct causing injury or conduct endangering serious injury or death. It is, of course, actionable under civil law" (pp. 26–37).

In a number of cases of medical murder, the perpetrators attempted to explain away their actions by blaming their difficult childhoods or other personal atrocities for their proclivities toward violence. Freckelton (1998) said that healthcare providers can blame their behavior on any number of factors, especially stress or substance abuse, as well as mental illness and abuse in their formative years, which is notable among these practitioners:

> Many mitigating factors which are regularly raised in the criminal courts in an attempt to persuade judges to impose punishments which are not excessively harsh or crushing are relevant to a number of transgressing doctors, nurses and others in the health fields. If the focus for the imposition of punishment in the disciplinary context be to any degree upon moral turpitude as

it is in the criminal courts, then a significant percentage of healthcare practitioners will legitimately be able to put before those dealing with their ethical
transgressions plea material which is reminiscent of that advanced on behalf
of their less advantaged brethren in the criminal courts. (pp. 26–37)

Medical practitioners should not be let off the hook easily, asserted
Freckelton (1998), due to their ability to work the system: "Given the nature
of their access to the instruments of power and the privileges that attach
to the status of their profession, they are well placed to consider the moral
ramifications of what they do and to estimate rationally the consequences of
their actions in terms of the harm that may be occasioned to victims. The difficulty occurs when a doctor is not particularly morally culpable and yet his
or her actions are exceptionally damaging to the public." Freckelton (1998)
added, "Most professional improprieties by medical practitioners, as well as
nurses and other healthcare professionals…are not committed in a context of
economic deprivation, intellectual impairment…rather, they are committed
by educated, advantaged representatives of a professional elite. Often they are
committed for professional advancement, exploitative sexual gratification or
pecuniary gain" (pp. 26–37).

Although having a license revoked is designed not to punish but to set
an example in many cases, there is a great deal of punitive force behind the
removal of a healthcare professional's right to practice, as it is "the death
of his professional life," according to Hadwiger (1933), cited by Freckelton
(1998), who added, "It does not amount to deprivation of capacity for unfet-
tered movement, but it does impose a career-long blight upon a professional's working life." Freckelton (1998) said that the healthcare professional's
attitude toward the misconduct is relevant to the final disposition of the
case: "In criminal law, contrition by the offender is conventionally viewed
as a significantly mitigating factor. This is because it reassures the sentencer
that repetition of the offending conduct is less likely than it might otherwise be as a result of the offender's insight into the wrongfulness of his or
her conduct and its consequences for victims.… From the profession's point
of view, the expression of contrition by an errant but remorseful doctor
serves the collateral purpose of reinforcing the immorality of breaching the
profession's standards, and also signals to others that the doctor involved
accepts the proposition that what he or she has done is unacceptable in the
eyes of the profession" (pp. 26–37).

Freckelton (1998) noted the difficulty the system has in deciding what to
do about problematic practitioners: "When doctors behave improperly, what
they do can quite reasonably be classified as both an abuse of power and as
extremely damaging to their patients. When nurses behave incompetently,
it strikes anxiety into potential patients' sense of well-being. It is affronting
to any of us as consumers of medical services to think that we could be the

subject of exploitation, gross incompetence or assault by doctors and other healthcare professionals whom we need to trust. However, if the object of dealing with the misdeeds of doctors, nurses and other healthcare practitioners is ultimately to protect patients, then it should only be in extreme cases that the criminal law needs to be the means of regulation. Where there is rape by a nurse or where a doctor commits an act which would constitute a criminal act for other persons in the community, such as gross negligence resulting in death, by all means let him or her be charged" (pp. 26–37).

There is a gray area, Freckelton (1998) asserted: "However, where the conduct of the medical or other practitioner falls within a class of behavior that is borderline criminal and more properly to be regarded as disgraceful, incompetent, impaired or unethical, there is often a better way to deal with it. The disciplinary process, where the infraction needs only to be proved on the balance of probabilities, is both easier of access and offers readier opportunities of proof. As police and prosecutors will eloquently claim, proof beyond reasonable doubt is a high standard" (pp. 26–37).

The Role of Healthcare Security

No work is complete without a look at the role hospital security plays in detecting medical malfeasance. Hospitals are relatively safe places, medical errors and other adverse events notwithstanding. "I don't think serious violent crime is running rampant in hospitals today," said Joseph Bellino, CHPA, HEM, President of the International Association for Healthcare Security and Safety (IAHSS) and system executive, security at Memorial Hermann in Houston, Texas. "Do I think it happens? Yes. I'd be lying to you if I said there was no crime in hospitals, but I don't believe it is widespread. When we discover there is a crime, we deal with it. If you have a good security department and a good relationship with your local police, you can conduct an investigation that will lead to the apprehension of the perpetrators. In the past it has been my experience that some hospitals are reluctant to file criminal charges against employees and visitors but that's changing."

The IAHSS, which has been keeping tabs on hospital crime statistics for more than a decade, determined in its 2004 survey (the latest year for which data are available), that IAHSS survey participants reported a continued decline in total crime, driven by fewer incidents of property crimes as well as a drop in assaults. The survey is not indicative of the crime rates found in all of the country's 6,000-plus hospitals, as the 192 hospitals participating in the survey only represent a 20 percent sampling of IAHSS-member facilities.

In 2004, these participating hospitals reported 7,764 crimes; in 2003, 219 participating hospitals reported 10,794 crimes. In the 2004 survey, 5.71

crimes per hospital were reported by survey participants in six violent crime categories—murder, rape, other sexual assaults, robbery, aggravated assaults, and simple assaults; in the 2003 survey, 7.70 violent crimes per hospital were reported. According to the IAHSS, violent crimes accounted for about 12 percent of all hospital crimes; simple assaults, which accounted for 83 percent of hospital violent crimes in 2004, ranked third in the number of total incidents (904) in that year, after larceny theft (4,412) and vandalism (1,317). In hospitals, the simple assaults tend to be a crime committed by patients; in the 2004 survey, the patient was reported as the perpetrator 59 percent of the time. Approximately 1 in 100 hospitals reported a murder in 2004, and six rapes were reported in the 2004 survey. Hospitals reported 33 incidences of other *sexual assaults* (defined as any sexual assault not defined as forcible rape); in these crimes, 50 percent of victims were patients, 33 percent were employees, and 17 percent were visitors. The perpetrators of these sexual assaults were employees (47 percent), patients (39 percent), and visitors (14 percent). Overall, in 2004, employees were victims in 39 percent of the crimes and patients were victims in 20 percent of the crimes. Employees were most often victims of aggravated assaults, simple assaults, larceny theft, and motor vehicle theft; patients were primarily victims of suicide and other sexual assaults. Visitors/outsiders were the perpetrators involved in most of the incidents of rape and robbery.

Bellino cautions that crime statistics are relative to the healthcare facility's region.

> I was at Hanover Hospital in Pennsylvania for eight years and we had a very aggressive security program, with 24 security officers for a 116-bed hospital. I was in an area with a population of about 58,000 and we only had about a 3 percent increase in crime a year. So one could argue that because we had a good security program maybe we're keeping crime out, or are we just indicative of the lack of crime in the community in general? It could be a different story in an inner city hospital with 400 or 500 beds, where crime rates tend to be somewhat higher. We have a good security program with an active investigational arm to it, and we use electronics for surveillance. We have identified people who have committed crimes and we filed charges, so the word got out that hey, if you go to such-and-such medical center with criminal intent, and they catch you, you're going to jail. (Interview with author.)

Bellino continues,

> I think that a hospital succeeds against crime when it has a solid security department with a proactive crime prevention program that also reaches out to the community. It assures patients that when they come here, it's a safe haven and that they can get well and go home. The analogy I use is that a hospital room is a hotel room without locks, and that you have people who are at

risk because they are ill and they can't protect themselves or fight back, and so everyone who works in the hospital, and not just security, has to be watchful for crime against patients, staff and visitors. (Interview with author.)

Violence can take many forms at a healthcare institution, and staff must be ready to handle anything, Bellino says:

Sexual assaults on patients happen, but they are relatively rare and it's usually perpetrated by an outsider. Sexual assault of employees happens, but again, it's usually by an outsider, not a fellow employee. White-collar financial crimes such as embezzlement and fraud happen in hospitals, as do break-ins into offices to steal computers or petty cash. I was at one healthcare organization where we conducted an undercover operation; we found that the entire materials management department was stealing from the hospital and we were able to shut them down. But again, that kind of organized crime doesn't happen every day. The big one that everyone is struggling with is violence within hospital walls. Healthcare institutions frequently deal with people who have psychological and emotional disorders combined with abuse of narcotics or alcohol, and that's a deadly cocktail. When people have to wait in the emergency department and they don't think they're being taken care of, they get upset, and they let you know about it. Again, having a good security program helps deter and prevent crime as much as possible. (Interview with author.)

Sometimes that calls for surveillance, Bellino says:

We have cameras in our hospital but at the same time, we don't have them directly focused on patients. They are in common areas, and we let everyone know that when you walk into our building, you will be observed. We have a sign at every entrance that says 'for your safety and security this building is under video and audio surveillance.' We also have a very strict covert surveillance program. If we suspect that something illegal is happening, and that the only way we can catch or prove that it is, we will use covert surveillance. There was a time when a security director at a large urban hospital caught a Munchausen by Proxy Syndrome suspect. The mother kept blaming staff for harming her child, but thanks to video surveillance, they were able to detect that she was to blame, not the staff. In one case where security staff members were accused of stealing computer equipment, I used covert surveillance and it revealed that the technical staff was to blame. In another case we had a gang breaking in and we couldn't figure out how they were getting in to steal computers. We were able to determine how it happened via covert video, and we caught all three suspects and they were convicted. So surveillance has its benefits, but hospital security personnel must be very careful and responsible; I say keep it legal and keep it quiet, so if nothing comes about, you don't embarrass anyone. (Interview with author.)

To help bolster hospital security, the Security Industry Association (SIA) has developed the "Securing America's Hospitals Act of 2008," legislation that authorizes $500 million in federal grant funds. Modeled after the Port Security Grant Program and the Public Transportation Security Assistance Program, this proposal calls for the Department of Health and Human Services to administer funds for the acquisition, installation, or use of electronic technology, including access control systems, identification credentials, bomb detection devices, video surveillance cameras, locking devices, and mass annunciation systems. The proposed legislation would limit each grant award to $100,000 annually so that the maximum number of hospitals, regardless of geographic location or bed size, can participate in the program. The federal share of the program would be 100 percent for projects less than $25,000, 90 percent for projects between $25,000 and $50,000, and 80 percent for larger projects.

This proposed legislation is supported by the IAHSS, and Bellino said the organization is working on a plan to get its members working with lawmakers to help pass the bill that has stalled in Congress. "Congress is interested in it but they want to hear from us, so we have to get the word out among our constituents," Bellino says. The IAHSS issued the following statement in support of hospital security grant legislation: "There has been, of course, improvement in many healthcare facility protection programs; however, overall progress is nominal. Above and beyond the daily incidents that challenge healthcare, many facilities do not have the resources to appropriately protect their environment. Whether due to a lack of mandated security regulations or the unique cost pressures placed on our nation's healthcare delivery system serving uninsured and underinsured patients, the funding allocated to protect these critical infrastructures is severely limited."

The Role of Healthcare Human Resources

While hospital security directors and personnel do what they can to help prevent crime, another group associated with healthcare institutions, human resource managers, is battling the threat of negligent hiring of healthcare professionals. Norman Bates, JD, President of Liability Consultants Inc., who has been retained in numerous cases nationwide by both plaintiff and defense firms in civil cases regarding inadequate security, workplace violence, and negligent hiring, said healthcare institutions are finding themselves increasingly liable for the actions of their employees. At the heart of the debate is something called *respondent superior doctrine*, which is defined as vicarious liability for the actions of one's employees. "Say a fellow driving a truck for a transport company gets into an accident; responsibility for his actions is left to the employer," Bates explained. "The concept of negligent hiring law has really evolved over the last 20 years or so, and now the test of whether an employee is furthering the interests of the employer is being applied; if the answer to this question is yes, then the action may be within the scope of their employment. For example, a person hired to be a nurse's aide did not have in his job description the right to sexually assault a patient. But in the case of a bartender who serves too many drinks, he may be furthering his employer's financial interests, but the same bartender who assaults a patron is not furthering his employer's interests."

According to Renas (1991),

> Historically, an employer has been held liable for the criminal acts of his employee if one could show that the employee was acting within the scope of his/her employment. Consequently, lawsuits were frequently brought against employers under the theory of respondent superior, a doctrine that holds the employers liable for the negligent, on-the-job actions of his/her employees. Recently, a subtle change in the law has occurred. Today, employers can be held for the criminal actions of their employees even if those actions are not job-related. More and more, injured persons claim the employer is guilty of negligent hiring. This theory appears to hold an employer liable for damages—to employees and others—if the employer failed to conduct a 'reasonably proper' pre-employment background investigation of an employee who later causes damages. Legal theory also seems to hold an employer liable for an employee's actions if the employee is kept on the payroll when the employer knows of—or reasonably can suspect the employee of criminal or tortious behavior in the past, present, or future.

Renas (1991) added, "Today, an employer can be held liable for crimes committed by an employee even if those actions are not job-related. Injured persons are now claiming that employers are guilty of 'negligent hiring.'"

According to Bates,

> The concept of negligent hiring for hospitals places focus on the fact that this particular class of employers is hiring people who are in some kind of responsible position that has unsupervised access to a vulnerable population like children, the elderly or the mentally ill. In this case there is responsibility on the employer's part to do some screening and be careful in their selection of potential employees. Negligence is in the failure to use the proper background screening. (Interview with author.)

Bates continues,

> We have seen a lot of these kinds of cases. One involved a visiting nurse association that hired a fellow to be a home health aide, a non-medical position in which he would have unsupervised access to the home and to the patient. He was hired without a background check and he ended up robbing and

murdering a 32-year-old man with cerebral palsy. We went to trial and the
jury awarded $26 million because it was so outraged at what it heard. We've
published a couple of studies looking at any case involving a violent crime and
certain percent of these are when employees committed the crime, we have
found over the years that the jury verdicts tend to be a bit higher in the cases
where the employee committed the crime. There is a certain outrage factor
that the jury reaches. (Interview with author.)

Bates states that the majority of cases settle out of court.

That's a rule of thumb in tort law, and of the 5 percent to 10 percent of cases
that do go to trial, I can't think of any that have come back for the defendant. From time to time you do see the employer win because the jury feels
that the person didn't have a negative background that was relevant in some
way or that the employer was negligent, period. In order for these cases to
proceed there has to be something in the employee's background, some kind
of criminal history that could have been discovered through reasonable diligence and also that would have made it foreseeable that this person was at
risk—that this person had a violent background, for example. You might
say, 'Well, violence and rape go hand in hand,' but even though rape is a sex
crime, it's a violent crime, and without that history, the law would allow the
defendant's employer to get the case dismissed. So, I think cases go through
a natural vetting process and if it goes to trial, more likely than not it will
come back for the plaintiff. (Interview with author.)

While far from black and white, healthcare hiring occasionally has its
"no-brainer," so to speak. "Sometimes the answer is easy because someone's
got a violent background and so you're not going to let them work with kids
or the elderly or anyone, actually," Bates said. He adds,

Employers don't want to be discovered hiring anyone who has a criminal background check, but from a social policy you don't want to prohibit someone
who made one mistake in their life from ever being able to work again—you
would be perpetuating the problem if you did that. So what we have seen over
the years evolve is employers giving consideration to what a potential hire's
crime was, how long ago they committed it, and what they have done with
their life since then, so that a youthful indiscretion, such as possession of marijuana or shoplifting, doesn't get held against them. These are seldom going to
be the types of crimes that exclude someone from employment. Some states
list the offenses that would preclude someone from working, and healthcare
employers such as operators of hospitals, nursing homes, mental health facilities, or even daycare should be cognizant of these offenses. Employers can also
have their own criteria that address any violent behavior, including domestic
violence, and there is often a standard of care affecting hiring practices established by agencies such as the Joint Commission. (Interview with author.)

Renas (1991) explained that many injured parties claim that employers are liable for damages caused by their employees if they fail to conduct a thorough preemployment background investigation of employees who later commit crimes. He pointed out that "Healthcare facilities and other organizations that invite the public onto their premises have a heightened responsibility to protect their patients and guests from the criminal acts of their employees. Yet one study shows that only one in five hospitals checks the criminal records of job applicants. In many instances, employers who attempt to investigate the background of job applicants are thwarted in their efforts by previous employers who refuse to divulge vital information. More and more, employers who provide 'damaging' information on job applicants find themselves being sued for invasion of privacy."

"Almost without exception hospitals screen as best as we can given the technology and the information available," said Jeffery Payne, past Vice President of the American Society for Healthcare Human Resources Administration (ASHHRA) and Vice President of Human Resources at Lakeland Regional Medical Center in Florida. "Most hospitals' human resources departments will conduct an investigation at least five to seven years back into a person's work history to look at criminal warrants, and so on. Larger hospitals will invariably use outside companies for that, so they depend upon that third party's expertise and technology. But even still, some stuff just doesn't surface."

Payne points to a notorious case in Florida in which a former anesthesia nurse was found guilty of the first-degree murder of a 24-year-old woman by lethal injection of the fast-acting anesthetic drug propofol. Oliver Travis O'Quinn, who had worked at Shands HealthCare in Gainesville, Florida, was sentenced to life in prison without parole for the murder of Michelle Herndon in November 2005 (Chun, 2008). Payne cites the Florida Employment Law Letter's recent cover story on the O'Quinn case, "Patient's death results in negligent hiring claim against hospital," in which it was reported that Shands-Gainesville, a University of Florida teaching hospital, was being sued. "Apparently this nurse had been stealing drugs—drugs were reported missing and employees had reported the nurse was taking them," Payne said. "The defendants claim that Shands didn't act reasonably when it 'omitted a competent background check of the nurse that would have revealed his previous theft of drugs' and 'failed to reassign or fire him when the theft was reported before [the] death.' According to the article, the Florida appeals court overturned an earlier dismissal of the defendant's claim and has allowed the case to proceed with a negligent hiring case."

As Ahearn (2009) points out,

> In the healthcare industry, where millions of patients—often in vulnerable and compromised positions—put their lives in the hands of trusted caregivers

every day, the importance of background screening for current and potential staff members goes beyond cost, compliance, and legal liability issues. It can be a matter of life or death. Such was the case with Charles Cullen, a former nurse who in 2003 told authorities he had murdered as many as 40 patients through lethal injections during the 16 years he worked at 10 hospitals around the country. While those hospitals that did review Cullen's work history had charges against them dropped because reference checks of past employers did not reveal any past firings or suspensions, a more thorough and investigative background screening could have uncovered his negative behavior patterns and prevented his access to patients. To ensure the safety of both patients and health care staff, and to avoid catastrophic hires like Cullen, it is imperative that all health care employees—from doctors and nurses to the hospital's maintenance workers—undergo a criminal background check during the hiring process, and a background screening process should be ongoing for existing staff as well.

Criminal background checks are the most popular form of inquiry into a potential employee's work history. In 2008, ADP Employer Services, a provider of human resource, payroll, and benefits administration services, released its annual screening index, a yearly evaluation of employment screening and hiring trends. The index showed that of the nearly 5.8 million background checks completed, criminal background checks were the most popular screening tool by human resource departments in 2007, outnumbering all other background checks by more than three times. ADP clients conducted 1.7 million criminal background checks last year; driving records were second to criminal checks, with almost 500,000 completed. The study also indicated that 10 percent of background checks came back with at least one hit, and that more than one in three candidates have violations or convictions on their driving record, including 10 percent who have had their licenses suspended, revoked, or withdrawn in the last 7 years. The study also showed that 44 percent of job candidates who were checked for credit have at least one mark on their credit reports; that one out of 20 (5 percent) of the candidate reference verifications that contained information differences also had at least one negative remark about the candidate; and that of the 1.7 million criminal record checks, 6 percent of candidates showed a criminal record over the last 7 years.

Ahearn (2009) outlined three critical reasons hospitals are strongly encouraged to screen prospective hires and their existing employees:

- *Danger to patients*: A prospective employee who has been convicted of a violent or drug-related crime is unsuitable for a job in close proximity to patients, as this situation could expose both the patients and the hospital to enormous risk.

- *Danger to staff*: If an employee with a violent criminal past is hired, fellow staff members are extremely vulnerable, as they are often busy caring for patients and not watching their coworkers. Instruments and medications can be used to cause harm.
- *Potential lawsuits*: If patients or staff members are harmed as a result of insufficient background screening, they can sue the hospital for negligent hiring. These lawsuits can be expensive, and, in some cases, the courts may award compensation totaling millions of dollars to victims of workplace violence.

Although hospitals know they should be conducting thorough preemployment screening, there is some indication that hospitals are not doing everything they can to screen these potential employees. According to a survey of 395 human resource managers conducted by ASHHRA, hospital human resource managers primarily rely on four screening tools in checking the backgrounds of job applicants: information contained in the application form, the preemployment interview, letters of reference, and phone calls to previous employers. For some positions, the scrutiny of licenses, diplomas, and certificates is a significant factor in screening job applicants. Only about 20 percent of the respondents routinely check the criminal records of job applicants, and relatively few require drug testing as a part of the application process. Interestingly, applicants for security jobs are much more likely to be subjected to drug testing than other job applicants, and there is a greater tendency to review the criminal records of security job applicants than applicants for other positions. One respondent routinely checks each applicant's driver's license through the state Division of Motor Vehicles.

There is no recommended minimum number of background checks that should be conducted, according to Payne, who adds,

> There is some interest in starting to advocate for a national installation on referencing, but that's a little different than background checks. I struggle with the creation of a national standard because any time you try to do a one-size-fits-all approach in a country as big and diverse as ours, you will run into exceptions everywhere. At best what I would suggest is that an organization like ASHHRA have suggested guidelines, and then organizations are free to follow those or not, or to exceed them. Hospitals certainly took notice of the necessity of background checks when a nurse, Charles Cullen, went from facility to facility, killing patients. Yes, he was a serial killer but he was also an aberration. He caused a lot of people to ask themselves, "how was this person able to do this?" Part of it is because hospitals are reluctant to share employment references. As I mentioned, all hospitals I know perform background checks of some sort or another. Where hospitals might differ is how far back to check, how many previous employers to check, what state and federal agencies

to contact, etc. Many hospitals use background check companies; these companies provide a menu of options to choose from and price accordingly. The Joint Commission, in its standards, specifies that background checks need to occur and they have expanded to include volunteers, students, and so on, in the healthcare environment. (Interview with author.)

According to the accreditation organization, the Joint Commission, staff, students, and volunteers who work in the same capacity as staff who provide care, treatment, and services, would be expected to have criminal background checks verified when required by law and regulation and organization policy. This means that if state law, regulation, or organization policy requires background checks on all employees, volunteers, and students, the Joint Commission expects them to be done on all three categories. If state law requires background checks on only specified types of healthcare providers (such as nursing assistants), then the Joint Commission would require background checks on only those specified in state law, unless organization policy goes beyond state law. If state law requires background checks on all "employees," the Joint Commission says the healthcare organization should seek an opinion from the state on what categories of healthcare workers are considered "employees." If the state clearly does not consider volunteers or students to be employees, then the Joint Commission would not require background checks on them (again, unless organization policy goes beyond state law and requires it). The Joint Commission explains further that if state law is ambiguous as to the definition of employee, the organization can define the scope of background checks to fit its own definition. As such, they may include or exclude students and volunteers, and the Joint Commission would survey to hospital policy. In the absence of a state law on criminal background checks, the Joint Commission says each healthcare organization can develop its own expectations, and it would evaluate compliance with the organization's internal policy only. There would be no Joint Commission expectation that an organization check categories of providers beyond what is required in their own policy, which must comply with law and regulation. All criminal background checks must be documented by the organization.

Renas (1991) asserted that "traditional screening tools such as letters of reference, personal interviews, data sheets, and application forms are generally inadequate in preventing liability for negligent hiring. In fact, these instruments are not designed to detect tendencies toward violence or other antisocial patterns of behavior."

Bates pointed out that no tool used by human resource managers can magically detect a healthcare serial killer. "You won't really know what's going on with people but if they have a history of violence that is discoverable, that's the critical point at which you can do something about it," he said.

"If they have some history of violence at their previous place of employment, where they threatened someone or actually assaulted someone, it becomes dicey whether or not that employer will tell you. This is why we keep telling our clients, when you do the background checks and you do the reference checks, make sure you write down everything they tell you—when they say 'we can't do anything more than verify employment,' then you write that down, the date and time and who you spoke to. It's an imperfect science of detection."

Renas (1991) also said that the in-person interview, even though the most commonly used screening device, is often the weakest: "While it allows the interviewer (employer) to assess the interviewee's (applicant) social skills and communication abilities, it cannot detect honestly or trustworthiness. Application for employment forms have their limitations too. Often the applicant will omit details, fail to list brief stints of employment, or give a nebulous reason for leaving a job. In short, the application form is designed to create a favorable impression rather than raise red flags. Since the applicant is usually allowed to select references to be contracted by the prospective employer, s(he) will always list individuals who will provide a positive—if not glowing—recommendation. Even when names are not provided by the applicant, references tend to be positive because they don't want to be charged with libel or slander, or because they are unaware of an applicant's criminal background. Like the application form, a resume is designed to elicit a positive response from the prospective employer." The accuracy of a potential healthcare employee's resume is also suspect. According to Equifax Services, an audit of 100 resumes submitted to Equifax Services by one client revealed that 68 of them contained 129 items of erroneous information. This single audit showed 41 incorrect dates of employment, 26 incorrect dates of education, 11 instances of incorrect salary, 11 nonexistent employers, and seven incorrect grade point averages (Renas, 1991).

Healthcare institutions make poor hiring choices because they have incomplete information, yet getting the entire picture is challenging due to former employers' reluctance to share the details that count. As Renas (1991) stated, "Previous employers are often reluctant to provide detailed information to a prospective employer because they fear that the applicant will file defamation charges. In some states, the law does not protect the rights of an employer to respond frankly to a request for information about a former employee. For example, in *Carney v. Memorial Hospital*, a former hospital employee claimed that he had been 'terminated for cause.' Although the hospital argued that its statement was not defamatory, the New York Court of Appeals said the plaintiff was entitled to a full trial in which a jury should decide whether or not the statement 'terminated for cause' was defamatory. Similarly, a Pennsylvania court ruled that a former employee had a legitimate defamation claim against his former employer who said that the employee had 'suddenly resigned.' In this case, the court found that the language suggested that the employee resigned under a veil of suspicion or scandal." Because employers lack legal protection in many jurisdictions, and because courts permit jury trials on defamation charges, some employers have adopted a policy of providing little, if any, information on previous workers. As a result, prospective employers are hindered in their search for information that might call attention to high-risk applicants. Renas (1991) acknowledged the dilemma faced by hospital human resource managers: "If they fail to thoroughly scrutinize the backgrounds of applicants, they run the risk of negligent hiring. If they investigate too thoroughly, they may violate an applicant's right to privacy. In short, the prudent human resource manager must develop a screening procedure that will protect the employer without jeopardizing the rights of job applicants."

Bates does not believe that threat of legal action over reference or background checks has a chilling effect for human resource managers working in the healthcare environment. He said:

> This kind of thinking is a product of overly conservative human resources people. They are so worried that someone is going to say something that will come back to haunt them, so they say nothing at all, and it's an overkill reaction. I think they are hurting themselves by doing that and the fact is, there are protections in place. If you have an employee who's fired for cause—say they pushed a supervisor—you're perfectly within your legal rights to communicate that fact because it's true. The chances of you being sued by the former employee are pretty slim, and the chances of them winning would be next to nothing. As long as it's true, there's a defense to any claims of slander. That's well established in the law and it has been around forever. It gets dicey when the previous employer gets a call for a reference check and the human resource manager starts inserting subjective commentary such as, 'Well, he missed a lot of Mondays and we thought he might be hitting the bottle.' That's when you get in trouble. Many employers will simply terminate the employee, not prosecute them, but if they are prosecuted, again, you are perfectly within your rights to communicate that fact. I have never seen a case—and I have done about 1,000 of these lawsuits over the last 20 years—where the employer got sued because they told the truth.

Healthcare expert Kenneth W. Kizer, MD, MPH, former founding President and CEO of the National Quality Forum as well as the former Under Secretary for Health in the U.S. Department of Veterans Affairs, said that he believes that "a Good Samaritan-type law would be helpful" to institutions fearful about reporting reckless or malicious healthcare providers. Kizer said that he made this point in an early draft of an article addressing healthcare serial murderers but that "the idea was trashed by the journal's reviewers based on the lack of evidence showing that such would address a real need and questioning whether it truly is helpful." Kizer said, "While I believe that it would be very helpful for a number of reasons, including the inherent logic of the idea, I have to agree that there is no evidence showing that it would be effective."

Henry (2004) recommended that healthcare employers consider including, in their employment application or in a separate document, a release that the applicant must sign that acknowledges a previous employer's right, and the right of the prospective employer at any time, to discuss the applicant's job performance, reasons for separation, and anything else the state law permits. A number of states have employer-protection laws, but in states that do not, a healthcare institution could still require that applicants sign a release, holding employers harmless for references as long as those references are made in good faith. Healthcare organizations also are advised to ask employees who have been terminated or who resign to sign a release allowing them to provide good-faith comments if asked for a reference. As Henry (2004) noted, "Employees who are leaving on good terms will appreciate it. For those who refuse to provide the release, make a note in the file. If you get a call from a prospective employer, tell him or her that the employee refused to sign the release, and stick to name, rank and serial number."

Regarding the tightrope between privacy and due diligence, Bates emphasized,

> That's another misconception or overreaction to invading a person's privacy; any facility with a human resources manager knows to get signed releases so that you get permission to do it, and then you have a right to do these checks. The invasion of privacy thing is frankly quite silly. So many human resource managers play it safe but sometimes you have to be more aggressive if you are going to protect the employer and the employees, and in healthcare, the patients. I think that the expectation of a healthcare facility is that the standard of care is so much higher because they have a vulnerable population they serve. I think juries get rather incensed when they think, "Wow, you have patients who are vulnerable and you didn't make any kind of effort when you were hiring." There's the expectation that healthcare institutions will be much more diligent in their efforts to protect patients. (Interview with author.)

Renas (1991) stated,

> All evidence suggests that employers typically have inadequate information on which to base hiring decisions. Either they fail to thoroughly investigate the backgrounds of applicants, or they are thwarted in their search by employers who refuse to divulge pertinent information. Based on a nation-wide survey of healthcare institution, it appears that a growing list of employers have adopted a policy of not providing complete information on previous employees due to

a fear of being sued for libel or slander. Without question, human resource managers must walk a tightrope, balancing the need for protecting their employers from negligent hiring on one hand, and avoiding invasion of privacy lawsuits on the other. To a great extent, this can be achieved by modifying the pre-employment screening process to include an analysis of criminal records (where permitted), proper questioning of previous employers, detailed record-keeping, and the use of integrity tests that detect tendencies toward theft, drugs, and violence.

Payne concurred:

> We truly have to walk a very delicate line. For example, say someone had a bad manager who didn't like them and it was a purely personality issue; the manager painted a poor picture of them and got them fired for insubordination. So now the person's employment record shows they are a non-rehire. They know that firing was trumped up but they can't really pin a lawsuit on it. They apply to our hospital for a job. We call their previous employer and they say this person is not re-hirable, and so we don't hire the person. How many times will this happen before this person's ability to make a living is being impinged upon and they are being economically disadvantaged by this information that patently isn't true. There was a recent case in which the court said hospitals have a legitimate concern about releasing any information that would appear slanderous or damaging to someone's reputation, as well as a concern to ensure that the person coming on board isn't a danger to the organization. The court said the hospital has a legitimate right to say they will only give a neutral reference—in other words, they will not say why a person left or was fired, only that they worked there. So it's almost damned if you do and damned if you don't. And the law is on both sides pointing fingers, and we, as healthcare human resources managers, are right in the middle of it. The healthcare human resources profession would welcome laws that would provide amnesty for sharing damaging information, but you have to be careful—what we think is damaging may not be true; most people just need another chance—they're not evil, but they are going to get swept up in any kind of attempt to prevent the one-in-a-million mass killer. (Interview with author.)

As we have seen, there has been civil litigation associated with the Charles Cullen case, but Payne said he has not generally noticed an increase in lawsuits against hospitals filed by families of patients whose loved ones may have met their death suspiciously. "Those are horrible situations in which the family has every right to be enraged. And those situations in which a healthcare provider does harm to a patient and then goes to another healthcare organization and does harm to someone else, are also very rare events. It is unusual to have a situation where a hospital looked the other way when someone so negligent was allowed to be hired and hurt people in their care. These cases do happen occasionally, and hospitals do face lawsuits, but I think it's a stretch to say this is happening rampantly. And then there is the challenge of hiring people who have an absolutely clean record and still have bad intentions to inflict harm."

Short of peering into a crystal ball, Payne said it is imperative for human resource managers in the healthcare environment to do the following:

Watch for the standard red flags, such as long and unexplained gaps in employment, or any kind of falsification of an application. These are the things that almost always would result in termination if they are found out after the fact. Increasingly, we are moving toward doing a better job of conducting pre-employment screening by way of something akin to psychological profile testing; social scientists have recreated more defensible tools that we can use to help form a personality perspective to see if there are tendencies toward dishonesty. We also are working toward a better interviewing system with behavioral-based inquiries where we look for specific types of behavior from the past, as we now have better ways of predicting how someone is going to be on the job than we did in the past. It's not foolproof, but it helps. (Interview with author.)

Ahearn (2009) suggests that healthcare institutions follow a few best practices:

- Obtain the applicant's full name, current address, Social Security number, work history (including names and addresses of former employers), job titles, dates of employment, references, reasons for leaving, and written consent to contact references.
- Utilize a licensed and experienced background-screening firm.
- Decide how they will proceed if they encounter a "hit" (such as a criminal conviction) during an applicant's background screening; they must decide how to weigh each past crime with the type of job they are applying for, to ensure both the safety of employees and the privacy rights of applicants.
- Screen all healthcare applicants following the same stringent requirements used for verifying the competency and backgrounds of physicians, which is known as credentialing.

As Ahearn (2009) explains,

Extensive credentialing provides healthcare employers with information on a candidate's licensure, performance, working style, clinical knowledge and professional privileges. Physician profiles give detailed information on a physician's education, medical residency, work history, licensure, and disciplinary action. A medical malpractice history determines if the candidate has an undesirable history of involvement in medical malpractice lawsuits. Screening nurses can prove to be tougher than screening doctors, because nurses are hired more frequently and from all over the world. Checking the background and experience of a nurse may be far more complex than checking a physician's past history, since employers may have to run background checks in other countries. Also, while there are national and state data banks listing physicians, as of yet there are no such databases for nurses, which may complicate matters.

Ahearn (2009) emphasizes that all individuals who have access to healthcare facilities must be screened, including temporary workers hired by outside staffing firms, vendors and contractors, volunteers, and students and interns.

Ahearn (2009) explains that the most common background checks incorporate two principal components—criminal background checks and employment/education verifications: "Criminal background checks can range from quick and simple online checks, to extensive and thorough searches of courthouses and databases by experienced investigators. Best practices demand the latter course of action for effective screening." Other elements of this process include checking the Social Security Number (SSN) Address Locator, which provides an accounting of resident history by uncovering current and former addresses, as well as county, state, and nationwide criminal searches, plus national warrants, and a search of the National Sex Offender Registry. In terms of employment verification, Ahearn (2009) notes, "This process verifies dates of previous employment, position, starting and ending pay rate, performance, and reason for departure. No matter the size of the healthcare organization, hiring and retaining honest and qualified employees is critical. In the healthcare industry, it is imperative that employment verifications reveal inconsistencies about what the applicants report." This verification process should encompass checks of education and training, as well as professional licensure and a check of personal and professional references. As Ahearn (2009) states, "The reference check focuses on the 'human' side of an applicant's background by contacting colleagues, co-workers, and other references listed on the resume to assess capabilities, character and work record." Other important checks include Form I-9 and E-Verify, which are federal programs that enable healthcare organizations to accurately and quickly perform employment eligibility verification, receive proactive notifications of expiring work authorizations, and help reduce the potential for identity theft. Ahearn (2009) points out the importance of credit report checks: "The credit report check includes derogatory credit information and public filings such as bankruptcies, liens, and judgments, and is useful if the applicant will have check-writing privileges or access to company funds. Health insurance fraud is a major problem for hospitals, and people with troubled economic pasts may be more prone to commit such crimes. Due to notification rights, employers must notify an applicant or employee if a criminal 'hit' appears during a screening. Because laws differ from state to state, employers are advised to consult a licensed screening company to ensure compliance with both state and federal laws."

According to Ahearn (2009), "Healthcare organizations should create well-defined best practice procedures to be followed for each new hire. By implementing and utilizing sound and comprehensive best practices, employers can meet compliance requirements, perform proper due diligence in background screening, and protect themselves against liability from negligent hiring litigation. A successful background screening process helps healthcare organizations promote workplace safety, increase security for patients, and avoid the consequences of fraud, injuries, judgments, damages and poor performance."

Ahearn (2009) noted, "Verifications can be life-saving in the healthcare industry. A recent study by the Society of Human Resource Management (SHRM) found that 53 percent of all job applications contained inaccurate information. This figure takes on greater importance in the healthcare field, where an employee can pose a danger to vulnerable patients and fellow staff members."

As discussed in Chapter 1, there is a significant shortage of healthcare professionals, and this may bring pressure to bear on healthcare human resource managers who must hire quickly in order to try to fill positions that are critical to patient-care delivery. "A situation such as this is dependent upon the severity and the criticality of the need and the complexity of the skill that person is bringing to the job," Payne said. "I've seen it played out where an opening requiring a very skilled individual has been there for a while and when a candidate comes in, there's pressure to float an offer and sometimes human resource managers fold under that pressure. When that happens, there's a tendency afterward to point fingers if the person didn't work out. I think more people are realizing that employment decisions belong to more than just the human resource manager, it's a joint effort between management and human resources. It takes a more collaborative approach between hospital departments and human resources during the interview process, and once the new hire is on board, if there are ever suspicions about this person, everyone works together to investigate, document what might have gone awry, and make decisions about how to address it."

Payne emphasizes the need to work together should a human resources–related situation develop:

> There are many possible scenarios, but let's say there is a suspicion that a nurse is diverting drugs. Perhaps an anonymous tip comes into the human resources department; from my perspective, if anonymous tips have enough reasonableness and detail to them, you are probably better off acting on them versus just disregarding them. So, in this scenario, it may be that the anonymous tip

was someone who said they saw the nurse on the unit at 3 P.M. and he or she was taking things from the bedside. If we know that indeed, that nurse was working on that unit at 3 P.M., you then start a process of inquiry. You engage security, human resources and the pharmacy, which would run reports to see narcotics utilization related to that nurse's shift. You start looking at time-cards, discharge patterns and behaviors to determine the performance characteristics of this employee. If there's a drug allegation there frequently is the question of whether they are using it themselves or selling it, so you try to monitor them and not trap them, but set up a situation where you can determine what exactly is going on and how to deal with the situation. In every scenario, human resource managers should share their concerns about applicants and work with management to make the right decisions and hire the best people possible. (Interview with author.)

What happens after a healthcare professional is fired is a source of controversy for many hospitals. In the Cullen case, Cullen was able to bounce from hospital to hospital, despite a questionable trail of circumstances in his wake. Payne says it is similar with impaired nurses: "When someone who becomes impaired who is then fired because of their impairment, it takes a while for that information to filter down to the nursing board properly, so that person could leave one hospital and get another job before the board is even aware there is an issue," Payne says. "You can go to a big state like California and never be seen again—you can essentially start fresh. There is a lag in information sharing that is not intentional, and it's not as though the hospital is turning its back on the situation, it's just the way bureaucracy is set up, and information is not instantaneously shared. There is also room for improvement in instantaneous sharing of knowledge across all medical boards."

Bates states that talking to the healthcare professional's former employer is usually the best source for information, as challenging as that may be, given the alternatives. "A problematic work history is not being reported, or the licensing authority doesn't have its act together and doesn't have its records updated," he said. "In the healthcare industry, people go from facility to facility, so it behooves human resource managers to participate in their local chapters of human resources organizations and get to know those people. That way, you have an easier time calling your colleague in human resources at the other hospital and asking for the scoop."

What Is Happening with Medical Murder Now?

It has been some time since the high-profile cases of Michael Swango, Kristen Gilbert, and Charles Cullen have been in the news, and some experts believe caution must be taken when characterizing serial murder in hospitals.

Sackman states,

> Due in part to media attention, there is a greater awareness of cases of medical professionals intentionally murdering their patients. The number of known instances of murder by healthcare professionals is extremely small. Medical centers will quote the Joint Commission definition of a sentinel event as "an unexpected occurrence involving death or serious physical or psychological injury, or the risk thereof. Serious injury specifically includes loss of limb or function. The phrase 'or the risk thereof' includes any process variation for which a recurrence would carry a significant chance of a serious adverse outcome. Such events are called 'sentinel' because they signal the need for immediate investigation and response. This reporting of course is subject to the politics and interpretation of management. Just because the death rate increases on a particular ward when a particular nurse is on duty doesn't automatically trigger reporting. The VA, which was the site of a number of medical serial killers, still hasn't implemented a suspicious death policy. No businessman wants to admit in writing that its customers could be murdered by its own staff." (Interview with author.)

Sackman says that it is important to realize that healthcare serial killers are the exception, not the norm.

> Of course it's an aberration or hardly anyone would survive a hospital stay, but that doesn't mean we should ignore it. I personally think that the murder rate in nursing homes and other long-term care facilities is much higher than at hospitals but detection efforts at those types of facilities are almost nonexistent. Even the police care little about going into a nursing home to investigate the death of an octogenarian. There will never be a public outcry because the public is unaware of the actual murder rate. (Interview with author.)

There is also nothing to indicate that serial killing will ever cease.

> The instances of fraud and identity theft will always be far greater than the murder rate, period. I, however, have not seen any evidence to support the theory that healthcare-related homicides have been decreasing, in fact at best it has remained constant based on the stories periodically appearing in the press. The methods, motives and opportunities for healthcare-related crimes have not changed so why should the frequency? We still don't have suspicious death policies or training for medical professionals in detection of medical serial killers. The shortage of medical professionals often results in proper background investigations waived in order to fill this need. Given these factors, how can anyone claim that medical center homicides are on the wane? (Interview with author.)

References

Ahearn T. "Recommended best practice guidelines for background screening in the healthcare industry." Hospital Association of Southern California and Pre-Employ.com. May 7, 2009. (Accessed at: http://www.pre-employ.com/blog/post/Recommended-e28098Best-Practicee28099-Guidelines-for-Background-Screening-in-Health-Care-Industry.aspx.)

American Society for Healthcare Risk Management of the American Hospital Association (ASHRM) 2004 Advocacy Task Force. "A call for federal immunity to protect healthcare employers and patients." April 2005.

Associated Press. Victims' families settle with hospital in serial killer nurse case. February 20, 2008.

Bailey E. Planned background checks for in-home healthcare workers are criticized. *The Los Angeles Times*. October 28, 2009.

Barber J. Introduction to digital forensics. In: *Forensic Nursing*, second edition. Lynch VA, ed. St. Louis: Mosby. 2010, pp. 97–104.

Chun D. Ex-Shands nurse O'Quinn gets life without parole. *The Gainesville Sun*. May 24, 2008.

Cox M. (Michigan Attorney General). Press release: Criminal Background Check Legislation to Protect Michigan's Most Vulnerable Adults. Sent to Governor of Michigan, February 2, 2006. (Accessed October 27, 2010, at: http://www.michigan.gov/ag/0,1607,7-164-46849_47203-135742--,00.html.)

Dehlendorf CE, and Wolfe SM. Physicians disciplined for sex-related offenses. *JAMA*. 279(23):1883–1888. June 17, 1998.

Federation of State Medical Boards (FSMB). "Essentials of a modern medical practice act." 2006.

Federation of State Medical Boards (FSMB). "State of the states: Physician regulation." 2009a.

Federation of State Medical Boards (FSMB). "Summary of 2009 board actions." 2009b.

Federation of State Medical Boards. Protecting the Public: How State Medical Boards Regulate and Discipline Physicians. (Accessed October 27, 2010, at: http://www.fsmb.org/smb_protecting_public.html.)

Freckelton I. The criminalization solution to medical misconduct. In: *Healthcare Crime and Regulatory Control*. Smith R, ed. Annandale, NSW: Hawkins Press. 1998, pp. 26–37.

General Accounting Office (GAO). "VA Healthcare: Improved screening of practitioners would reduce risk to veterans." GAO publication 04-566. March 2004.

Grant D, and Alfred KC. Sanctions and recidivism: An evaluation of physician discipline by state medical boards. *J Health Politics, Policy Law*. 32:867–885. 2007.

Henry WR. Employment references: Can you get (and give) an honest answer? *RiskVue*. April 2004. (Accessed October 27, 2010, at: http://www.riskvue.com/articles/rb/rb0404b.htm.)

Hockley C. Staff violence against those in their care. In: *Workplace Violence: Issues, Trends, Strategies*. Bowie V, and Fisher BS, eds. Cullompton: Willan. 2005, pp. 77–96. (Accessed October 27, 2010, at: http://www.elderjusticecoalition.com/legislation.htm.)

James DS, and Leadbeatter S. Detecting homicide in hospital. *JR Coll. Physicians Lond*. 31(3):296–298. May/June 1997.

Joint Commission. "Requirements for criminal background checks." November 24, 2008. (Accessed at: www.jointcommission.org.)

Kent DR, and Walsh PD. Modern U.S. healthcare serial killings: An exploratory study and work in progress. In: *Linking Data to Practice in Violence and Homicide Prevention: Proceedings of the 2004 Meeting of the Homicide Research Working Group*. Bunge VP, Block CR, and Lane M, eds. Chicago: HRWG Publications. 2004, pp. 178–184.

Kizer KW, and Yorker BC. Health care serial murder: A patient safety orphan. Joint Commission. *J Qual Patient Safety*. April 2010.

Kohn LT, Corrigan JM, and Donaldson MS, eds. *To Err Is Human: Building a Safer Health System*. Committee on Quality of Health Care in America, Institute of Medicine. Washington, DC: National Academy Press. 2000.

Levine RH. "Internal investigations by healthcare organizations: Practical considerations." Member briefing for the American Health Lawyers Association's Sarbanes-Oxley Act Task Force. October 2005.

Levine A, and Wolfe S. "Hospitals drop the ball on physician oversight." Public Citizen. Publication 1873. May 27, 2009. (Accessed October 27, 2010, at: http://www.citizen.org/hrg1873.)

Medversant Technologies, LLC. "Medversant credentials study reveals 18.7 percent of U.S. healthcare practitioners demonstrate at least one adverse finding." Press release. October 7, 2009.

Morrison J, and Wickersham P. Physicians disciplined by a state medical board. *JAMA*. 279:1889–1893. 1998.

National Coalition on Elder Abuse. Elder Justice Act signed into law. E-news. Vol. 12, No. 10. April 2010. (Accessed at: www.ncea.aoa.gov.)

National Council of State Boards of Nursing (NCSBN). "The Council of State Governments supporting criminal background checks for nurses applying for state licensure." 2005.

Ornstein C, and Weber T. Criminal past is no bar to nursing in California. *The Los Angeles Times*. October 4, 2008a. (Accessed October 27, 2010, at: http://www.propublica.org/article/criminal-past-is-no-bar-to-nursing-in-California.)

Ornstein C, and Weber T. Many California health workers not checked for criminal pasts. *The Los Angeles Times*. December 30, 2008b. (Accessed October 27, 2010, at: http://www.propublica.org/article/California-fingerprinting-of-medical-licensees-1230.)

Ornstein C, and Weber T. Reform of California nursing board's discipline system shows early progress. *The Los Angeles Times*. October 11, 2009a. (Accessed October 27, 2010, at: http://www.propublica.org/article/reform-of-California-nursing-boards-discipline-system-shows-early-09.)

Ornstein C, Weber T, and Moore M. Problem nurses stay on the job as patients suffer. *The Los Angeles Times*. July 12, 2009b. (Accessed October 27, 2010, at: http://www.propublica.org/article/when-caregivers-harm-california-problem-nurses-stay-on-job-710.)

Public Citizen. "*Public Citizen* releases annual ranking of state medical boards." Press release. April 20, 2009. (Accessed October 27, 2010, at: http://www.louisiana-medicalnews.com/la-among-best-states-for-md-oversight-cms-1282-printer.)

Renas S. Negligent hiring: Are hospitals vulnerable? *Public Personnel Management*. September 22, 1991. (Accessed October 27, 2010, at: http://www.allbusiness.com/legal/265744-1.html.)

Saferstein R. Evidence collection and preservation. In: *Forensic Nursing*. Lynch VA, ed. New York: Elsevier. 2006.

Sala BR. "Physician misconduct and public disclosure practices at the Medical Board of California." California Research Bureau publication 08-015. November 2008.

Schwartz HA. "Sexual abuse of patients by health care professionals." Matthew Bender & Co. Undated. (Accessed at: http://www.stanford.edu/group/psylawseminar/Sex.htm.)

Senate Special Committee on Aging (SSCA). "Building on success: Lessons learned from the Federal Background Check Pilot Program for Long-Term Care Workers." July 30, 2008.

Smith RG. *Healthcare, Crime and Regulatory Control*. Annandale, NSW: Hawkins Press. 1998.

Smith RG. Regulating dishonest conduct in the professions. Paper presented to the Current Issues in Regulation: Enforcement and Compliance Conference. Convened by the Australian Institute of Criminology in conjunction with the Regulatory Institutions Network, RSSS, Australian National University, and the Division of Business and Enterprise, University of South Australia, Melbourne. September 2–3, 2002.

Standing Bear ZG. Crime scene processing. In: *Forensic Nursing*. Lynch VA, ed. New York: Elsevier. 2006.

Thunder JM. Quiet killings in medical facilities: Detection and prevention. *Issues Law Med*. March 22, 2003.

Ulrich C, O'Donnell P, Taylor C, Farrar A, Danis M, and Grady C. Ethical climate, ethics stress, and the job satisfaction of nurses and social workers in the United States. *Soc Sci Med*. 65(8):1708–1719. 2007.

Weber T, and Ornstein C. Dozens of criminal RNs identified by California regulators. *The Los Angeles Times*. December 26, 2009a. (Accessed October 27, 2010, at: http://www.propublica.org/article/dozens-of-criminal-registered-nurses-identified-by-California-regulators.)

Weber T, and Ornstein C. Schwarzenegger sweeps out nursing board. *The Los Angeles Times*. July 14, 2009b.

Weber T, and Ornstein C. States fail to report disciplined caregivers to federal database. *The Los Angeles Times*. July 19, 2010.

Weber T, Ornstein C, and Lin RG. Schwarzenegger wants sweeping reforms in discipline system for healthcare providers. *The Los Angeles Times*. August 13, 2009. (Accessed October 27, 2010, at: http://www.propublica.org/article/schwarzenegger-wants-sweeping-reforms-for-healthcare-providers-812.)

Yorker BC. Nurse-related homicides. In: *Forensic Nursing*. Lynch VA, ed. St. Louis: Mosby. 2006.

Yorker BC. "Forensic nursing applications: Preventing crime in hospitals." Presentation to the Southern California Association of Healthcare Risk Managers. February 19, 2008.

Zhong EH, Kenward K, Sheets VR, Doherty ME, and Gross L. Probation and recidivism: Remediation among disciplined nurses in six states. *Am J Nurs*. 109(3):48–57. March 2009.

Prevention Strategies and the Future of Healthcare Crime

7

Throughout this book, we addressed many reasons why the U.S. healthcare system is a haven for individuals intent on exploiting, defrauding, and harming patients; now we will explore why change is overdue and essential if medical malfeasance is to be eliminated.

As Young and Olsen (2009) assert, "The United States has the highest per capita spending on healthcare of any industrialized nation but continually lags behind other nations in healthcare outcomes" (p. 3). It is an opinion echoed by numerous healthcare economists; Harvard University expert Regina Herzlinger (1999) refers to the "maddening contradictions" of the U.S. healthcare system. Without acknowledgement of healthcare system failures, there can be no lasting, meaningful remedy to healthcare crime, especially when the healthcare system has already been decimated by quality issues. In 2000, the Institute of Medicine (IOM) issued a report, "To Err is Human: Building a Safer Health System," that sent shockwaves throughout the healthcare community because of its detailed enumeration of the system's prevalence of medical errors and adverse events—the report estimated that at the time, as many as 98,000 people die from medical errors in U.S. hospitals annually. In this report, Kohn et al. (2000) state that, "The status quo is not acceptable and cannot be tolerated any longer. Despite the cost pressures, liability constraints, resistance to change and other seemingly insurmountable barriers, it is simply not acceptable for patients to be harmed by the same healthcare system that is supposed to offer healing and comfort. 'First do no harm' is an often quoted term from Hippocrates. Everyone working in healthcare is familiar with the term. At a very minimum, the health system needs to offer that assurance and security to the public" (p. 3).

Let's take a look at what can be done to help reform the system and curtail the opportunity for medical malfeasance.

Strategy 1: Admit Healthcare System Failures

We established that healthcare is a complex machine with many moving parts. Hickam et al. (2003) said that medical errors and breaches in patient safety occur because coordination of structural and cultural elements of the U.S. healthcare system has not been optimized, and that the sources of these errors include failure of process safeguards, faults in equipment, or lack of teamwork. Hickam et al. (2003) added, "Patient safety is thereby dependent on the optimal interactions of the components of the healthcare system, with errors being minimized." Even though Hickam et al. (2003) did not specifically cite intentional medical malfeasance, it is assumed that this behavior runs counter to the tenets of safe healthcare and that vigilance for medical errors can carry over to other adverse scenarios. With all of its attempted transparency, the healthcare system retains its ability to hide its failures, whether medical errors or intentional harm by healthcare professionals. As Walshe and Shortell (2004) observed, "Better systems are needed for reporting and investigating failures and for implementing the lessons learned. The culture of secrecy, professional protectionism, defensiveness and deference to authority is central to such major failures, and preventing future failures depends on cultural as much as structural change in healthcare systems and organizations" (pp. 103–111). There has been a public realization that "healthcare facilities are often dangerous places," according to Walshe and Shortell (2004), which has healthcare institutions launching aggressive quality improvement initiatives as well as adopting ideas and techniques from safety science that were developed and have been applied in other industrial and commercial settings where safety and reliability are critical concerns.

Events such as wrong-site surgery, in which the wrong site or side of the body is operated on or amputated, are the "airplane crashes of the healthcare industry," according to Walshe and Shortell (2004), who added that they are also "the most serious and shocking manifestations of failure, which result in the most concentrated and visible harm to patients." They further stated, "Every airplane crash is carefully catalogued and painstakingly analyzed to learn lessons for the future. However, this does not occur in healthcare. If we fail to investigate and learn from major failures in care, opportunities for improvement likely will be missed, and the chances are higher that similar failures will happen again" (pp. 103–111).

There are a number of major system failures in healthcare, asserted Walshe and Shortell (2004), who pointed to the persistence of long-standing problems that "have been present—and known about—in healthcare organizations for years or even decades before they are brought to light." Walshe and Shortell (2004) added, "For example, physician Harold Shipman murdered more than 200 patients during 23 years in general practice in England, even though many people were concerned about the number and pattern of the deaths and raised those concerns with, among others, the police" (pp. 103–111). Walshe and Shortell (2004) said that other system failures include events that are well known but not handled, including adverse events about which clinicians and healthcare administrators knew of but did nothing—to the detriment of patients. Additional failures include causes of immense harm that can result in massive malpractice claims, lack of management systems in dysfunctional organizations, and repeated incidences of medical harm.

The tenets of medical error prevention can provide a foundation for the prevention of intentional harm. In addressing medical errors, several recommendations from the Agency for Healthcare Research and Quality (AHRQ) to make healthcare safer have merit for the fight against intentional healthcare crime. Healthcare institutions should create accountability through increased transparency while at the same time raising standards for competency in patient safety efforts. Hospitals must identify threats to patient safety, medical errors, and causes of patient injury associated with the delivery of healthcare. They must also identify, design, and evaluate practices that eliminate or mitigate the effects of medical errors and system-related risks and hazards that compromise patient safety. Having done this, healthcare facilities must then teach, disseminate, and implement effective patient safety practices—they must educate healthcare providers, patients, and policy makers about successful patient safety interventions and best practices while sharing knowledge about the causes of and successful interventions to identify, reduce, eliminate, or mitigate the effects of error. Even as they raise awareness that patients are at risk for healthcare-associated injury and harm, they must work toward adopting an institution-wide patient safety culture. These initiatives are nothing without maintaining vigilance; healthcare institutions must continually monitor and evaluate threats to patient safety to ensure that a positive safety culture is maintained and a safe environment continues. Such systems are absolutely necessary to ensure that interventions are achieving their objectives with no unintended effects.

As discussed in Chapter 5, the investigation of medical murder is fraught with difficulties; Walshe and Shortell (2004) stated that there are numerous barriers to disclosure and investigation of adverse events, and that "major failures appear difficult to expose and investigate, and chance plays a large part.... It seems likely that the major failures we know about are just a proportion—perhaps only a small one—of those that actually happen" (pp. 103–111). Walshe and Shortell (2004) suggested that a major failure in a healthcare institution can be revealed by a chain reaction of events: an egregious event occurs; a healthcare professional objects, thus becoming a whistle-blower; a group of united and well-informed complainants may emerge, forcing the healthcare institution to face the brewing crisis; and finally, media attention may aid in further discovery of misconduct.

As Walshe and Shortell (2004) noted, "It is striking that major failures are not usually brought to light by the systems for quality assurance or improvement that are now found in most healthcare organizations, such as incident reporting, clinical profiling, mortality and morbidity review, credentialing, risk and claims management, and the external arrangements for regulation, inspection, accreditation, and oversight" (pp. 103–111). As an example, they point to Vermillion County Hospital in Indiana, where intensive care nurse Orville Lynn Majors murdered his patients; although there were clear, suspicious mortality patterns, the hospital's quality management systems did not identify a problem.

As discussed in Chapter 6 relating to the perils of whistle-blowing, there are numerous obstacles to reporting medical misconduct. As Walshe and Shortell (2004) observed, one of the most crucial barriers to disclosure and discovery is "the endemic culture of secrecy and protectionism in healthcare facilities in every country. There is a pervasive culture in which … healthcare professionals prioritize their own self-interest above the interests of patients, and some healthcare organization leaders act defensively to protect the institution rather than its patients" (pp. 103–111).

Another barrier to reporting, experts say, is fragmented information scattered widely across multiple healthcare institution departments, coupled with a lack of incentive to coordinate this information to aid in investigation. And when faced with unpleasant revelations, many healthcare institution leaders feel it is "easier to disbelieve the data than to believe the unwelcome truth, and so problems go unaddressed until the evidence is quite incontrovertible," according to Walshe and Shortell (2004). Reporting misconduct frequently becomes a moot point when a problematic healthcare professional is allowed to slip out the door quietly without facing formal action, something that Walshe and Shortell (2004) said encourages problems to "get moved around the healthcare system rather than being tackled and resolved" (pp. 103–111).

Experts say that without compelling incentives to report medical misconduct, healthcare organizations will continue to be plagued by system failures. Making it safe and easy for healthcare providers to express their concerns and observations at the earliest possible stage can prevent patient injury and death and underscore the health system's commitment to quality and safety.

Walshe and Shortell (2004) said that reporting must be viewed as an integral part of an institution's culture in order for it to be successful, and that it should be hardwired into the clinical front line. They suggest that healthcare institutions should also have "explicit, properly resourced internal systems for investigating and triaging quality concerns to ensure that serious problems get rapid, high-level attention. All should have a clear policy on the circumstances in which external agencies need to be notified of a problem or called in to advise or investigate" (pp. 103–111).

Are mistakes and errors the first step leading to eventual intentional harm by a fine line in some cases? The answer is debatable, as experts ponder a human-engineering response to adverse events in healthcare. In his testimony before Congress on the subject of healthcare quality improvement, Lucian Leape, MD, a professor at the Harvard School of Public Health, noted, "The single greatest impediment to error prevention in the medical industry is that we punish people for making mistakes" (1994, pp. 1851–1857).

However, in healthcare, there is no margin for mistakes, as Lord Denning has asserted, "There are activities in which the degree of professional skill which must be required is so high, and the potential consequences of the smallest departure from that high standard are so serious, that one failure to perform in accordance with those standards is enough to justify dismissal" (Marx, 2007).

The healthcare community is beginning to embrace the concept of a "just culture," which Marx (2007) explains is a model that focuses on three duties—the avoidance of causing unjustified risk or harm, the duty to produce an outcome, and the duty to follow a procedural rule—balanced against organizational and individual values of safety, cost, effectiveness, equity, and dignity. Essentially, a just culture creates an open, fair, and just culture; creates a learning culture; helps design safe systems; and helps manage behavioral choices. Marx (2007) states that it is "not about seeing events as things to be fixed, but rather seeing events as opportunities to improve our understanding of risk—system risk and behavioral risk."

Marx (2007) explains that according to the just culture paradigm, three kinds of behaviors can lead to errors:

1. *Human error*: Inadvertently doing other than what should have been done; a slip, lapse, or mistake.
2. *At-risk behavior*: A behavior that either increases risk where that risk is not recognized or is mistakenly believed to be justified.
3. *Reckless behavior*: A behavioral choice to consciously disregard a substantial and unjustifiable risk.

Wachter (2007) reported that attorney David Marx was the first to describe the application of a just culture to healthcare, and noted, "Marx argues that most errors are due to at-risk behaviors—shortcuts and workarounds that normal people use to get their work done—and should be dealt with by examining why the system pushed them to make these choices. On the other hand, reckless behavior is blameworthy, and should be handled accordingly."

According to the just culture concept, accountability is the bottom line in healthcare, with institutions needing to manage their employees' behaviors with the appropriate level of action. In the event of human error, it should be managed through a "console" approach that addresses processes, procedures, training, and design. In the event of at-risk behavior, it should be managed through a "coach" approach that addresses removing incentives for at-risk behaviors, creating incentives for healthy behaviors, and increasing situational awareness. In the event of reckless behavior, it should be managed through a "punish" approach that takes remedial and punitive action.

In the just culture paradigm, managerial and staff expectations must change in order to create a stronger sense of unified accountability. Marx

(2007) explains that managers must know and understand the risks inherent to their institutions (including investigating the source of errors and at-risk behaviors, and turning events into an understanding of risk), design safe systems, and facilitate safe choices. Staff members must actively look for the risks around them, thus reporting errors and hazards, helping to design safe systems, making safe choices, following procedure, making choices that align with organizational values, and never signing for something that was not done.

For the just culture concept to take root in organizations, Marx (2007) said that there must be a willingness of stakeholders—individual providers, healthcare institutions, professional boards, and departments of health—to work together in one model of shared accountability that not only protects the healthcare organization's learning culture but also supports patient safety accountability.

In this context, the principles of a just culture can be applied to preventing medical malfeasance by creating an environment where healthcare professionals feel safe enough to report suspicious behavior on the part of their colleagues as part of an institutional culture of accountability. Although pointing fingers is counterproductive, the right blend of accountability and risk management can circumvent unwanted criminal overtones, according to Dekker (2007), who adds, "A just culture pays attention to safety, so that people feel comfortable to bring out information about what should be improved to levels or groups that can do something about it; allow the organization to invest resources in improvements that have a safety dividend, rather than deflecting resources into legal protection and limiting liability." Dekker (2007) suggests that a just culture allows organizations to uncover system failures, while at the same time "satisfy demands for accountability and contribute to learning and improvement" (p. 24).

Dekker (2007) advocates a "forward-thinking accountability," and explained, "Accountability that is backward-looking…tries to find a scapegoat to blame and shame an individual for messing up. But accountability is about looking ahead. Not only should accountability acknowledge the mistake and the harm resulting from it; it should lay out the opportunities and responsibilities for making changes so that the probability of such harm happening again goes down" (p. 24). Von Thaden et al. (2006) say that a just culture creates an environment of trust in which "healthcare professionals are encouraged and willing to report errors and incidents; their own, and those of others. These reports provide key information about safety problems and aid in the development of potential solutions." Von Thaden et al. (2006) state that for an organizational culture to be successful, it must "promote an atmosphere wherein the organization and its workers learn from mistakes, rather than focusing on blame and punishment of individuals (however, this does not apply to cases of criminal neglect, abuse or violations)" (p. 964).

Von Thaden et al. (2006) discovered that acceptance of the just culture concept varies by healthcare discipline; in a survey of 12 healthcare facilities (with a total of 1,984 surveys returned for an overall response rate of approximately 32 percent), the researchers found that respondents had moderately positive views on their organization's just culture. The researchers reported on areas to address, including perceptions of negative repercussions for reporting errors and perceptions of the assignment of blame for errors committed. They said that "while intentions may be positive, lack of time prevents disclosure of many mistakes and errors, and an existing perception that human error is aided by problematic technology and time pressure. To the credit of healthcare professionals, patient safety is seen as top priority and training is taken seriously" (p. 966). Von Thaden et al. (2006) reported that clinicians rated their organization's culture differently; physicians tended to have the highest ratings, followed by management, and then nurses and clinical staff. Nonclinical staff gave less-positive ratings. Physicians had a slightly positive view, but all other groups of healthcare employees had a negative view of how their organization appropriates blame after an incident. Von Thaden et al. (2006) also noted that comments gathered from the survey suggest employees perceive that disciplinary action is adjusted according to who makes the error.

Healthcare professionals generally have a positive view of organizational just culture. Von Thaden et al. (2006) noted that differences in perceptions of just culture between physicians, management, nurses/clinical staff, and nonclinical staff indicate areas where improvements to the experience of just culture may provide a better encounter for professional and patient safety. Von Thaden et al. (2006) added, "While on the surface it may appear positive, clearly, the concept of a just culture suffers ostensible differences when compared among the disciplines in healthcare. A just culture necessarily resides within an organization's overall safety culture and addresses the shared understanding of how behavior is determined acceptable and how accountability/culpability is evaluated" (p. 967). Von Thaden et al. (2006) state that the bottom line is the need for a shared accountability, and that additional research could help determine the extent of the inconsistency found among clinicians in terms of opinions about just cultures in healthcare.

Strategy 2: Address the Shortcomings in the Healthcare System

Hickam et al. (2003) have acknowledged that healthcare has a long way to go to improving the way it addresses its shortcomings: "Clinicians and managers accept that efforts should be made to reduce errors, but the best strategies for error reduction have not always been well understood." Although in recent years there have been efforts to embrace quality improvement, some experts believe there has been little progress in understanding how the processes and outcomes of care are related. As Hickam et al. (2003) observed, "The progress in quality improvement in healthcare has led to an environment of proactive approaches to recording information about the processes of clinical care that makes investigations of medical errors more feasible."

As discussed throughout this book, the current system of protections for vulnerable patient populations is inadequate and must undergo reform in order to make strides in the improvement of patient care. There are a number of ways in which the system fails patients:

- There is underreporting of abuse, neglect, and victimization of patients, as well as reluctance to report potential abuse or suspicious behavior of healthcare professionals.
- The system is complex and confusing to victims and mandated reporters of abuse.
- Researchers fail to collect reliable, valid data concerning the scope of the problem.
- The system is generally unsuccessful in prosecuting perpetrators.
- Many individuals within the abuse response and criminal justice systems lack training and expertise working healthcare abuse–related cases.

Recommendations for addressing these shortcomings include the following:

- Making the elimination of patient abuse and neglect a public health priority.
- Cooperatively engaging local, state, and federal legislatures and the private sector in system reform.
- Ensuring that incidents of abuse and neglect are investigated by law enforcement.
- Educating investigators who lack expertise in conducting abuse and neglect investigations involving patients in healthcare environments specifically; also educating district attorneys and judges.
- Implementing an integrated system of data collection to document the incidence of abuse and neglect and track the outcomes of criminal investigations and prosecutions.
- Putting resources in place for better investigation and prosecution of perpetrators, and strengthening medical boards' ability to sanction problem practitioners.
- Providing victims with new protections from perpetrators.

- Cultivating better patient ombudsmen programs.
- Ensuring medical boards are more vigilant against problematic practitioners.
- Incentivizing healthcare institution administrators and staff to provide quality care or punish poor care.
- Tying facility licensure to good reporting, investigations of allegations of abuse and neglect.

The challenge is that many healthcare organizations become paralyzed and unable to act swiftly to address and prevent adverse patient outcomes. Walshe and Shortell (2004) state that in the majority of cases of healthcare system failure, the organizations are unequipped to deal with problems that are "easily bypassed or sidetracked, and they fail to raise an alarm that something is wrong." Quality improvement experts insist that organizations' systems of response should be "rigorously tested, through simulations or the equivalent of fire drills, to check that they are capable of dealing with the circumstances of a major failure" (pp. 103–111). Unfortunately, many healthcare institutions are as uncertain in their remedy processes as they are in their discovery of adverse events, and many more lack the mechanisms to ensure that lessons are extracted from system failures and change is implemented.

When addressing shortcomings, it is essential that healthcare institutions create a vision for improvement for the future. As Leape et al. (2009) explained, it is imperative to "envision a culture that is open, transparent, supportive and committed to learning; where doctors, nurses and all health workers treat each other and their patients competently and with respect; where the patient's interest is always paramount; and where patients and families are fully engaged in their care" (pp. 424–428). Leape et al. (2009) also envision an organizational culture "centered on teamwork, grounded in mission and purpose, in which organizational managers and boards hold themselves accountable for safety and learning to improve. In a learning organization, every voice is heard and every worker is empowered to prevent system breakdowns and correct them when they occur. The culture we envision aspires to, strives for and achieves unprecedented levels of safety, effectiveness and satisfaction in healthcare" (pp. 424–428). To transform, Leape et al. (2009) assert that healthcare organizations must embrace the following concepts: transparency must be a practiced value in everything we do, care must be delivered by multidisciplinary teams working in integrated care platforms, patients must become full partners in all aspects of healthcare, healthcare workers need to find joy and meaning in their work, and medical education must be redesigned to prepare new physicians to function in this new environment.

Strategy 3: Investigate Problems in Healthcare Working Conditions

In Chapter 1, we reviewed the numerous stressors that can aggravate health-care professionals and possibly push them toward medical malfeasance. Warren et al. (2007) cited research suggesting that high levels of employee stress in healthcare organizations are associated with higher levels of personal insurance costs, decreased functional status, errors, and malpractice. They noted, "An Institute of Medicine (IOM, 2004) report found that management practices, workforce capability, work design and organizational safety culture have a strong impact on the work environment of nurses and thus on patient safety. A growing body of evidence documents that organizational climate and work organization affects working conditions, employee health and patient outcomes."

Hickam et al. (2003) suggest that healthcare organizations reexamine several key factors affecting workers' performance, including the following:

- Healthcare workforce staffing (addressing workload, the professional skills/academic degrees/specialty certifications required for particular job assignments, duration of experience in a particular job category, and the effects of work schedules, including length of shift, days of the week worked, and temporal cycle effects).
- Workflow design (addressing hazards to healthcare providers and patients inherent in some work processes).
- Personal/social (addressing issues related to rates of stress, burn-out, dissatisfaction, motivation, and control over work in the healthcare environment).
- Physical environment (addressing working conditions such as light, aesthetics, noise, air quality, toxic exposures, temperature, and humidity).
- Organizational factors (addressing organizational culture and how this affects beliefs, values, and expectations).

To what extent do working conditions affect healthcare professionals? It may be a stretch to say that a crowded, noisy environment and an impossible workload might drive a healthcare professional to the brink of exploiting, abusing, or murdering a patient, but these factors should be taken seriously and treated as a potential source of agitation that could trigger other psychosocial motivations already at play within the individual. Hickam et al. (2003) found that higher nursing workload is associated with higher rates of nonfatal adverse outcomes in inpatient and nursing home settings, but that the evidence was unclear in terms of associating higher nursing workload with higher rates of patient mortality or higher incidence of medication errors. Hickam et al. (2003) were unable to address the age-old question of the potential relationship between job satisfaction and job performance, because they felt the research remained inconclusive; however, there might be reason to believe that work conditions can affect healthcare delivery. To affect patient safety, working conditions must have an impact on healthcare professionals, and this effect on health professionals must interfere with or alter their clinical work practices, and thus the altered work practices must result in harm to patients. Hickam et al. (2003) noted, "Steps in this theoretical chain of causation are independent, and every step in the chain must be present for an impact on patient safety to occur. This allows for the possibility that a working condition can affect health professionals without affecting clinical practices, or that clinical practices may be affected without necessarily resulting in harm to patients." And in terms of the impact of stress, the researchers noted that anecdotal data from qualitative studies suggest that healthcare professionals attribute some patient adverse outcomes to overwork, occupational pressures, and fatigue.

Organizational factors might be the strongest influence on healthcare professionals, but the subject warrants further research. Hickam et al. (2003) acknowledge that healthcare institutions focus their safety efforts on the system, rather than on the individual care provider, thus engendering a culture of blame and a culture of silence—concepts that "indicate a clear belief that something about the work environment and in the context of the work itself influences positively and/or negatively the occurrence of errors and adverse events." Hickam et al. (2003) added that the complexities of healthcare necessitate culture management and that "despite culture's importance in high reliability systems, research into the relationship between organizational culture and patient safety remains sparse."

Strategy 4: Establish Accountability

Healthcare institutions should be aware of patient safety imperatives and be held accountable for addressing them. There is no lack of information in the medical literature and in the mainstream press about the incidences and prevalence of medical errors and intentional harm, and how to remedy these situations. What is lacking, however, is a national agenda that speaks to healthcare system failures.

What is needed, according to the aforementioned IOM report, is a comprehensive approach to improving patient safety that not only presents sufficient pressure to make errors costly to healthcare organizations and providers so they are compelled to take action to improve safety, but at the same time, provides a mechanism by which knowledge can be enhanced and a breakdown of the legal and cultural barriers that impede safety improvement can be achieved.

Although the IOM report stated, "Given current knowledge about the magnitude of the problem, it would be irresponsible to expect anything less than a 50 percent reduction in errors over five years," some would argue that this goal has largely been ignored, despite the initial frenzy that the report instigated. Jewell and McGiffert (2009) described how the IOM report triggered congressional hearings, prompted the introduction of five pieces of federal legislation addressing medical errors, and caused Congress to allocate millions of dollars to AHRQ for patient safety-related research grants. Jewell and McGiffert (2009) said that despite this frenzy of activity, progress on addressing quality and safety issues slowed and interest in a follow-up report was negligible on the part of lawmakers, the media, and the general public. Several years later, none of the medical error–reporting legislation had been passed, and, according to Jewell and McGiffert (2009), "the initial outrage surrounding the report had faded. Movement toward systematic change to the healthcare system remained frustratingly slow." Jewell and McGiffert (2009) add, "Ten years ago the Institute of Medicine (IOM) declared that as many as 98,000 people die each year needlessly because of preventable medical harm. Ten years later, we don't know if we've made any real progress, and efforts to reduce the harm caused by our medical care system are few and fragmented."

Consumer watchdogs focusing on healthcare say that the system still lacks transparency and sufficient public reporting. Jewell and McGiffert (2009) assert that the IOM's recommendation that a national system of accountability through transparency be created has not been actualized and that in many cases, "hospital-specific information is confidential and underreporting of errors is not curbed by systematic validation of the reported data. No national entity has been empowered to coordinate and track patient safety improvements." The current system of public reporting is fragmented at the state level, with many states using a list of events that should never occur in healthcare as its measure for what kind of medical harm requires reporting. Jewell and McGiffert (2009) called for a national reporting system that uses three components of accountability—mandatory, validated, and public at the facility level (MVP): "MVP reporting systems are needed to create the external pressure needed to create systemic change. MVP reporting would represent a sea-change in a healthcare system accustomed to hiding errors."

Pressure from Within for Accountability

According to the IOM report, accountability starts with leadership. Healthcare institutions must make patient safety a priority corporate objective, they must make patient safety everyone's responsibility, they must make clear assignments for and expectation of safety oversight, they must provide human and financial resources for error analysis and systems redesign, and they must develop effective mechanisms for identifying and dealing with unsafe practitioners. As Kohn et al. (2000) observed, "The healthcare organization must develop a culture of safety such that an organization's design processes and workforce are focused on a clear goal—dramatic improvement in the reliability and safety of the care process." Patient safety must be an explicit organizational goal demonstrated by clear organizational leadership on the part of governing boards, management, and clinical leadership. Kohn et al. (2000) explained that this process unfolds when institutional boards commit to close oversight of safety protocols at the organizational level, as well as regularly review in detail the progress in reaching quality-improvement goals. Kohn et al. (2000) suggest that "Ways to implement this at the executive level include frequent reports highlighting safety improvement and staff involvement, regular reviews of safety systems, 'walk-throughs' to evaluate hazardous areas and designs, incorporation of safety improvement goals into annual business plans, and providing support for sensible forms of simplification."

This process ensures the establishment of a culture of safety that trickles down to the healthcare professional on an individual level as well as on an organizational level. To that end, healthcare institutions must make patient safety everyone's responsibility. The IOM report indicates that messages about safety must signal that it is a serious priority of the institution, that there will be increased analysis of system issues with awareness of their complexity, and that they are endorsed by nonpunitive solutions encouraging the involvement of the entire staff. As Kohn et al. (2000) explain, "The messages must be well conceived, repeated, and consistent across healthcare systems, and should stress that safety problems are quality problems. Establishing and clearly conveying such aims are essential in creating safety systems." Kohn et al. (2000) state that healthcare institutions owe it to the healthcare consumer to be accountable for patient safety as well as to address error and improve their performance without unreasonable fear of the threat of civil liability. The threat of legal proceedings "creates tension between ensuring the transparency that allows institutions to be viewed publicly as trustworthy and the confidence that their workers have in identifying and addressing error without fear of formal or informal reprisal," according to Kohn et al. (2000).

It is essential that healthcare institutions establish meaningful patient safety programs with defined responsibility that supports strong, clear, visible attention to safety. Kohn et al. (2000) have stated that improvements in safety do not occur unless there are both a commitment by top management and an overt, clearly defined, and continuing effort on the part of all personnel, workers, and managers. In addition, a meaningful safety program should include senior-level leadership, defined program objectives, an adequate budget with which to fund quality-improvement initiatives, efficacious data collection, as well as regular monitoring of results by an executive committee and timely reporting to the board of directors.

Pressure from Outside for Accountability

The aforementioned IOM report asserted that there are numerous opportunities to strengthen the focus of the existing processes on patient safety issues, including ensuring that performance standards and expectations for healthcare organizations should focus greater attention on patient safety; that regulators and accreditors should require healthcare organizations to implement meaningful patient safety programs with defined executive responsibility; and that public and private purchasers should provide incentives to healthcare organizations to demonstrate continuous improvement in patient safety. Kohn et al. (2000) suggest that existing standards in healthcare do not provide adequate focus on patient safety, and that while licensure and accreditation concentrate on the review of core processes such as quality improvement and risk management, they lack specific focus on patient-safety issues. Another weakness of professional licensure, according to Kohn et al. (2000), is that it focuses on a healthcare provider's qualifications at initial licensure, "with no requirements to demonstrate safe and competent clinical skills during one's career."

Putting pressure on healthcare institutions to do the right thing in upholding patient safety was a major tenet of the IOM report. One such group could be professional societies, groups, and associations that could improve patient safety by contributing to the creation of a culture that encourages the identification and prevention of errors. Few professional societies or groups have demonstrated a visible commitment to reducing errors in healthcare and improving patient safety. Although it is believed that the commitment exists among their members, there has been little collective action. The IOM report says that these societies could help healthcare institutions create a culture of safety by defining standards of practice; convening and collaborating among society members and with other groups; encouraging research, training, and education opportunities; and advocating for change. Professional groups can also serve as advocates for change; one example is the National Patient Safety Foundation (NPSF), created by the American Medical Association (AMA) in 1997.

Regulators must step up their oversight of healthcare institutions and enforce sanctions against those facilities and individuals that turn their backs on the patient safety imperatives. This includes developing effective mechanisms for identifying and dealing with unsafe practitioners. The IOM report notes, "Although almost all accidents result from human error, it is now recognized that these errors are usually induced by faulty systems that 'set people up' to fail. Correction of these systems failures is the key to safe performance of individuals. Systems design—how an organization works, its processes and procedures—is an institutional responsibility. Only the institution can redesign its systems for safety; the great majority of effort in improving safety should focus on safe systems, and the healthcare organization itself should be held responsible for safety." It also acknowledged that "some individuals may be incompetent, impaired, uncaring or may even have criminal intent. The public needs dependable assurance that such individuals will be dealt with effectively and prevented from harming patients." The IOM says that although these represent a small proportion of healthcare workers, they are unlikely to be amenable to the kinds of remedies described in this chapter, "registration boards and licensure discipline is appropriately reserved for those rare individuals identified by organizations as a threat to patient safety, whom organizations are already required by state law to report."

Kohn et al. (2000) noted, "Historically, the health system has not had effective ways of dealing with dangerous, reckless or incompetent individuals and ensuring they do not harm patients. Although the health professions have a long history of work in this area, current systems do not, as a whole, work reliably or promptly." Patient safety experts say that the absence of timely response to problematic professionals is concerning, and even if legal due process is used, it is frequently a slow and uncertain path to resolution.

The IOM report recommends that healthcare organizations rely on proficiency-based credentialing and privileging to identify, retrain, remove, or redirect physicians, nurses, and others who cannot competently perform their responsibilities. With effective safety systems in place, the IOM says it believes it will be easier for those within organizations to identify and act on information about such individuals; if these systems are working properly, unsafe professionals will be identified and dealt with before they cause serious patient injury.

Healthcare institutions not making enough progress on patient safety received a rude awakening in October 2008 when the Centers for Medicare and Medicaid Services (CMS) announced that it would not reimburse hospitals for additional care related to complications from what it considered to be preventable events; these hospital-acquired conditions include some of the "never events" endorsed by the NQF. As Jewell and McGiffert (2009) reported, "Medicare's no-pay policy has increased pressure for accountability, and given some time could have a significant impact on Medicare patients and costs. Numerous states and private health plans are following suit by adopting similar no pay policies for some or all of the Medicare and NQF preventable adverse events."

Additional external pressure comes from the Joint Commission, whose National Patient Safety Goals must be met in order for healthcare institutions to receive accreditation by the agency (Joint Commission, 2009).

Strategy 5: Embrace Quality Improvement

Batalden and Davidoff (2007) defined quality improvement as "the combined and unceasing efforts of everyone—healthcare professionals, patients and their families, researchers, payers, planners and educators—to make the changes that will lead to better patient outcomes, better system performance and better professional development." Batalden and Davidoff (2007) add that healthcare "will not realize its full potential unless change making becomes an intrinsic part of everyone's job, every day, in all parts of the system" (pp. 2–3).

Quality improvement has been a goal in U.S. hospitals for more than two decades, but many institutions' efforts stall or never get off the ground because of policies, politics, and other barriers to implementation. In addition, even though some hospitals are strongly committed to the goals of quality improvement, there appears to be significant variation in the implementation and effectiveness of hospital reforms, as a Commonwealth Fund–supported survey found. Cohen et al. (2008) surveyed top quality officers at 470 U.S. hospitals to examine the extent to which hospitals are embracing the principles and methods of quality improvement. They observed, "While it is reassuring to note that a high percentage of quality managers (87 percent) believed that patient care at their hospitals today was better than three years earlier, the finding that only one-third felt that quality of care and patient satisfaction levels today compared with where they should be had exceeded their expectations suggests that improvement is still needed." Cohen et al. (2008) added that even though quality improvement is a strategic priority at many healthcare institutions, "it also appears that quality improvement implementation is an evolutionary process that takes years, perhaps a decade or longer, to transform a hospital into a high-performing organization."

In many cases, a specific trigger serves as the impetus for change, whether it is a highly publicized case of a healthcare serial murderer or other adverse event. Silow-Carroll et al. (2007) identified a common cyclical sequence of factors resulting in change: a "wake-up call" in the form of an adverse event causes a healthcare institution to launch or renew a quality improvement initiative; this triggers organizational changes (such as establishment of quality-related committees, empowerment of staff, and investments in new infrastructure that facilitates the problem-solving process); problems are studied and root cause analyses are conducted; action plans are formulated;

people are held accountable to new protocols and evidence-based practices; and finally, improved outcomes relating to errors, complications, and mortality are achieved, employee and patient satisfaction soars, and bottom-line indicators such as reduced length of stay and increased market share show the success of the quality improvement initiatives undertaken. Silow-Carroll et al. (2007) note that experiencing positive results improves the motivation to expand quality-improvement efforts and turn the aforementioned cycle into a self-sustaining, ongoing project: "The improved outcomes led to further impetus to change, accelerated change and a spreading of the 'change culture' to other parts of the institution. This entire sequence reflects the establishment, growth and reinforcement of a culture of quality."

Organizational changes that occur in pursuit of this culture of quality include creating committees responsible for monitoring and ensuring success of quality improvement efforts and providing sufficient resources; instituting policies that encourage staff to express concerns, identify deficiencies, and challenge the status quo; nurturing physician and nurse champions to develop protocols to address deficiencies and to encourage and educate their peers on new practices and procedures; and using public performance reports as opportunities to identify deficiencies and improve outcomes and patient satisfaction. Silow-Carroll et al. (2007) note that public policy can help facilitate quality improvement efforts in healthcare institutions by standardizing reporting requirements as well as ensuring accuracy and clarity of public reporting; educating healthcare consumers in interpreting information and using it appropriately; supporting pay-for-performance programs that use "carrots" (rewards) rather than "sticks" (penalties); and continuing to document and publicize quality issues.

The IOM advocates a four-tiered approach to improving patient safety within the context of quality improvement:

1. Establish a national focus to create leadership, research, tools, and protocols to enhance the knowledge base about safety.
2. Identify and learn from errors through immediate and strong mandatory reporting efforts, as well as the encouragement of voluntary efforts, both with the aim of making sure the system continues to be made safer for patients.
3. Raise standards and expectations for improvements in safety through the actions of oversight organizations, group purchasers, and professional groups.
4. Create safety systems inside healthcare organizations through the implementation of safe practices at the delivery level.

Meeting these directives is no easy feat, and a number of organizations have been created that provide healthcare institutions with some amount of research and guidance to facilitate these improvements. One example is the National Quality Forum (NQF), a private membership group that works to establish national priorities and goals for performance improvement and publishes a list of voluntary consensus standards related to patient safety. Kizer and Stegun (2005) reported that as part of a comprehensive approach to improving patient safety, the IOM recommended that healthcare errors and adverse events be reported in a systematic manner and recommended that the NQF identify a set of patient safety measurements that should be a basic component of any medical errors reporting system. In 2002, the NQF, which functions as a broker for healthcare quality improvement, formally endorsed a list of Serious Reportable Events in healthcare that should never occur.

As Kizer and Stegun (2005) explain,

> While it is believed that having reliable information about the occurrence of the most egregious healthcare errors that cause patient harm will lead to improvements in patient safety, the primary reason for identifying a standardized set of serious reportable events that would be reported on a mandatory basis was to facilitate public accountability for the occurrence of these adverse events in the delivery of healthcare.... The public expects healthcare providers to take all appropriate measures to ensure that care is safe, and the public looks to government and other oversight bodies to make sure that such actions are taken. The occurrence of a serious preventable adverse event in healthcare—e.g., operating on the wrong patient or wrong body part or transfusing the wrong type of blood into a patient—suggests (but does not prove) that a flaw exists in the healthcare organization's efforts to safeguard patients. It is reasonable for the public to expect an oversight body to investigate such occurrences. In many ways, this is analogous to the reporting of airplane crashes, train derailments, and school bus or tractor-trailer truck crashes. When these types of events occur, the public expects that they will be reported to a responsible transportation oversight agency, investigated, and steps taken to eliminate or remedy whatever caused the event to prevent such occurrences from happening in the future. These serious reportable events are healthcare's equivalent of airplane or other public-transportation crashes. Accountability entails both an obligation of healthcare providers to report on their performance and of oversight bodies to investigate specified occurrences and to enforce compliance with accepted standards of care for ensuring safety. Both parties have a responsibility to use the information to improve public safety. Having a standardized set of reportable adverse events should facilitate fulfillment of this obligation.

The NQF's list of serious reportable events address a number of medical errors, including wrong-site or wrong-patient surgery, retention of a foreign body in a patient following surgery, intraoperative or postoperative death, injury or death resulting from use of a medical device, medication errors, and many others related to the clinical care environment. But for the purposes of this book, of particular interest are the "criminal events," considered to be any instance of care ordered by or provided by someone imperson-ating a physician, nurse, pharmacist, or other licensed healthcare provider; abduction of a patient of any age; sexual assault on a patient within or on the grounds of the healthcare facility; and death or significant injury of a patient or staff member resulting from a physical assault (such as battery) that occurs within or on the grounds of the healthcare facility.

Kizer and Stegun (2005) note that

Although healthcare facilities cannot eliminate all risk of these events, they can take preventive measures to reduce their risk of occurrence.... Meaningful accountability requires that both healthcare organizations and oversight agencies use the reports to improve patient safety. There are two main methods by which this can be accomplished. First, when an event occurs, it should be investigated to determine the underlying system prob-lems and/or failures (e.g., via root cause analysis). The identified problem should then be corrected to prevent recurrence of the event. Prevention strategies can include identifying points in the system of care where proto-cols should be changed, new or different technologies implemented, training revised, or other processes changed. These activities are the responsibility of the healthcare organization. Second, aggregate information about seri-ous reportable events from multiple healthcare organizations can be used to improve safety if the lessons learned from their investigations of the under-lying system problems and/or failures are disseminated to other healthcare organizations. Such outreach would allow others to take appropriate mea-sures to prevent similar events in their own institutions. Dissemination of this information is possible if the oversight agency or its designee collects information about the adverse events themselves, and information about the findings from the investigations of the events (i.e., from the root cause analyses).

Since the IOM's report on medical errors and the increased call for trans-parency in healthcare, failures in the system are coming to light, but many healthcare institutions are grappling with how to adopt quality improvement initiatives. McLaughlin and Kaluzny (2006) explain that quality improve-ment is a "structured organizational process for involving personnel in plan-ning and executing a continuous flow of improvements to provide quality healthcare that meets or exceeds expectations" (p. 3). They added that quality improvement involves a common set of characteristics including the act of implementing the organization's strategic vision and plan; using a quality council of institution stakeholders; training programs for personnel; utiliz-ing mechanisms for selecting improvement opportunities; forming process improvement teams; providing staff support for process analysis and rede-sign; and implementing personnel policies that motivate and support staff participation in process improvement.

McLaughlin and Kaluzny (2006) state that society assumes that the concept of professionalism is embraced by healthcare, "in which service providers are assumed to have exclusive access to knowledge and competence and, therefore, take full responsibility for self-regulation and for quality. However, much of the public policy debate has centered on the weaknesses of the professional system in improving quality of care" (p. 3).

Strategy 6: Reduce Risk for Intentional Harm

Creating a culture of safety at any healthcare institution must include steps to eradicate the impediments to protecting patients and reducing the risks of intentional harm. As an example, Nerenberg (2002) pointed to a report from the General Accounting Office (GAO, 2002) that cited significant gaps in protections for some of the most vulnerable patients—nursing home residents—including the inadequacies of state registries in tracking employees, inconsistencies by Medicaid Fraud Control Units in investigating abuse and neglect, failure of local law enforcement to become involved, failure of states to inform consumers how to identify and report abuse, failure of homes to notify state authorities of abuse allegations, lack of witnesses, and failure of the CMS to strengthen resident protections. Other cited factors include employment practices designed to protect workers that compromise accountability, such as expunging complaints of abuse from workers' files if they cannot be proven; lack of policies for preventing abuse; low worker pay and morale; lack of training and resources; low status of the work; lack of openness within institutions; lack of training; and poor communication between state agencies that review certificates of need (which must be submitted by providers and approved before they can open a new facility), and those that license and monitor homes, potentially permitting providers who are having trouble with their licensure to open new homes. It was further noted that workers lack models to help them understand the authority, boundaries, and intimacy issues posed by this type of work.

A number of researchers enumerated the variety of options proposed to reduce the risk of healthcare institution abuse, including the following:

- Improving coordination between the various law enforcement, regulatory, protective services, and advocacy organizations that are involved in patient care.
- Improving conditions for workers, through adequate staffing; enhanced communication between direct care and administrative staff; more time to nurture relationships between staff and residents; humane salaries; opportunities for upward mobility; and greater

recognition, respect, and understanding for the difficult lives many workers lead.
- Training that focuses on interpersonal caregiving skills, managing difficult resident care situations, problem solving, cultural issues that affect staff and resident relationships, conflict resolution, stress reduction techniques, information on dementias, and witnessing and reporting abuse.
- Improving compliance with federal requirements affecting hiring of abusive healthcare providers.
- Improving reporting through consumer education and stricter enforcement of mandatory reporting.
- Creating support groups for healthcare providers.
- Strengthening resident councils for nursing home residents.
- Improving the screening of prospective staff to focus on applicants' criminal backgrounds, history of substance abuse, and history of domestic violence; their feelings about caring for the elderly; reactions to abusive residents; work ethics; and their ability to manage anger and stress.
- Creating an environment that is conducive to good care.
- Establishing consistent definitions of abuse to improve tracking and research.

Strategy 7: Educate Healthcare Providers

Perhaps medical malfeasance occurs as a by-product of healthcare professionals' lack of education about ethics and dignity shown to their patients. As Kohn et al. (2000) noted, "Clinical training and education is a key mechanism for cultural change. Colleges of medicine, nursing, pharmacy, healthcare administration and their related associations should build more instruction into their curriculum on patient safety and its relationship to quality improvement." The challenge of doing so, however, is addressing the pressure that educational institutions are under to broaden the scope of their curricula and the costs involved. Educators also are divided on the topic of whether patient-safety training should occur in undergraduate or graduate training programs only, or if it should be relegated to continuing education pursued independently by the healthcare professional. Kohn et al. (2000) also suggested that interdisciplinary training be incorporated into healthcare curricula, because much of healthcare today is delivered by teams of professionals; however, it must be recognized that training often remains focused on individual responsibilities, leaving practitioners inadequately prepared to enter complex settings. Kohn et al. (2000) assert that the "silos" created through training and organization of care impede safety improvements:

"Instruction in safety improvement requires knowledge about working in teams, using information and information technology, quality measurement, and communicating with patients about errors."

Sullivan (2004) assert that healthcare professionals must overcome the distrust, generated by breakdowns in institutional reliability, that has been festering among members of the public, and said that care providers "must embrace a new way of looking at their role to include civic responsibility for themselves and their profession, and a personal commitment to a deeper engagement with society." Sullivan (2004) added that institutions of higher learning can assist healthcare professionals with this task by addressing professional purpose and identity in the curricula, including "an understanding of the moral and social ecology within which students will practice."

Education of physicians is essential if quality improvement is to be taken seriously, some experts assert. Leape et al. (2009) assert that medical education must be restructured to "reduce its almost exclusive focus on the acquisition of scientific and clinical facts and to emphasize the development of skills, behaviors and attitudes needed by practicing physicians. These include the ability to manage information; understanding of the basic concepts of human interaction, patient safety, healthcare quality and systems theory; and possession of management, communication and teamwork skills." Leape et al. (2009) point to the typical medical school curriculum, in which little or no instruction is provided in concepts related to safety science, improvement science, human factors, leadership, or teamwork: "Students obtain little experience in examining the patient-care processes, which constitute the everyday practice in the real world of healthcare.... Nor do they receive instruction in skills needed to communicate effectively with co-workers and patients, or how to deal with their own feelings of doubt, fear and uncertainty. Yet, these are the knowledge and skills that most people consider essential for a physician."

Physicians' education and training has been the focus of scrutiny by the American Medical Association's Committee on Medical Education. In 2005, the AMA began the 5-year Initiative to Transform Medical Education (ITME) project to promote excellence in patient care by implementing reform in medical education and training through the implementation of 10 major recommendations. The ITME stated that gaps in physician education and training included their inability to self-assess the quality of their own practice, to be patient advocates, to be team players, and to communicate effectively. As a result, the AMA feared that many physicians would eventually lose their sense of altruism and the caring aspects of medicine. The committee advocated for changes that included new medical school admissions criteria, including applicant qualities of lifelong learning, team orientation, and service orientation; course requirements that included more exposure to the humanities, social sciences, and economics; and new medical school curriculum requirements of teamwork, information sharing, communication, self-assessment, professionalism, functionality within various healthcare systems, and community service. The AMA says that an integrated curriculum must include humanism, ethics, and professionalism.

It is an undertaking that must include all stakeholders in the process: students, professors, residents, medical school accrediting bodies, medical school administrators, and medical specialty societies and professional organizations. In addition, the National Board of Medical Examiners (NBME), which is the nonprofit organization that creates the standardized exams required for medical licensure in the United States, must be cognizant of changes in medical school curriculum and reflect these on the U.S. Medical Licensing Examination (USMLE). As Skochelak (2010) notes, "New partnerships are needed to develop medical education systems and standards that incorporate the best evidence and new modalities in support of lifelong adult professional education. These partnerships must include experts from the education academy, experienced in the knowledge and skills needed to develop asynchronous educational formats supported by education technology resources."

Nurses' education is also being evaluated as we enter a new decade. In a project sponsored by the Carnegie Foundation for the Advancement of Teaching, University of California, San Francisco (UCSF), nursing professor Patricia E. Benner, RN, PhD, chair of the Department of Social and Behavioral Sciences at UCSF, will examine teaching and learning modalities in nursing education. This 3-year study is part of the second phase of the Foundation's Preparation for the Professions Program; the first phase looked at educating clergy, engineers, and lawyers. The foundation has a long history of studying professional education, beginning in 1910 with the Flexner Report, a landmark study of medical education that is still widely cited today. The nursing study will be conducted simultaneously with a study of medical education and will examine the evolving professional goals, basic practices of teaching and learning, and assessment practices in the education of nurses.

Benner et al. (2009) note that this is a well-timed study for both nursing and medical education, in that the nursing profession is experiencing an international nursing shortage, and both recruitment and retention of nursing students are critical to the health of the nation. The practices of medicine and nursing are intertwined with many shared responsibilities for good patient care. Currently, healthcare delivery, equitable access to healthcare, and patient safety and well-being are major national issues, she said, adding that these studies will make cross-professional innovations and comparisons possible.

As Benner et al. (2009) note, "The profession of nursing in the United States is at a significant moment. It must contend with enormous pressures, from the chaotic healthcare system and the economic forces that drive it to profound changes in science, technology and patient activism. These demands, combined with ongoing shortages in the ranks of nurses and shifts in the nature and settings of nursing practice, have an impact on the profession's ability to uphold and transmit its core values: to provide astute clinical judgment, to keep patients safe, and to ameliorate human suffering." In their estimation, nursing education must be remade, and they call for more advances in the pathways to nursing licensure and a radical new understanding of the curriculum. They report that based on extensive field research conducted at nursing schools and a national survey of teachers and students administered by the National League for Nursing (NLN), the American Association of Colleges of Nursing (AACN), and the National Student Nurses Association (NSNA), there must be new recommendations to "realign and transform nursing education."

No analysis of nursing education can be accomplished without acknowledging the factors impacting the field. As Benner et al. (2009) point out, nurses "must learn and work under less than optimal circumstances" within healthcare institutions that "are not well designed for good nursing and medical practice, or for education." In fact, they say that "Nurses and nursing students must function within the complicated, and many would say, chaotic and dysfunctional U.S. healthcare system. To further complicate matters, since 1998 there's been a growing shortage of nurses, causing 93 percent of hospital-based registered nurses to report a lack of sufficient time and staff to maintain patient safety, detect complications early, and collaborate with other healthcare team members."

In addition, even though nursing education programs must increase their capacity by at least 90 percent to meet current and projected nursing shortages, these programs already face a faculty shortage, coupled with a dearth of baccalaureate-level nurses eligible to enter graduate programs, thus triggering a sixfold increase in the number of applicants denied admission to nursing schools since 2002 (Benner et al., 2009).

There is significant disagreement over a nursing curriculum that adequately addresses real-world clinical work, and as Benner et al. (2009) note, "Even more serious than the different points of entry to the practice are the quality gaps in the educational preparation and teaching development of nursing faculty seen across all types of nursing programs. Despite these enormous external challenges facing nursing practice and nursing education, we argue change in nursing education must come now, from within the schools and the profession. For as nursing education copes with these mounting pressures, the risk is to lower standards and aspirations; but at such a time of crisis, it is especially critical to have a clear vision of what high-quality nursing education is and what programs must do to meet those standards."

The Carnegie National Nursing Education Study examined three dimensions of nursing education and formation: the learning of theory and scientific methods, the mastery of skillful practice, and the formation of professional identity and agency. Benner et al. (2009) have stated that the study's results indicate that "today's nurses are undereducated for the demands of practice. Previous researchers worried about the education–practice gap; that is, the ability of practice settings to adopt and reflect what was being taught in academic institutions. Now, the tables are turned; nurse administrators worry about the practice–education gap, as it becomes harder for nursing education to keep pace with the rapid changes driven by research and new technologies."

Benner et al. (2009) summarize three key findings:

1. U.S. nursing programs are very effective in forming professional identity and ethical comportment. "While nursing education helps students develop a deep commitment to the values of the profession, there was a significant difference between what educators and students articulate as their understanding of ethical comportment and the actual teaching toward it. Educators and students often described 'ethics' primarily in terms of learning the principles of bioethics; yet, in the process of teaching and learning in clinical situations, they actually focused on everyday ethical comportment, on becoming good practitioners, and on continuously improving their practice, always with the patient in mind."

2. Clinical practice assignments provide powerful learning experiences, especially in programs where educators integrate clinical and classroom teaching. "One strength of U.S. nursing education is that students work directly with patients and the healthcare team. Moreover, as they progress through their programs, they are given ever-increasing responsibilities in clinical situations. In describing how they learned to become a nurse or 'think like a nurse,' students invariably pointed to clinical situations. However, when the clinical and classroom instruction were not integrated, students reported a fragmented experience."

3. U.S. nursing programs are not effective in teaching nursing science, natural sciences, social sciences, technology, and the humanities. "The lack of rigorous scholarship demanded of nursing students in these areas, and a failure of nursing education to connect the liberal arts to the development of sound nursing practice, was a sharp contrast to the skillful and effective approaches used in clinical situations. Material in these courses was typically delivered through standardized lectures. Developing knowledge that is to be used in a complex, high-stakes practice such as nursing calls for an ongoing dialogue between information and practice, so that students build an evidence base for care and thus learn to make decisions about appropriate interventions for a particular patient."

Benner et al. (2009) suggest that nursing educators make four shifts in their instructional approaches to fostering student learning:

1. Emphasize the active use of nursing knowledge and science.
2. Integrate clinical and classroom teaching.
3. Transition from an emphasis on critical thinking to an emphasis on clinical reasoning and multiple ways of thinking.
4. Transition from an emphasis on socialization and role-taking to an emphasis on formation, which includes those changes in identity and self-understanding that occur in moving from a layperson to a professional.

These paradigm shifts are nothing without the requisite policy changes that ensure that the entire nursing profession works together to transform nursing education. For this to occur, Benner et al. (2009) state that nursing programs must agree on a set of clinically relevant prerequisites; that a national advisory group should determine what prospective students need to know in the humanities, natural sciences, and social sciences, as well as their relevance to clinical practice; that a bachelor of science in nursing (BSN) should be required for entry into nursing practice; that the minimal educational level for entry into nursing practice should be the baccalaureate degree; and that additional master of science in nursing (MSN) programs be developed. In addition, a more diverse faculty and student body must be cultivated; more financial aid must be made available; and renewed attention by federal, state, and local authorities is needed to support the education of nurses. One of the most important changes proposed by Benner et al. (2009) have a direct bearing on this work; they insist that nursing ethics curricula be revamped, explaining, "Nurse educators need to focus on not only critical and dilemma ethics, but also everyday ethical comportment related to relational or care ethics. Narrative strategies, such as debriefing and reflecting on practice, provide effective ways to uncover and articulate everyday ethical comportment central to nursing practice." Equally important, they say, is to empower nursing students to become agents of change: "In order for today's students to be prepared to meet the reform challenges in practice settings—and be influential leaders in the political and public arenas for improved healthcare systems—they will need to learn theories of organizational development and policy-making, as well as strategies to change organizations. All levels of nursing education should prepare students for the complex bureaucratic settings where they will practice, learn and teach."

Also of significance is the recommendation of Benner et al. (2009) to revise the requirements for licensure. They say that the Boards of Registered Nurses should require graduates who pass the NCLEX-RN examination (one of two licensure examinations) after 2012 to earn a master's degree within 10 years. They also advocate for required performance assessments for licensure: "Nursing students should be exposed to competency evaluations during their undergraduate programs to better prepare them for competency clinical performance exams, which occur during their professional lives. To do so, the National Council for State Boards of Nursing needs to develop a new set of student performance assessments, with three national examinations of performance. The first exam should start at the beginning of the last year of nursing school; the next should be given at the same time the student sits for the NCLEX-RN examination (one of two licensure examinations); and the last exam should take place at the end of a one year post-licensure residency."

The Carnegie Foundation study is a serious call to action for significant change in nursing education. As Benner et al. (2009) emphasize, "Redesigning nursing education is an urgent societal agenda. The profound changes in nursing practice call for equally profound changes in the education of nurses and the preparation of nurse educators. Unfortunately, the current climate rewards short-term focus and cost-savings over the quality of nursing education and patient care. The challenge will be to create healthcare institutions and management systems that will educate nurses in a climate that fosters professional attentiveness, responsibility and excellence."

Is it possible that some healthcare professionals simply do not possess the information they need to provide good patient care? This may be prevalent among the lower-paid and less-educated healthcare providers who provide a vast majority of the care in certain healthcare environments, such as long-term care. Nursing and medical schools provide rigorous training, but merely cursory education exists for or is demanded of certified nursing assistants (CNAs) and orderlies. Even in the more formal education for nurses and physicians, it is probable that a student could graduate without ever hearing or thinking about patient abuse and its ramifications, so a nursing assistant is likely to have missed this critical instruction as well. Nerenberg (2002) said that better caregiver training can address the skill sets that get missed, including interpersonal skills, managing difficult situations, problem solving, cultural issues that affect staff and resident relationships, conflict resolution, stress reduction, and witnessing and reporting abuse.

DeHart and Cornman (2009) examined the existing training on elder mistreatment in nursing homes and discovered that there is little training specifically targeted toward prevention of mistreatment before it occurs. This is so despite growing awareness of elder mistreatment in nursing homes and the role that staffing and staff training may play in the prevention of such mistreatment they assert. DeHart and Cornman (2009) emphasized that "Development of quality training programs for CNAs and other nursing home staff is therefore an essential aspect of preventing elder abuse and neglect" (pp. 360–378).

For their study, DeHart and Cornman (2009) engaged in exhaustive interviews of nursing home staff, policy makers, and other professionals, including a psychologist, a social worker, several ombudsmen, several regulatory investigators and law-enforcement officers, and an elder law attorney, to identify training needs for elder mistreatment prevention among CNAs and to propose competencies essential for caregiver training to prevent mistreatment in nursing homes.

The competencies DeHart and Cornman (2009) propose are as follows:

- Define and provide examples of different types of mistreatment that occur in nursing homes, including neglect and quality-of-life issues, psychological abuse, physical abuse, financial abuse, and sexual abuse.
- Identify organizational, state, and federal policies around documenting and reporting elder mistreatment in nursing homes.
- Identify workplace contexts (such as staffing and oversight) that create a risky climate for mistreatment in nursing homes.
- Identify worker attitudes and behaviors that create a risky climate for mistreatment in nursing homes.
- Identify resources and coping strategies for addressing personal stressors (such as financial difficulties or family problems) so that these do not carry over to create mistreatment risk in the workplace.
- Identify strategies to engage the nursing home resident in his or her own care.
- Differentiate appropriate and inappropriate responses to resident behaviors that are perceived as problematic; the goal is to establish understanding and cooperation for mutual benefit.
- Identify verbal and nonverbal strategies to reduce conflict and establish safety for staff and residents.
- Identify age-related conditions that may affect compliance and strategies for communicating with persons who have diminished capacity.
- Identify generational issues that affect resident behavior (such as racism, sexism, and cultural and generational differences that will become apparent during daily care activities).
- Describe the inherent power differential between vulnerable adults housed in a nursing facility and the staff working in that facility and implications of this for mistreatment risk.
- Describe the CNA's role as a customer service provider who assists the nursing home resident in maintaining activities of daily living.
- Justify the importance of knowing the nursing home resident as a person and individualizing care.
- Share core values related to caregiving, including concern for humankind, compassion and empathy, protecting those who cannot

protect themselves, and respecting the elder's right to privacy, dignity, and self-determination.

- Identify strategies for communication among staff around the nursing home resident's needs, the care plan, and changes in behavior or condition.
- Justify teamwork as part of a supportive work environment, including appreciation and respect among coworkers, pride in one's work, and cooperative efforts to promote quality service. (pp. 360–378)

DeHart and Cornman (2009) state there is much training to be conducted on the prevention of mistreatment, and that in many cases, mistreatment results from misunderstanding, thoughtlessness, heavy workloads, and a lack of skills and knowledge. The researchers suggest that "Building relationships with residents should be a top priority for direct-care staff.... If direct-care staff share core values related to caregiving and they are able to build relationships with residents, they will be able to see past the series of tasks to be completed. They will be able to see residents as individual human beings deserving of respect and care" (pp. 360–378).

Strategy 8: Address Healthcare Professionals' Stressors

As discussed in Chapter 1, healthcare professionals are exposed to a number of significant stressors, including heavy workloads, staff shortages, and workplace violence.

Is there a remedy for violence in the healthcare institution? Perhaps there is no quick fix for the problems and challenges outlined in Chapter 1, but experts say that hospitals must adopt programs and policies to facilitate workplace violence mitigation and prevention.

According to the Occupational Safety and Health Administration (OSHA, 1998), a victim services program that can serve healthcare professionals and patients should:

- Provide debriefings following any critical incidents within the hospital setting, as well as provide peer support groups and referrals to community-based assistance programs.
- Provide policies to allow staff to have time off from work to deal with mental health issues, problems in the criminal justice system, and practical concerns as the result of victimization.
- Provide crisis intervention, counseling, and advocacy.
- Implement preventive safety strategies and security plans to ensure the safety of patients and staff.

- Train all hospital personnel on how to defuse a violent patient or visitor, as well as how to handle violent acts when they do occur.
- Develop contingency plans for disasters and critical incidents.

According to OSHA, recommendations for reducing violence include the following:

- Adopt a written violence-prevention program, communicate it to all employees, and designate a "Patient Assault Team" task force or coordinator to implement it.
- Advise all patients and visitors that violence, verbal and nonverbal threats, and related behavior will not be tolerated.
- Set up a trained response team to respond to emergencies.
- Encourage employees to promptly report incidents and to suggest ways to reduce or eliminate risks.
- Review workplace layout to find existing or potential hazards; install and maintain alarm systems and other security devices such as panic buttons, handheld alarms or noise devices, cellular phones, and private channel radios where risk is apparent or may be anticipated; and arrange for a reliable response system when an alarm is triggered.
- Use metal detectors to screen patients and visitors for weapons.
- Establish liaison with local police and state prosecutors, report all incidents of violence, and provide police with floor plans of facilities to expedite emergency response or investigations.
- Ensure adequate staff coverage at all times.
- Set up a system to use chart tags, logbooks, or other means to identify patients and clients with assaultive behavior problems.
- Institute a sign-in procedure with passes for visitors and compile a list of "restricted visitors" for patients with a history of violence.
- Control access to facilities other than waiting rooms, particularly drug-storage or pharmacy areas.
- Provide medical and psychological counseling and debriefing for employees experiencing or witnessing assaults and other violent incidents.

Strategy 9: Legislate Change

As discussed in Chapters 1 and 6, legislators are attempting to get traction on the 2009 to 2010 Patient Safety and Abuse Prevention Act, whose purpose is to lay the foundation for a coordinated, nationwide system of comprehensive state registry and criminal background checks that would greatly enhance the chances of identifying individuals with problematic backgrounds who change jobs frequently and move across state lines to avoid detection. The legislation would also stop individuals who have a record of substantiated abuse, or a serious criminal record, from preying on helpless elders and individuals with disabilities, and would provide assurance to long-term care employers and the residents they care for that abusive workers will not be hired into positions that give them access to extremely vulnerable individuals receiving long-term care services in healthcare settings across the United States.

According to the bill language, it would allow the secretary of Health and Human Services (HHS) to establish a program to identify efficient, effective, and economical procedures for long-term care facilities or providers to conduct background checks on prospective direct patient access employees on a nationwide basis. The legislation would prohibit the hiring of abusive workers and the authorization of the imposition of penalties by a participating state.

Essentially, the legislation would require that facilities conduct state and national criminal history background checks on the prospective employee through such means as a search of state-based abuse and neglect registries and databases, as well as state and federal criminal history records, including a fingerprint check using the Integrated Automated Fingerprint Identification System of the Federal Bureau of Investigation. It would also require that states describe and test methods that reduce duplicative fingerprinting, including providing for the development of "rap back" capability by the state such that if a direct patient access employee of a long-term care facility or provider is convicted of a crime following the initial criminal history background check conducted with respect to such employee, and the employee's fingerprints match the prints on file with the state law enforcement department, the department will immediately inform the state, and the state will immediately inform the long-term care facility or provider that employs the direct patient access employee of such conviction. The Inspector General of the Department of Health and Human Services is instructed by the legislation to conduct an evaluation of the nationwide program and to submit a report to Congress containing the results of its evaluation of this program.

According to the Healthcare Leadership Council (2009), healthcare system reform bills in the House and in the Senate as of January 2010 addressed healthcare workforce issues. Both the Senate and House bills propose a task force to assess the adequacy and appropriateness of the nation's health workforce and recommend federal policies that ensure the workforce is meeting the nation's needs. The Senate bill provides for grants to nursing schools to improve nurse education and training programs, and it also establishes training programs for direct-care workers in long-term care. Another provision is for improved training in general practice and family medicine, plus it authorizes funding for training in geriatric care.

Strategy 10: Address Major Anomalies

Much of this chapter examined patient safety in the context of quality improvement, and much remains to be done to address the significant anomalies that crop up in healthcare, such as medical murder. As Thunder (2003) observed, "There are a variety of methods by which we may choose to improve our prevention and detection of quiet killings in medical facilities. We should not simply rely on serendipitous observation by eye witnesses. We should use sophisticated as well as ordinary means to detect these killings and we must announce our use of them so as to deter perpetrators. The use of these methods will not only improve our prevention and detection of quiet killings but also improve medical care generally and security generally."

Thunder (2003) enumerates some interventions:

- Enhance facility security.
- Improve background checks.
- Improve controls over dispensation of medicine. (As Thunder explained, "Strengthening such controls will not only cut off a source of supply for killers, it will also cut off a source of supply for medical facility employees with addictions.")
- Require reporting of individual deaths and establish systems to monitor rates, places, and times of death.

Kent and Walsh (2004) recommend the following countermeasures:

- Random forensic autopsies.
- Death-review team conferences in underage or overage parameters.
- Confidential anonymous ethics hotlines.

Yorker (2006) recommends the following preventive measures:

- Conduct heightened surveillance of time, place, and person.
- Use strict pharmacy- or unit-level accounting for all doses of medication; conduct routine toxicology screens immediately following cardiac arrest for all patients, regardless of the presumed cause or manner of the event.
- Obtain monthly code and death statistics by unit, shift, and total hospital; compare units to each other and to themselves and monitor any trend changes.
- Prompt toxicological studies.

As Kizer and Yorker (2010) note, "We believe that greater efforts should be made to build a capacity to understand the causes of healthcare serial murder and to strengthen the weaknesses in healthcare safety systems revealed by these occurrences" (pp. 186–191). Kizer and Yorker (2010) suggest several actions they say would be reasonable first steps to this end:

> First, we believe that healthcare professional organizations, accrediting bodies and licensing agencies should do more to increase awareness of healthcare serial murder among healthcare professionals. Granted, it is disturbing to think that doctors, nurses or other healthcare workers might intentionally kill or seriously harm patients entrusted to their care and there is a fine line between acknowledging the problem and inappropriately frightening patients and undermining public confidence in hospitals and other healthcare facilities, but the first step in addressing any problem is acknowledging that it exists. Based on experience managing other safety problems, transparency is critically important despite the challenges that such openness may initially present. Conceptually this is not unlike what has been done to increase awareness about other patient safety problems, although communications about healthcare serial murder would need to be carefully crafted. (pp. 186–191)

Kizer and Yorker (2010) point to a lack of centralized data collection on healthcare serial murders, and suggest that, "an appropriate federal agency should be designated and empowered to collect and analyze data about these occurrences and to maintain a clearinghouse of information on the subject. The ownership of this problem could be given to a number of existing entities whose mission includes analyzing and being an authoritative resource about rare occurrences, e.g., the Agency for Health Care Research and Quality (AHRQ), Centers for Disease Control and Prevention or Federal Bureau of Investigation" (pp. 186–191). Kizer and Yorker (2010) also emphasize that "the effectiveness of current methods for determining the training, experience, qualifications and performance of healthcare workers and for communicating complete and timely information about these things should be assessed" (pp. 186–191). They state that an evaluation of peer review, licensure, and adverse event reporting should be conducted by an independent entity experienced in evaluating complex and sensitive issues, such as the Institute of Medicine (IOM) of the National Academy of Sciences or the National Academy of Public Administration (NAPA).

Kizer and Yorker (2010) say that because most healthcare professionals and facility administrators are not instructed about how to identify and manage situations of intentional harm,

> Consensus guidelines for managing suspicious situations might be helpful. In many of the cases of convicted health care serial killers, concerns about the worker arose long before any action was taken, and when action was finally taken it often consisted of simply terminating the worker, after which he or she went to work at another health care facility and committed additional patient

murders. Guidelines that detail circumstances that should prompt consideration of an event being intentionally harmful, reasons for reporting suspicious circumstances to public health and law enforcement authorities, and procedures for collecting and safeguarding potential evidence and documentation that may be later needed for forensic purposes, among other things, should be detailed in such guidelines. These guidelines could be developed by the NQF as part of its ongoing work identifying evidence-based safe practices or by the IOM or various other entities. (pp. 186–191)

Finally, practices for catching healthcare anomalies such as serial murder and medical malfeasance should be built into existing systems for addressing patient safety-related problems. As Kizer and Yorker (2010) explain,

> Policies and procedures for use of high-alert medications should be particularly reviewed since administration of non-narcotic medications has been the primary weapon used by healthcare serial killers in the U.S. It also would be helpful to know whether the use of automated drug dispensing technologies that have become widely utilized in hospitals in recent years has changed this pattern. Similarly, processes used for monitoring and evaluating sentinel events in healthcare facilities should be specifically assessed since in most known instances of healthcare serial murder suspicion of a malicious act arose because co-workers of the perpetrator observed an increased frequency of deaths or cardiac arrests associated with a particular care unit, work shift and/or caregiver. Whether unusual situations needing detailed investigation could be better identified by routinely monitoring monthly mortality and cardiac arrest rates by time of day, unit of care, primary diagnosis and cause of death, or whether it would be practical to do so, should be assessed. This review could be conducted by the IOM, NQF, AHRQ, or other entities. (pp. 186–191)

Strategy 11: Remove Barriers to Reform

In so many other industries, there are systems to catch performance failures, but in healthcare, it appears that both a safety net and a safety culture are lacking. Walshe and Shortell (2004) have said that safety is taken more seriously in other industries for three reasons; first, healthcare organizations "usually carry on with their work after even the most serious failures, and the staff are rarely harmed or even much affected by what happens. Patients bear nearly the entire cost of failures, and that may mean that the problems do not matter enough for healthcare organizations to want to fix or prevent them" (pp. 103–111). Second, there is an expectation that in healthcare, patients stand a decent chance to encounter harm, whether it is from their disease/injury process or from a by-product of healthcare provider error. As

Walshe and Shortell (2004) observe, "No other industry deals with morbidity and mortality as such a routine part of the production process. This presents a unique challenge in distinguishing what might be termed disease-harm and production-harm and disentangling their causes and consequences. Moreover, as organizations and as individuals, we become inured to such harm. It is normal for patients to die and for treatments to fail, and so we become accustomed to such events. When things go wrong, it is then more difficult to step outside this normalizing mind-set and see the problems for what they really are: evidence of major healthcare failures" (pp. 103–111). Third, healthcare organizations face powerful vested interests that could easily block reform efforts that would produce greater accountability.

Walshe and Shortell (2004) assert that system healthcare failures are "a product of the distinctive culture of the organizations, the healthcare professions, and the health system" and that "endemic secrecy, deference to authority, defensiveness and protectionism" further undermine an institution's efforts to address medical missteps. They said that patients' interests "are too often subordinated to the needs and interests of healthcare organizations and professionals" (pp. 103–111). Walshe and Shortell (2004) say the most important action to take to prevent future failures is to "create a more open, transparent, equitable, and accountable healthcare culture. This will require changes in medical and health professions education, greater public demand for accountability, continuing advances in the measurement and reporting of healthcare quality and patient outcome data, and more principled clinical and managerial leadership of healthcare organizations" (pp. 103–111).

Strategy 12: Create New Opportunities for Dialogue

In early 2010, Florida State University (FSU) launched the Center for Innovative Collaboration in Medicine and Law, designed to bring practitioners together to discuss the issues that confound both sectors and remain unresolved if the chasm between them persists. Endeavors such as these could make great strides in discussing issues such as medical malfeasance, and in helping to shape medicolegal policy for the future.

Serving as director of this new center is Marshall Kapp, JD, a faculty member in the College of Medicine and College of Law at FSU, editor of the American College of Legal Medicine's *Journal of Legal Medicine*, and a frequent lecturer on topics in health law, medical ethics, and law and aging. "Its unique mission is collaboration starting at the student level, through the practitioner level, through the policy level—collaboration on behalf of the consumer, who is the doctor's patient and the lawyer's client," Kapp said.

Kapp adds:

Much of what we will be trying to do is putting people together in the same room to identify what the problem is, the realistic extent of the problem, what is causing the problem, who is responsible for the problem, and then coming up with potential approaches to eliminating or alleviating the problem. I think you would find pretty broad agreement among the medical and the legal professions as well as the public that fraud and other forms of crime by healthcare professionals is a bad thing, that it ought to be eliminated, and that inroads in doing that would be beneficial to the healthcare consumer. Beyond those general platitudes, it is a question of figuring out what's really going on, why is it going on, who is responsible and what sorts of approaches might best address the problem. For any of the issues we address, we will try to identify legal interventions that might be helpful but we recognize that there might be other kinds of interventions that could be even more beneficial—whether it is education or additional funding, there must be other kinds of interventions beyond simply the attitude that "there ought to be a law." (Interview with author.)

Targeting the intersection where law and medicine meet is Kapp's goal. "If you really want to figure out not just what's happening but why it's happening and what effective interventions might look like, you must have that cross-professional dialogue. This isn't the kind of issue where there's going to be fundamental disagreement on principle, as no one is going to be defending fraud and abuse, but I think the medical perspective can be very useful in investigating why it's happening—not to justify it, but to explain why and how it's happening, and what interventions, beyond more law enforcement, might be useful."

Essential to cultivating this kind of open and honest dialogue is creating an environment in which unpopular views can be aired without undue antagonism or even legal ramifications. Ironically, the current climate mirrors that we have seen hospitals face in Chapter 6. "Among physicians, there is the fear that—individually and collectively—anything they say can and will be used against them," Kapp states. "Lawyers are responsible for some of that impediment as well, because many lawyers start out with the assumption that doctors are all driven solely by money and lacking in ethics, so there are attitudinal problems on both sides."

Motivations must be examined if a resolution to this medicolegal conundrum can be identified. However, practitioners on each side are seemingly eager to point fingers, thus potentially constipating any meaningful dialogue between physicians and lawyers. "The explanation that the temptation to engage in questionable behavior is driven by greed or personal gain in some way, as well as a lack of ethics on the part of some healthcare providers, is an accurate explanation to some extent, but I think it is more complicated than that," Kapp says. "For example, physicians might say, 'Well, we have to falsify records once in a while in order to obtain necessary treatment for patients because third-party payors are greedy and unethical.' That doesn't necessarily justify the action, but it does explain how if the doctor wants a needed test for a patient and the only way to get the third party to pay for it is to indicate on the documentation that the doctor suspects a medical problem that doesn't really exist—the doctor's probably going to falsify the documentation for a good reason in his or her mind. I think greed explains a lot, but it doesn't explain the whole phenomenon of medical fraud and abuse." Kapp continued, "There are a lot of different actors on the healthcare stage—it's not just the doctor and the patient; now you have third-party payors, regulators, reviewers, private accrediting bodies, lots of different moving parts in the system that complicate an attempt to pin down the fraud and abuse and other criminal activity by healthcare professionals."

Acknowledging the inherent tension between medicine and law, Kapp said a balance must be found between two extremes—lawyers' pandering deference to physicians and the zeal with which they pursue litigation against them. "It's difficult to make global statements about the legal profession because it is so diverse, but I don't think on the whole the problem is excessive deference of lawyers to physicians," Kapp said. He continues:

> With most lawyers, if anything, it's the opposite—they are too willing to ascribe bad motives and conduct to physicians. A lot of that is done out of ignorance or jealousy. I don't think there's squeamishness on the part of the legal profession, particularly those involved in representing the public, regarding physicians and healthcare professionals. I think the public as a whole still, to a large extent, puts the medical profession on somewhat of a pedestal, treating them as mysterious and above the fray. For example, prosecutors don't bring to the courtroom prosecutions that they don't think will result in convictions. So if I am a prosecutor, I have to think, "can I convince a jury or other fact-finding body that the doctor acted wrongly," and that is often a difficult thing to do because the public from whom juries are drawn do tend to have a natural deference to the medical profession. They frequently have difficulty with believing that doctors are doing wrong, so I think the squeamishness may play out in that regard but it's not because lawyers are more deferential to healthcare providers—if anything, it's the opposite. (Interview with author.)

Whether or not animosity between medicine and the law can be addressed, Kapp said he hopes the new center can assist healthcare organizations as they navigate these unchartered medicolegal waters:

> Hopefully one of the things we can do, by working through the lawyers who are counseling and representing healthcare institutions, is to relieve some of the anxiety healthcare providers have about taking aggressive action to protect their patients. Many providers would probably say one of the reasons

they are not more aggressive in looking for these sorts of problems and doing something about them is that they are afraid the plaintiffs' lawyers are going to use this information to sue them. Healthcare institutions are afraid that if they discipline a member of the medical staff, he or she is going to instigate litigation to sue them for tampering with their privileges, and those are not irrational fears. So hopefully one of the things the center can do by bringing the different perspectives together and working with public policy-makers to change the laws and policies, is to find ways to alleviate some of that legal anxiety on the part of providers so that they are more willing to address problems with fraud and abuse. I suspect most healthcare providers would love to ferret out these kinds of activities from their facilities. One significant challenge is resources, of course, but the other I think is fear of legal consequences—the fear of no good deed going unpunished. These are issues the center hopes to address. (Interview with author.)

The strategies contained in this chapter are simple, straightforward suggestions for improving the level of quality of care and safety provided by healthcare institutions, but they require funding and implementation in order to become reality. Jewell and McGiffert (2009) said that healthcare consumers and progressive healthcare institutions are "alarmed by the lack of public accountability surrounding patient safety" and have issued a call to action to emphasize the imperative of implementing the IOM's recommendations. They note that when the IOM called for immediate action, it asked, "Must we wait another decade to be safe in our health system?" As Jewell and McGiffert (2009) observe, "Ten years later, we find ourselves asking the same question. As the nation begins to reform our healthcare system, we have an opportunity to take effective and accountable action to make healthcare safer for all Americans. The time to act is now. We cannot wait another decade."

References

Batalden PB, and Davidoff F. What is quality improvement and how can it transform healthcare? *Qual Saf Health Care.* 16:2–3. 2007.

Benner P, Sutphen M, Leonard V, and Day L. *Educating Nurses: A Call for Radical Transformation.* San Francisco: Jossey-Bass. December 2009. (Accessed October 27, 2010, at: http://www.carnegiefoundation.org/newsroom/press-releases/educating-nurses-call-radical-transformation.)

Cohen AB, Restuccia JD, Shwartz M et al. A survey of hospital quality improvement activities. *The Commonwealth Fund.* 105. July 24, 2008. (Accessed October 27, 2010, at: http://www.commonwealthfund.org/Content/Publications/In-the-Literature/2008/Jul/A-Survey-of-Hospital-Quality-Improvement-Activities.aspx.)

DeHart D, and Cornman C. Prevention of elder mistreatment in nursing homes: Competencies for direct-care staff. *J Elder Abuse Negl.* 21(4):360–378. October 2009.

Dekker S. *Just Culture: Balancing Safety and Accountability.* NSW: Ashgate. 2007.

General Accounting Office. Nursing homes: More can be done to protect residents from abuse. Washington, DC: GAO Report 02-312. 2002.

Healthcare Leadership Council. House and Senate health reform proposals before the 111th Congress. December 22, 2009.

Hickam DH, Severance S, Feldstein A et al. "The effect of healthcare working conditions on patient safety." Agency for Healthcare Research and Quality (AHRQ). Evidence Report/Technology Assessment No. 74. May 2003. (Accessed October 27, 2010, at: http://www.ncbi.nlm.nih.gov/bookshelf/br.fcgi?book=erta74&part=A111553.)

Institute of Medicine (IOM) Committee on the Work Environment for Nurses and Patient Safety. *Keeping Patients Safe: Transforming the Work Environment of Nurses.* Washington, DC: National Academy of Sciences. 2004. (Accessed October 27, 2010, at: http://www.ncbi.nlm.nih.gov/bookshelf/br.fcgi?book=erta74&part=A111553.)

Jewell K, and McGiffert L. "To err is human—to delay is deadly." Consumer Reports White Paper. May 2009. (Accessed October 27, 2010, at: http://www.safepatient-project.org/safepatientproject.org/pdf/safepatientproject.org-ToDelayIsDeadly.pdf.)

Joint Commission. "National Patient Safety Goals." 2009.

Kent DR, and Walsh PD. Modern U.S. healthcare serial killings: An exploratory study and work in progress. In: *Linking Data to Practice in Violence and Homicide Prevention.* Proceedings of the 2004 Meeting of the Homicide Research Working Group. VP Bunge, CR Block, and M Lane, eds. Chicago: HRWG Publications. 2004.

Kizer KW, and Stegun MB. "Serious reportable adverse events in healthcare. Advances in patient safety: From research to implementation." Vol. 4. Agency for Healthcare Research and Quality. February 2005. (Accessed October 27, 2010, at: http://www.ahrq.gov/downloads/pub/advances/vol4/Kizer2.pdf.)

Kizer KW, and Yorker BC. Healthcare serial murder: A patient safety orphan. Joint Commission. *J Qual Patient Safety.* April 2010, pp. 186–191.

Kohn LT, Corrigan JM, and Donaldson MS, eds. *To Err is Human: Building a Safer Health System.* Committee on Quality of Healthcare in America, Institute of Medicine. Washington, DC: National Academy Press. 2000. (Accessed October 27, 2010, at: http://www.nap.edu/openbook.php?record_id=9728.)

Leape LL. Error in medicine. *JAMA.* 272(23):1851–1857. 1994.

Leape L, Berwick D, Clancy C et al. Transforming healthcare: A safety imperative. *Qual Saf Health Care.* 18:424–428. 2009.

Marx D. "Patient safety and the just culture." PowerPoint presentation from the Just Culture Community. 2007. (Accessed October 27, 2010, at: http://www.health.state.ny.us/professionals/patients/patient_safety/conference/2007/docs/patient_safety_and_the_just_culture.pdf.)

McLaughlin CP, and Kaluzny AD. Defining quality improvement. In: *Continuous Quality Improvement in Healthcare.* Sudbury, MA: Jones & Bartlett. 2006, pp. 3–36.

Nerenberg L. Abuse in nursing homes. *National Center on Elder Abuse (NCEA) Newsletter.* May 2002.

Occupational Safety and Health Administration (OSHA). "Guidelines for preventing workplace violence for healthcare and social service workers." 1998.

Silow-Carroll SS, Alteras T, and Meyer JA. Hospital quality improvement: Strategies and lessons from U.S. hospitals. *The Commonwealth Fund*. 54. April 3, 2007.

Skochelak SE. Commentary: A century of progress in medical education: What about the next 10 years? *Acad Med*. 85(2). February 2010. (Accessed October 27, 2010, at: http://journals.lww.com/academicmedicine/Fulltext/2010/02000/Commentary__A_Century_of_Progress_in_Medical.14.aspx.)

Sullivan W. "Preparing professionals as moral agents." Carnegie Foundation for the Advancement of Teaching. December 2004. (Accessed October 27, 2010, at: http://www.carnegiefoundation.org/perspectives/preparing-professionals-moral-agents.)

Thunder JM. Quiet killings in medical facilities: Detection and prevention. *Issues Law Med*. March 22, 2003. (Accessed October 27, 2010, at: http://www.accessmylibrary.com/article-1G1-100112231/quiet-killings-medical-facilities.html.)

Von Thaden T, Hoppes M, Li Y, Johnson N, and Schriver A. The perception of just culture across disciplines in healthcare. Proceedings of the Human Factors and Ergonomics Society 50th Annual Meeting, San Francisco. 2006.

Wachter R. "When is a medical error a crime?" Wachter's World Blog. November 5, 2007. (Accessed October 27, 2010, at: http://www.thehealthcareblog.com/the_health_care_blog/2007/11/when-is-a-medic.html.)

Walshe K, and Shortell SM. When things go wrong: How healthcare organizations deal with major failures. *Health Affairs*. 23(3):103–111. 2004.

Warren N, Hodgson M, Craig T et al. Employee working conditions and healthcare system performance. *J Occup Environ Med*. 49(4). April 2007.

Young PL, and Olsen LA. "The healthcare imperative: Lowering costs and improving outcomes: Brief summary of a workshop." Roundtable on Evidence-Based Medicine, Institute of Medicine. National Academies Press. 2009.

Index